CHRISTIAN EVC

CHRISTIAN EVOLUTION

Moving Towards a
Global Spirituality

URSULA BURTON & JANICE DOLLEY

TURNSTONE PRESS LIMITED
Wellingborough, Northamptonshire

First published 1984

© URSULA BURTON AND JANICE DOLLEY 1984

This book is sold subject to the condition that it shall not, by way of trade or otherwise, be lent, re-sold, hired out, or otherwise circulated without the publisher's prior consent in any form of binding or cover other than that in which it is published and without a similar condition including this condition being imposed on the subsequent purchaser.

British Library Cataloguing in Publication Data

Burton, Ursula
　Christian evolution,
　1. Christian life
　I. Title　II. Dolley, Janice
　248.4　　BV4501.2

ISBN 0-85500-204-2

---

*Turnstone Press is part of the
Thorsons Publishing Group*

Printed and bound in Great Britain

Dedication

To our children and their generation in whom we see the light shining.

Contents

	Page
Foreword	9
Prologue	11
Chapter	
1. Unfinished Business	13
2. Ursula's Journey	16
3. Janice's Journey	26
4. Journeys of Other Travellers on the Way	36
5. My Dilemma in the Church – *Janice Dolley*	72
6. The Role of the Church in the Next Decade – *Janice Dolley*	86
7. Citizens of One World – *Janice Dolley*	101
8. The Emergence of a New Consciousness – *Ursula Burton*	110
9. The New Creation – *Ursula Burton*	127
10. The Way Ahead	135
Epilogue	141
Notes	145
Organizations and Publications	150
Index	159

Life in this new age is insistent to us
to move on in our thinking.
For Truth abides in no Tabernacle.

> Ian Fern

Foreword

I am delighted to commend *Christian Evolution – Towards a Global Spirituality*. This book is written for those within the Christian tradition, but whose experience of the life and worship of their local church is that of being cheated, even betrayed. The Christian Church claims so much, speaks so much, – but the experience of all it claims and talks about seems so often to be missing. Ursula Burton, Janice Dolley and some of the other women whose stories are recounted decided not to continue in this spiritual desert, but to set out on a spiritual journey of personal transformation in the search for 'the Christ within'. They retain their links with the Church, and these links have been strengthened, but their search has led them into areas of the mystical tradition which have some features in common in most of the major religious traditions. This book is therefore also written for those who are questioning, doubting, searching; it is for those on the edge of faith, those who wish to give the institutional church yet one more chance.

It is a book which should make priests and ministers particularly thoughtful. What have we done to shape Christian communities where there are so many disappointed men and women? One thing is needed and that is the sort of spiritual formation which enables people to appropriate, own and reclaim their faith. The authors have done this for themselves, and while not everyone will find aspects of their journey to their liking, their pilgrimage makes for invigorating reading.

Donald Reeves
Rector, St. James's Church, Piccadilly

Prologue

We first met in Iona ten years ago. It is a place to which we have returned many times, an island whose fabric and pounding seas seem permeated by the vision of St Columba and the early Celtic Church. When we met we knew that we had both reached a similar stage in our experience and felt that we were standing together on a bridge between the old and the new. It was a few years later, over tea and toast in Glastonbury – another point of connection with the early Church – that the idea of this book began to impress itself upon us both simultaneously. We did not know then the form it would take or even what it would say.

Since then the book has progressed in fits and starts. We live 400 miles apart. Ursula has six children and many roles; Janice four children and a full-time job. Meetings have not been easy to arrange. We have managed a few days here and there: a farmhouse in Surrey, a convent in Sussex, a pilgrimage to Ephesus, a villa in Spain, and then back again to Iona. Each time we shared our experiences we found that though in the interim we had moved on in our thinking, we had nevertheless arrived once more at the same place at the same time.

At last this slim volume has emerged. Why did we feel this compulsion to embark on it in the first place? That question remains unanswered. At least in writing it we have practised what we are here preaching, which is that one should not ignore these strange, often irrational yet imperative hunches that come from somewhere deep within. Moreover, we have been encouraged by some in authority within the Church who feel it is time that the laity voiced their thoughts and opinions, be they 'right' or 'wrong'. A book seems to follow a course of its own after a time, which can be disconcerting for the writer, forced as he then is to review the original structure and even the title. This happened with us, and we eventually had to follow the direction the book was taking us despite our original plan.

All we can do now is to 'cast our bread upon the waters'. Some of this may be stale news, already communicated far more effectively by previous writers; yet it rose in us with a freshness that can come only from personal experience. Our hope is that it may be a 'nibble' for someone who is hungry – needing nourishment for the spiritual side of their nature.

Our thanks go first to each other for patience, understanding and care, and then to the waitresses, barmen, air hostesses and nuns who served us gladly and unobtrusively during the precious minutes we stole as we crossed between railway and plane journeys, and transport cafés. How odd our conversations must have seemed to those who overheard us!

We found our times of discussion vital, for they enabled us to help each other articulate thoughts that were waiting for recognition. It is so often an honest sharing and interchange with others that helps us to formulate our ideas as they emerge. At times, in a way that has been confirmatory and frequently surprising, we found that other writers – whom we quote – were thinking along similar lines. Is this not the process by which we have all progressed, each one adding a small measure to the understanding that has gone before? Perhaps one characteristic of the evolution of Christianity is a willingness to engage in a changing perception of the world and of God. God does not change, but our perceptions of Him do; just as we reach one horizon, another vista opens up before us and we find ourselves in a landscape that is personal and new.

We hope that in reading of the dilemma we have experienced others may find their own journeys to be less lonely and may be encouraged to respond and open up areas of debate and shared experience through which we can all grow together.

> No man is an Island, entire of it self; every man is a piece of the Continent, a part of the main.
>
> John Donne

Ursula, Lady Burton, Edinburgh
Mrs Janice Dolley, London

1.
Unfinished Business

As technological progress speeds us towards the twenty-first century, there is a sense in which mankind's own development is taking an evolutionary step. Many today are perceiving within themselves the first faint glimmer of a new understanding of the nature of God, of their own humanity and of their place in the Universe. They are also discovering a growing interior awareness that is causing them to question the nature of religion as it has been presented, and to query its relevance for a changing world.

When we first met, these questions were already within our minds and we had both been through a great deal of mental conflict due to a clash between the 'orthodox' and 'New Age' streams of thinking. This had helped us to see more clearly the different elements of truth that each stream brings and the many paths that lead to a greater Truth. Since then we have met up with other lay people who feel like ourselves, and we have asked some of them to contribute to this book. Others we have met are priests or leaders within established Churches and we realize that they must continue, for the time being, to support the institutions to which they belong whilst encouraging others to pursue more freely the way that lies ahead.

As we share the insights and understandings that are welling up within us, we hope that these will 'ring bells' for others who are sensing a 'New Age' emerging but who, having stepped beyond a previously held mode of belief, may be feeling isolated and bewildered.

If anything that we or others have written presents ideas that are new to you, we ask not that you accept or reject what is said, but rather that you live with these ideas and see if they become real for you. We have found that a process occurs through which an understanding dawns slowly from within and rises to the surface in its own time. The more we learn to co-operate with our anima, our intuitive side, and the more we obey our hunches and act upon them, the more will our eyes be opened and ideas take on a new and universal meaning. Naturally, our intuition must always be balanced by our intellect, our reason; balanced lest we swing too far in one direction, but not blocked off, lest we deny one of the best ways that life has of teaching us.

Our own discoveries have led us towards an inner way from which we find a global spirituality beginning to emerge. We have begun to trace a pattern formed by an interweaving of the truths contained in all the great religions; for religion is perhaps not an end in itself but rather a system, or discipline, to bind us back – religio – to our Source. It is as though we are all on an evolutionary journey and that the next stage is impressing itself upon us. Our hearts and minds are beginning to lead us towards a higher level of understanding and we find ourselves out of step with many in the Christian church. We have felt the need to write about the dilemma in which we find ourselves because we can no longer keep silent about the way we feel. We question much of what the church teaches or does not teach us. We do not want to undermine its tenets, for we feel that each new process of man's development must build, with gratitude, on what has gone before. Yet on the other hand we can no longer sit comfortably in the pews hearing what to us seems a limited version of the Truth.

The way we feel we can resolve our dilemma is by making a plea to the Churches. We want them to see that what they are currently offering their people is 'unfinished business'. We can only have glimpses of the journey we are on and must always be prepared to open up new areas of debate. There are perhaps three ways in which we see the Churches' business as still unfinished.

The first is that if man is on an evolutionary journey, returning to the Source, then growth will inevitably take place; and growth, by its very nature is always unfinished. Possibly the Church has not hitherto allowed sufficient space for this growth to occur. One of the reasons may be that all growth involves, in one sense or another, a falling away of what has gone before. The pod has to swell and burst in order to release the seed, which in turn must swell and split to release the shoot; and so it is with the Church. The Christian Church in its various forms has been like a pod, containing and nurturing the Truth for nearly two thousand years. This pod has become encrusted with man-made concepts and ideas, and the seed, unable to break through within the Church, has therefore put forth side-shoots in different directions. We feel that man's religious quest will always move us upwards and outwards and that the time has come for a greater acceptance by the Churches that their business is indeed unfinished.

The second sense in which we use this term is that expressed by Christ, when He said, 'Behold, I make all things new.'[1] We believe that only now are the inner truths of Christ's teaching being grasped by more than a limited number of individuals. Throughout the centuries there have always been a few enlightened figures who, by their understanding, have towered above the masses. They have often been persecuted or at best misunderstood, for the mystical inner way has often challenged the ideas of the day. But today a new understanding of the Truth as manifested by Christ is beginning to dawn on greater numbers than before. The notion of adherence to a set of truths, crystallized into dogmas, is being replaced by an increasing intuitive awareness.

The third sense in which we mean 'unfinished business' concerns ourselves both as individuals and as a social order. If our understanding is to move us on, it must affect both how we live and how we as a race organize our world. For the way we think and feel is more powerful than possibly we realize: it forms the basis of the life we build for ourselves and for generations as yet unborn. The Church must move with the new dynamic that is unfolding.

You will find that those contributing to this book are, in their different ways, seeking freedom to break through the set boundaries and explore the uncharted waters of the ocean of life. At the same time, they are seeking to sail aboard the vessel that has carried them thus far and which has long guarded the maps of Truth insofar as Man has perceived and understood them. Although we acknowledge the validity and value of the past, we are searching for an expression of the new awareness that is surfacing from the depths and urging us forward, 'for Life goes not backwards nor tarries with yesterday'.[2] The journey is ever new, and there can be no final boundary but infinity.

2.
Ursula's Journey

I hope this contribution may be read by those who were once faithful members of their Churches and whose spirituality was alive and meaningful within that structure. Then, maybe there came a time when disconcerting thoughts filled the mind: something, somewhere, did not ring true for them. I can only hope that the fellow traveller who turns these pages will come across one thought, albeit one alone, which perhaps as yet lies dormant on the surface of the mind but which might be awakened and recognized; that some of these words may be like a shower of rain on dry ground, so that only a little encouragement is needed for the seed to start to grow. I hope it will be seen that we are not negating Christianity, but merely endeavouring to ask what it is trying to say to us today, and discover what Christ was actually teaching at a deeper level. On this exploratory path I have found that many revelations connect with the higher truths of other world faiths.

In my thirties, as a practising Anglican, I lived through at least ten years of inner conflict, tension and guilt feelings before I found someone within the Church who understood my newborn beliefs and who by this very understanding could allay the fears I had of such thoughts being in any way 'heretical' or a distortion of the truth. To have someone understand and confirm this 'knowledge' which had become a living part of my Christian belief was an enormous relief. And what can surpass the joy of sharing at soul level? If the Holy Spirit is as alive today as He was 2,000 years ago – and we believe this to be so – then surely, if we are open to Him, we will be given new insights; for nothing is static in Creation. Is there any reason why new revelations should not be given, as man's ability to comprehend increases? Surely this is an integral part of evolution. Truth is eternal: the depth of understanding is what matters.

The realization of oneness, of wholeness, was my first

conviction. It might be fairer to say that I had a new and deeper awareness of that oneness of Creation which I had experienced as a young girl standing under the night sky and looking up at the stars. I felt a momentary fusing with the universe as I stood there, rapt in contemplation of the 'grandeur of God'. Yes, I truly knew then that all men are brothers, regardless of colour, creed or nationality. (This was before the days when the brotherhood of mankind was openly talked about, as it is today.) Having experienced this awareness of being part of the whole, how could I talk about 'them' and 'us'? St Paul's statement that we are all members one of another brought the meaning of 'the Body of Christ' to life out of what had for me become a dead setting. (Maybe it was a case of over-familiar words formerly not having registered with their full impact.)

In later years there were times of experiencing a total blending with Creation. It was with great joy that I read Teilhard de Chardin's writings portraying life within each rock and living thing. This experience of being a part of the whole – a part of Creation – later helped me through a difficult period concerning Holy Communion. I could not understand the Church's assertion that we *become* partakers of the Divine nature through receiving the Sacrament; as I see it, we are *already* part of God's Creation, which must include Christ. And yet it is still necessary to acknowledge the particular, to give full individual consciousness to the fact. There can be no separation, but in making a conscious act of acceptance of this fact we bring into play a force, we activate an energy. Mankind alone at present has been given the gift of saying 'I will' to God, the Creator. By allying ourselves to that which is deep within, the soul, the divine spark, or Jung's 'other' part of himself – and by saying 'Yes' to the cosmos we became truly in tune with the Infinite.

I later found that I increasingly had an inner knowing if a friend was unwell or in any way upset. Today, I find this form of non-verbal communication growing remarkably strong, which again points to the soul link there is between us all. This deep inner connection we have one with another was well known by the Hunas of Polynesia, who referred to the link as the *acka* chords. Recently a friend, while at her office desk, became 'agitated' about me for no apparent reason and found on checking up, that at that very moment I had had an accident. A nun in San Francisco wrote to say that I was so much with her that if I walked into the room she would not be surprised. She ended by saying that she was off to Mass and would take me with her. Oh yes, we are members one of another and affect each other for good or ill, even by our thoughts: what a responsibility we have for ourselves as well as for the world! We are continually contributing energy to the universe, without considering whether it is good or bad, positive or negative. We are by our very natures transmitters – we cannot help it. A single thought going out from us lives on for ever, going out in never-ending ripples which can be picked up by any sensitive person. It can be a 'high' or good thought, or it can come from a lower level. A responsibility – yes, but also what a privilege! It helps us to understand that we must first put our own house in order, work on ourselves, and that this is neither selfish nor introspective but ultimately for the benefit of the world. *Self* transformation must come before we can have *world* transformation.

Increasingly, I found that the prayers of the Liturgy, prayers of petition as 'prayed' at Church services and in prayer groups, did not 'ring true' – they even smacked of manipulation. We seemed to be telling this 'God out there' what we needed and what to do, yet who are we to judge? 'Do not judge and you will not be judged', Christ had entreated us.[1] We were still behaving as children: we needed a 'crutch', a visible prop, something that was tangible and had form. We still did not understand the command to 'obey the spirit of the Law, not the letter of the Law'. Furthermore, we were given no encouragement to 'grow up', to think for ourselves or to start to take responsibility for our own lives, for our very own souls. Man has to know himself before he can know God, and our pilgrimage takes us inwards to the depth of our being, on our journey to realization.

One longed for *silence*, to be given a chance to find and make contact with this 'God out there'; and in this seeking one wanted instinctively to turn inwards in order to listen to the 'still small voice'. Listening is surely more important than our incessant babbling. When we have learned to listen we become ready to receive God's grace and guidance:

> When you pray, go to your private room and, when you have shut the door, pray to your Father who is in that secret place, and the Father who sees all that is done in secret will reward you.[2]

During these spiritually depressing years – years of intense loneliness and even of doubt – a few like-minded people appeared and formed a small, silent prayer group. Not all were Christians in the strictly orthodox sense, but there were absolutely no barriers of race, colour, creed or sex; only perfect unity of heart and soul within this silence where we were seeking our Creator and His will. The more we experienced the reality to be found in this silence the more we sought these times in regular daily periods set apart and, for longer times, in retreats. A new dimension began to open up: one discovered the reality of non-verbal communication with one's fellow men and saw that the benefits were horizontal as well as vertical.

The gifts of the Spirit, which are surely only a 'spiritualized' form of ESP, are being restored to life again. Is it possible that Christ is the supreme example of a fully realized human being, whose ESP faculties were so developed – 'spiritualized' – by the fact of His living so close to the Father? A few years ago, the gift of healing was looked on with suspicion and mistrust: how incredible! My own family have been the recipients of various forms of healing, from Agnes Sandford's absent prayers to the restoring of balance in the energy fields in order to counteract a malignancy. This was not smiled upon by the local priest. But after all, Christ did say, 'Greater things than this shall ye do when I go to the Father.'[3] The climate is changing, and the charismatic movement has done a great deal to open the windows to let in the wind of the Spirit. This has undoubtedly been responsible for a new openness which, when rightly channelled, can be used. I would urge everyone to pause and reflect when hands begin to burn in the vicinity of a person needing healing, or when some 'miraculous' event comes about after prayer (even if it is only your guardian angel supplying you with a parking space after a fleeting prayer was sent up!). Alternatively, if your mind is lit up by a profound statement applicable to your present need, stop for a moment and consider from whence it may have originated. The gifts of the Spirit are still being poured out on us to this day, and we must learn to be ever more open to receive them and to use them wisely. More and more are we coming to realize that there are no such words as 'coincidence' or 'extraordinary' and that nothing happens by chance.

There followed another ten years or so of continued

searching. I joined many groups that proved helpful to me at different stages and I absorbed, most gratefully, their different aspects of the spiritual life. Then this came to an end, and I was again left in a state of dissatisfaction. It seems to me that we are always being gently steered onwards and upwards, never allowed to rest too long in one place. I knew I could not continue along this many-forked path. I wanted to throw all that was affiliated to Christianity out of the window, and began mentally to turn to the East where, at least, the mystery and transcendence of God had been retained. Why was it that so often the Church's ritual seemed to be empty and meaningless? Surely 'religion' was a much bigger thing than any of us realized? The words of Scripture came across as devoid of life and meaning. Something appeared to be lacking – an unawareness of another dimension in Christ's teaching, perhaps, or a wrong interpretation being put on the context of certain passages? I blamed myself for being unable to accept the Word of God and suffered a great deal of mental anguish.

Later on, when I felt I could no longer keep my thoughts to myself, I was overjoyed to find others on the journey who thought as I did. To be able to share doubts and difficulties and know one was not alone in the darkness was incredibly healing and creative. It was at this stage that I took myself off to my Anglican 'bolt hole', the Dorothy Kerin Centre (Burrswood) in Kent, to spiritually 'sweat out' my future direction within the context of prayer. What emerged was a complete surprise to me, as well as to my friends; for I was shown that beyond a shadow of a doubt the way ahead for me lay within the Catholic Church. This may seem a strange step, given that the climate today is increasingly more ecumenical, but it was the first time in my life that I had experienced what it was like to be completely certain, utterly sure that this was the step that had to be taken. (It is in my nature to doubt my own decisions for I usually see too clearly the pros and cons of any issue.) Perhaps something has to be finished off in this life that had either been left undone or done badly – who knows? This heightened awareness of certainty and rightness was a gift in itself, as were the nightly visions that appeared to help me to this realization.

I would like to stress that at no time did I intellectualize this decision. In fact, the taking of this step would not have been possible if I had been asked to 'think it out', for my own personal beliefs could not have been contained within the Church. These 'beliefs' or inner 'knowings' were authentic for me, as they emerged from some place deep within and gradually unfolded their message, but only as fast as the conscious self could understand and assimilate the contents. The process which is still going on, is rather like peeling an onion – always there is another layer to be stripped off and deeper insights to be revealed. The teacher is most certainly within. (I must add that I have found that in the Catholic Church the area of the supernatural is accepted as a 'natural' part of life. And surely the interpenetration of these two dimensions is what has to take place in order for the higher to transform the material?)

The next problem was how to cope with an inner 'knowing', which had grown stronger over the years, that one returns more than once to this earth plane to experience and learn all the lessons that go to make a whole person? Realization of this did not come via any external factor; it emerged almost imperceptibly from the hidden depths within the psyche, maybe from the sphere of the collective unconscious. At first I recoiled from the very notion. This was partly because of the conditioning imposed by my religious upbringing and partly because I simply did not like the idea. I was forever sweeping this concept under the biggest proverbial carpet I could find. Nevertheless, it would, however, recur again and again until I eventually saw the whole revelation in its wider aspect. I realized that rebirth is not to be thought of in the way Eastern belief has it, a perpetual wheel of successive human lives, but rather as our one life having many embodiments in the process of our spiritual evolution; maybe 'there are many mansions', just as Jesus said. We have free will, so may we not wish to return to perform a service for our fellow human beings? A more highly developed love and compassion would not be at peace if there were others still outside the 'fold', not to mention imperfections and desires of our own that have to be tested in the fire many times before they become purified. What matters is a person's soul, for it is the soul that is eternal, the link which makes us all one. I believe this awareness to be the gift of wisdom. For me, it has indeed been a great blessing. It has taught me – and is still teaching me – not to judge others, as Christ preached, for we have no knowledge of the whys and wherefores of our own situation let alone of what is right or wrong in another's life. I see God's mercy and forgiveness here: we are always given another chance to mend our ways and use our free will to the greater glory of God and for the benefit of mankind. I have personally experienced Christ – or a Great Being – taking to Himself the errors of my life here and now, along with those of past lives, and raising them up so that they too may be forgiven and redeemed. The Church did, after all, hold the belief of rebirth until the Ecumenical Congress of Constantinople in AD 553, and only after this did the idea of the 'wandering of the wondrous soul' become such an anathema.

The most crucial question is: do we remain true to our conscience or inner teaching and hold on to a truth we believe to have been shown to us by the Holy Spirit within, or do we subscribe to the teaching expressed in man-made doctrines and dogmas, which does not ring true in our hearts? In the end there is no peace until we are courageous enough to believe in ourselves, and not merely to believe, but to let our understanding filter through to our daily lives and all which that may affect. Having been through so much mental agony because my beliefs conflicted with those of the Church, I now want to try to spare others this same agony; they will thus soon learn to accept that the Truth may be found just as surely within themselves as within the minds of other mortal men. We must never allow our beliefs to crystallize but try to be at that point of perfect balance where we can be moved on easily should the wind of the Spirit blow our way. I generally need such a thump on the back before I can be moved on that I suffer needlessly in the process of obeying! This has brought me to the point of looking upon universal and spiritual truths as there for all of us to find. I no longer feel that I have 'beliefs' as such but can only speak from an 'experience' which for me then becomes a deep 'inner knowingness'. I am not now so concerned about what is taught or written about the nature of God, for by allowing God to reveal something of Himself deep within my consciousness, within myself – for 'the Kingdom of God is within'[4] – I have been given and shown as much as I can bear at present. Spiritual experience can only come through our own realization, through something which has taken place within our own consciousness and no one else's:

> Truth is within ourselves . . . and to know rather consists in opening out a way whence the imprisoned splendour may escape.
> Robert Browning, *Paracelsus*, Part I

I had been led to believe that grace was rather like a beautifully wrapped surprise gift planted on one by the whim of a benevolent Father Christmas figure – a bonus handed out to those who deserved it or were in favour. But as God sends the rain on the just and unjust, so He pours His grace upon the world. He cannot do otherwise, for as Christ said, 'All that the Father [*our* Father] hath is mine.'[5] It is a gift we must learn to accept by opening our hearts, minds and consciousness.

Joel Goldsmith writes about the Is-ness of God in his book *The Contemplative Life:*

> You cannot know what God is because no one in the history of the world has ever been able to embrace God by means of his human mentality. King Solomon said that his entire temple was not big enough to hold God, and you may be assured that the mind of man is not capable of embracing God. So, it is useless to try to ask what God is. Rather acknowledge that God IS.[6]

I therefore now no longer crave to share my own experiences with others for I have come to realize that each person's approach to their Creator and to the Christ is a unique and personal experience and that we must all respect this fact when talking with our fellow men. If we share what we feel and are chastised for it, then we should neither feel guilty nor become dispirited, because all we are being told is that we look at life, at God, at religion in a different way. As a rule, we all give credence to the One God, but the interpretation, the symbols and the words we use differ. We are, perhaps, looking at different aspects or angles of the same goal. The various interpretations placed on translations and on historical facts can never be united by hammering out the points with words.

It is at this stage that silence is invaluable, for when we can quieten our minds and hearts and be still we shall 'hear' with the inner ear and understand with a mind divorced from trivia and prejudices.

What I find is that when one *is* able to share similar revelations and experiences, then this is a very great bonus – a true blessing – and one in which we are brought closer together at soul level, or so it feels to us. In actuality, this is not possible as we are already branches of the same Vine and our lives are 'hid in Him' who is rooted and grounded in the Godhead. I feel we must therefore be tolerant of the paths of other wayfarers for, as unique individuals, we each have our own particular approach to the One. And many paths lead to our Source. I am sure that the highest truths of all religions contain the Truth and that if they are looked at carefully they will be seen to be saying the same thing. But I also believe that – though we may learn much from the East – if we live in a Western culture it is within that context that we should practise our faith. Otherwise, would we not have been born in regions where Islam and Buddhism are practised? In saying this I do not mean to lessen the status of the Christian faith, which I firmly believe, when truly understood, to be the Way. Its message is that of Love, the highest and most enlightened concept of all religions when it is practised and understood in its purest form. Jesus is the Christian's Master, but other faiths have their own Masters; and within them all, and over and above them all, is the Cosmic Christ.

Having said so much about the difficulties I have been through while in the Church, I would now like to add something on the positive side. First, I would say to my fellow travellers: persevere within the Christian Church if that is where you are, for you are not there by chance. The time will come when seemingly conflicting views will tie together, not in the old way in which you understood them before, but in a 'new' way – call it another dimension if you will. And let us always bear in mind that there are many, many others, even those in 'high places' or formally entrenched situations, who are being moved by the Spirit of God and need understanding and companionship, to be made to feel that they are not alone in what seems to be strange new territory. We were told, 'Ask and it shall be given to you; search and you will find; knock and the door will be opened to you.'[7] This certainly happened to me. The picture grows larger and the structure firmer, making a stronger base from which to grow spiritually. I believe that as many people as possible must be given the opportunity to explore in depth their true faith and the nature of their being.

I believe we are being given an increasingly clear glimpse of Reality, though it can hardly be called a glimpse: it is as yet only an awareness of something out of our reach. One gets the feeling that when this other dimension comes, when it manifests itself further, it will be above and beyond all we have known up to this present moment, something infinitely greater and essentially universal. Let us hold on loosely to our hobbyhorses and our opinions so that we may be ready to rise up and receive whatever it is that will come to supersede all else and cause us to question certain tenets of our faith. We have no need to wonder what form 'it' will take, as it comes from the Source, and that is Good (God). Still, we must be receptive, for only those who have 'ears to hear' will hear and 'eyes to see' will see. More and more I am being directed far back, back into the Church's story, where, beneath the superficial superstructure, lies the naked Truth, the Uncreated Light, the Mystery. So it must remain while our eyes are yet finite; but we can taste these delights in contemplation and meditation; and through the revelation of the supernatural we know of their existence, which is our inheritance. True humility, a dying to self or an abandoning of oneself to God, is a continuous process throughout life. Gradually, it will be His Light that is reflected and which shines forth from us to the world. We do not shine forth our light, but we allow the Uncreated Light of God to flow out into His world. How it accomplishes its task is not our business, but we are assured that it is used where it is needed. So we must enter into the Greater Silence within, and in the stillness the Spirit takes over and prays in us, illuminating our hearts and minds with the Love and Truth that come not from man but from the Source, the Christ within.

3.
Janice's Journey

From childhood my spiritual approach to life was built on two foundations: a local Anglican church in which I was confirmed, with a vicar abounding in 'the joy of the Lord', and a Roman Catholic convent, where I was educated by nuns who seemed to be alive with the sweetness that living in the presence of God can bring. Through the Church I found a basic Christian faith, enjoyed Christian fellowship and went through a conversion experience. At the convent, where we had a small chapel at the centre of things, I came to value quietness, stillness and prayer. By the time I left school I felt I had found God in some way; the God I knew in each context was one and the same, and disputes over doctrinal and liturgical differences seemed to me man-made and irrelevant. I therefore find it natural to collaborate in the writing of this book with a Catholic and equally to be linked locally with a joint Roman Catholic and Church of England secondary school where we are finding that the way forward is by sharing the vision we have in common, not by accentuating the differences that exist.

Through university and while raising a family I was a fairly regular practising Anglican until one day our curate asked if I would lead a house group for women. I felt that house groups were a very good thing and gladly agreed. But now I really had to do some deep thinking if I was to lead others. Little did I realize what a lonely journey I was setting out on. Once one really starts to search, one can only let go, put one's hand in the hand of God and be led. My leading at that time seemed to be away from my own Church and away from the Bible. I seemed increasingly drawn to try other services – Quaker, Pentecostal, White Eagle, Methodist and Sufi – and instead of the Bible, which I had read regularly, a large quantity of other reading matter seemed to be put in my way. At each step of my thinking, exactly the right person, group or book seemed to land in my path at the very moment I was ready. I found myself being propelled steadily away from my preconceived ideas and learned to move with the ideas that came.

The first major realization that dawned upon me was the idea that this lifetime might not be all there is, but merely one small part of a far, far longer journey. I had previously dismissed concepts of rebirth as being part of some quaint Eastern superstition, but now I found myself brought to this possibility by the logic of my own thinking. I had already rebelled against the emphasis on 'salvation' while in this life and against the hazy notions I had received concerning death and a life beyond. Yet at this point I panicked. I was able to move neither back to the security of my previously held beliefs, nor forward to all that must follow the acceptance of such an idea. Slowly, I was able to piece it all together. An article explaining a Christian view of rebirth certainly helped; so, too, did the lines from Shakespeare and Wordsworth that came flooding back, bringing with them a feeling of relief. I realized that I was not the first to think this way. Suddenly it all made sense of so much – why people were at different stages, had different abilities and burdens. Life took on a clearer pattern and a purpose as just part of an experience, a series of schoolrooms where we truly must 'judge not, that [we] be not judged', for we cannot know the point another person has reached, nor indeed where we are ourselves. Suddenly it does not matter whether we were born this time a beggar, last time a king; but what may be important is possibly how we treated a beggar when we were a king! 'Whatsoever a man soweth, that shall he reap': is there not an underlying pattern of cause and effect? Are we not placed alongside others in the process of interaction we call our life through which we learn the vital lessons that we need? All at once I found that everything had its place and that I could love everyone.

Then came the second new idea, and it came like a revelation: Love – that is what God is, pure Love and nothing less. A divine intelligence, an energy permeating and sustaining the universe, activating every cell and atom of every form that exists and vibrating at the rate of absolute purity and Love. This is the 'I am' of which the Bible speaks; this is the inner esssence Teilhard de Chardin describes. This, too, is the message Jesus came to bring and spelt out as the basic precept for our lives: 'Love the Lord thy God with all thy heart and all thy soul and all thy mind and thou shalt love thy neighbour as thyself.'[1]

Of course, I had known this since I was a child; the difference was that I no longer accepted it because that was what I had been told – now I *knew* it to be so. In fact, in higher moments I could actually see this Love: a vibrant energy pulsating through every plant and flower, every person, every living thing. The world is such a wonderful place if only we could see it as it is; and if we are going to live attuned to it we must pulsate at that same rate, for everything is a beautiful expression of this basic oneness which is God.

This, then, was the third revelation: oneness. We are truly one; we can be nothing else. Jew and Gentile, Russian and American, rich and poor, Third World and First World, we are all one, part of the same one life that sustains us – God. This totally revolutionizes our thinking. Each of us can no longer deliberately harm another, though in ignorance we still do, for in so doing we harm ourselves and we harm God: 'In as much as ye have done it unto one of the least of these my brethren...'[2] We find ourselves turning to conservation and ecological movements, to wholefoods and natural healing methods and cutting our living standards to do more to satisfy the needs of the Third World. We find ourselves, also, treating the person who serves in the supermarket as a son of God and thus equally deserving of respect as ourselves. We look around and find so many in the world bent on the meaningless pursuit of material wellbeing for its own sake, and our politicians holding this up as the goal of our desires. We can only step aside into our own space and let the world race by for a time.

Some call this change of awareness the 'New Age'. It has many names and many definitions, but there is no doubt that a change of understanding is dawning, that the world is moving into a new order of existence and that we are being asked to move with it or stay behind. The change has been painful to me, not only internally but also externally because of the rejection it brought from family and orthodox friends. One finds oneself living in two different worlds, until at times one either doubts one's sanity or, like St Joan, cries out: 'What other Judgement can I have but my own?'[3] We have no choice but go the way that we feel led.

For me the key has been this one phrase, 'Be still and know that I am God', and I am grateful to the nuns at school and to the meditation groups through which, more recently, I learnt this.[4] As a matter of fact I no longer feel comfortable in most church services, which rarely seem to provide the necessary space for being quiet and still, and I usually content myself with creeping into the building when no one else is there. For now I find that God is not only 'up there' but also deep within and that communion with Him is all-important. This 'I am' presence is within us all, whether we recognize it or not, and in our quietness we slowly find that God speaks to us 'within our own thinking'. Throughout the ages individuals have testified to hearing the 'still small voice within' yet it is perhaps only now that we are finding this real in a mass sense. It can come through a thought flow of words, through a voice speaking as the conscience, through being in harmony with nature, through vision in imagination, through mental pictures – in the many ways the Spirit speaks to us. As we first open up, the Spirit seems to flow in fast, and we find that we do need to learn discernment through experience, but this does come; we make mistakes, and our faults seem to glare at us more strongly; we correct them, pause and move forward again.

Yet beyond all this lies a conviction about God and His presence in the universe and a firm belief that what all the great religions have taught us is true: this reality exists, this great spark within us all, the Christ. For this indwelling presence within us – the Christ – *is* there, whether we use that word or not. When we meet, the Christ in you meets the Christ in me, and we are truly one; for as Jesus tells us, 'I am the vine, and ye are the branches', and to the extent that we can live within this reality and accept this spirit of Love in us, then this is so.[5]

Through this growing realization I began to see Jesus in a different way. Perhaps it is because I have always associated with rather evangelical churches, but it seemed that those I met there were talking about a historical figure who was at one and the same time human and divine and whose life history was so important that we celebrated different stages of it during the Church's year. Once I began to switch to a slightly more 'inner' level of seeing things, I found that behind the historical events and the outer form of the teaching was an inner mystery for all men; so that, for instance, in celebrating the birth of Jesus at Christmas the attention is focused not so much on the events of the Nativity as on the birth of the Christ Light, the 'Son', or first-created offering, of God. The more I thought about this, the more I felt that this was the essential Light – 'Let there be light' – which was emanating from God entering into matter, taking form and becoming life. Thus the very essence of life, the original creative principle, is the Light of God, and this is the Christ or, as some would say, 'the Cosmic Christ'.

This Light is there in all men; it has to be if this is right. It is within us all, only we do not as yet realize it and so do not fully manifest it. Jesus was born as the most perfect being yet to exist. He was the first to carry the full vibrations of this Light and as such was a bridge between God and man. Others through the ages had also seen this, conveyed it in ancient writings and prophesied the birth of Jesus, but what Jesus Himself showed by His life and teachings is that to live life in harmony with God we too must manifest love in all we do. This then becomes the touchstone of our lives and the unfolding of the inner Light – the purpose of our lives on earth. Some talk of this as the birth of the inner Christ, the Christ within – an essential nativity, and the first step on the inner path.

This, for me, is different from the evangelical injunction: 'Turn to Jesus, believe in Him and you will be saved.' It is not a matter of mental belief, of assent to a set of facts or ideas, but an inner process of turning one's consciousness away from matter and outer form and towards an inner way.

At first this realization of an inner way, an understanding of the Buddhist teaching that this material plane is *Maya*, an illusion, had the result of making me abandon the outer way entirely! The way I dressed, what I ate, how I spent my time or money – these seemed no longer important. But I shortly realized that, as Jesus said, we must live perfectly (or as perfectly as we can!) in the world and yet not be *of* the world, that is, our consciousness and our awareness must be set on something higher which will thus spiritualize and bless the material level at which we find ourselves.

It is this integration of the inner and outer that the Church should perhaps try to serve. Nevertheless, I feel that it has got somewhat 'stuck' at the material level, the level of form, and is failing to move with the way ahead. I very much hope that a spiritual awakening does not pass it by, for many young people I have met are moving with this change. Some are travelling to the East and discovering there the spirituality that is missing in the West. 'Now at last,' one said, 'I understand what Christianity, deep down, is all about. But what I have discovered is shared by all the faiths alike. Surely different religions are only different paths for travelling to the same place. Can we not break down the barriers between them?' I feel that the Christian Church is being urged to grow up, to leave behind not the essence of the faith, but the dogmas and rituals – some might even say superstitions – that have come to dominate the form.

The early Church was like a mighty force – groups of loving people who spread the new Life they had found throughout the world. Such a possibility of transformation seems to be calling this generation, yet the Church as a whole seems not to understand the wave of loving awareness that is surging through the young and occupies itself instead with its own self-perpetuation. Meanwhile the young without the wisdom and guidance of those in established faiths are likely to be swept into backwaters and extremes.

One possible reason for this is that the Church seems to be stuck at an intellectual understanding of the truth, objective facts which one was supposed to take on board as a 'package deal' of faith. In the past, the Church has even killed those who would not agree with whichever package of truth was prevalent at the time. What seems to be more important nowadays is not so much the mental knowledge about the truth as the experience, the knowing or gnosis, of the truth. Gnostics have been condemned throughout history, and may be afraid even now to express their views. I do not feel that the Church, in any of its denominations as I have come across them, is what Jesus the Christ intended to establish. First of all, it is quite possible that we do not have all the Gospels, and also likely that others, previously hidden or suppressed, will be revealed during our lifetime. But by taking the Gospels that we do have, if one isolates for a moment what Jesus Himself taught and the life He demonstrated, and if one dwells more deeply on the inner meaning of it all, then it seems that He did not intend that He Himself should be worshipped in the way He has been. He always, always pointed to the life-giving Spirit He called Father – thought of, rightly, as He/She/It – as the Creator or Sustainer of our universe. He tried continually to bring us in touch with Him. How? Through repentance, that is, by making us turn away from ourselves as being the centre of our lives. If we 'ask', we shall 'receive' an awareness of the Spirit. Then comes a constant daily living in the awareness of the Spirit. Jesus

Himself was so 'together' and so 'realized' in His being that He was able to focus this power of life and bring it to bear on such situations as healing a blind man or turning the water into wine. 'He that believeth in me, the works that I do shall he do also', – an awesome thought, and one that most of us feel, as yet very far from.[6]

It seems almost inevitable that once a Church was set up it was to be subjected to the power of Man; whether well- or ill-intentioned, he would twist things in certain ways, to suppress some truths and overintellectualize others. This was the state of the Jewish Church that Jesus found. He went along with it, but showed that it had served its day and should now grow to embrace the awareness that He was bringing; the same is true today. Jesus said: 'Think not that I am come to destroy the law, or the prophets. I am not come to destroy but to fulfil.'[7] I think that that is what He would say today if He were here. We have become trapped into perpetuating what we have and, like Hamlet, I feel 'There are more things in heaven and earth, Horatio, than are dreamt of in your philosophy.'[8]

Sometimes when I am quiet I go back in time and almost find myself sitting upon the shores of Galilee, listening to what the Master is saying and sensing the deeper meaning in it all. For a brief moment I glimpse what was meant by the words He spoke, and the profundity is almost overwhelming. So, too, is the awareness of how basically simple it all is and how complicated we have made it all become. But this simplicity appears only to dawn as we leave behind our preconceived ideas and let an inner understanding and deeper sense of reality break through. I am sure that deep within the Church can be found an awareness of cosmic levels of being and of a greater sense of the glory and the wonder of it all. Yet too often religion has become merely a question of attending services for the sake of attending rather than an opportunity to be uplifted to the heavenly realms. Sometimes there is more emphasis on doctrines and good works than on a sharing of the kingdom of heaven that is within us all.

I have met people who are finding and following this hidden reality, but they are rarely anchored in the old traditions. They are with gurus in the foothills of the Himalayas, or in small community groups, living and loving but in danger of becoming sheep without a shepherd. Jesus still seems to be saying 'Feed my sheep', but He does not mean 'Teach them hours of doctrine; sit them in joyless pews'. He means: 'Nurture them where they are. See the Christ Light growing within them and, from the Christ Light within yourself, love them into a fuller sense of being.' This is what He Himself did. He blessed them, young and old, sick and well, saint and sinner – all were equally beloved in His sight. He did not see their faults and blemishes, as we have all been inclined to do. Instead, He saw the Christ within them and knew that each one was part of the same Life as He Himself, that this Life was the nourishment that we need: 'Whosoever drinketh of the water that I shall give him shall never thirst.'[9]

These living waters must be for everyone, not just for Christians in the West and not just for the few who feel comfortable within the pews. I can understand that the clergy feel that they must minister to those who look to the Church for worship and support. But between the services, the committees on carpets and Church teas, could they not go forth more often into the community to heal and bless, to comfort and listen? There are, of course, many who do so, and it is possible that many more would like to but feel trapped into merely the preserving of an institution rather than a pouring out of living waters.

Jesus did not tell people what to believe. He did not set up services for them to attend. He healed them when they were sick, fed them when they were hungry and gave them simple truths to comprehend that would help them on their way. This is what Mother Teresa is doing in Calcutta, and what the hospice movement is doing in Britain today. This is what, with God's grace, we could all be doing today.

Grace – this leads me to the sacraments, which to me are potentially significant as they can give us at one and the same time the outer form and the inner meaning – contact with the divine – the two blended into perfection. About a year after I had left the Church (in the sense of regular attendance), I decided to go to the midnight Holy Communion service on Christmas Eve, a time when it seems heaven and earth can truly blend. My sense of the mystery and peace of it all carried me in, and I anticipated the church being filled with angels, holy music, candles and an awareness of the Christ child's birth. But instead the lights were ablaze, and there was no music. There were people, but no feeling of joy or holiness. We were ushered to the altar by cheerless sidesmen and stood in serried rows, no smiles between us. I felt that I had asked for living bread and been given stones: on my journey home, I wept.

This made me think about the many levels of being Christ tried to show, and I went back in my mind to the first Communion, the 'Last Supper', on the last day before His death. He left with us the best message that He could. His friends were hungry, so He gave them food: physical matter taken in physical form. They needed fellowship, so the meal was shared: they smiled and joked as they passed the bread around. But above all they needed nourishing with the Life Force of the universe: God, the essence of being, the 'I am' that was fully in Jesus and potentially within us all – the Christ. So, speaking as the Christ, the living Life, He said, 'This is my body and my blood' which might be taken to mean 'the essence of what I am, the essence of what you are'. If the 'I am' presence is within each atom, then it is within the food. We do not need to turn it into the spirit, it *is* already; we only have to recognize that this is so – the blessing is already there.

Although there may be a deeper level still conveyed by the Eucharist, the one which is now important to me is the sense of inner communion. This offers a link with the way some young people are seeing things today. As one young writer has put it:

> It is fundamentally a change of consciousness from one of isolation and separation to one of communion, attunement and wholeness.[10]

With a growth in the sense of communion with God comes a sense of non-separation and an increasing telepathic link with others. Death suddenly seems unimportant, just a transition from one state of being to another, a discarding of the outer form. Here again I found my thinking in conflict with the Church, which rarely offers much comfort to the bereaved, and yet I discovered after the death of a loved one that he became, in a way, more real than he had been before. It is our blockages of fear, sorrow and doubt that prevent this from being so. If we could but sense the release of the being into realms of greater Light, our funeral services would be a thanksgiving for the life just led and not the sombre committal of dust to dust that so often we enjoin nowadays.

Slowly, I have come to a widening understanding that

encompasses other levels of being – levels of consciousness perhaps – interpenetrating our own and pushing us gently towards a greater growth beyond. Books like Helen Greaves' *The Testimony of Light* confirmed the horizons that were opening up ahead, but the dilemma has been that so few others in the Church seem to understand.[11] I had felt heretical: a self-appointed outcast from the fold with no authority to turn to save what I found within. This is perhaps good, in a sense, for it makes us grow to greater spiritual maturity and obliges us to find our own interior guide. I have since come across many who do know something, that is, something real and authentic; in fact, their understanding far surpasses my own. But I must confess that few such individuals are in the Church. This increased my dilemma. I longed to leave the Church behind as something I had outgrown, but there was always the 'pull' to stay and to help awaken its people's understanding of the fact that our perception of the Truth does not stand still.

It can never stand still. We must be forever breaking boundaries if we are to live and grow. The Church does help if it offers a stable base to which we can return in order to test out the truths we think we have discovered; for we must let go of the dross and keep hold only of what is real. The Church does not help if it maintains boundaries too solid to be broken through and leaves us trapped and helpless, within them. If instead we could incorporate into our thinking the many aspects of Truth that are penetrating our understanding today, might we not find that we have slipped unperceived into the universal and mystical Body of Christ wherein everyone can find room in the many mansions within the greater dwelling?

My present situation is one of compromise. I sometimes attend our parish church, but I feel more at home at services held at the local ecumenical school, for everyone there is striving for a more universal expression of what we all believe. When I can, I travel to a meditation group some miles away and always come home feeling refreshed and integrated at all the levels of by being. I have also joined a universal teaching system which teaches an integral wisdom and is giving some of the underlying philosophy for which I yearned. It makes me realize that my journey has only just begun!

4.
Journeys of Other Travellers on the Way

A Tolerant View
If a man does not keep pace with his companions,
Perhaps it is because he hears a different drummer;
Let him step to the music which he hears,
However measured or far away.

Henry David Thoreau

The journeys which we have each described seem to have much in common. More important, perhaps, is the fact that they both express openly the struggles we have endured against the rigidity of the Churches in which we have found ourselves. We feel that it is now time for us, the laity, to be allowed a hearing and to show, albeit in a small way, how the climate of thinking may be affecting us today.

Everyone is, naturally, afraid of being ridiculed. We ourselves would not have dared to express how we felt had we not first had our experiences confirmed by others. This confirmation grows the more it is shared, and so, at the risk of repetition, we are including here some contributions from those we have met. None of the contributors have had the opportunity of reading anything that we have written, which means that their testimonies have emerged spontaneously from within themselves; it also means that they may not necessarily wish to be identified with everything that we ourselves have said. Most of them are no more writers than we are ourselves, but their accounts, like our own, are honest and first-hand. It was not our intention that they should all be women, but possibly women find it easier to express their feelings; possibly, too, they have had more time to allow their intuitive side to develop and for it not to be swamped by pressures of a more mental nature.

The contributors come from different backgrounds, and their ages span a wide range: from the teens to the eighties.

We have arranged them in order of age, starting with the freshness and sponteneity of the young and moving gradually to the increased wisdom of those in later years. They do not form part of any one group or way of thought; indeed, most of those in our own lives and communities either remain comfortably within the Church and regard us as misguided in our thinking, or have left it behind and feel that we are wasting our time and energy in attempting to explain our predicament. Those who have contributed still care, and hopefully their views will give a clear indication of how some of the laity feel today.

Philippa's Discoveries
Philippa is in her late teens. After leaving the sixth form she spent a year travelling in India and the Far East. She grew up in a Christian home, attending Sunday School, Crusaders and Bible Study classes at an Anglican church.

Ever since I was a child there has been this tremendous desire to answer satisfactorily the question of God's identity, although there was never any question in my mind that He existed.

However, events of recent years did cause me to question the state of the world: widespread violence and terrorism; increasing antagonism between Eastern and Western superpowers leading to the threat of a nuclear exchange; the everwidening gap between the rich of the North and poor of the South; mounting friction between different religions; and even an increasing number of natural calamities, which seemed to indicate a reflection of mankind's impurity in the very elements themselves. The peace and natural harmony of the world order that I felt ought to exist was distinctly lacking. There was, it seemed, a very profound change going on in the world. The massive revival in spiritual awareness and 'alternative' groups and organizations was, I felt, indicative of the unrest and uncertainty being experienced by everyone, everywhere. Indeed, at such a time of need as this, it is natural that we should react by turning to the One, remembered as God, in a final bid for help, peace and an answer to all our questions. If there is belief in God, there has to be belief in a reason for everything that happens. I felt there had to be some 'Master Plan' which would explain why everything was happening in the world the way it was.

So strong was my conviction that this particular period of

time we are all experiencing was one of such critical importance that I could not rest until this nagging dilemma was resolved. Responding to the gloom and uncertainty of the general atmosphere in the West, and also to the 'pull' that somewhere in the world the force of God, the Supreme, was at work, I decided to journey out to the East to see if the secrets of such ancient civilizations could provide an explanation for the changes which were taking place. One thing was clear in my mind from the start: the remedy of the situation of the world had now passed out of the hands of human beings. It was now up to that One source of energy to set all things to rights once again – my only trouble now was: 'Who is He?'

At Sunday school I had great problems grappling with the concept of God which I was being taught. I was given the impression that God was a stern old man living above the clouds watching me, waiting to pounce on any evil doings. If some sadness or catastrophe occurred, it was because it was 'God's will'. I could never understand why God should be blamed. I wish I had been taught then that everything that happens to me is a result of my own actions in the past, the cause and effect: as I sow, so shall I reap. The law of God had been experienced, but never the love. It was difficult to try and make a relationship with God because, instead of love, there was this fear of getting close.

I was confused even further when I was taught that God existed in the form of Father, Son and Holy Ghost: this I couldn't rationalize at all, and I was even less able to rationalize when I learned that God was also supposed to be omnipresent, that is, everywhere, in everybody, in everything. The idea of God being 'Universal Love' or 'Cosmic Consciousness' seemed so very abstract and vague – an easy answer to a difficult question. On examining these points further, the only conclusions I could draw were that these were matters you just had to accept whether you understood them or not, that it was above my head to comprehend and I didn't really need to know anyway. And yet my faith that God existed held out. If God never existed, why should a single human being ever have reason to remember Him?

During my travels in the East I was surprised to come across devotees who believed with an equal amount of faith that God exists in the forms of Krishna, Rama and Buddha, just as Christians believe Him to be incarnate as Jesus. Yet I soon came to understand that if God was the Supreme Father of all – be they Christian or Muslim, Hindu or Buddhist – He had to exist in a form that was acceptable to all. Those believing that Jesus was the Incarnation of God would not accept that the same was Krishna, and vice versa. What I saw was that all these religious founders were perfect examples of the qualities and virtues of God and that all pointed to One who was above them and beyond them. I remembered Jesus as saying, 'Don't pray to me but to God your father who is in heaven'. Indeed, Jesus himself would pray to God, His Father, the Supreme Father of all. So how could they be one and the same being? In my efforts to understand God, I had to transcend the differing opinions of all the religions on such subjects, to try and rise above them in order to discover on what ground they all agreed. I felt that the reason why humans thought of God as a human being also was because it was easier to remember Him in this form, the same form as themselves. I found that the best policy when it came to trying to decide what was true and what was not true was to believe only that which I had experienced for myself to be true, rather than what I was told to be true.

Yet until the start of my travels I really didn't have a relationship with God. I realized that my mind was unable to travel to God because it did not have the answers to the questions it needed to know. Even in the physical world, you cannot have a relationship with someone if you do not know their name, what they look like, where they live, their occupation, and so on – so why should it be any different with God? My mind kept on going back to one particular line from the chapter of Genesis that said God made us in His image – surely this did not mean that God was physically the same as me, in human form, with eyes, nose, mouth and the rest? One thing became quite apparent to me: before I could hope to understand God the Supreme Personality it was first necessary for me to know who *I* was. Was I really this physical body of flesh and bones – or was there more to me, a spirit, a soul?

Einstein, one of the greatest scientists and philosophers of all time, was once asked the question: 'Do you know everything that there is to know in the whole world?' He very wisely replied, 'I may have the knowledge of the entire universe, but even so, I do not know who that "I" is that has this knowledge.' What is this consciousness called 'I'? What is the source of all my thoughts, ideas, feelings, sentiments? The heart? The brain?

The answers to all my questions about myself and God finally came when I began learning about India's highest and most ancient yoga, Raja Yoga (literally, 'the highest union of soul with the Supreme Soul'). Through this I discovered the source of the River of Life itself and was enabled to put a 'full stop' to all those questions that had long lain dormant in my mind. For the first time in my life, not just my heart but also my intellect was fully satisfied. No longer having to abandon my reason and follow with 'blind faith' as I was being asked to do by the Christian religion, I was now able to realize, on the basis of my own experience and with simplicity and ease, all that the Bible was saying.

During my period of study I was taught that the seat of consciousness was actually the soul. The idea of 'soul' or 'spirit' was not new to me since Christians also speak of it, though without mentioning its precise form. I learned that, just as the smallest possible particle of physical matter was an atom, so too is the smallest possible particle of spiritual matter a soul – a tiny, sparkling point of indivisible, eternal, conscious Light-energy. The word for 'soul' in Hindi is *atma*: 'atom' versus *atma*. I realized that I do not *have* a soul, but that I *am* a soul. I, the soul, live inside this body, which is the apparatus or medium through which I perform actions and experience everything that is merged within me. The relationship between soul and body was shown clearly through the example of that between a car and its driver. The two are very separate entities, yet each needs the other in order to function: without a driver the car is completely motionless, and without a car the driver cannot go anywhere. Once inside it, however, the driver can control the direction in which his car moves, its speed, etc. In the same way, the soul sits inside the body and directs its activity. To make it even clearer to me, an analogy was also given. This was that I was an actor who had taken this body as a costume in order to act out my part in what might be compared to an all-embracing world drama, with God as the director. Like actors, who sometimes forget themselves and begin to identify with the roles they are playing, we too have forgotten that we are really souls and begun to identify ourselves with our costume, this body.

Moving on from this, I learnt that the soul is situated in the brain or, more precisely, in the forehead and between the eyebrows. For thousands of years this spot has been known by people of different civilizations and of all religions to be specially sacred. Buddhists call it the 'eye of wisdom'; Hindus the 'third eye' – hence their tradition of marking this seat of the soul with a dot. Christianity and Islam also knew this knowledge once, as they have depicted saints with a circle of light or halo centered on this exact spot.

But how did this knowledge of my true form help me understand who God really was? It was at this moment that I finally realized what that phrase in the Bible about God being in the same image as myself actually meant. As I looked around me, I was able to see that not all souls were alike: some were better than others. I finally understood that just as I am a soul, a tiny point of Light, so too is God a soul – only He is the highest and the loveliest soul of all, the Infinite in the infinitesimal.

This realization of the true nature of God was the key to the lock on my intellect. With the gradual opening of that lock came jewels of knowledge: subtle secrets concerning the workings of the entire universe and the eternal interaction of souls with matter and with the Supreme Soul. It was silent meditation which enabled it to be slowly eased open, making the intellect more subtle and endowing it with a greater capacity for understanding the deep points I was being taught.

I was taught that, unlike me, God never takes a body of His own and is thus able to remain beyond the cycle of birth and death, never coming into the consciousness of the body. Because of this He is able to remain ever pure, peaceful and full of knowledge – free from the continually changing influences of matter. He becomes a detached observer of the drama as it unfolds, and because He remains ever perfect, ever full of knowledge, He is able to play His role of world transformer and purifier of both souls and matter. I learnt of the place where God resides: a region of golden-red light beyond the physical universe; a region of complete silence, beyond sound; a region called the soul world, for not only is it the place where God resides but also the place where all souls exist before coming on earth to take on a body, a costume in order to act out a certain role.

In meditation, I practised taking my mind to this place of supreme silence and experienced overwhelming feelings of deep love, peace and bliss which unleashed from deep within me a feeling of great benevolence towards all mankind – a feeling of perfect unity with the whole world. I was now able to understand why we all seek peace in our lives: it is our original state.

I practised stabilizing my mind in the awareness of myself as a soul and in so doing I found I was shedding the body consciousness to which I had become so accustomed. I began, very tentatively at first, to think of God as a soul: like myself, only Supreme in all qualities. My body consciousness had previously acted like a dam preventing me, the river, from flowing into God, the Ocean; now, on the basis of this similarity, it was possible for me to merge my self and my nature with that of God and to inculcate in myself His virtues and divine qualities.

From this personal experience I went on to understand how the concept of God's omnipresence had come about. I knew God to be all-knowing and all-powerful, and I experienced for myself that His presence could be felt anywhere. The mind can only find peace when it concentrates on one point; so by directing my attention to God as a point of Light I could immediately experience my original qualities of peace, purity and happiness simply through this mental link or union with God. The intensity of these emotions was far greater during the meditation than had ever been experienced before; these feelings were definitely being channelled into my being from an external source of energy. Just as the sun remains always in one place, so too does God. But I can feel the warmth from the sun's rays on my face as I write in this room, which means that the sun's effect can be experienced in this room without the sun itself actually having to be in here also. In the same way, I can experience the power and qualities of God wherever I am, without God literally having to be there also.

As a result of this meditation came the revelation that before there can be peace in the world there must first be peace within the self. Self-transformation comes before world transformation: I have to become completely pure, non-violent and viceless first. Yet peace is much more than the mere absence of conflict, of tension or even of war; it is a rich, complete, positive energy source. It is this hidden energy reserve of the power of silence, the power of the mind, which must now be drawn on in order that world transformation can occur and the New Age that everyone is talking about come into existence. I became aware that it needed only a small percentage of the population to start thinking in this positive way for the results to be very far-reaching. But in order to increase the power of the mind, complete purity of mind, word and action is essential; and then, when our attention is focused on one specific aim and object, all our aspirations will be quickly realized.

Travelling to the various Eastern countries that I visited gave me an insight into many differing world religions. One point that struck home very clearly and frequently was that it is now time to stop seeing others as Muslims, Jews, Hindus, Buddhists, Christians and so on and see them all as souls – my brothers or sisters – each one no less a child of the One Father than ourselves. Seeing just the physical form is very limiting and can cause great misunderstanding and sorrow. And if we compare the temples of the East, where such joyfulness, singing, dancing and bright colours celebrating the Living Force can be seen, to our churches of the West, the latter appear very solemn, drab and depressing, as if they were forever celebrating nothing more than the funeral service of Christ.

I was also interested to learn that the symbol of the cross is much older than Christianity and is not a symbol of suffering; rather, it is symbolic of the meeting of heaven (the vertical tending upwards) and earth (the horizontal lying firm and stable). At the intersection point stands man, who is destined to bring about heaven on earth. Whoever really wants to imitate Christ must take this Cross upon himself and spread heavenly joy.

Tania's Thoughts
Tania is in her early twenties and a graduate in environmental studies. Her background is Anglican, and she grew up quite closely connected with her parish church.

I remember trying to grapple with concepts about God, the meaning of life and so on from quite an early age, and all along I had the feeling that what I was being taught by the Christian Church did not accord with the way I sensed things must be as a result of my own ponderings. I made a conscious decision to leave the Church at the age of fourteen. I had tried hard, having been brought up on a series of Sunday school-type classes, but the older I got the less sense any of it made and I felt increasingly uneasy with what struck me as all the rituals and clichés involved in the way the teaching and worship were conducted. It just did not tie in with my inner sense, albeit vague and unarticulated, of what it was all about. Trying to go along with it created feelings of great guilt and conflict which had built up to a climax by the time I was confirmed. Immediately after that, I realized that it was futile to continue in such an uncomfortable state and decided to let the whole matter rest. With that decision came a sense of lightness and relief.

It was not so much the concept of God that I was rejecting as the ways of the Christian Church and its interpretations and explanations which did not satisfy me because they seemed to me too simplistic. I could not accept the idea of God as a *person* somewhere 'out there'. This did not ring true for me: it seemed an almost childish concept. I was already developing my own ideas about the meaning of life and interpreting Christian teaching as best I could, in a way that made sense to me. I had a sense of postponement, as if I were shelving the issue for some future date, and I had a picture of myself coming back to it in my twenties. So that was that for Christianity! I had decided that it made no sense to me and continued creating my own ideas and philosophies in the meantime.

After I left university I travelled in India for a year, and it was there that I found a connection which I had never experienced before. A whole new awareness was aroused in me, an awareness that was like a shift in consciousness. The only word to describe the feeling is 'magic'; it was a feeling of contact with oneself, of connectedness to life and nature greatly stimulated in my case by the deep inspiration drawn from the incredible natural beauty to which I had been exposed for several months in the Himalayas. It seemed to have opened me up to a state of mystical receptivity that was further fed by contact with Buddhist and Hindu beliefs and a short but intense spell at the Ashram of a Hindu guru.

Suddenly, I understood Christianity: I understood what it meant. I could see through the 'trappings' to the core of its teachings, but only because I had discovered this core directly, and contacted it via a different route. I can now see that the essential 'core' of all major religions is one and the same. From a central perspective, I can see that all religious teachings are fundamentally concerned with the same thing: oneness, and a connection with man's spiritual Source. In this way I now see that religion is about a state of awareness, and that a cultivation of that state of awareness throughout one's life is the objective of following a 'religious' path. The 'bodies' of religion should thus be concerned with teaching, leading, guiding and reminding people of this state: in a sense, with assisting their mental orientation. Although religions may aim to do this, for me the truth had been totally hidden by the traditions, rituals, dogmas and other things that constitute the trappings of 'religion'.

The core of Christianity as I see it is Christ's teaching. He taught the qualities of love, respect, humility and so on, and the greatest of these is Love. God *is* Love; Love *is* God. This was my earliest and most powerful realization – a sudden flash of understanding that God and Love are the same thing. A Being ruled by pure unconditional Love automatically possesses all other qualities. The process of spiritual transformation is, I guess, a process of opening up to Love. This involves dropping the ego-oriented, aggressive, competitive set of attitudes which are cultivated and encouraged by contemporary society.

The difference between 'believers' and 'non-believers' is, I think, that the former have undergone a paradigm shift: that is their frame of reference, their mental orientation, beliefs and attitudes have changed in a subtle yet drastic and powerful way. Their outlook on life, their sense of perspective, is different. All this adds up to a more fully human being holding human values as a higher priority. The fundamental problem for many people these days is the lack of a meaningful philosophy of life. Thus to them life lacks depth, meaning, a sense of man's place in the natural order: they suffer a lack of perspective, a lack of wisdom.

I believe that it is through contacting directly that core in ourselves, which is Love, that we are helped to make the connection, within ourselves, with our spiritual Source. Assisting people to make this connection should be the chief task of all religions. The interpretations and the language differ, but the connection is the same. I find that I can now sit in a church and interpret the language, that made me 'squirm' when I was young, in my own words, and that now makes perfect sense. I still do not choose Christianity as my 'path', because I still find the way it is taught too ritualized, too far removed from what I can now see to be the essence of its meaning. The shift in awareness that I experienced in the East has helped me to re-establish in myself a sense of Man's spiritual nature. I now see that the purpose of all religions should be about connecting with Love.

Angela's Experience

Angela is in her thirties and lives in the Western Highlands of Scotland with her husband, who has been a salmon fisherman all his life, and their small son. She works as a printmaker (wood engraving, etching and relief printing) and also in the field of book design, production and illustration.

Before I entered my twenties, I embraced the Christian faith with gratitude. There then came a time of conflict over beliefs and over allegiance to the Church, a time when I was unable to reconcile traditional religious teaching with my growing sense of that which was essentially true within. It seemed there were so many outer rules – rules to govern good behaviour and rules about Church attendance – but the dynamic which I felt should have supported these rules for all this outer behaviour was missing. I knew this dynamic to be an inner dimension, an interior 'livingness' which was the pivot or mainspring from which in turn our outward existence draws its meaning; yet my elders seemed to be performing, and asking for, rituals. What I was really feeling perhaps, was *my own* sense of meaninglessness, despite my theorizing, and despite the teachings of Christ. These teachings had to be really understood and the meaning reached.

Out of such conflicts action can be born, and the result is often one of disassociation from the Church or from whatever outward authority has guided the seeker so far. The seeker begins to think, and it often happens that he outgrows the usefulness of the particular form that has nurtured him. For myself, this disassociation was not a wrench but a natural progression of events. It was essentially a case of moving away from an outward authority. The yearning to understand the truth, to gain meaning, involved an inner voyage, an inner undertaking which brooked no obstruction: it is a real life urge.

Meanwhile, the individual grows in experience and experiments with thoughts. At this period, when I was a student, I was meeting people on this same road who were living life with an intensity, a sincerity, a lack of compromise and a courage that were inspiring; though life could also include a crippling despair and a meaninglessness. However, it did seem to be the selfsame search that was driving us all forward, and little attention was paid to such outward things as money or status.

Wide reading can be of the utmost benefit on this road, and is a way of finding out that one is not alone. I found that the search was clarified and confirmed by my reading of world literature: poetry, mythology, psychology and some philosophy – just as the books came. (Not exactly a university course, but more of a private education!) I also made a practice of contemplating nature in the English landscape. In this 'contemplation' can be discovered an experience of mystery, not so much in the outward beauty as in that very act of contemplation. The beauty is a spur, a lever to the heart. This is not really 'my' experience but universality. The variation, it seems to me, lies only in the individual detail. This contemplation brings a recognition of the one humanity through that inner sense of unity with all things in the universe; a joy in the world of all living things; a rejoicing in God in the briefest of timeless moments. It is a genuine interior event, something which is measured in the life of the indwelling Christ nature, the Whole Man. This experience can come also through the concentration on and the study of works of art, through the deliberate practice of solitude in quiet and beautiful places which brings a sense of inner communion. It can come equally through that dreadful frustration which somehow releases the self into that greater identity towards which it so desperately strives, through dire pain, through the threat of the void. The ability to experience this union, in whatever way, is universal and is mankind's common heritage, to be realized now or at some time in the future. It certainly seems to be happening on a large scale today. Many are seeking guidance on these matters and for lack of it are experimenting, learning from their mistakes, through a process of trial and error. Their lot has often been condemnation, but the spirit of their search enlivens our society.

Spiritual truth, beauty and goodness were indeed an inner dimension, as I had sensed, and I discovered:

'Beauty is truth, truth beauty – that is all
Ye know on earth, and all ye need to know.'[1]

The kingdom of heaven is indeed an inner place of love, power and unparalleled beauty. Our world is its distortion, and yet just as much the plan of God, just as divine. The meaning is nevertheless within, and it is this meaning that we bring to bear in the world.

Mystical experiences are rare. I believe they are reached not through a sequence of mental events but through either the devotion of the heart, which spirals up and penetrates the unseen beatific world, or the anguish of the heart, which seems to me to have the same results. I also believe it true to say that this interior and definitive experience of union or oneness with God has the effect of simultaneously thrusting the individual outwards into human life again so that the inner understanding of unity is paralleled by some form of outward action or creative activity. It is as though the heart, which by its efforts has penetrated upwards, must descend again into the human spirit, bringing with it a kind of bonus from the inner world. The outward expression can then be as closely in line as possible with the greater life within, whatever commitment a person makes.

Human lives are punctuated by moments of change or crisis. When approached with a positive attitude they can be moments of movement and growth. The Chinese word for 'crisis' is written by combining the symbols for the word 'danger' and 'opportunity', which is most interesting. As far as these periods of change are concerned, the crisis often comes when one realizes that the heart's contemplation is dependent upon outward beauty or outward solitude. Once again, the individual recognizes the need to make a move from this dependence, however sublime, into interdependence, which uses the mind as well as the heart in a more active, conscious process of concentration or meditation.

We need to put our ideas into practice, and this requires a new sort of effort: that of consciously and internally recollecting the Love of God and acting upon it. Furthermore, this must be done without any outward prop, any outer authority, without our being dependent upon any external circumstances. I myself have received a great deal of help from the Alice Bailey books, which embody the teaching of the ancient wisdom. They make a strong appeal for the unity of all approaches to God and for the work that must be done to build right human relations in the world, based on sharing, justice, and a sense of oneness. They are not an authority telling the seeker to act in a certain way; however, they can be a confirmation of his own inner promptings and realizations. At some stage the seeker drops all forms of outward authority in order to discover and depend upon the true Authority within. He then comes to realize that this inner Authority, the Christ within, is also the light which is found in the innermost heart of all humankind; it is not my light, but Light universal. This consciousness is an inclusive one. Thus he comes to know that it is precisely *through* form that he must serve, be it religious, political, social, educational or whatever. The inclusive consciousness is described by a sense of responsibility, co-operation and sharing. These are the values that characterize the New Age groups: groups which are working to heal cleavages and build right human relations, working in a practical way within their own fields because they affirm life, because they have thought and because they love. They are, in fact, meeting the problems and crises thrown up by humanity's very growth and progress. They are working, for example, in the Churches towards the dropping of barriers formed by Old Age materialism, and in world economics towards the incorporation of the values of sharing and goodwill. They are working in the fields of politics, in groups and organizations, to foster a growing recognition of the one humanity and of the necessity for goodwill leading to right relations; and they are active also within groups that deal with every sort of human need. Little by little, the outer forms of our civilization are changing because, first of all, there came about – and is coming about – a change in the human heart.

Before this change can come about we often have to lose aspects of the little self; for example, attitudes that one holds dear must be changed, and very often we have to face a certain kind of loneliness. This can only be a good thing for the little self is an enclosed world and one which is, I think, at a certain point, self-destructive. Through successive crisis points and through our own initiative, we come to discover the inner Authority; this is our service to the world. It is an urge to know the Truth as a living dynamic that very often drives us on in the first place. I know that Christianity embraces the Truth, but then so do other great world religions – Buddhism, for example – and many great individuals down the ages have embodied these truths for humanity in their illumined lives. In order to express the Truth as I know it, I must live it, and living involves commitment. This may mean adopting a religious life; it may mean dropping it. It may mean facing a certain chaos; it may mean imposing the highest order you know on your daily life. It cannot be defined, for it is not a system, but it does mean living a new life in the place where I am. Perhaps this means living the Christ life as one that is all-embracing: becoming the practical mystic. It is as though a new consciousness is bursting through the old interpretations, which were right and good in their day but now no longer serve our purpose. It is this new inclusive consciousness, one of creative thinking and intelligent, active goodwill, which will build the new civilization. This consciousness is characterized by deep joy and life affirmation. The Christian Church and all true religions have nurtured these truths up to this very moment. We now live them, and in so doing, build bridges towards a better world.

Ann's Perspective
Ann is a Roman Catholic in her forties. She has three children and lives in the 'stockbroker belt' of Surrey. Since writing this, she has travelled to India and spent some time with a swami in the Himalayas, where she discovered the more universal and cosmic levels of understanding that she found to be missing in the West.

Last Sunday I went to Mass with one of my children. He likes to go every week, and I find I can use this time for meditation. The form of the service does not mean much to me, so I usually sit there quietly with my own thoughts. One of the things that I increasingly feel is that so many of the people in church are there because they have been taught that they should sit there every Sunday, and as I look around at their faces I see very little joy. People go there because they are lonely; because their parents say they should; because they want to keep the peace at home; but not many of them go to find the peace within themselves, the God within themselves.

I sometimes listen very hard to the sermons which are being given and feel quite sad because, although it is all very clever stuff with a beginning and a middle and an end, the content often seems meaningless, for it stems from religious preaching and not from the heart. This idea started me thinking about the bridging needed between the Church in the Old Age and the Church in the New Age, and one of the things that I felt quite strongly is that whenever a man speaks the Truth, his words reach out clearly to the hearts of the people, but when he speaks by rote, expressing religious beliefs that are really indoctrinations rather than knowing, then his words mean very little to the people sitting there.

All things of any consequence stem from love, and

sometimes when I look at the faces of the priests who stand up there I see sadness, confusion, bitterness and frustration. If all these emotions exist within our priests, then these must cloud the mirror into which they look and distort the truths they speak. If only they could unwind the corkscrews of their lives, they would have the ability to speak the truth in love. For when you know yourself, you know the God within yourself; when you do not know yourself, there is confusion. There has occasionally been someone who has preached in the church that I go to and spoken from utter love, and the simplicity of the Truth they spoke was beautiful. Every human being responds to truth and simplicity, but there is little of this in the Church at the moment. The Church in this age is like an adult who has forgotten what it is like to be a child, the child of truth, wisdom and beauty – forgotten the wonder of a child and the joys of a child.

Jesus Christ was a man of beauty, a child of nature. He spoke from absolute Truth. His faith did not stem from a system of belief, but from His experience with God. I feel that the teachings of the Church are now based too firmly on the 'Jesus Himself' syndrome, rather than on the teachings that He gave us. He taught love and brotherhood, and saw beyond the individual personality. He saw the God who was in each man rather than the personality differences that separated him from God. For in every human being there is a Godhood which is clouded and troubled by the personality which has become sullied.

There are now people on the earth who are willing to love sufficiently to assist us all to bring our Godhood through and so unite it with our personality. If they could start with the priests who lead their flocks within the Church, think of the ripples that could spread throughout the whole of this country! For beneath the veil of illusion, everyone has an 'at-onement' with their essence, with their Goodhood. Each person is a crystal of great beauty, but that crystal is sometimes muddied with the mud of life. If we look around we see that a tree, a daffodil and a butterfly grow because they grow: they are because they are. No one forces them to do anything – they just are. If mankind could learn that it is part of the universe as surely as are sun, trees and flowers, if it could shed all those layers that separate it from God, we could all become children again in childlike simplicity, and as children stretch out their hands to another in friendship, so could we.

Pride is Man's most besetting sin, the one thing that causes separation very surely. If a man who is a priest or bishop could stand in a pulpit and speak from his own experience, from his wisdom of himself, and have the humility that goes with it, he would then have the ability to guide his flock; for in the age to come there is a place for the Church. People will always want to congregate in a place of worship, but when they do so they will want to be in a place which is truthful and where they can relate not only to their own beings, but also to that of the person who is there in the capacity of shepherd.

Love is a quality which was the touchstone of Jesus Christ's ministry. It is a sadly overworked word but one that is very little used in the Church system of today, so heavily bogged down by administration, etc. There are so many lonely people, and their hearts and souls are crying out for a means to end their loneliness. Their spiritual selves are deadened, and their misery is such that they are unable to touch the God aspect of themselves. The Church will have a great role to play in the future if it can move into the New Age in Truth and in Love, for there are many frightened and lost souls who still require a shepherd to assist them. But that shepherd must be a person to whom they can relate: someone who knows himself and who is unafraid to share and relate to both the human and the divine aspects within himself.

It is one thing to say, 'I believe in God' – that is the old way. 'I know my God', is the new way, and 'I know my God' will be the bridge between the old and the new. For belief can only last so long, and then it becomes imprisoned within the very concepts that it is preaching. 'I know my God' is something else again: it is like saying, 'I know that I am loved' rather than, 'I believe that I am loved'. If a child only *believes* that he is loved, then he is an insecure child who needs to be constantly reassured. A child who *knows* that he is loved walks surely and unafraid.

So, how to progress from the old to the new? The only way is to dare to express that which is so for you at that moment, dare to open your mouth and not know the next word that you speak. The Apostles were given the gift of tongues and then went and preached their experience of Jesus Christ. When you think about it, this must have proved quite an ordeal for them, for they were simple men. They must have had a great love for the Master, and their experience of Him must have been so total that it enabled them to go abroad and teach. Yet more than just teaching, they lived the example of Jesus Christ. For unless you live what you teach, you teach a lie. Similarly, if a person speaks from the pulpit about the Love of God without knowing it within his own self, it is a lie and conveys nothing to the people listening. If he does not speak from total Truth, he should not be in a position of such trust.

The cloak of illusion has been spread so wide over people that now it is difficult for it to be put aside – and yet it must, for under the cloak there is a frail radiance and a great beauty. It is right to speak from Truth: to speak from the knowledge of an experience of yourself, from surety. Then indeed do you shine like a lantern in the darkness, and then indeed are you a true shepherd of your flock: 'Come unto me all ye who are heavily laden.' Look into the faces of those around you. These people are hungering for that which they do not yet know of. The Love that exists within all men has been trapped for so many centuries, yet it is still there. It is the aspect of Godhood which has been trapped and which can be released in the New Age. The love, the essence, the being that has been trapped in mind and in matter can now be released. And the Church has an important part to play in the release of the beautiful being that is every man's birthright, if only it can see brotherhood as a reality and not just as a word.

One must not be afraid to lose oneself in order to find one's self. Jesus said: 'I am the way, the truth and the life.' Every man is the way, the truth and the life, but as yet he is largely unaware of it. For the Godhood which exists within him has been barred, bolted and shuttered for many centuries. Let the Church be a means of unlocking the barriers, for man is an organized creature and likes to remain within the perimeters of such an establishment. If only the Church could be fluid, seeking, and receptive to change! Change, transformation – these can be a new beginning. Come and be part of that which is new. It is a simple thing, for all you have to do is to be unafraid to look within your own structure and find the reality that is you: not what you think you are, but what you *are*. Share with others the Truth that you have found for yourself, and when you shed the layers of falsity, the Light of Love will shine upon you and be able to shine through you upon others who have long been in darkness.

'Let not your heart be troubled', for it is joy that the New Age is bringing. Rejoice in the knowledge that man will stand tall when he recognizes the beauty and simplicity of it: of being able to say to another human being that which lies in his heart; of being unafraid to show affection and gladness; of truly holding out his hand to another human being in friendship.

The Godhood of man has always been there, and it is time for it to be truly awakened. As a child grows into adulthood, so shall the being of man grow in this age which is to come, which is here now. Let all those who teach within the framework of the Church look to the example of the little children who know love surely, speak truth and have simplicity of being. They have not as yet acquired the so-called maturity that is often an illusion, bound up with pride, envy, greed and all the other besetting sins of mankind. They are just able to *be*. The universe has a flow, and too often we resist the flow and go against it. Love is the flow, and to live in that flow we need the love and simplicity which are the keynotes of the New Age and the essence of the new Church.

Dorothy's Journey
Dorothy is in her fifties and lives in Sussex. Her background is in the Anglican Church, but she now takes no part in its services. She belongs to a meditation group and is trying to apply the lessons she is learning to her life and work, particularly in her relationships with the people with whom she is increasingly involved on the mundane level. She feels it is sometimes very difficult to see the 'Christ within', but that it is an effort that must be made if people are ever to live together in peace and harmony.

The first memories I have connected with religion bring back feelings of bewilderment and terror. I can recall sitting outside our back gate sobbing because I did not want to go to Sunday school but being quite unable to explain to my parents why. The Sunday school was connected with a chapel of the 'wrath of God' variety. I remember feeling the impossibility of meeting all the demands of this vengeful Being which was waiting to pounce on me – there is no memory of joy or peace.

In my teens I was confirmed into the Church of England. I had no particular feelings about it: at the time all my friends were being 'done', so I joined in. I remember only two things about the preparation: one, it was the first time I had seen the practice of bowing to the altar, and I was unable to see the point, and two, being told, 'If you haven't the time to kneel down to pray in the morning, pray while you are running for the bus.' (This is about the only useful bit of advice I have ever received from a clergyman!) Taking communion was a profound disappointment. I had expected to feel something or have some sort of experience, but the only thing that came into my mind was, 'Is this all?' The mystery remained one to me and led me to believe for a long time that I was unworthy, that there was something wrong or lacking in me.

Churchgoing was a physical ordeal. During the services I would suffer from waves of panic, and certain chants and pieces of organ music would make me feel most peculiar. I would feel cold, shivery and 'disembodied'. At that time I knew nothing of the effects of sound upon consciousness and was very frightened. However, I told no one about this, as I didn't want to be labelled 'odd', and tried to endure to the end of the service. I wish I had come across *The Doors of Perception*, by Aldous Huxley, then: I might have realized that my reaction was quite normal and in fact exactly what was intended, that is, a raising of consciousness to a different dimension.

As I grew older I wondered more and more what the purpose of the exercise could be. If I asked anyone, the answer would be 'to worship God', 'to feed on Christ' or some such pious platitude. The latter used to fill me with disgust – I had not then realized that everyone 'feeds on' something or someone. If one was dissatisfied with the answer and persisted, asking, 'Yes, but what are you actually *doing*?', there would be a blank stare and 'I've just told you.'

In discussion with people who were better versed in theology and Church practice, I would try to understand but almost invariably end up wondering why they felt it necessary to believe all that – and then, of course, I would come back to the idea that something must be wrong with me for me to feel that way too. They used a lot of words, and they argued extremely logically, yet most of these arguments seemed to be based on churchmen's opinions rather than on the precepts of Christ. The simplicity, as I saw it, of Christ's teaching was being lost in a fog of interpretation and rules of conduct.

There were two stances in the Church which I found hard to accept: one was the insistence on Christianity as the *only* way to God, and the other the exclusively masculine bias of the priesthood and imagery. The first seemed to me to be denying the validity of other religions, and I could not see the justice of condemning Hindus, Muslims, etc. because of an accident of geographical and cultural chance. Moreover, it seemed to me a great arrogance on the part of Christianity to assume that it was invariably right about everything.

The Church's attitude to women affronted my feeling of value as a person. Since my femininity was as much a matter of chance as my Church, I felt indignant at being regarded as a lesser being and therefore unfit to participate fully in the affairs of the religion in which I found myself. I also felt that Pauline pronouncements were regarded more highly on this subject than was the example of Christ, who appeared to value women, if the Gospels are to be believed.

For a time I played the organ for services, and this finally finished my regular churchgoing. I found the behind-the-scenes 'stage management' and attitudes to people unacceptable. It seemed to be a game for which men dressed up, and the congregation was regarded as a passive crowd to be manipulated and drilled, whose needs and opinions were a distraction from this aim.

After several years, I came by various paths to meditation and to encounters with people and books which seemed to hold promise of a new understanding of what religion *is*, rather than what it is said to be. It is still not possible for me to take part in church services, but other doors are opening. Paradoxically, it was through a death that I came to life. I was with my father when he died. As I bent over to give him a last kiss, he gave a long sigh and I felt that he had passed a task on to me. Shortly afterwards I read an article in *The Guardian* about Sufism, and from then on things happened 'by chance' which led to a broadening out of every aspect of my life.

I began to try to know myself – not the daughter, wife or mother, but me, myself – and realized that for many years my mental and active functions had been neglected while I had been occupied with bearing and rearing children. The joy of using mind and body again was incredible: I began to feel loosened and stretched in every direction. A dynamic yoga course jolted me out of my mental and physical rut and led me to the Indian scriptures. Reading these and the holy books of other religions for the first time, with no preconceptions, could be called an enlightenment. For the first time, I could see that my thoughts had been true and that all religions are facets of the same jewel, though they each use different symbols. We are all children of the universe, and each one of us, just as we are, is a part of the pattern. The words of the Gospels became clearer. 'Love thine enemies' didn't mean 'Do good to them' but 'Love them just as they are'. 'Love thy neighbour as thyself' meant that one must love and value oneself before thinking of others. This last concept took a bit of digesting – we have been so conditioned to think of love of oneself sinful. I was at last able to accept myself, with all my imperfections, and start from where I was instead of striving to be something else.

I started to dream. From one very clear dream I awoke with the words, 'You must learn to understand the symbols'. While I was looking for books in the library, Anne Faraday's *The Dream Game* and Jung's *Man and his Symbols* and *Mandala Symbolism* almost jumped from the shelf into my hand. This led to an intensive spell of recording and trying to interpret dreams and of reading psychology in an attempt to understand what was going on inside myself and others in our relationships.

An important discovery was that none of this richness was to be hugged to myself at the top of the mountain – it had to be brought down and put to use in everyday life. I found making bread a powerful meditation on the individuation process! A book which helped a great deal was Graf von Durckheim's *The Way of Transformation – Daily Life as Spiritual Exercise.*

An adult literacy scheme was started in our neighbourhood, and I became a tutor. This made me realize that I knew nothing about the processes of learning, so when an RSA course on teaching literacy skills was advertised I enrolled and found out a great deal about the functions of the brain and the limited degree of perception with which most of us operate for most of the time.

I began to take piano lessons, and became interested in harmony. This led to vibrations, which led to physics, which led to Gurdjieff, and so it went on:

> I give you the end of a golden string,
> Only wind it into a ball –
> It will lead you in at Heaven's gate
> Built in Jerusalem's wall.[2]

A great many people are winding up that golden ball and looking for Heaven's gate, but few of them find it in the Established Church.

Mary's Way

Mary, in her sixties, is basically an Anglican, though she feels all Churches are 'one'. She has three children and has worked in the social and welfare fields for many years. Her special interests are healing, intercession, counselling and writing.

My 'Way' was perhaps a little different (a reversal process, the cart before the horse, maybe!). Because of this I seemed to fall between two stools: in that the Church might think I was an occultist or a heretic, and the esoteric world think I was too 'Church', not open and universal. However, the Way is essentially and eventually 'one', and so maybe it does not matter what people may think.

For many years most of us have to keep silent, 'go within' and magnify the Lord, until the conscious mind and conscious activity become completely flooded with the spiritual and are not just mental apprehensions unrelated to action and to daily life. This seems essential to any deep mystical experience, for our human mind tends in any case to be Herod and seeks to slay the divine seed and conception we have received. To be silent is not to be inactive; it is the opposite, for as one becomes more active on both the outer and inner levels, one is loving one's neighbours and loving and serving the whole world.

What I learnt was that one has to follow the path of *self-discipline*, wherever one stands and whatever Way one takes. This proves one's motivation and leads to discipleship. Secondly, the individual is often crucified in one form or another – mentally, emotionally or both. One is rejected by one's friends, one's relatives, even one's family, and at times by one's Church or group. The 'world' in us inevitably crucifies the Truth. The deep sense of hurt which is involved, particularly in personal relationships, is overcome in the end by Love (God), at which stage we have to 'love until it hurts', as Mother Teresa says (although I am quite sure that in her state of consciousness there is no hurt but only Love indeed). One realizes that one must condemn no one but instead try to understand the other's point of view, for we all think quite differently and even relate to what we hear or read quite differently. Blessing seeming enemies – who are really teaching us lessons – means surrounding one's critics with love, love, love and prayer. This, too, communicates on and unites the upper and inner levels, eventually penetrating the consciousness of those who criticize through lack of understanding or because of the deep hurt they themselves have experienced at the hands of others. If understanding and forgiveness have not yet evolved in their mental pattern we cannot – *must* not – criticize them in return. Thus one learns to love and to give without ceasing and never to turn away from a single soul, for God loves and gives without ceasing and is with each one 'always'.

As a rule when one has deep mystical experiences one does not speak of them for years: not until one has learned deep humility and grown to realize that the heritage is for all and all souls are equal; that all will evolve and it is merely a matter of time and stages of soul development. A beggar or a St Paul can be raised up far, far beyond us at any time, and thus we must never seek or ask for a 'higher place' or to sit at the right hand of the power which is so increasingly evident today. If we see Christ in everyone, we shall be incapable of this anyway. Neither shall we ever be able to feel superior to any soul, for how can we be superior to the Christ in them? Apart from this, contact with the Majesty of God, the Holy of Holies, leads to the utmost awe and humility so that one's desire can never be to criticize the soul itself but to continue to Love and to wash the feet. For me, Mother Teresa is the supreme example of the Way: as long as she lives and serves on this planet, Christ is living and serving in her.

So we come back to this Way, this Truth, and to this Life. I found that I underwent a certain degree of asceticism, fasting and withdrawal from the world in order to find the Real behind the world of appearance and the Real person behind the person. Self-discipline, the reading of St John's Gospel – *really* reading it, which meant marking, learning and inwardly digesting the Christ Life therein – plus prayer, intercession and the visiting of the sick and elderly were daily elements. Later, and quite unexpectedly, service in a psychiatric hospital marked another chapter. The divine psychology I had learned inwardly through meditation and silence – 'He knew what was in man' – was reinforced by psychiatry. This was a reaction to the divine heights and, indeed, proved a descent to the lowest and most miserable forms of living. Once this would have been utterly revolting and totally unacceptable to one who was previously shy, reserved and fastidious, but later I was to see the divine purpose behind it and know that I had been 'sent' into this 'school' as part of that purpose, as part of the plan. It called for a complete broadening of my awareness of the spectrum of human experience and for my 'further education', enabling me to become involved with all classes and types of people, and to lose the sense of self-consciousness which had previously hindered me.

On my path I went through a medly of teachings, as many people do. In the early years I went to church only about twice, feeling that it was nothing but sitting, standing and kneeling, plus sermons on the social history of a man called Jesus – a man who lived 2,000 years ago but not today, evidently – someone very much in the past. Healing and discipleship did not appear to be mentioned, neither were deep prayer and meditation. It also seemed that the Church was for Sunday only and not for the rest of the week. Here I was hardly in a position to criticize, for I had tried to be a Christian seven days a week and failed miserably. This was impossible, I thought, until I experienced the fact that Christ entering into one's daily life made all the difference: one then received a new life and a new consciousness, was completely changed, and most things were made possible.

I did recognize that the clergy did an enormous amount of work in visiting the sick and counselling the bereaved. I was fortunate enough to come into contact with a young clergyman and his wife to whom I was able to relate. They were delighted to confirm my experiences and revelations, having already studied the words of Mother Julian and others. These teachings provided further confirmation. Even so, 'my' God was unimaginably greater, so much greater than man's conception that I had to continue my journey as a cosmic as well as a planetary one. So I sojourned in Origen, Swedenborg, Theosophy, Buddhism, Christian Science, metaphysics, healing and other areas: I read everything and went everywhere. But all the time my heart remained Christ-centred: I knew 'I am the Way, the Truth and the Life', for these were the words He spoke to me at the end of my first cosmic, shattering experience and revelation and which kept me to the 'narrow' path.

Eventually, and very much against my own self-will and the desire not to don any one label other than the cosmic and universal, I was nevertheless drawn irresistibly to the Church – for again He spoke to me in a Communion chapel – and thus 'led' me to be confirmed. I surrendered myself to the usual teaching and was duly confirmed, which enabled me to go to

Communion. This has been my great strength and grace, and has kept me in humility. When I moved away, I found it was to a church which was being rapidly emptied because of the rector – an utterly sad state of affairs. However, I continued my inner prayer life and intercession, and that church was nearly always filled with a golden radiance and light. I read St Teresa, *The Cloud of Unknowing*, *The Imitation of Christ* and other texts, and knew that all Truth lay within these teachings and that the Church was merely awaiting revelation of the inner mysteries.

What I have found to be the only way, by whatever door or group or Church one enters (and this is usually a matter of birth, heredity and environment) is the way of the Christ Life as lived in the Gospels. One has to go through the birth (the realization of the divine spark, the seed within, the conception), the baptism (cleansing, repentance, soul-searching, realization), then the contemplative ascent to the divine realms and finally the descent into hell and suffering before we can be completely reborn, liberated, and so live – completely – in true Christ Consciousness. Or, as it were, the Christi, the spark, the Light within every man is resurrected and ascends within us so that we dwell in God and He in us. Then it is God praying in us, God serving in us, God loving in us.

As for the Church, it seems to have progressed by leaps and bounds. Ten years ago, if one had a healing group one was regarded as completely *persona non grata*, and this despite the fact that the Guild of St Raphael and Guild of Health had been in existence for decades and despite Archbishop Temple's considerable committee work on healing. Now, of course, it is quite the 'in' thing, with retreats and meditation and intercessory groups becoming ever more popular. If this continues, together with the promotion of ecology and conservation, the growing awareness that pure food and pure air are vital and the increasing opposition to cruelty to animals (not to mention the killing of human beings!), it may well provide the alternative to some degree to the esoteric and exotic cults that have mushroomed. Their teachings are colourful, exciting and tempting and have no doubt caused the Church to rethink and look back into its own deeper teachings, lost down the ages, and to reactivate them at last.

But, it is for each of us to pray, to meditate, to practise self-discipline and ask for guidance. Then the Holy Spirit will show us our own work, our own means of service as part of the cosmic plan and pattern. Belonging to the invisible Church one will then be already in 'unity' with all Churches and groups and be able to see that Christ is working in all: unity can be brought not through meetings and paperwork but through Love, God, coming forth from within the soul of each person. The mystical body of Christ is all-embracing, and many belong to it albeit unconsciously: membership of it is conferred by seeing the Lord and loving the Lord in all men.

Molly's Story
Molly describes herself as a 'youngish OAP'. She attends her Anglican church in London fairly regularly and leads an active life, which includes working for a visually handicapped drama group.

One suspects that the commonest experience of those of us who try to reconcile our awakening consciousness to our traditional religious allegiances is that of feeling isolated. At any rate, this was my own experience, particularly in the early stages. One doesn't seem to fit in anywhere – not in the cosy ranks of the wholly orthodox, neither with the avant-garde, let alone among the agnostics and atheists. Who does one talk things over with? The very people one should be able to consult, the priests or ministers of one's denomination, are unfortunately often those from whom one least expects a sympathetic and helpful hearing. The way-out 'New Agers' probably express surprise that one should still want to be bothered with anything so old-fashioned as an organized religion; the agnostics can't make up their own minds, kindly though many of them are, and therefore can't help anyone else; while anything to do with religion is completely beyond the ken of the atheists. No wonder one feels one must be wholly on one's own.

The relief is enormous when one discovers that there are in fact large numbers of people just like oneself and that these even turn out to have been members of one's local church. One reaches the stage of being able to recognize likely fellow pilgrims on the path and also of having enough courage to talk to them about one's less orthodox views. Occasionally one makes mistakes, but one learns to take these in one's stride. Less damage is done, too, when one has learned the additional art of wading into the deep gently and of not plunging in headfirst!

But the early stages *are* painful – at least mine were. As one writer said recently, one can't 'with integrity continue to submit unquestioningly to the authority of the institution, however venerable it may be'. At the same time, early conditioning dies hard and our emergence from 'understanding like a child' can take some time and not a little distress.

Looking back, I feel that the most important first move is to try to establish contact with other like-minded people. This may seem easier said than done, but the public library, the telephone directory and some 'New Age' magazines may help the individual track down organizations which may appeal to him immediately or which he can at least try. One thing really does lead to another: even if a certain avenue is found to be useless, it may well end up introducing the seeker to someone with other contacts that may be exactly what he has been looking for.

Personally, I have also derived great help from some of the many books now published on religion. There was certainly a time when I would have shied away from religious books as far too stodgy and probably quite beyond my comprehension, but in fact the really worthwhile writers these days speak from the heart to the heart, in simple and direct terms. However great their spiritual stature, their writings reveal them as human beings exactly like ourselves.

Different people doubtless begin their quest at different ages, some starting because of a personal tragedy or a spiritual experience while others may just 'think about' it. I suppose I began when, as quite a small child, I became aware of feeling that 'this life' was not my first one. It felt rather like one's first visit to a foreign country, where some things are entirely new and others are similar to those in one's homeland. I had never heard the word 'reincarnation', but by the time I reached school age I felt a deep affinity with some other periods of history and 'far' memories were beginning to seep through. I was also very sensitive to the atmosphere (including to that of past events) of some places. Of course, I took these experiences completely for granted – I certainly had no idea that the clergy of the church to which I was taken would probably have been deeply shocked by such notions!

Only when I grew older and learned more of dogma and theology did doubts and difficulties begin to surface. My first skirmish with the 'establishment' took place when I was twelve and argued with the rector, who was a great believer in hellfire. It ended with my refusing to go to that church any longer, although it took twice as long to get to the one I wanted to go to instead. It would never have occurred to me, however, to refuse to go to church altogether.

When I grew up I went through a fairly long period when I simply kept my own personal beliefs to myself and went to church without getting into any real contact with either the clergy or the other members of the congregation. There were brief periods when I felt dishonest about it and would give up going to church altogether; with the exception of Easter and Christmas, because birth, death and rebirth – both physical and spiritual – never ceased to be meaningful for me.

I gradually learned to be neither too credulous nor too sceptical about phenomena which couldn't be easily explained. With regard to reincarnation, I am sure that the important thing to ask is: 'What can I learn from it?' If 'far memories' are just a sort of pleasant daydream, they are of no use whatsoever; they should be guidelines for action (or non-action) in the present. It is in retrospect that we can see our mistakes and missed opportunities for spiritual growth. I am not the same person I was twenty years ago, let alone 200 years ago. I have assimilated experiences and grown to be the person I am now. To me a major lesson is that of avoiding saying, 'if only things had been different'. It is not the situations in one's life which are important, but the way in which one responds to them. If one happens to have 'far memory', one can use it by saying: 'Yes, last time round when such and such a thing happened, I did so and so; *this* situation has similarities, and if I was mistaken in my response before, then this time I must act differently.' Then memory becomes something positive, a useful tool, no longer a cause of self-pity or self-flattery as the case may be.

I do not believe you can prove reincarnation any more than you can prove love, a dream, a soul or God. (Nor, I understand, a subatomic particle, although that is accepted happily by the most hard-headed scientists.) Matters of inner experience are for just that – for experiencing, not for bandying words around.

Though an Anglican myself, I feel that the recent visit of Pope John Paul is a tremendously clear signpost of the change – 'the opening up' – that is taking place between the leaders of different denominations and between their followers.

Not all the cheering thousands belonged to Pope John Paul's own Church. We must doubtless not allow ourselves to get carried away by euphoria, and we all surely have a long way to go yet, yet it does seem a giant step on the way to a more universal Church and gives one great hope for the beginning of the end of rigidity. What is one's faith worth if it cannot bear questioning, if it will not listen to the ideas and experiences of others? They may be right and we wrong; alternatively, something may be the right way for them and the wrong way for us, or vice versa. I think it was the late Father Glaszewski who said we would be on the right path when we were able to say: 'not "I have found the Truth", but "I have found *a* Truth"'.

Kathleen's Perspective

Kathleen is the only contributor with a theological background. Now in her seventies, she has worked nearly all her life in the educational sphere, where she has made a substantial contribution. She lives with her husband, a retired clergyman, in London and is still involved in the future direction of the Church.

'They told us at the shop that you might have a place where we could camp for a couple of nights.' This encounter, on the doorstep of our Dorset home 'Seniors' in 1975 not only changed the future for me by getting me involved in the Bridge Trust and, more especially with its purchase of a farm a mile away, but also reoriented my past. What right have I, in my seventies, to think of myself as a 'New Age Christian', except that the processes of movement into that age began for me thirty years ago, when I was much closer to the age of those young campers than I am now?

At a memorable service in Canterbury Cathedral in June 1982, the Archbishop of Canterbury and Pope John Paul II honoured the memory of five modern Christian martyrs, including the German Luteran pastor Dietrich Bonhoeffer, executed by the Nazis in 1945. His *Letters and Papers from Prison* were translated into English and published in 1953. (A new and better translation has recently appeared.) They were written to a friend, with no thought of a wider public. There is no self-pity, no anger, no retreat into a private world. Bonhoeffer is looking out at the world, clear-eyed, and asking, 'What can I make of Christian faith in a world like this?' He has two resources: his own experience and his fresh and open reading of the Bible.

This book, which I read at a single sitting, dealt me a blow which was almost physical in its impact. He wasn't telling me something new; he was fishing up from my innermost depths what I really thought and believed, in contrast with all the 'churchianity' I thought I believed in. At the time I was working for the BBC on a series of programmes called 'Fundamental Debate' – discussions between Christians and humanists about what they believed and how they saw the world. That experience worked the inner preparation for Bonhoeffer's letters. The world gets on all right for all practical purposes without any God-hypothesis, and even in matters of morality it is possible to have strong moral convictions and to sacrifice oneself for what one endeavours. Christians, says Bonhoeffer, cling to the idea that there must be some problems left which man cannot solve, some human weaknesses which need God's support. No, says Bonhoeffer, we are in a New Age, an age without religion. What should it mean to be a Christian in such an age?

The answers to that question are not easy. According to Bonhoeffer, they are found not by intellectual endeavour but by living; and living demands daily application. What, for a Christian, should be the goal? Is one to try, Bonhoeffer asks, to be a saint or some other sort of special person? No. Again he points the way for me to walk: no startling changes of life-style but a daily effort to discover what it means to be a human and to share one's humanity with others.

Is there then no more God in the New Age? I can only tell you what I found for myself, helped by friends and writers of many persuasions. It may be that birth into the New Age causes great suffering. The demolition work goes on (and, being a theologian by training, I cannot but be aware of it); the God 'out' or 'up' there is no longer credible. There seems to be no need for a personal Creator, for a Providential power ruling over things, for something to which one can confidently attach the adjective 'Almighty', with which so many of our Church prayers begin. As one surveys the wreckage of past beliefs, desolation can set in. The only way ahead is to live through it, following the track of the search for one's humanity and remaining open to all clues to what that humanity is or could be.

For me, the first sure piece of ground is that we humans are a part of the whole of nature, a part of the process of evolution; every other part has its own unique place. I have learnt a new respect for creatures, for the soil and, above all, for this wonderful planet earth. Christians – and Jews too, for that matter – have taken the Genesis story to mean, among other things, that man has domination over the rest of Creation, and from this has come the very common supposition that everything that is done to nature is 'OK' if it is for man's good. But then man becomes the arbiter of what is 'good'. I now see things differently. Man's power over nature is so enormous and his pride in what he can do to animals, plants, the soil, the oceans and the atmosphere so overwhelming that he is in danger of destroying the life system on which, whether he sees it or not, he depends. I have given up all belief that a God from somewhere above or beyond will rescue us from our folly. That abandonment has allowed something else to begin to grow in me – how can I find words to describe it? I read and re-read the Bible, finding daily confirmation of an experience of God quite other than my former conception. One example will suffice: in Psalm 36, God is spoken of as 'the Fountain of Life', springing up all the time. This is the 'living water' of which Jesus spoke; it is also the water from which in the evolutionary story all life emerged. It is there to refresh and renew my own spirit. It flows through all things and people, often impeded, never defeated. Prayer is receiving it and giving it the freest course I can between myself and others.

I think of the other aspect of the New Age as a newly awakening understanding of human relationships. I do not need to describe the oppressive nature of vast institutions as perceived by so many individuals, nor the feeling many Christians have that the Church shares many of the same characteristics of impersonality, pressing down on the individual in the form of rules and self-denial. Nor perhaps, do I need to stress that jump to the conclusion that the opposing force is 'the individual' (this has been made into a political catch phrase) creates its own fallacies and dangers. The flight from rules and obligations into individual freedom has too often proved to be a flight into loneliness and thence to despair. Yet the instinct for freedom is right and good, and Christians are learning about it through the sufferings and struggles of people in the Third World, where the Churches, too, are finding themselves engaged.

Part of the disenchantment with the Churches felt by so many people in the West is due to their feeling that the

Church ought to be a community but fails to be one; or that, if it is a community, it is all too often inward and backward-looking. For the New Age Christian, life has to be lived on the frontiers, in sharing human concerns with ordinary people; not trying to discover their weaknesses and problems so that I can find God-shaped answers (Bonhoeffer again) but looking for their strengths and helping them, if I can, to find their freedom, not least because in so doing I find my own.

'But,' I hear the reader ask, 'how can you carry on going to church, claiming to belong, saying the creeds?' I go for worship: to receive the life-giving symbols of love unbounded flowing from the life and death of Jesus. I share these things with others and do not need to explain: just to be in the same realm of receiving and giving. And I do say the creeds, because I know that if I were living in AD 325 I would be using the concepts believers used and that like me, they may be finding their way as citizens of the New Age. I find in worship – though not always of course – that time, which our century has made into an idol, falls away, that space is counteracted, and that the communion (or community) of saints, who in the New Testament are not the 'extra good' but ordinary people seen with new eyes, takes over.

Hilda's Views on Life
Hilda is in her eighties and lives with her daughter in Surrey. Her eyesight is now too poor for her to read, and she cannot go out often, but she is always joyful and young in spirit.

As I look back over more than eighty years, I find it impossible to understand people thinking that this is the only life there is. It seems ludicrous that this very brief existence, with all its frustrations and disappointments should be our only chance. There is an order in nature – the acorn becomes the mighty oak tree – and we, as the highest form of Creation on earth, are all on our way to perfection. What we are now must be the result of previous lives: we must now be building the next life through the way we deal with this one, sometimes having to make what are apparently backward steps in order to progress.

So often people go through a miserable time because of a guilt complex, perhaps connected with a loved one who has died. The 'real' me feels that where there has been love on both sides we do meet again; our loved ones have gone on to their fresh experience and can understand in a way that they could not while they were here. I am quite sure that in many cases there should be no sense of guilt at all, but even where there may be good reason for guilt, I think that if the person concerned is fundamentally sincere and kind, he will realize that he had to go that way and will in future be able to help others with the same difficulties; without that experience, he could not possibly have understood. Christ condemned no one, whatever they had done or left undone. However bad they were, He loved them and said repeatedly: 'Now forget all your past. Start afresh, every day start afresh.' However many times you fail to think positively instead of negatively, never get mad; forgive yourself and remember that all mistakes will be rectified in due course. It is a worse sin to dwell on our wrongs and refuse forgiveness than to have committed them in the first place. Christ said, 'The kingdom of heaven is within you, *now*.' We live not in time but in eternity; the clouds will clear and the way will lighten.

If any person reading this does not believe in Christ, or in anything at all, then the Love is still there. Jesus did not ask people if they believed in Him before He helped them – in fact, He had all the sympathy in the world for them. He said: 'There is so much I cannot tell you now – you would not understand – but just go on, day by day, quietly doing your best.'

I feel that many young people, though they think about these things and need help desperately, are too embarrassed even to speak the name 'Jesus' or 'Christ', probably because of the way He has been introduced to them in word or picture form. He was serene and calm in the face of every conceivable hurt that life could do to Him, but when it was necessary for others He could also be very forceful. Divine Love was the basis of everything He said and did.

A magazine that has helped me enormously – and I know very many others – is *Science of Thought Review*, which accepts all religions as having some truth but feels Christ to be the embodiment of them all. There may be millions of other Christs on millions of other planets, but as far as I am concerned, I can only try to follow the one I know in the New Testament. His message was Love, and twelve simple fishermen carried out His instructions because they knew without any doubt that the Resurrection was absolutely true; before that they had felt lost and bewildered.

This is an extract from *God Calling*, a book I have loved for more than thirty years:

> Peter could never have done my work, never have had the courage to live on, or the daring to live for me but for the love with which he knew he was surrounded. He needed protection from himself.

It is the same today. People who long to be strong and wise feel shame, remorse and contempt for themselves, of their weak selves. They then have to remember the divinity within them and know that, quietly and patiently, they will in due time learn to understand the meaning of 'Christ's kingdom is within you' – all the strength we need is there. When we are aware of that marvellous sense of peace and joy that the consciousness of this presence brings, we know that whatever outward appearances may be, all is well now and forever. Yet we must persevere in stilling our minds so that the Light can penetrate. I have always found this extremely difficult, but it is absolutely true:

> Never judge. The heart of man is so delicate, only its Maker can know it. Each heart is so different, actuated by different motives, controlled by different circumstances, influenced by different sufferings. How can one judge another? Leave to Me the unravelling of the puzzles of life, secure in the certainty that all that is wrong I can set right.[3]

I should like to add one more extract that I have found encouraging:

> Building the character means cutting and chiselling. It is a work that requires consideration, mine and yours. It is a work that brings much sense of failure and discouragement too, at times, because as the work proceeds you see more clearly all that remains to be done. Shortcomings which you hardly recognized, or at least for which you had no sense of sorrow, now cause you trouble and dismay. Courage. That is in itself a sign of progress. Patience, not only with others but with yourselves. As you see the slow progress made by you upward in spite of your longing and struggle, you will gain a divine patience with others whose imperfections trouble you.

My final thought is taken from a book by the same authors, called *God at Eventide*:

> The unseen world is the real world. Realize more and more as you go through this earth life that this is only a material plane parenthesis. The real paragraph, chapter and book of life is the Spirit life. This point of view will alter your ideas of suffering, failure and the work of life here. It will give you a new view of death. Birth begins the parenthesis, death closes it. Then back to real Life-History. Absorb this. When you have done so, you will get that same idea about the various periods of your earth life. Times of struggle, defeat, joy, failure, work, rest, success, treat them all as parts of a parenthesis in the one life of Spiritual progress.[4]

The older I become, the more clearly I recognize this to be true. If we could see life more from a spiritual point of view, all would be well.

5.
My Dilemma in the Church

> We shall not cease from exploration
> And the end of our exploring
> will be to arrive where we started
> And know the place for the first time.[1]
>
> T. S. Eliot

In earlier chapters we have been describing, in different ways, a kind of awakening: a sudden recognition that the world is not exactly as we had previously been taught to see it. On the face of it nothing has changed, yet deep down there has been a shift in our perception: we see the same place, but it is as though we are seeing it for the first time. We look around for others with whom to share this perception and we find very few. We know we should not try to change the perceptions they already have, for how they see things must be right for them. Yet as Christians we wish to share our discoveries with others, especially with those in the Church. Our religion has always helped us to make sense of the world around us, but when the feeling that grows in us does not accord with the teaching that the Church offers, it is inevitable that there should be pain and confusion. I have tried hard to consider why I now find Church membership so difficult. One reason may be that as I am slowly awakening to the cosmic unity of all life, in this world and in others beyond, so I am finding myself struggling against the limitations of understanding which my Western, Christian upbringing and education have imposed upon me. Along with others, I am increasingly sensing this unity of all life expressing itself in an evolutionary process in which we ourselves are asked to play a part by reaching towards higher levels of consciousness. This is a subtle process and one which does not follow man-made rules and forms. These have their place at the personality level at which we have hitherto been working, but once our souls gain a glimpse of the Christ Light which is seeking to shine through us, we find that creeds can limit that reality. They have perhaps played their part in bringing us thus far; but gradually, to me at any rate, they are being replaced by an awareness of the divinity that sustains us all and of the guiding precepts of Love, Light, wisdom and understanding that can help us become more truly what we are and take us a step further in our quest for beauty, goodness and Truth.

As one of the laity, I am aware that I am saying nothing new, yet at the same time I believe I should express how I feel because it increasingly seems that the way that is emerging in us is in line with the way that Christ so often indicated. He always spoke so that each level of meaning could be grasped by those at different levels of understanding: 'He that hath ears to hear, let him hear.' Sometimes we grasp a level of meaning that is deeper than the one we saw before, and it is then we begin to feel that we are knowing the place for the first time. This can be a risky business, for it may lead us to try to unravel some of the man-made understandings that have gathered, centuries old, around the simple truths. It could be that new revelations will be given that enlarge our horizons and bring a greater sense of the unity of mankind and the whole created order. If this were the case, it might lead us towards the salvation of mankind in a literal sense. For the direction in which humanity is now heading is based on a divisive understanding where 'I am separate from you and if I do not overcome you, you may overcome me'. If only we could let the outer petals of our separateness fall away, we might find that a new seed grows within us, impelling us to obey Christ's command: 'Love your enemies, bless them that curse you, do good to them that hate you, and pray for them that despitefully use and persecute you'.[2] The sun shines on us all, so surely anything that fosters a sense of separateness, even if this is felt to be 'in the name of Christ', could be the greatest sin of all?

Western society, with its emphasis on material prosperity, fosters a separatist view of ourselves which subtly develops into a kind of prison and keeps us from making contact with our inner and more universal selves. My dilemma is that so often the Church, also, seems to direct us outwards to the world of sensory perception that fosters this notion of the separated self and does little to create the atmosphere necessary for a greater connection within, to quote T.S. Eliot again – 'The still point of the turning world'.

From this 'still point' we do not need to merely act according to a set of rules or to believe a particular set of doctrines, though these things have their place. What we find is that if we just 'Seek the kingdom of God', it is within us, it is without us, it is the abundant reality of life – 'and all these things shall be added unto you.'[3] Is this not what Jesus meant? He never spoke about religion as such, although he respected its place; He spoke about life. He experienced and tried to transmit the quality of transcendence that makes for 'life abundant' – a quality that has always been known by a few, like Brother Lawrence, 'practising the presence of God' in all he did.

This very same quality is now being discovered by so many that some writers today are describing major shifts in the way people perceive the world, in the patterns or paradigms on which our lives are based. One such writer, Marilyn Ferguson, has recently explained in *The Aquarian Conspiracy*:

> A new paradigm involved a principle that was present all along but unknown to us. It includes the old and the partial truth, one aspect of how things work. While allowing for things to work in other ways as well.[4]

This is how some of us see things. Formerly held beliefs are now seen as partial truths. We feel we must let go and move forward with the truth that pushes us on. But holding us back is the thought that those who do push forward have so often been subjected to attack. We think of Copernicus, Galileo, Joan of Arc, Darwin; we think how established institutions have so often resisted the push of truth towards new frontiers, and we feel we must either crack within ourselves or break away from an institution which, at that point, seems to have lost touch with the Life whose presence in the world it was set up to serve.

> Long after the old paradigm has lost its value, it commands a kind of hypocritical allegiance. But if we have the courage to communicate our doubts and defection, to explore the incompleteness of the rickety structure and the failure of the old paradigm, we can dismantle it. We don't need to leave it to collapse on us.[5]

These words express very well the way I often feel. Yet where can one go in the Church to find someone to listen to our doubts and not condemn them? So many clergy seem to think that the answers should be handed to us from those in authority.

Perhaps there are more people feeling the same way than one imagines, as Gerald Priestland discovered in his search for *Priestland's Progress*:

> To my joy I seem to have brought encouragement to what I call the Great Anonymous Church of the Unchurched; those who believe, or would like to believe, but are disenchanted with the Churches and dare not discuss their faith elsewhere for fear of being thought neurotic or gullible. To them I say, Christianity is not a way of unreasonable certainty, it is a far more interesting way of reasonable uncertainty. Let us talk about it frankly and openly together.[6]

His plea is one which I would echo; so, apparently, would many of those thousands who responded to what Priestland has said. Most of those interviewed for the book were clergy or theologians of repute, but the laity can also respond to God and our experience may also be valid. David Hay, in *Exploring Inner Space*, refers to a nationwide sample of 2,000 which showed that twenty-nine per cent of those aged between sixteen and twenty-four years had become 'aware of or been influenced by a presence or power, whether you call it God or not, which is different from your everyday self.'[7]

In another recent book, *The Awakening Earth – Our Next Evolutionary Leap*, Peter Russell quotes a survey by two American sociologists which showed that forty-three per cent of those interviewed had 'had an experience of going beyond their normal self' and that very few of them had ever dared to share this with anyone else.[8] This type of experience can take many forms, from an entering into the 'innerness' of everything to the awareness of a whole extra dimension of being which is there all the time interpenetrating with our own – there, that is, for those who have 'eyes to see and ears to hear'. Perhaps it is towards an awareness of this extra dimension that one yearns for the Church to lead us. It is already there, behind the symbolism, and is even there in the language. But we translate the appearance of angels, or of God speaking from a burning bush as being physical realities in material form. May these not be a breaking through of another dimension of being into our own – may not the whole 'company of Heaven' be waiting to work with us if we could but listen, respond to what they would have us do? Today, with a developing sense of inner awareness, more people are 'seeing' and 'hearing' this other world. Many are now saying that in the first Elizabethan age we explored the oceans and that in this second Elizabethan age we are beginning to explore ethereal space, the inner realms we find within ourselves. As Columbus began to push back the frontiers marked on maps of the then known world, so we are now beginning to explore the territory shown on the inner maps of our own being, the inner world in which God's laws appear exactly as Christ said – only, for the first time, we begin to truly understand them. The boundaries of Truth may not, on our infinite plane, be eternally set. The domain of the Church may be wider than it knows: its business may indeed be not yet finished.

It may seem only natural that in this second Elizabethan age some should have experienced a shift in the way they see things. Man's field of physical exploration has itself shifted from planet earth to other parts of the universe and the astronauts' first picture of our world has become imprinted on our minds in all its beauty. What we seek to explore spiritually will thus almost inevitably be of more cosmic proportions. This, then, is part of the dilemma that I feel today: my journey is a cosmic one, yet the Church still tries to teach me that my spiritual understanding should be small in scale and closely bound up with a thirty-three year span of history some 2,000 years ago. Could it be that the revelation that is now beginning to dawn is as significant as the one we were given then? Could it be that we are now seeing a flowering of the seed ideas that were implanted in our consciousness by the life and ministry of Christ and that, by denying the harvest that is bearing fruit, we are denying the very purpose of His life and work?

If anything is going to hold us back, possibly it will be fear: fear that this is all too vast for us to comprehend, so we must reduce it to a size we can contain; fear that if the map of knowledge traditionally belonging to the Church is extended to so vast a canvas, the Church will have no special province to call its own. I can understand this dilemma and have struggled with the tensions that it brings, but I now feel the needs are great enough to cause us to speak out:

> The human heart can go the length of God,
> Dark and cold we may be, but this
> Is no winter now. The frozen misery
> Of centuries breaks, cracks, begins to move,
> The thunder is the thunder of the floes,
> The thaw, the flood, the upstart spring.
> Thank God our time is now when wrong
> Comes up to face us everywhere,
> Never to leave us till we take
> The longest stride of soul men ever took.
> Affairs are now soul size.
> The enterprise
> Is exploration into God.
> Where are you making for. It takes
> So many thousand years to wake,
> But will you wake for pity's sake?
>
> Christopher Fry[9]

'Wake up, wake up!' I seem to want to say to clergy and lay people everywhere. 'Your Church is in the world. Look at the world and see the need that *is* there.' The group of young people sitting in silence after the sudden death of John Lennon, dedicating themselves to world peace and playing 'Imagine, imagine . . .' – were they not reaching out for a spiritual dimension as sincerely as those who sit in the evensong pew? Was not Christ among them in the sense of love and brotherhood breaking through human limitation, failure and destructiveness? 'Wherever two or three are gathered in my name, I am there in the midst of them, for my name is Love;' He might have gone on to say: 'And where love is, that is where I am.' If we think of the places where love is shown – the office, the club, the pub and especially the home – may we not perceive a different concept of the Church, that is, if the Church is to be where 'I am'?

I spoke to one of the young people I had seen sitting in silence after John Lennon's death. Her background was Anglican. She had been brought up and confirmed within the Church, but she no longer felt able to attend with sincerity and went to please her parents on Christmas Day. 'I don't feel any freedom of thought within the Church,' she explained. 'It seems that everything is categorized or seen in terms of some analogy with Church or biblical teaching. My experience cannot be contained in that way. I need to feel free to join a peace group, a homoeopathic group, a feminist group – all these, to me, embody aspects of spiritual understanding, but they are not normally seen as being containable within a Church structure. The Church tends to see them as beyond the scope of Christianity, yet I feel that in working for harmony in the world, for wholeness in our treatment of the body and for balance between male and female, all these things express aspects of the Gospel message. There seems to be a fundamental ambiguity within the Church which, on one hand, says, 'Go out and preach Christianity to all people', yet on the other does not have the capacity to care for these people where they are. Caring for the needs that exist in the world seems to be a fundamental part of what Christ taught, and if the Church were relevant to the world today it would be running rape crisis centres, crèches for single parents and counselling centres for the unemployed. Christ was always there, where life was, not closeted within set structures or buildings. Our local church sees 'giving to God' as giving money to extend the Church building for bigger services (it can already hold several hundred), whereas I feel Christian funds are needed to implement Christ's philosophy in the community. It seems to me that spirituality can be expressed wherever there is caring. It does not have to be connected with the Church or with Christian people – it is where Christ is, and cannot be measured out into little boxes. After all, you can't Christianize a whole nation, but you can minister to a whole nation where its needs are. Isn't that being Christ in the midst of the people?' Her view is one that is shared by many.

Might it be that a spiritual dimension could penetrate life as a whole, and that the challenge to the Church is to act as midwife at the birth of this spiritual dimension, wherever it may take place? Its task would then be less that of teaching us to worship God as above and beyond His Creation and appearing to us in the form of His Son Jesus than in going the way Jesus himself showed – the way of transformation, the way of following the gentle promptings within us of a loving God immanent in the human heart.

Once we go this way we begin to see religion not merely as a set of rules or dogmas, or even of forms of worship, but as the discovery of an unseen order with which we connect and with which we may learn to live in harmony. These, then, are the two chief things I would like the Church to teach me: how to connect with this kingdom and how to live in harmony with it. 'Thy kingdom come, thy will be done on earth as it is in heaven' – is it only as we each try to bring it through within ourselves that the kingdom really will come to pass on earth as in heaven?

One of the best ways of finding this connection is through silence, and it may be because this is so hard to find in a church service that so many people are now seeking out groups that teach meditation. The first time I went to a meditation group, I was quite scared in case it was not 'Christian'. I can recall wearing a cross and chain, though I am not sure whether this was for some sort of protection, or whether it was so that others there might know what I stood for! But my fears soon melted away in the loving atmosphere, and I have since come to see the consciousness and understanding that is growing in such groups as in no way hostile to the Christianity that Christ preached. If it is hostile to anything, it is so to the interpretation which Churches have constructed around Christ's simple message. A single visit to a meditation group does not bring about vast changes in the individual, but over a certain period there develops a new awareness of the oneness within all things, accompanied by a longing to connect with this One and live in harmony with it. If the One we seek to connect with is Love, then maybe we should do as we have been told: love God and love our neighbour as ourselves. This is so very straight forward, yet nevertheless so very difficult – that little self will creep up on us and get in the way!

In writing as we do neither of us asks that anyone in the Church accept or reject anything that has been said. However, what I would ask is for a greater spirit of openness within the Church so that such issues might at least be raised and considered valid for those who raise them. The change in thinking that we are requesting does not involve changing the truth in a way which would imply previous error – but an acknowledgement that we were once only partially right. As we share the insights of the laity today, the horizons of understanding can be broadened for us all. I have found the need to struggle until my view of God and of the meaning of the world has adjusted to fit the inner sense that has grown within me. Even if we glimpse something more integrated and meaningful just for a moment, we must – if we are to be true to ourselves – seek to live by what we know we have seen:

> To thine own self be true,
> And it must follow as the night the day
> Thou canst not then be false to any man.[10]

The process by which we do this seems to be that of following our hunches. These intuitions may at first seem contrary to our reason, but as we live with them they slowly take on a type of transcendent reasoning. We establish a new threshold of awareness from which we can choose which new aspects of the truth dawning upon us to admit into our consciousness and how openly we shall look at the contradictions that these highlight in our beliefs and in our lives. It is at this point that we badly need friends: those who can share how we feel and who will stand by patiently while our perceptions break through. For if the Church as a body is unable to act as midwife to what is gathering to be born in us, then it does help if we can offer ourselves as 'midwives' to each other.

What, then, are we assisting to be born? This is hard to put into words, but perhaps the nearest one can get to it is a breakthrough from traditional religious belief and practice to a more direct connection with the spiritual dimension which exists in everything we do – from a following of a 'God out there' to an awareness that the kingdom of heaven is within. The Gospel according to St Thomas puts this very well:

> Rather, the kingdom is inside of you, and it is outside of you. When you come to know yourselves, then you will be known, and you will realize that you are sons of the living Father. But if you will not know yourselves, then you dwell in poverty, and it is you who are that poverty.[11]

The discoveries at Nag Hammadi lend some assurance to those who today feel both an awareness of God's Life within them and a discrepancy between this awareness and the Church's teaching. If we study the early history of the Church further, we may well find that the organized structures moved in one particular direction of belief and that the major themes of Gnostic teaching, which emphasized the divine within each person, did not lend themselves so well to the development of orthodoxy.

> When you make the two one, and when you make the outer as the inner and the above as the below and when you make male and female into a single one . . . Then shall you enter the kingdom.[12]

This kingdom is within us – we have always known that as an idea – but somehow, once we connect with it, love, goodwill and understanding flow between us and our friends, in our families, our nation and our world.

As the Love flows, so our sense of communion grows stronger. I am finding that when I speak of the Church I now mean all those who, world-wide, are united in a communion of love and that the Christian Church as a historical institution is only one subset of this group. There is no reason why, for the moment, it should not remain a distinctive group – there can be diversity in our unity – but the essential awareness that is growing today is that the same 'Lord of the Dance' permeates and sustains us all. This is where the Oriental concept of God is beginning to confirm our own awakening understanding that the 'whole cosmic order is nothing but the dance of Siva'.[13] God is at the same time both manifest and unmanifest in the world. Whatever human organizations we construct, these can only belong to the world of signs and outer appearances. For much of my life I lived as though this were the only reality, and yet there was always the search, the yearning for that which lay behind them, a reaching beyond the signs and symbols. It is encouraging to discover a priest who expresses what one feels:

> As long as we remain in this world we need these signs, and the world today cannot survive unless it rediscovers the 'signs' of faith, the 'Myth', the 'Symbol', in which the knowledge of reality is enshrined. But equally fatal is to stop at the sign, to mistake the sign for the ultimate reality. It is this that sets one religion against another and divides Christians from one another, from people of other religions and from the rest of the world. This is essentially idolatry. Whether it is the Bible or the Church or any dogma or creed, when it is forgotten that they belong to the world of signs and appearances, to the world which is passing away, they become idols far more deadly than any graven image.[14]

I have quoted from Father Bede Griffiths' *The Marriage of East and West* because he has expressed so well what I have not quite dared to say myself! Are we being called into an era of new understanding in which we leave behind our props and idols, and discover our Sonship of God as it was revealed by Christ? Perhaps if we knew a little more about other religions we would find that they each express in different ways the same inner reality behind the symbols in the Christian understanding. It is the 'Lord who is my shepherd', but what I feel that David meant, speaking long before Jesus was born, is: 'It is the Lord who speaks within my being who is my shepherd.'[15]

'Behold, I stand at the door, and knock, if any man hears my voice and opens the door, I will come in to him, and will sup with him, and he with me.'[16] This is not a once-in-a-lifetime 'opening to the Lord' but a daily, hourly, minute-by-minute process – one I fail in time and time again, but which is, I am convinced, the only way. This is what the Church has preached all along, but the subtle distinction is the 'I' who will come is not merely the Jesus of the Gospels but the Christ that He expressed, the 'I am' essence which is the Life that created and sustains us all.

This 'I am' may be clothed in many religious forms or alternatively in none at all. For those whose backgrounds lie in traditional faiths it is embodied in the symbols of those faiths; for those with no such background of form, it might be a sense of connection with an inner reality which they describe as a 'transformation of consciousness', of a 'new age being born'. This transformation process is most certainly in the air, and the awakening which people are experiencing is rather like that of the disciples at Pentecost. However, the important thing to stress is that it takes many forms, and it is to be hoped that the Church will begin to see that an expression in religious terms is not the only form. It may indeed be a 'born again' experience or a charismatic renewal, but equally it may be a transpersonal awareness of a scientific or psychological kind: for example, an awareness of Mother Earth derived from a wilderness experience or from a feeling of total belonging whilst working on the land. The transformation and the path that opens up ahead will be different for each individual. One difficulty is that the Church tends to minister only to those who see this Reality purely in Church terms. Yet may not these terms be symbols? May not the transformation processes be the same thing, whatever form they take? For the understanding comes not with the head alone but also with the heart. As we connect with the spirit of God we sense a deeper level of meaning to everything. Now we see 'through a glass darkly', but sometimes as we look more closely we do see one or two lighter patches.

In one of these lighter patches, I see that Christ offered us a more cosmic meaning to 'I am the way, the truth and the life' than we have hitherto understood. By His coming to earth and His Crucifixion, Christ anchored cosmic energies in the material density of our world so that it would henceforth be possible for us to be Christ-filled human beings and for God's 'will' to be 'done on earth as it is in heaven'. He thus opened up the 'way' for us to follow wherever our own path of initiation may lead us. We may well find that laying down our lives for others is a part of that path. Gandhi found this; so did Martin Luther King. On the Cross, the Christ-filled Son of God united in His being the greatest extremes of love and hate the world has ever known. Love and hate are ever present in our world today, yet the Church so often takes our attention backwards in time instead of forwards to the future and the living moment. As another laywoman has recently put it:

> The seemingly conflicting forces of material and spiritual growth met within him. They must meet within each one of us. No wonder the cross is such a powerful symbol. For it is not a question of rejecting the natural world, of choosing heaven rather than earth, of isolating one's heart from the unpleasant and destructive, or even of deciding one is in the right and the other person, group or nation is in the wrong, but pinioned to a cross of paradoxes, actively immobile in the tension of loving all mankind, the psyche surrenders to a disintegration in the effort to embrace the apparently impossible.[17]

If we are to follow the 'way', there may be a more cosmic sense to it than the Church has taught. I no longer think that Jesus intended us to worship Him and His way but rather to find this 'way' and follow it ourselves. 'I am come that they might have life, and that they might have it more abundantly.'[18] I now believe that this 'abundant life' can be found by the transformation process in many ways and that this is what the resurrection is all about. As I hope I have explained, the Crucifixion may well be the most significant event yet to have occurred on this planet – but may not an understanding of the

Resurrection, rather than an overconcentration on the Crucifixion, be our way to wholeness? This is hardly a good analogy, but let us imagine that I am a father who wants his child to go to college but whose present earnings are insufficient to cover the fees. I then spend three years away on oil rigs in order to raise the necessary funds. I would want my child to feel grateful, certainly, but not to be forever dwelling on the sacrifice I had made for him. Rather, I would want him to take up the opportunity that I had made available to him joyfully, to enter fully into its delights and rewards and live the student life abundantly. Might this not be the challenge to the Church: to place less emphasis on the known domain of the Cross and enter more fully into the unknown liberation of the Resurrection with the opportunity for wholeness that this offers?

The way of wholeness has meaning, and not just for ourselves as individuals. It could lead us to find a way through all the problems that lie ahead for the human race. Indeed, that may be the reason why the problems are there, so that we learn to gather in the name of Love and work with goodwill for a common and greater good. The solutions cannot come if we continue to tell ourselves that as a Christian Church we have the only way. God is One. He must therefore belong to all. The ways to Him are many, but they can only be as different as are the leaves on a tree – for all are on the branches of the One True Vine. Once we accept that the 'abundant life' is one for all to share, then we can become attuned to a common vision. I have found in the office where I work that if we agree to work for a common goal and work with this, then the inspiration flows and we co-operate with one mind – is this not the solution to differences of opinion in business or politics? Yet how easily the blocks can be put up like spanners in the proverbial works: self-interest, self-will, greed, fear, doubt, mistrust, criticism and envy. Anything negative blocks the flow, and we are back again working separately, as isolated fragments for whom life is neither abundant nor whole.

The way ahead is Love; not just preached from pulpits, but lived; not just lived within a congregation, but in the world – the shops, offices and clubs – of which we are part. This seems to be the way that Jesus tried to show; this is the way one hopes the Church will show. This seems vital if we are to break through the separations that we create and which the Church has done so little to overcome. We have to see ourselves as one and work together if we are to find a way ahead. The world does not have the resources to feed us unless we collaborate to use them wisely; the nuclear button is too sensitive to our discord unless we move towards a greater tolerance and understanding; Mother Earth will no longer recover from our pollution unless we work in harmony with the natural realms. Turning to this inner way, to a living of the abundant Life, does not make us perfect people overnight, but it does give us a little of the Love, the will and the wisdom that we need in order to begin.

6.
The Role of the Church in the Next Decade

In moving on from my discussion of how the Church might develop in the years ahead, I would like to stress two things. One is that I am very much aware that I speak merely as a lay person of limited knowledge and experience. The other is my sense of gratitude to the Church, with all its faults, for the way it has enshrined the Truth for 2,000 years and brought it thus far. I think with deep appreciation of all those who have given their lives that this might be so. Yet I also feel that as a body we must now respond to 'Life, insistent in its challenge to us to move on in our thinking', and implicit within such a challenge must be the need to change, to 'sell all that thou hast... and follow me.'[1] May not this be a message to us not just as individuals but also as a corporate body with its dearly cherished concepts of the truth?

Possibly one of the things we as Christians are asked to give up is the extremely narrow historical view we have of ourselves. We look around us at the world as it is now and see it as set upon a canvas, forgetting that the evolutionary process might still be going on and that if this process is still unfolding, the blueprint of God's evolutionary plan may not as yet have reached its fullest manifestation. There perhaps comes a point when we are asked to cease being mere passive recipients of this process and to awaken, so that we become sensitive to what it may be and are able to co-operate with God in the unfolding of His plan.

It may help to look for a moment at the growth of man's spiritual understanding as a part of this evolutionary process. The general argument of this book is that the business of the Church can never be finished and fixed for all time. If the domain of the Church is man's religious understanding, and if this changes as we mature and become more fully able to live out our spiritual nature, then it is essential that the Church should move with these changes as they occur. For in these days of instant telecommunications through satellite and computer links, any process of change must inevitably be speeded up; and an institution that cannot move with change is in danger of being left behind, a dinosaur of our times.

One of the changes that seems to be taking place in this decade is the awakening of more individuals to some of the deeper mysteries of life. The mystery tradition of the West stretches back at least as far as the ancient Egyptian civilization, a highly structured, hierarchical society whose members drew on a combination of teachings that reflected their deep spiritual understanding. Their Pharaoh was venerated as God in human form. This idea may well have influenced the Hebrews, who introduced the concept of One Creator and laid the foundations for the coming of Christ. The early mystery schools – such as those founded by Pythagoras and Confucius – taught a select few how to bring a spiritual power into their earthly existence and thence into their daily lives. Jesus extended this concept through the example of His life and teaching. He showed that we all have the potential to open ourselves to the kingdom of heaven, to align ourselves with the will of God and act in accordance with His love. He also showed the importance of a group – 'Where two or three are gathered in my name . . .' Perhaps in demonstrating a sense of brotherhood He sowed the seeds for the coming of the oneness of humanity that is being realized more fully today.

The sense of brotherhood within the early Christian Church was extremely strong, but as Christianity became institutionalized, with Constantine adopting it as the official religion of the Holy Roman Empire, the dynamic of the faith seems to have become dissipated in the plethora of structures, doctrines and other ideas, frequently politically inspired, that heralded in what are known as the Dark Ages. Apart from a few great lights (such as the desert fathers and, nearer home, St Columba and his monks of Iona), who by living simple lives remained aware of the ever-present reality of God, it seems that inspiration did not grow stronger until around the eleventh century. The great cathedrals evidence the reaching upwards by the people to a divine order beyond themselves. Yet those operating within the power structures of the Church seemed not to fully recognize that an understanding of the mysteries might be contained in the songs of the troubadours or the stories that the Knights Templar were bringing back from their travels among the Sufis and Essenes.

The Renaissance brought a flowering of the religious spirit in the field of the arts, but still the structures of the Church and of the monarchy imposed the old forms. In the centuries that followed there seemed to be a widening division between science and religion. The philosophy of Descartes, which had the effect of reducing everything to its smallest parts, militated against the concept of wholeness and possibly encouraged the growing emphasis on outer form and on things material. As society identified ever closely with the material world, so the Church seemed to concentrate more and more on outward form, on symbols and behaviour, and less on connection with the spiritual Source and on that sense of synthesis whereby everything can be seen as:

> parts of one stupendous whole,
> Whose body nature is, and God the soul.[2]

Poets such as Pope saw that materialism was swamping the spirit of Man, just as nowadays someone like Alexander Solzhenitsyn is able to sense a rising tide that is waiting to break through:

> If the world has not come to its end, it has approached a major time in history, equal in importance to the turn from the Middle Ages to the Renaissance. It will exact from us a spiritual upsurge, we shall have to rise to a new level of life where our physical nature will not be cursed, as in the Middle Ages, but, even more, our spiritual being will not be trampled upon as in the modern era.[3]

An emphasis on man as a spiritual being has always been nurtured by the mystic tradition. Within the Christian Church, one great exponent of the consciousness of man as a spiritual being has been Teilhard de Chardin, who saw the mystery of the 'I am' consciousness within all things and hinted at the evolutionary awakening ahead: the 'Christification of Mankind'. If this comes about, then it will indeed be based on the law of Love and may lead to the establishment of some kind of universal religion that transcends all existing forms of religion. This would be totally different from ecumenism, which at its best is a mutual striving for something greater than the insight that each denomination can bring, or may, alternatively, be a mere watering down of what exists already, not a real contribution to the process of Christian evolution. An outpouring of Love, already manifest in many ways, could be a transformative agent, leading, eventually, to the promotion of more universal concepts and a more integral understanding between men. The Church could then become a mighty force for the breaking down of those economic barriers that prevent the feeding of a hungry world. It could help us to understand our fellow man rather than use aggression as our first and only resort; it could cause us to end pollution, deforestation and all the other activities that desecrate the earth. Why, then, are we so inhibited? Does this small piece give any clues as to why this might be?

> Within the Whole My glory can shine. Man has worked in fragments for too long, which is why there has been so little magnetic effect – a small magnet will only pick up small particles, but as the strength of the magnet is increased, so the power is intensified beyond all normal proportion.
> Think of a magnet, lights, rivers – all these are symbols which help the understanding of my truth. But do not dwell too deeply on the symbols themselves, on the words themselves; always look behind them for the deeper meaning which can be found only by going within. This is where mankind has lost its way. If one does not turn within, then the symbols will be all that there is. I know men that love to argue over symbols and that they still argue over them. Yet when they have turned within they will find that the Truth is one, and the symbols, having played their part, will then fall away: these must be allowed to fall away, just as the snake sheds its skin.
> The snake must shed its skin, or else it cannot grow; but having done so, the creature will find its progress greatly hampered if it drags the old skin along with it. Have a gentle understanding for those still in their old skins, for those who are straining to break through but are held back by prejudice and fear. Be less gentle with those who are still dragging their old skins along behind. Tell them firmly to drop them, as the pod falls from the seed, as the shell falls from the newborn chick, or as the nest falls to the ground when the birds have flown. This nest is there for their nurturing, and, having played its part, should be allowed to fall free. Nothing is ever lost or wasted, but it must not impede growth. As this is grasped, there can be no turning back. My way is one of growth, of freedom, of joy. A swimmer must

leave his water wings on the shore if he is to explore the deeps – leave them behind, not to be scorned but to be looked on with gratitude for the part they played in service to the greater growth: 'I *am* that growth – I *am* that life – so grow in Me.'[4]

If we could but turn within and find the abundant Life which is there for all, we might find that so many of the symbols and doctrines that we hold dear, so many of the separate understandings and codes, would fall away as having played their part, and a greater sense of the unity of all things and the power of good, of God, break through. One of the difficulties has been that the various traditions, instead of seeing that each offered a different aspect of the Truth, have each seen themselves as in some way superior to all the others. If we are honest as Christians, we must admit to having regarded ourselves as the possessors of a special revelation of God as 'Ours', even a special way to God that others do not have unless they themselves join us. Once we sense, however dimly, the inter-relatedness of all approaches to God and His essential Oneness that we are to seek, then we must be prepared to grow and move with it. Growth means change, which in practical terms means moving on from the place where we are now. If the Church is to take up this challenge, is to give up all it holds so dear and move with the Spirit of God, it may face two main tasks in the next decades. One might be to assist each individual to open up and connect with the Life abundant in whatever way is right for him. The other might be to learn how, as a corporate group, we should respond to Christ's prayer 'that they may be One'.[5]

If we consider firstly the individual's need to find his own way of becoming innerly attuned, the Church could respond by offering more opportunities for meditation and creative silence, for it is in the silence that we can 'Be still, and know that I am God'.[6] Is it not from a point of stillness that all growth springs? It is from stillness that we connect with the creative flow and find that we are, after all, all part of the One. The mind can rest steady and pure, and solutions to whatever problems are before us can begin to evolve. The busier our lives become, the more we need opportunities for retreat, a chance to step back from the 'out' breath of life, the working and the doing:

Getting and spending, we lay waste our powers:
Little we see in Nature that is ours.[7]

We must make a space instead to take the 'in' breath we so badly need, to pause, to reconnect and to find our higher selves. Though weekend retreats may be within the reach of a limited few, the organization of local day retreats could bring benefit to many. There are now a large number of teachers of meditation available to us, and some of these are within the Church; the contemplative orders have centuries of experience they are often willing to share. Nowadays there are also many teachers from the East, each offering different techniques maybe, but each one pointing us in the same direction. Might not each parish invite a teacher to instruct in meditation within the community of the Church? In this way fears that it was not 'Christ-centred' would be dispelled. Besides the spiritual awareness this would bring, the physiological state of relaxation and rested brain activity would benefit all those living modern stress-filled lives. Buddhist monasteries may have much to teach us in this respect for they are havens of peace and tranquillity within the busy towns of which they are often a part. Basic material needs are met by the laity in return for the meditation and the serenity of the monks, who bring a sense of 'mindfullness of God' to everything they do.

Once the Church begins to orientate towards a sense of the 'mindfullness of God' in everything, it might begin to see its work as more person- or people-centred and less institution-centred. In this way we might progress towards different models for teaching about God. One of the changes that may come is a shift from the concept of sitting people in pews and teaching them about God, to that of people in the world learning about God from the ups and downs of life and returning to the Church for counselling, for discussion and for the nourishment provided by the sacraments. The concept of distance-learning materials using several media, enhanced by local tutorial and group support (that was pioneered by the Open University for undergraduates) is becoming increasingly popular as a way, for example, of learning about being a parent or caring for the older members of the community. As a desire for spiritual understanding grows, so might courses be offered that would satisfy this need.

For if all of life is for learning, is not the Church in the business of education in the broadest sense, and may it not be time to review both the concepts of education that it upholds and the tools of education that it uses? One way of educating is to instruct, to discipline or 'school' a person in facts and ideas: the priest and lay reader preaching a sermon are part of this understanding of education. Another way is that of *educare*, which involves bringing forth the potential that already lies within us, for:

> No man can reveal to you ought but that which already lies half asleep in the dawning of your knowledge . . .
> For the vision of one man lends not its wings to another man
> And even as each one of you stands alone in God's knowledge, so must each one of you be
> Alone in his knowledge of God and in his understanding of the earth.[8]

If the potential awareness of the reality of God is already within us, might not the Church act more as a piper calling this forth and its priesthood act more as ministers ministering to the awakening within each person, in whatever way this may take place? From this might come less of an emphasis on the Church building as a temple to which all who regard themselves as Christians are summoned and more of an emphasis on God being where the people are, perhaps with the home revered as the most special place of all. There would be less insistence on the use of the Sabbath for churchgoing – so often it becomes an extension of the hustle and bustle of the week – and more on spending time alone with God, in whatever way the individual feels called to do. A recent survey has shown that the main Christian denominations lost one million members in Britain between 1970 and 1980 and that if the present decline in Church membership continues, by 1985 it will represent a mere sixteen per cent of the population in Britain.[9] By contrast, the house group movement is growing. The rush of people to the country and to the sea at weekends has become a flood. Is this just for a day out or a good time, or could it be their own Sabbath, longing to find some wilderness experience that brings them as close to God as any sermonizing can do? This is not an argument for a formless Church but for a greater sense of opening up to the kingdom of heaven as being within us, everywhere, to be contacted through beauty and silence and not only in the

THE ROLE OF THE CHURCH IN THE NEXT DECADE 93

pews, in man-made constructions.

It could be that young people are leading the way by laying greater emphasis on spiritual values and less on adherence to formal religious codes. Perhaps we should be aware always of what is coming through the young. To some extent they need guidance from their elders, but in other ways the dynamic of Life is coming through them, for:

> You may give them your love, but not your thoughts
> For they have their own thoughts.
> You may strive to be like them, but seek not to make them like you.
> For life goes not backward nor tarries with yesterday.[10]

Some are bringing into the world vibrations of great gentleness and understanding and are slowly spreading the 'white carpet of peace', if only we could be sufficiently sensitive to watch it grow. The Beatles singing 'All You Need is Love'; an American Indian girl taking round the world her message, 'Do not take from the environment without considering what it may mean for seven generations down the road.' These may be pointers of the way ahead and as significant as anything shown on *Songs of Praise*. Jesus himself always pointed to the young, and Steven Spielberg in his widely acclaimed film *ET* seemed to be giving the message in a subtle, gentle way that dimensions of higher intelligence could be understood only by those with the heart of a child. The scientists pouncing on the creature ET for their research seemed to show how very ignorant the approach of reason and knowledge can be. They failed to see what it was all about, perhaps because they could not be still and let their intuitions, guided by a heart of Love, take control. This seemed also to be the message brought by the Pope when he visited Britain in 1982. Everywhere he smiled in Love, exhorting us to join together and see ourselves as a common humanity; but how soon after his departure did various Church committees find fault with the steps towards unity that he had proposed! Truly the 'mind is the slayer of the real'.

The Archbishop of Canterbury has been leading in the same direction, urging us to raise ourselves up to the higher vision of man that Jesus always portrayed. He said that man could:

overcome the deadly selfishness of class or sect or race by discovering himself as a child of the universal God of Love. When a man realizes that he is a beloved child of the Creator of all, then he is ready to see his neighbours in the world as brothers and sisters... he is also given strength to turn more and more of his life and actions into love and compassion for other men like himself. It is necessary to the continuance of life on this planet that more and more people make this discovery.[11]

This statement, made in the context of the service of thanksgiving after the Falklands war, is important not just in itself but for the outcry that followed it. Many said that the Church should not comment on politics but confine itself to speak on Church matters. This seems to be a fundamental issue, for if the Church does not take a lead in proclaiming man a spiritual as well as a physical being, then, for God's sake, who will? Ministers of State are appointed to do just that – minister to the temporal state, the nation in which we live – but there is always the need for vision: 'Where there is no vision, the people perish.'[12] As individuals and as nations we have a tendency to desire for ourselves, our families, our union, our class and our nation dangerous 'isms' of so many kinds. The pull of materialism and the values of this world are strong and all-pervading. Whence, then, is to come the voice for spiritual principles, for higher values, for Light and Love and the good of the whole?

The late E. F. Schumacher, in *A Guide for the Perplexed*, said:

> It may be possible to live without churches but it is not possible to live without religion, that is, without systematic work to keep in contact with and develop towards higher levels than those of 'ordinary life' with all its pleasure and pain sensation and gratification, refinement and crudity – whatever it may be. The modern experiment to live without religion has failed and once we understand this, we know what our post-modern tasks really are.[13]

Most people in the Church would agree with Schumacher that we cannot live without contact with the higher levels of life. We need not only to connect with a higher awareness as individuals but also to be inspired by higher values as a society. If this is so, then it is important to see why formalized religion is now serving such a small proportion of the population and to see whether the Church, as a movement as well as an institution, is to lead this inspiration or whether it is to come from an amalgam of the many small groups now establishing themselves under the vague banner 'New Age'. If the latter comes about, there is a danger that the Church might become overinsistent on outer form and refuse to join forces with them, thereby proving to be a force of reaction heading towards separateness as opposed to wholeness. The reactionary element within orthodox Islam seems to be heading this way today.

One way that this awareness of higher values and spiritual principles might come about would be for the Churches to lay less emphasis on the teaching of historical facts and ideas and more on the universal principles and integral wisdom that hold good for everyone. One London school starts the day by declaring:

> This day we will try:
> To find our way back to the Absolute
> To live according to the fine regulations of the Universe.
> To live according to the Unity of the Self.

Might this not be more helpful than a recitation of the Apostles' Creed? Among our 'post-modern' tasks might be the need to teach values to be lived, at least alongside the articles of faith: a love of truth and justice; a recognition of the needs of all in an inclusive and progressive society; a spirit of goodwill and co-operation; a sense of personal responsibility for community and national affairs; and a willingness to serve the common good not just the interests of ourselves. At first sight, such values seem to involve no overt acknowledgement of God at all, but are they not close to the message that Jesus always preached? This is a fundamental question which must be considered. Is the Church as close as it might be to the inspiration which Jesus gave us and demonstrated in His life and work, or has it possibly become crystallized over the centuries, overpreoccupied with perpetuating its own forms and ideas?

Anyone who has ever created anything – a pot, a poem, a picture, a song – will know that there comes a point in the creative process where the thing created seems to develop a life of its own and go its own way. This is even more the case where the creation involves people – a club, a society, a group of any kind – it develops its own dynamic and can move some distance from the one that originally inspired it. Might this be the case with the Church? Jesus left behind a 'golden rule':

> Whatsoever ye would that men should do to you, do even so to them: for this is the Law and the Prophets.[14]

Might not the essential purpose of the Church be to spread this golden rule everywhere, not just to its own membership? If we did so, we might well find that the links with other faiths would develop naturally, for this golden rule runs like a thread through all the major world religions:

Bahai	'Regard not that which benefits yourself, but hold to that which benefits mankind.'
Buddhism	'Hurt not others in ways that you yourself would find hurtful.'
Hinduism	'Do not do to others what you would not like yourself.'
Islam	'No man is a true believer unless he desireth for his brother that which he desireth for himself.'
Jainism	'A man of religion should treat all beings as he himself would be treated.'
Judaism	'What is hurtful to you do not do to your fellow man.'
Sikhism	'As thou deemest thyself, so deem others. Then shalt thou become a partner in heaven.'
Taoism	'Regard your neighbour's gain as your own gain, and your neighbour's loss as your own loss.'
Zoroastrianism	'That nature only is good that does not do unto another whatever is not good for its own self.'

This, then, can be the second major task of the Church: to work with a movement for synthesis towards the Church becoming one. If we dwell on this golden rule it appears to be the most important message from God, who is One, to His peoples, who are many. May His greatest wish not be that His peoples, who are many, should become closer in their understanding and intent to He that is One? Might not our greatest 'sin', or separation from God, be to emphasize and perpetuate anything that lessens a growing movement towards this One?

If only the universal aspects of all religions were released from their narrow confines, then religion could become a progressive and unifying force in the world. For if we are in fact on an evolutionary path, then might not the Oneness with all that is divine be the ultimate purpose? If so, then may not dearly held doctrines, sense of sovereignty, privilege and difference, and misused positions of wealth or poverty be among those things that separate us and hold us back? We must confront the fact that, on behalf of 'national passion and differing ideology',[15] we are prepared to risk the destruction of millions and even of our planetary home; we must question where we are going. We perhaps need to recognize the evil forces at work in the world and which appear to tempt us in two chief directions. One direction is to encourage us to think that we are now clever enough to master everything, that we must control events in a Godlike way and not expect God Himself to be in control. The other direction leads us to a denial of all things spiritual so that our higher perceptions are deadened up to the point where we feel that the world of matter is all that there is and that God does not really exist at all.

Where would Jesus be leading us if He were here today? Would it not be towards an awakening of the spiritual impulse in our hearts that leads us to acknowledge and be at one with God? Would He not expect the Church to be a body of Christ-filled lives, giving a lead away from materialism towards a spirit-filled understanding, a body for whom 'at-one-ment' had taken on a new meaning and purpose?

Many people who see themselves as Christians are perplexed by major issues, such as the nuclear debate, and feel the need to discuss how they feel within the setting of their church. There is one church in London which has opened up the doors both of its rectory and main building to all those who wish to explore different aspects of their Christian commitment. One group have started up a coffee bar for people to meet and talk; another have started regular counselling and healing sessions to meet the needs of people where they are; another is a peace and security group which hold lectures on different points of view, and host supper parties at which those responsible for the nation's defence may meet and discuss informally. A small caravan parked outside the church houses a computer enabling the setting up of a network of all the groups and associations working for peace; 'Prayer for Peace' is also being distributed. One interesting development is that its services of worship are seen not as the prime purpose of the Church but increasingly as a source of nourishment and support for all those busy living out the golden rule. Might not many different models of a church arise, once we concede that the one we presently hold is not the right and only one for all time?

Indeed, once the Church has shifted its concept of itself, the Holy Spirit may well lead us in other ways. Many encouraging signs tell us that this is so. Members of an ecumenical school in Surrey have found that parents are realizing that their children have a greater universal sense and integral understanding than they themselves do. Local clergy are thus being asked to run a day school, at the school, where these parents can explore what Christianity might be like in the twenty-first century and learn how to form a partnership with the school and parish in order to educate their children in a way right for them. The increasing number of inter-faith conferences, of study groups based on the Brandt report, of linked schemes for parishes to support a Third World need, of life style groups, natural healing groups and many more indicate that great changes are taking place. Slowly, perhaps, it is beginning to dawn on us that we are all members of a world-wide body in which no religion is exclusive, no caste or class is superior, no cultural or racial group is perfect and no one of us has all the answers. We are like instruments in an orchestra, each making our own contribution to the symphony of Life in response to the conductor's call.

This, then, is the link to which one returns: the fundamental need to make this connection with the conductor of all, to listen to His voice and become attuned to the rhythm of His universe – for one false note can spoil the whole. This connection, which as Christians we find in prayer, others are finding in their own way. However the connection may come, it seems to bring a greater awareness of 'the kingdom of heaven within' and is leading to what many are terming a 'transformation of consciousness'. If the Church can accept that this change of consciousness may be God-directed, whether clothed in Church symbolism or not, then it is important that each priest and deanery, each minister and Church group should focus in prayerful openness on the way that they should go. The way will not be preset, for it is a *sine qua non* of such a transformation that it is an adventure, that the way ahead is unplotted and by definition cannot be foreknown.

In the few suggestions made in this chapter, one can only hint at how things might be; that is all any of us can do. For, implicit in the new consciousness in which we begin to find ourselves, is that there are no rules of the kind that we have known. A recipe for chaos? Maybe, until a connection with an inner way is truly found, and this will not come overnight. The doctrines and creeds of the Church were appropriate to the level of understanding of the times in which they were devised, but it is natural that, if we are to grow and change – to turn within and find a higher order of understanding than we have previously known – these things should be challenged. We shall then need to begin to chart the spiritual principles and eternal values that should guide our course as individuals and as members of a Church. We shall also need to blend the outer forms that we have with the inner spiritual understanding that is breaking through. If we seek to unite amidst our diversity, we shall begin to recognize that all pathways can lead us to the One that is drawing us towards a higher level that transcends all that we have known before.

The challenge seems to be this: do we stick to the old order, the fixed rules, the laid-down dogma and long-held model of what a Church should be – or do we use all that is stable as a springboard from which to launch forth and build something new, something in which all people everywhere can comfortably find a place and know themselves as valued children of the one eternal God? There are no guidelines to the new way except the guiding rule of Love, but there is a way through the darkness of the unknown. King George VI, in a Christmas broadcast to the nation, may have provided the clue:

> I said to the man who stood at the gate of the year, 'Give me a light

that I may tread safely into the unknown'. And he replied 'Go out into the darkness and put your hand into the hand of God. That shall be to you better than light and safer than a known way.' So I went forth and finding the hand of God, trod gladly into the night. And He led me towards the hills and the breaking of day in the lone East.[16]

7.
Citizens of One World

As we look back over the centuries, it can be seen how humanity has progressed from age to age: the Age of Reason, the Age of Enlightenment, the Age of Revolution and so on to the Industrial Age. Historians hotly debate the point at which one age succeeded another; for there must always have been transition periods and for many living at those times such transitions may well have been imperceptible. So, today, the transition to another age may well be imperceptible to some, while to others it may be very real. Those for whom it is real are referring to a coming 'New Age'.

One theory behind the concept of the New Age is that the 'vibrational rate' of the planet is being raised; others point to the procession of the sun through the equinoxes now moving at the end of a 2,000-year cycle from Pisces into Aquarius. The more orthodox view is to perceive the Old Testament as the Age of God the Father, the New Testament as the Age of God the Son. We may now be moving into the Age of God the Holy Spirit. All these views may assist our understanding but what does seem certain is that 'something *is* happening'.

Whatever it is that may be happening, the keynote of it appears to be a movement for synthesis derived from an understanding of the underlying unity behind all things and the sense of oneness that this brings.

This oneness of all life is the crux of the New Age movement. It has its basis both in mysticism and science. Fritjof Capra, in his important book *The Tao of Physics*, informs us:

> Quantum theory has abolished the notion of fundamentally separated objects, has introduced the concept of the participator to replace that of the observer, and may even find it necessary to include the human consciousness in its description of the world.[1]

He goes on to show how the Eastern traditions refer to this

'ultimate, indivisible reality' which manifests itself in all things and of which all things are part. In Hinduism this is called *Brahman*, in Buddhism *Dharmadaya*, and in Taoism the *Tao*. What is now emerging within the Christian tradition is that this 'indivisible reality' is the 'I am': 'And God said to Moses, I AM THAT I AM.'[2] 'Jesus said unto them, Verily, verily, I say unto you, before Abraham was, I am.'[3] If we could begin to see this link with other faiths and with the understanding of modern science, we might start to take the early steps towards the vision of one world.

The first step we may take is towards a greater spirituality, that is, a more sensitive connection with the eternal world from which will spring an adherence to values and laws that are of the divine. We have lived at variance with spiritual laws for too long. 'As ye sow so shall ye reap', and the harvest is around us now: pollution, greed, violence, hunger – we are all part of this. Humanity must seem like cancerous cells that have ceased to function according to the workings of the planetary body of which we are a part.

Perhaps we have forgotten that we are a living part of a larger dynamic organism – the planet Earth. If we begin to see ourselves as a vital link between the mineral, plant and animal kingdoms on the one hand and the higher, unseen worlds on the other, then we begin to glimpse a deeper sense of the kingdom of God. Western culture has tended to foster a sense of separateness, which we are now seeking to transform into harmony. One separation is that between science and religion, which arose during the Age of Enlightenment but whose fruits are still with us today. Western scientists have come to see the world as something to be mastered and controlled, whereas in certain Eastern traditions, such as the Islamic, it is seen as something that needs to be understood:

> For the scientists of classical Islam, science was a vehicle of understanding and the mandate for the pursuit of this understanding was to be found in the Qur'an, where man is commanded to contemplate the heavens and the Earth and all that is enclosed within. These scientists did not see the natural world as something hostile or evil to be controlled and dominated but something that needed to be understood so that life could be lived in harmony with it. In fact, it was something sacred whose spirituality needed to be preserved.[4]

This is the view the New Age Christian is beginning to share. Through conferences such as the 'Mystics and Scientists' series organized by the Wrekin Trust, and the work of innumerable small ecological groups and communities, we are beginning to regard all matter as a manifestation of divine energy and the whole cosmic order as charged with divinity, we ourselves being an integral part: 'For in him we live, and move, and have our being'.[5] Like Wordsworth, we begin to see every:

> ... meadow, grove and stream,
> The earth and every common sight ...
> Apparell'd in celestial light,
> The glory and the freshness of a dream.[6]

An increased reverence for all life is thus emerging and resulting in an 'organic' treatment of the soil, in the conservation of natural cycles and habitats, in the humane treatment of members of the animal kingdom and in a move to 'live more simply that others may simply live'. This naturally leads to the cry that technological research and applications can no longer be pursued for their own sake but must also embrace philosophical and sociological concerns, so that we work with and not against the natural environment. To be stewards and not possessors of the one earth is part of the spiritual awareness of the New Age. The second step might be for Christians to see that it is now time to stop seeing other faiths as partial truths and to begin to see the one Truth as manifesting in different modes of expression – each complementary to an understanding of the whole. Our quest in this direction has only just begun but increased communication at many levels is clearly heading us in this direction. From the East comes an understanding of the dynamic cycles of nature and the cosmos, a notion of harmony with the basic rhythms of the universe. The other great world faiths may each have something to teach us as we grope towards a global view. Our previously held understanding can supply important guidelines by which we judge the revelations that are beginning to dawn among us, but they should not act as straightjackets on our open, honest thinking today. As Leo Tolstoy commented as early as 1893 in *The Kingdom of God is Within You*:

> Quite difficult matters can be explained even to a slow-witted man, if only he has not already adopted a wrong opinion about them; but the simplest things cannot be made clear even to a very intelligent man, if he is firmly persuaded that he already knows, indubitably, the truth of the matter under consideration.

If we are prepared to drop our pet ideologies, whether these be political, religious or cultural, we may find that the Spirit of Peace is released and that our spirituality is a common one, our concerns universal and our faith eternal.

The West has made an important contribution towards this growing spiritual maturity by developing the sense of the individual and the importance of individualized identity. It has also offered the intellectual approach, the reasoning of our minds as a route to comprehension and to the solutions of our ills. But the mind on its own is possibly a limited tool of understanding and a third step may be for us to take a step beyond this limitation. Sri Aurobindo has been one of the bridge-builders between East and West. He sees that we must reach beyond this transitional stage:

> If, then, man is incapable of exceeding mentality, he must be surpassed and supermind and superman must manifest and take the lead of the creation. But if his mind is capable of opening to what exceeds it, then there is no reason why man himself should not arrive at supermind and supermanhood or at least lend his mentality, life and body to an evolution of that greater term of the Spirit manifesting in Nature.[7]

As we move with this evolutionary force within us, we return again to the concept of oneness. It was Christ's fervent prayer 'that they may be one, even as you and I, father, are one'.[8] As we understand a little more of the true brotherhood of man and the eternal nature of all life, so we begin to see what we mean when we pray: 'Forgive us our trespasses as we forgive them that trespass against us'. Most community groups striving towards the New Age vision are finding the need for constant daily forgiveness each of the other. We also begin to fear a little less and to realize more truly that after death comes life; perhaps leaving our bodies behind is actually less important than doing harm to others. If we were more truly obedient to the injunction, 'Do not be overcome by evil, but overcome evil with good',[9] might not our corporate goodness be better able to overcome darkness in the world? This goodness is not yet sufficiently concentrated to overcome the darkness – hence the agonies of the nuclear debate. One begins to suspect that neither side offers a workable 'solution'. Perhaps solutions as such cannot be found and we need to look 'neither right nor left but uplifted forward'.[10] For what could emerge is a movement for peace that spreads throughout the earth; though this may need to be a movement truly for peace, and not a disguised form of aggression against those whose solutions differ from one's own. Perhaps as nations we have to come to a world crisis before we fully understand that nations are made up of individuals; that we as individuals can open ourselves to the birth of the Christ Spirit in our hearts and follow the way shown to us by One who was totally illumined and who expressed in every possible way the laws of God. His exhortation was always, 'Go and do ye likewise'. If we had done 'likewise' over the centuries, the story might be somewhat different now. Co-operation, compassion, conciliation – these might be more firmly rooted in the minds of all. A bond of spiritual understanding unites people of every age, class, race and religion; we see this and we begin to feel we 'have a dream'.

For those who seek to live in accordance with God's laws there lies ahead the dream, the age-old vision of the 'New Jerusalem' – a human culture in harmony with itself and with God. If we hold on more tightly to this image now, it may appear as the next evolutionary step that is seeking to unfold among us. The declaration 'For the New City of Humanity', points in this direction:

> We declare our allegiance to the race of men.
> We believe in the potential for good in all men.
> We believe that the heart of humanity is sound.
> We believe that men can live together with right relationships and at peace.
> We believe in the power of goodwill to create justice, peace and progress for all humanity.
> We affirm our intention to practise goodwill in our relationships, in our daily affairs and in our attitudes towards those of other nations, races, religions and social background.
> We intend to play our part in the building of the New City of Humanity with love that is inclusive, with tolerance that is non-

critical and with service that is given for the 'good of the whole'. We resolve to fight waste and pollution on all fronts, and will adopt a simpler life-style that will embrace reverence for LIFE, whether plant, animal, human or the earth itself that nourishes and sustains the life of all the kingdoms of nature.[11]

The ancient sages pointed towards human unity. 'Under Heaven one family,' said Confucius, and Socrates instructed us: 'When you are asked your country, never reply, "I am an Athenian", or "I am a Corinthian", but say, "I am a citizen of the world"'. Today, the more enlightened politicians and world leaders are beginning to think along similar lines. In the second report of the Brandt Commission, *Common Crisis: North-South Co-operation for World Recovery*, Willy Brandt says:

> Together with my colleagues I hold the hope that the thoughts we have set forth may light a pathway to a more just and prosperous world for generations to come – free from dependence and oppression from hunger and distress. A new century nears, and with it the prospects of a new civilization. Could we not begin to lay the basis for that new community with reasonable relations among all people and nations, and to build a world in which sharing justice, freedom and peace might prevail?[12]

The ideals both of the 'New City of Humanity' and the Brandt Commission could be accused of being Utopian in vision and unrealistic in practice. Certainly, at the human level, the prospects look bleak, but if we shift our perspective a little and, like the Hebrews crossing the Red Sea, trust in God, then seeming impossibilities can occur. A new culture is not born overnight – it is the work of many generations – but each one inherits the culture envisioned by the one before. Are our grandchildren to inherit a radioactive earth? This is why the way we think now is vital for the years ahead.

Many small community groups are seeking this transformation in different ways. Some are Christian fellowships and house groups; others are self-styled New Age groups without any overt link with Christianity. What links them is a vision of a world made new, the key to which is an inner contact with the Spirit of God, in whatever way this may be conceived. Meditation and prayer, stillness and quiet are central to everything they do. All are ways of linking up our hearts, souls, and minds to God. We make the 'connection', and as we listen to God's voice we find we can respond as life offers opportunities to us rather than react against events which appear to be beyond our control. Once we do this, once we respond from a level higher than the one we normally use, we begin to conceive of the entire process of living as our 'work'. Work becomes no longer just what we do in the factory, the field, the office or the shop (though this may be a part of it) and takes on a broader significance altogether. It must, indeed, include a provision for our earthly needs – and the concept of the 'social wage' may help us here – but what the New Age offers is that work becomes the way in which our soul carries out its purposes on earth:

> You work that you may keep pace with the earth and the soul of the earth. For to be idle is to step out of life's procession that marches in majesty and proud submission before the infinite.[13]

Kahlil Gibran, in *The Prophet*, gives us an uplifting insight of work as 'love made visible' and brings us back to a sense of reconnection with the earth. This reconnection between ourselves and our world is behind the 'wilderness' movement which the modern prophet Laurens Van der Post is urging forward. He sees us as denying the wilderness, the 'natural being' within ourselves at the same time as exploiting the wilderness, the natural resources of the earth. In both senses we lose touch with our feeling of belonging.

The 'New Age Christian' today is one who is trying to bridge these divisions within himself and within the world. In a speech to a Universal Peace Conference, Robert Muller, Assistant Secretary-General of the United Nations, voiced the feelings of many:

> The only way I see the unfolding of the future is that humanity, or the human race on this planet, will have to work towards, and find, five basic harmonies.

Muller then outlined these five harmonies. The first is between man and the resources of the planet; the second the harmony between humans themselves; the third is harmony with time – both the preservation of the rich diversities of the past and the need to 'think hundreds of years ahead'; the fourth is harmony with the heavens, ('this is the new spirituality which is emerging from the UN'), and lastly the harmony of the individual:

> It is the responsibility of the individual to have harmony with the planet, with other human beings, with one's past and one's future and with the heavens through one's relationship to God or whatever religion one believes in.[14]

If we are to find this universal harmony then our relationship to God must be continually renewed, religion cannot be a historical thing; although it may have – and indeed needs to have – historical roots. The deeper the roots the better, for a tree cannot live without good, deep roots, but equally it needs the living shoots, the unfolding buds and leaves open to the life-giving Spirit each moment of the day – this day:

> Look ye well unto this day,
> For it is life, the very life of life,
> For yesterday is only a dream and tomorrow is only a vision.
> But today well lived,
> Makes all the yesterdays a dream of happiness
> And all the tomorrows a vision of hope.
> Look ye well therefore unto this day.
> Such is the salutation of the dawn.[15]

Looking to 'this day' helps us to achieve a profound belief in the Spirit of God in us. Our faith, being constantly renewed and restored, brings us to work co-creatively with God and with each other: 'Thy kingdom come on earth as it is in heaven'. Is co-creation something that we are slowly learning? The world is going to need people who are aligned to the Spirit of God, sensitively aware of the needs of those around them, who can bring serenity and balance to everyday affairs and can meet challenges cheerfully and humbly without losing the dynamic of Love within. That we might be such people is indeed a challenge. To support us in this challenge is the knowledge that at the centre of the universe there is indeed goodness – God.

> God reveals himself everywhere, beneath our groping efforts, as a universal milieu, only because he is the ultimate point upon which all realities converge.[16]

If God is the ultimate point, as Teilhard de Chardin suggests, then the purpose of all religions must be to help us to relate to this 'universal milieu' and to live by the rhythms that are deep within it. This leads us less towards an emphasis on the separatisms of formalized religion and more towards a convergence on Love, for:

> Love alone is capable of uniting living beings in such a way as to complete and fulfill them, for it alone takes them and joins them by what is deepest in themselves.[17]

Homo sapiens may be growing, slowly and painfully, into 'Homo Universalis'. Certainly, we live in changing times and sense another stage ahead. The birth pangs may indeed be real: 'And when ye shall hear of wars and rumours of wars, be ye not troubled.'[18] Fear is a threshold we may have to cross as we seek an inner wisdom. The way through is perhaps by recognizing the negative states as necessary yet not identifying with them. Rather we can try to align ourselves with the forces of goodwill and all that is positive in the affairs of men: 'Glory to God in the highest, and on earth peace, goodwill towards men.'[19] This was the mission Christ came to bring. The Cross and the Resurrection made it possible, but what we need to understand is that each of us is able to join with the evolutionary force of goodwill so that it may indeed bring peace among men. This was the message that heralded the birth of Jesus, and it is still the vision to be held today. It is also the message given by certain spokesmen for our times, for the 'solution of our crisis will not be found along the well-trodden paths of conventional notions'. So said Alexander Solzhenitsyn in his 1983 Templeton Address. His message might well serve as a manifesto for us today:

> Our life consists not in the pursuit of material success but in the quest of worthy spiritual growth. Our entire earthly existence is but a transitional stage in the movement towards something higher, and we must not stumble and fall, nor must we linger fruitlessly on one rung of the ladder. Material laws alone do not explain our life or give it direction. The law of physics and physiology will never reveal the indisputable manner in which the Creator constantly, day in and day out, participates in the life of each of us, unfailingly granting us the energy of existence; when this assistance leaves us, we die. In the life of our entire planet, the divine spirit moves with no less force: this we must grasp in our dark and terrible hour.[20]

8.
The Emergence of a New Consciousness

Today we are finding within all social structures, the Church included, a growing need for a reappraisal and a reformulation of previously held beliefs and thought patterns, so that these can open up to encompass the new consciousness that is emerging. This consciousness is an attempt to lift mankind out of its self-directed way of thinking wherein his 'world' is small and ego-centred, into an expanding awareness of his role in the evolution of the planet, where the aim is for the 'good of the many, rather than the few'. At the same time, this new awareness will direct our thoughts to a higher level and we shall begin to understand the laws of the universe, Christ's message to the world and our part in the symphony of Life. First of all, we have to recognize the change that is needed in our own thinking and within ourselves, which will then gradually permeate our surroundings and affect those we meet.

Up to now, the Church has been entrusted with the Truth, has guarded it and been exhorted to pass it on, but in the course of time that message has naturally been open to distortion. With the passing of the years has come a fear of losing the message which has occasionally caused Church leaders to resort to rigidity. Today the people – the flock – are able to sense a discrepancy between what they are being taught and what they feel inwardly to be true. The problem now has to be aired openly so that these emergent beliefs can be discussed freely, without the risk of being considered 'heretical'. 'Orthodoxy' should ring true in the depths of one's being, and the fact must be faced that certain orthodox doctrines simply do not do this, no matter how much one would like to give them credence or how hard one tries to accept them.

Many 'truths' are indeed a mystery to us, and to a large extent they must remain so while we have our finite minds; and yet it does seem possible for such mysteries to resonate at a place deep within ourselves where we recognize the essence of the Truth they contain though we are unable to articulate it. God reveals His Truth more deeply as time goes on, and thus no truth can be crystallized, tied up in a neat package and marked 'orthodoxy'. What was 'orthodox' today could become 'heretical' tomorrow, and equally, today's 'heresy' could emerge as the 'orthodoxy' of tomorrow, as man's thinking is moved on by the Spirit.

One longs for God-fearing people to be freed from the shackles of outdated concepts. Is it really healthy to repeatedly ask for mercy as 'miserable sinners'? Have we not already been forgiven at the cosmic level? Did Christ not come to 'redeem' this planet by the spilling of His blood? Those who are churchgoers do try to mend their ways; those who never darken the doors of a church never know what 'miserable sinners' they are! After the liberation from religious conditioning, there will follow an enormous release from the subconscious of that 'psychic' energy which had formerly been used to repress thoughts and feelings then considered heretical: those same thoughts and feelings that had produced guilt complexes and drained away potentially creative energy. The freedom that is experienced in such a release knows no bounds; the Spirit is able to move in and, in conjunction with man's total energy, the kingdom of heaven on earth could begin to become a reality. For this to happen, man has to cooperate with his Creator and with the whole of himself, not with the mere one-third of his being which – according to the psychologist Jung – is all that he uses at present. Then the 'pearl of great price' will be found within himself: a conscious awareness of God's presence will be unfolded.

It is encouraging to find a synthesis of religion and psychology taking place within the minds of psychologists. In her book *Something is Happening*, the Jungian therapist Winifred Rushforth expresses her belief that the spiritual and psychological ways of understanding are one and the same.[1] In a chapter entitled 'The Emergence of Human Potential', she gives an example of the creativity that is released with the return to consciousness of repressed material: 'The energy of the psyche surges into life, seeking an outlet.' As this happened with her patients, she discovered that hidden gifts emerged and their 'creative energy was replacing the fear that had kept them depressed, physically sick, the victims of inertia'. She likens this energy to the power referred to in St

Paul's teaching: 'Out of this Infinite Glory may he give us the power through the spirit, that the hidden self may grow strong'. She feels most strongly that 'this power working in us does infinitely more than we can ask or imagine'. Likewise, Jung taught that the *atman* – the Self within – has to be discovered in order to release this inner creative energy. What exactly do we mean by this inner creative energy? Could it not be the Cosmic Christ Consciousness that was brought to earth by Jesus and then, as it were, reduced in voltage so that we could bear its intensity and make it a part of our human consciousness?

The Church tends not to recognize that the teaching of Christ was often of a psychological nature and concerned with bringing out the full potential that lies within each individual. Within the Catholic Church, a method used to find the 'hidden self' and help it come alive is by following the Spiritual Exercises of St Ignatius Loyola. St Ignatius, a Spaniard born in 1493, recognized the significance of the unconscious and, indeed, used some of the methods that twentieth-century psychotherapists have rediscovered. Yet the modern therapist does not always touch on the spiritual dimension, and if he omits to do so, he ignores an intrinsic part of the whole person. The Spiritual Exercises enable the person to 'experience' as opposed to 'hear about' God. This is what has the power to change the lives of men: the experience of the power of God in Christ, and the power of Christ in us.

The medical world is also beginning to encompass the spiritual dimension and has a lot to learn from so-called 'alternative medicine', whereby the individual is treated in his entirety, rather than a cure being sought for the diseased part alone. In the case of cancer treatment, information about newer methods is at last being released to the public through radio and television programmes, as well as in books.

We are beginning to understand that man is more than just his physical aspect and possesses a mental 'field' (etheric body), an emotional 'field' (astral body), together with a spiritual aura, which in the paintings of the past was depicted as a halo around a person's head, or occasionally as a golden light emanating from his body. The size of the halo and the brightness of its light is supposedly indicative of the extent of that person's 'holiness', or wholeness. Was not this what Jesus meant when He said: 'Then the virtuous will shine like the sun in the kingdom of their Father'?[2] Those who have this extra perception are able to see emanating from a human body different colours which indicate that person's inner state and can then be a pointer to the cause of his disease. These magnetic 'fields' have now been scientifically recognized and monitored, not only in human beings, but also in plants and in all living things. Kirlian photography, as it is called, could be the means of a breakthrough to a quicker and surer diagnosis of disease, which would bring about more rapid relief together with a considerable saving of skill and energy, not to mention money and hospital beds. When the patient is treated as a whole, and the origin of the illness is found to be in the mental 'field', the alleviation must also concern the 'healing of the memories'. It is now well known that past tragedies or traumas can trigger off a cancerous growth. It then becomes a case of 'Physician, heal thyself'; but we still need a great deal of help in order to discover what has gone wrong – what it is that is playing up in the area of the unconscious.

Surgeons readily agree that having performed their skilled operations they have little more to do as nature then takes over, unobtrusively knitting together the broken bones or revitalizing dead tissues in the blood stream. Witness the way a cut heals itself. We can aid nature by going along with it, and many of the old herbal remedies do just this. Many people today are turning to homoeopathy, a science which proves that the holistic approach can, more often than not, effect a cure, though this may be a slower process than that effected by antibiotics. There is a place for all branches of medicine, and each can learn from the other; yet at present this happens but rarely and there tends to be rivalry or scorn rather than a pooling of knowledge. Nevertheless, scientific knowledge and religious insights are beginning to be seen to overlap and blend into one another, and we are beginning to appreciate the previous limitations of our thinking.

An oft-quoted phrase is 'man's coming of age', and there is more than an element of truth in this. For as we scan man's religious ideals and practices over the last 2,000 years, and even prior to that, we become aware of his spiritual infancy and where he stands today according to the scale of religious thinking. We are only just on the point of stepping over the threshold of adolescence into the realm of greater maturity. We now have to begin to take responsibility for our beliefs and ideas. We must be gentle with ourselves and resist sinking into a morass of guilt because we cannot accept all that the Church teaches; but our growing pains are real, nevertheless.

We say of our growing children that they must make their religion their own, which generally means laying aside what we have given them in order that they may discover a faith that is personal to them. No longer able to live with a 'second-hand' faith, this then becomes their faith. Similarly, as we mature we must do the same with what has been handed on to us, for in the end we have to take responsibility for ourselves. We shall find we still have some 'crutches' which will have to be discarded as we grow to maturity. It would be unwise to spell out what some of these crutches are, as each person should discover them for himself. After the initial awareness that these things were psychological props, there is a great deal of work to be done inwardly. We must ask ourselves, firstly, why the props had been necessary and whether we are ready for their removal, for damage can be done by taking away a dearly held belief or ritual too suddenly. We have always to be as gentle and patient with others as we should be with ourselves. Just as an adolescent needs a parent figure standing by to whom he may refer as necessary, so we need the ministry of the Church – but not an overpowering authoritarianism which stifles growth. Our plea is for the type of ministry that will allow us to develop freely within the Church's structure, which does contain the essence of Life. Yet the structure must grow and change with the evolving of man's spirit. This means a breaking down of old thought patterns so that new 'seed' thoughts can make their way to the surface of our consciousness and become reality. The breaking down process must by its very nature be a painful one: we do not like 'letting go', for old habits are 'safe' and we are fearful of a void in the future. Equally, giving birth will be a lonely and painful experience.

This process of change will occur – is indeed occurring now – within all the structures of society, and the evidence of this inner turmoil is reflected in the senseless violence, crime and general chaos seen in the world today. Although we must endeavour to tackle each problem in the material realm in its own sphere, it is in the spiritual realm that we must look first, for, to quote Winifred Rushforth again, 'I *am* spirit. I *have* a body'.[3] Something is certainly happening, though many would agree that the Church is not exactly at a peak just now.

Unless it opens its arms to man and helps his awareness to expand, then the pews really will be empty, and the lay person will look elsewhere for his God; so we must rightly ask, 'Where has it gone wrong?' Is it because the Church tends to teach *about* God and Christ rather than allow us to *experience* the living Reality? No amount of talking 'about' or even reading 'about' someone will enable us to know that person as he really is; only a personal encounter will enable us to experience their 'beingness'.

Our mind is like a house with many floors, each one relating to a different level of understanding. Each one of us must be allowed to experience that which unfolds from the level at which he finds himself. By this 'experiencing' it will become part of our thinking; we shall make it our own and it will be valid for us at that moment in time. God speaks to us in the 'now', where we are now, whether it be a physical situation or a level of consciousness. Any problems usually lie in the basement, the subconscious, for here mischief can be done without our being aware of what is going on, apart from recognizing the fact that all is not as it should be. We may be prone to ill-health or feel a 'blockage' which is difficult to locate. For our house to be in order and not divided against itself, there has to be free communication between the different storeys. This will reduce conflict and allow the creative energy to flow throughout the whole building, making it a temple fit for the Spirit to function for the glory of God and man. No part of ourselves is ever left out: our past and our present must in time be brought together, to be purified and transmuted so that the end product really is a whole and complete person.

The figure of Jesus Christ has been able to become many things to many men, but always the impression given has been that of a person open to allowing God to enter fully into His life and actions. His ego had been subjected to the Highest within him, so that His will was at one with that of His Creator. Is this not a pointer to the future development of mankind? Frances Young suggests, in her chapter of *The Myth of God Incarnate* entitled 'A Cloud of Witnesses' that:

> to recognise the possibility that diverse responses to Jesus Christ have equal validity may well be the only constructive way forward in a world which is beginning to value the enriching aspects of its variety and pluralism.[4]

It would be a real step forward if the Church would openly allow that each person's response to Christ is – and must be – theirs alone, whether or not this response is in line with the teaching of the Church.

We most certainly need to search for constructive ways forward. It is generally agreed that man has very nearly brought both the planet and himself to a point of no return. It appears that no economic, monetary or social strategy exists which is able to pull us out of this morass, and the danger lies in that some leaders still feel they have the ability to do this, in their own strength and at their own level of understanding which is still limited and bound by old concepts. If mankind is to change, it will have to be through a change of heart; and for a change of heart to occur, there has to have been an inner 'experience'. A breakdown of the old thought patterns has to take place before a breakthrough to a new dimension can be made. This other dimension relates to our spiritual nature and means allowing a higher consciousness to work through our human consciousness; or, to put it another way, to have a 'God experience'. For this reason it is imperative that the established Churches wake up, move on and open up to the thinking and insights of the laity. Beneath the dust of two thousand years lies the message of salvation. Today, Man's intellect surely needs to be balanced by his anima, his intuitive aspect, as opposed to the reasoning aspect that has latterly been the dominant one, for nothing short of a change of heart is going to alter the way things are in the world.

From this higher level of understanding, we begin to ask for a less exclusive insistence on Jesus as the way for all peoples and all cultures. This must, inevitably, lessen the gap between religions and bring us closer together. If God comes to us through the lives of men, we are all the poorer if we cannot accept that part of His Truth which is embodied in Buddha, in Muhammad and in all the very great number of saints and mystics throughout the ages, from all lands and religions. Does anyone have the whole Truth? If Christ had, it is certainly only imperfectly understood today.

One man who has pointed us towards this higher understanding is Mahatma Gandhi. The impact that Attenborough's film *Gandhi* has had on people is surely indicative of the climate of religious thinking today. E. Stanley Jones, a well-known missionary in India, described Gandhi as 'more Christianized than most Christians',[5] and we Christians would do well to heed Gandhi's remark in the film that 'if it is to be "an eye for an eye", then the whole world will go blind'. He remained a Hindu because he was unable to believe:

> that Jesus was the only incarnate Son of God and that only he who believed in Him would have everlasting life. If God could have sons, all of us were his sons. [6]

Gandhi's views have given encouragement to many devout people today who find the issue of Christ's divinity as taught by the Church to be a stumbling block. Their difficulty appears to lie not in accepting that Jesus was fully human by nature and that He possessed the perfect nature of humankind, but in accepting that He had a fully divine nature equal to the nature of God. Did He ever make this claim?: He said, 'The Father and I are one',[7] but he never said that he was God. He says elsewhere, 'Why call ye me good? No one is good but God alone.'[8] And again, 'The Father is greater than I.'[9] Yes, He was fully at one with God, and it could be said that God was in Him as in no other person. The shame felt by those unable to accept the 'Jesus, fully human yet divine' arouses deep feelings of guilt, the result of their religious upbringing and of their having been conditioned to accept the authority of the Church. Is it not possible that the Church's teaching can be realized at a deeper and more universal level? A new angle is perhaps coming into focus which is not destroying but fulfilling.

We are all on different rungs of the ladder that takes us towards ever increasing consciousness and to our goal. Is it too hard to believe that Christ was on a rung far above us all but which we one day must also reach? If the whole of Creation has come forth from this Life, then we each have within us a spark of that divinity which must be fed and nurtured so that we shall one day be of the stature of Christ. We are surely not expected to remain in the darkness that surrounds our understanding? Our Creator must have designed His Creation so that it will ultimately grow to its full potential. Christ never intimated that we should remain at this lower station of life; on the contrary, He told us to be perfect, even as the Father was perfect, and said: 'I tell you most solemnly, whoever believes in me will perform the same works as I do myself, he will perform even greater works, because I am going to the Father.'[10]

In a later book, Gandhi asks and answers the question:

> What then does Jesus mean to me? ... To me, He was one of the greatest teachers humanity has ever had. To His believers, He was God's only-begotten Son. Could the fact that I do or do not accept this belief make Jesus have any more or less influence in my life? Is all the grandeur of His teaching and of His doctrine to be forbidden to me? I cannot believe so. To me it implies a spiritual birth. My interpretation, in other words, is that in Jesus's own life is the key to His nearness to God; that he expressed, as no other could, the spirit and will of God. It is in this sense that I see Him and recognise Him as the son of God.[11]

The emphasis on the Christological aspect of the Incarnation is now being queried by theologians as well as by the laity. In *The Myth of God Incarnate*, John Hick, Maurice Wiles and other writers stress that in questioning the theological implications of the Incarnation, they are not attempting in any way to reduce the stature of Jesus. They do so 'in the interests of truth; but it also has increasingly important practical implications for our relationship with the peoples of other great world religions.'[12] By enlarging our concept of Christ's cosmic nature and mission they help us to see that 'God launched men into a relationship with Himself, so full and rich that, under various understandings and formulations of it, it has been and continues to be the salvation of a large proportion of the human race.'[13]

Jesus enabled men to come closer to His Creator by pointing always away from Himself, to the Father. He showed how He and the Father were One through an act of will and obedience, through allowing Himself to be emptied of his 'lower self', which permitted God to work through Him, making this God-man-God relationship possible.

If the concept of the 'Incarnational model' changes because of historical research and the need for a different psychological approach after 2,000 years, it can surely do nothing but help bring together the highest truths of the world's great religions and make a unity, but not a conformity, out of diversity? As Professor Wiles points out in his chapter 'Christianity without Incarnation', throughout history 'the precise way in which Jesus is understood, and impinges upon the life of the Church, has been a constantly changing phenomenon in the history of the Church'.[14] As the image of Christ changed between the time of the early Church and the Nicene era, so it must continue to change within succeeding cultures if it is to be the link between God and man and to be 'alive' to, and speak to, each generation. It only takes a greater openness of heart and magnanimity of thought for us to realize that the Holy Spirit, always within Creation, is ever new in the present moment and may also precede us into the future.

Jesus introduced into history a new humanity: God-centred instead of man-centred. He demonstrated the potential that could be brought out from within man if he lived according to the laws of the universe, spiritual as opposed to material laws. Above all, He saw Himself as a man of universal destiny – for all nations – a truth which, at the present time and with the emergence of a global human consciousness, is being highlighted. If 'religion' is not merely a set of intellectual beliefs but 'an evolving, living tradition', then a change in our understanding must be allowed to take place.[14a] We cannot contain or crystallize any part of the Truth; it is far too vast. Mankind tends to want to label and define so as to have power over the mysteries of life which elude his comprehension. That souls have had glimpses of this other dimension is a great gift: to them, as well as to others. The argument that is often put forward against openness to the Spirit stems from the fear that 'orthodoxy' will take a knocking and 'heresy' creep in. What is 'orthodoxy' but that which Man decreed? As history shows, this has often come out of politics and the power, greed and jealousy of those in authority.

The Fifth Ecumenical Congress of Constantinople in AD 553, convened by the Emperor Justinian and ordered by his infamous wife Theodora, who forbade the Pope's presence at the Council and allowed only six Western bishops to be present, is a prime example of the course of Church history being altered to suit those in power. According to historical evidence in support of the Edgar Cayce readings, its members 'expunged the Platonically inspired writings of Origen, an early Church Father, who upheld reincarnation until his death three hundred years before.'[15]

Maybe our outlook on life and our world situations would be very different if we took the view that we cannot judge the actions of others for we know not the origin of their cause: 'Judge not that ye be not judged'. Life is a learning process, and can we learn it all, or even experience all we have to, in one lifetime? Is karma not the same as 'Where a man sows, there he reaps'?[16] We are assured of forgiveness, and we know the Light will ultimately conquer the darkness – but would it be in our best interests as far as our growth in the Spirit is concerned for us to have our sins taken from us by a 'magical' action? Like a child, do we not have to go through an experience and learn from it before it becomes real to us or can teach us any lesson? Surely, this learning process is gained by reaping what we sow, either in this life or the next?

So-called 'heresy' comes, more often than not, from deep within the psyche – the part that is the 'real' you, or Jung's 'other' you – and you cannot, without being a traitor to your being, refuse to accept its validity. As Frances Young, in her chapter 'A Cloud of Witnesses' from *The Myth of God Incarnate* suggests, one is otherwise forced into a state of schizophrenia. Surely wholeness is a part of Christ's message? We are whole people, not divided within our own being. And surely, if sin is alienation, the rejecting of a very real part of one's inner being is the first step towards this unhappy state? It could be that the prevalence of breakdowns among the clergy today, be they due to physical, mental or spiritual causes, is attributable to their being divided within their own being, due to an emergence of a new consciousness which makes them unable to come to terms with conflicting thoughts within. It must be extremely difficult to come to terms with that which may go against the teaching they received while at theological college.

A lecturer I once heard suggested we imagine a large, luminous cloud, 'up there', 'out there', towards which we are all travelling, all faiths and denominations – the humanist, the philosopher, the religionist – all people, on their different paths and approaching the goal from different aspects, yet all part of Man's progression back to his Creator. Christ comes out of that cloud of which He is a part, bringing 'the Light of the World' to all the world, in order to share the Light and help us on our travels to the Source of our being. Christ has been called the 'Son of God', but other teachers such as Confucius, Buddha and Muhammad have also come from that Light, in order to help us on our way to becoming a part of the Light, and to claim our inheritance as 'sons of God' as well. If God reveals himself through people, where is the problem? Surely Christ's message was for all the world; dare we, as Christians, really say that we have the whole Truth? Can any human being with his finite mind comprehend the whole Truth?

If only we could learn to concentrate on what is common to the great faiths of the world. The Second Vatican Council brought many new insights into the Christian Church, one of which was that the Bible and the Koran have similarities of teaching and thought, and that each granted the Virgin Mary a high place in the scheme of things. The Muslim acknowledges Christ as a great Master and Prophet, a great Light to the world. In 1965, Vatican II – which debated religious freedom – opened up the way forward to ecumenism and, showing a less defensive attitude than in the past, stated, 'Every Church has a portion of the truth'. And in recognizing the truths in other faiths, it states:

> Upon the Muslims the Church looks with esteem. They adore One God, Living and Enduring, Merciful and All-powerful, Maker of heaven and earth, and speaker to Man. They strive to submit wholeheartedly even to His inscrutable decrees.

A visit to Maryamana, the house in the hills behind Ephesus where Our Lady spent her last days (according to the nun Catherine Emmerich, whose visions are recorded in her book, *The Life of Our Blessed Lady*) enables one to understand how Mary could be the instrument used for the bringing together of Christianity and Islam.[17] There in the chapel is a separate recess which Catherine Emmerich 'saw' as Mary's bedroom and where now a constant stream of Muslims come to pray through her to Allah. She is much venerated, and every mosque has a corner dedicated to her – a Lady Chapel.

As within Christianity, a new consciousness is emerging within parts of the Islamic tradition. They, too, are trying to leave behind the dogmas they have outgrown and are beginning to see the universality that lies within all religious traditions; there is a yearning to bridge the gap in understanding between East and West. They see Mary, mother of the Christian Church, as the intermediary. The fact that Christians say that Jesus is God certainly appears to be a stumbling block to those on other paths returning to the One God. Must we bar Him from other faiths by making Him an exclusively Christian property? Surely, sooner or later, we must admit to the reality of us all being part of the whole and coming from the same Source, members one of another –

brothers and sisters – one with the cosmos and all on our path to God? Nothing can be outside Creation, and in time *all* creation must be redeemed. Until that happens there will be suffering and divisiveness; we are now in a state of alienation or separation, not in actuality but in 'consciousness'; it is our thinking that makes it so.

There is disinterest and dissatisfaction with the established Churches today, chiefly because their message does not ring true. It may be time to go back to the Gospels and examine their historical evidence closely, as it is important for us to distinguish between what Jesus actually said and what the Church authorities later added – always allowing for the differing interpretations given in the early Gospels and bearing in mind what was allowed for general belief and what was destroyed as 'heretical' if it did not suit the political climate of the day. (This last applies particularly to the power games of the Emperor Justinian and Empress Theodora, in the 6th century.)

Primitive man saw and felt his 'God' in the elements – in the thunder and lightning and in anything that seemed incomprehensible to him. Old Testament man had an image of a wrathful, revengeful God, a God who judged and was all-powerful – and fear was introduced into his mind.

In the New Testament, Jesus comes to tell us that God is more than either of these. He is one with His 'Father', and the relationship is loving and forgiving, like that of any good father with his son. He tells us also that He is 'in the Father and the Father in Him'.[18] Man took this to mean that He was therefore God Himself, and it was because of this that the Crucifixion took place; for the Jews, rightly, maintained there was only one God. Surely, Jesus was trying to tell us that His inheritance was our inheritance if we would wake up and have 'ears to hear' and 'eyes to see'? We all have the same Father and Creator, and it was to Him that Christ always pointed. It was part of Roman culture to make an idol or god out of persons of stature. St Paul knew this, and to convert the Romans and help them understand that Christ was the Way, he had to present Him as a 'god'. Legend has it that Barnabas had to part company with Paul over their difference of opinion concerning the status of Jesus. Barnabas would not have Him deified, reporting that Jesus had specifically requested that He should not be. The 'Gospels' of Thomas and Barnabas have not been judged authentic and have been

THE EMERGENCE OF A NEW CONSCIOUSNESS 123

banned, labelled as 'Gnostic' heresy.

One only has to use the word 'Gnostic' to feel hackles being raised in defence. But Iraneas pointed out that it was St John's Gospel that many Gnostic Christians used as a source of Gnostic teaching. In 1945, an Arab peasant found in a jar at Nag Hammadi in Upper Egypt, ancient papyrus books containing the Gospels of Philip and Thomas, plus many other secret writings, among them the 'Gospel of Truth' and 'The Dialogue of the Saviour'. Elaine Pagels's book, *The Gnostic Gospels*, gives detailed accounts of the research carried out on these documents.[19]

In St Thomas's Gospel, the answer given by Jesus to the disciples who asked where they should go is: 'There is light within a man of light, and it lights up the whole world. If he does not shine, he is in darkness.' In 'The Dialogue of the Saviour', He is reported as replying to the same question, 'The place that you can reach, stand there.'[20] The word 'reach' implies we have to stretch ourselves as far as we can, and then ignorance will vanish of its own accord as knowledge appears, just as darkness vanishes when light appears. Elaine Pagels writes:

> Far from legitimising any institution, both sayings direct one instead to oneself – to one's inner capacity to find one's own direction, to the Light within.[21]

After the findings at Nag Hammadi, the questions to be asked are surely: 'Can some of the Gnostic Gospels be combined with the New Testament Gospels that we have been given? Can more of Gnostic Christianity be incorporated into orthodox Christianity in the light of this new understanding that is emerging? Will that ring of truth be restored to some of the traditional teaching to which we have become accustomed?'

The Gnostics' belief that matter is 'evil', and their rejection of the worth of the body and the part it has to play, can be seen to be untrue in the light of today's 'gnosis' and of our own understanding of the body being the temple of the Holy Spirit. We know of the interdependence of body, mind and spirit, which has been experienced by many. A prime example is that where there is disease either in the soul or the mind, it is reflected in the body's functioning, and pathological disease, such as cancer, is thus manifested at the physical level. This has happened to me, and a great deal of heart and soul searching had to be done in order to discover what was going wrong in the 'basement' or unconscious, to find in what areas of one's personality the fuses were being blown and why? Jung has cast a great deal of light on the subject of the unconscious and the role it can play in our lives; he has shown that it can work to the detriment of the personality which is reaching out towards freedom and true liberation in the Spirit. We would do well to ask if Man is not now trying to project a new and finer archetype upon the Universe, in his emergent desire to get beyond words and to worship God in the Spirit, as Christ told him to do. The Christian Gnostic's insistence that our pilgrimage is first and foremost to do with an inner journey ties in with our modern discovery of the working of the psyche. This again, is biblical, for Christ said, 'When you pray, go to your private room and when you have shut your door, pray to your Father who is in that secret place.'[22]

Was not Jesus trying to teach us how to raise our minds and hearts to a higher level of consciousness, telling us that life is all about being raised up and made whole people, reborn in the Spirit? If we have the desire, then by grace are we raised; it is a two-way flow. Every cell in our body cries out for Light, and through prayer and meditation we receive a heightened consciousness due to 'becoming' a part of that Light. We become a part of that Love which is an unconditional state of being, where we flow out to others in empathy and caring, because we cannot do otherwise; it is a state of 'beingness', and, God, the source of our being, is the Great Lover.

Veneration does not mean that man must make an idol (or a 'god') of a person, however spiritually evolved they may appear, for the 'saint' comes to show us the place we must all reach one day. We, as Christians, have been given the Way but have made it more comfortable by putting it on a pedestal for us to worship 'out there', rather than making it our own Way and taking it into our own lives.

The coming of Christ is the most important event that has happened in the history of our planet. Nevertheless, it still remains for us to discover the realm of the Cosmic Christ Consciousness and also recognize Him in our humanity as a presence that is continually speaking to us, beckoning us onwards and guiding us through our pilgrimage here on earth. He has been where we are now, in the dark times as well as the good times; He has been through all our sufferings and trials and conquered them all.

Our effect on others depends on the extent of our consciousness, for then we provide an environment wherein every individual we meet has the optimum chance to become conscious through his contact with us. We *are* consciousness – and all we have to give to another human being is ourselves: nothing more, nothing less. The raising of an individual's consciousness helps the whole planet – helps build up a store of this higher consciousness. Some can draw on this store at a cosmic level; others simply absorb it through a process of osmosis, unaware of doing anything other than having a 'will to good' – an attitude of mind which attracts like thoughts. We have to learn both to draw on and generate this energy of the higher universal consciousness. Surely Christ was doing this the whole time, and telling us to do the same? We still do not fully appreciate what this means and we call the effects 'miracles'; our faith is unable to stretch to the point of actually believing 'miracles' can happen. The day has come when our cry is for spiritual food and not merely for food for the body. If the Church could only recognize that people are ready for more solid food: all too often they ask for bread and are given a stone.

Jesus came to us in human form as one who had reached His full potential and performed God's will to the utmost perfection. He came from God, the Father, bringing to us the pure, Uncreated Light of God. He Himself was able to mirror that Light with complete purity, for in Him the 'self', the persona, had already been 'crucified'. This state of being enabled Him to be filled with the energies of God, and in that sense He was part of the Godhead. Yet that fact was never proclaimed in His teaching; it was to His Father that He always gave the glory. He came to proclaim the Good News that we were created from the One (God) and had within us the divine essence which still had to grow to its full potential, as we were the 'heirs and sons of God'.[23] He gave us guidelines to help us on the way back to the Father. His message that we are 'sons' and therefore 'heirs' should eventually enable each man to make a leap in consciousness and so become better able to understand who he is and the potential that he carries within him. The path was not to be an easy one, but within the context of suffering we too could be purified and emptied of 'self' so that the Holy Spirit could work through us; for, to the extent that we surrender our will to God – 'Let your will be done not mine' – it is not our being but His being.[24] When each of us becomes a pure instrument, God is made manifest in man. Jesus came, above all, to tell us who we really are. It has taken us almost twenty centuries to begin to discover our true identity and to have an inkling as to our inheritance.

9.
The New Creation

There is a hunger for the 'transcendency' of God which is manifested by the interest in Eastern religions and many forms of meditation. Perhaps the Church has to restore that aspect, as well as discovering what the Incarnation should mean to us in the twentieth century? The yearning to touch this higher consciousness is one that cannot always be contained in words; but the wonder of revelation, still to be discovered by those close to the spiritual dimension, is, I believe, what Christ's teaching and life is all about. It is still spiritually unexplored territory for the majority of individuals. Thankfully, we have as evidence holy men and women, people of prayer who balance their material life with their spiritual side; these people are recognized because a light shines within them and on meeting them we find that our own dim flickering light is fanned into a brighter flame. These examples are not necessarily Christian in the sense that we might use the term – indeed, very many are of other faiths altogether.

This brings us back to a fundamental reality: to live fully we need to be in contact with our Source, living a life of real and 'alive' prayer and meditation. We were entreated to pray without ceasing, which really means to be deliberately aware of God's presence throughout the universe, for He truly is in all things and in every situation. Our clerics, too, must be allowed to have time set apart, so that they will become men of prayer, living from the heart and not from the head alone. If this were given precedence over much of the committee work that tends to fall to the lot of the Church minister, and if he were truly allowed to be a 'minister' to his flock, he would then be able to feed them with the Bread of Life, different from that given in the sacrament of the Eucharist, offering them the deep healing of the spirit which would flow from him after time spent 'with the Lord'. In the apparitions of the Virgin Mary – at Lourdes in 1858, at Fatima and Garabandal from 1961 to 1965, as well as in the Cairo visitations between 1968 and 1971 – the message to the clergy has been one and the same, that they were in danger of leading people astray: 'Many cardinals, many bishops and many priests are on the road to perdition and are taking many souls with them' (Garabandal, 18th June 1965).

The desert and the market-place, each has a necessary place in our lives if we are to be whole people: we go into the desert for nourishment, and we return to the market-place to give back what we have received. This has been the pattern of the lives of saints down the ages. The Benedictine monk, Anselm, Archbishop of Canterbury in about 1200 wrote:

> Come now . . . turn aside for a while now from your ordinary employment, put aside your worldly cares. Let your distractions wait. Free yourself for a while for God. And rest in Him. Enter the inner room of your soul, shut out everything except God – and that which can help you seek Him. Now my whole heart say to God, I seek your face; show me your face.[1]

We in the West are the impoverished ones in that respect. We know *about* God, but how many of us *experience* Him? How easy it is to talk glibly from the head, even to the point of deluding ourselves – but we cannot live that Truth which we should be expressing. We tend to know so much through our intellect and so little as a living reality. Yet our duty is to remember, always, that we are body, mind *and* spirit. We are made 'in the image of God', as well as being 'sons of God', and it is when we take ourselves apart from the world for a period of time that we get a glimpse of what this means: 'Be still and know that I *am* God'.[2] We begin to taste the essence of that spark of divinity that dwells within us all which is still lying dormant, undeveloped as yet and longing to be recognized. We are 'strangers in a far country', but our faces are turned towards the place of our inheritance, and each of us strives towards it in our own way.

In the East, they know and practise the art of emptying themselves within before beginning to commune with God so that they may be filled with His life. Only then do they dare to go to the altar to offer their petitions, breathing the given life into their prayers as they do so. When missionaries were seen to utter only a few quick sentences, they were called *haolis*, which means 'without breath or those who failed to breathe life into their prayers'.³ We also must empty ourselves of our own desires and attachments, so that the Holy Spirit may fill us, whereupon we shall be able to say: 'I live, yet not I, but Christ liveth in me'.⁴ Then, we too, will breathe this Spirit upon those we meet and into all that we undertake.

The value of *silence* can, I feel sure, never be overemphasized; it is sad that the Church does not teach us its use. During services we are lucky if we are allowed two or three fleeting moments, an embarrassing pause which does not give us time to even begin gathering our thoughts together, let alone to lose them in the state of stillness that 'Be still and know that I *am* God' entreats us to observe. We are quickly asked to sing hymn so-and-so in order to put an end to the awkward shuffling of feet and snapping of handbags. The excuses tend to be that 'they cannot take very much' or that 'it is an embarrassment to people', and so on. The only way to learn what is meant by a deep silence is to be given time in which this can be experienced; more will be found within a deep silence than can ever be told in words.

On a recent trip to Iona I went up to the abbey for the evening service. It was a Saturday night and I knew the incoming youth group would be organizing their own liturgy, usually a refreshing experience. They had elected to start the evening with a few lines of Scripture and follow it with half an hour of silent meditation (I use that word purposefully as 'prayer' is apt to conjure up the idea of words and yet more words, and pleading with the Almighty for the desires they express to be heard. He would have a terrible time pleasing everyone if this form of prayer was a reality!) This silent half-hour was deep and 'alive', an 'active' passivity, and as we left the abbey after the service I heard those young people talking quietly among themselves – for they did not want to shatter the stillness they had found – saying how meaningful it had been and how they wished it could have gone on for longer.

Interest in 'God' is certainly very much alive, as is an honest and healthy rejection of a good deal of traditional Church teaching. Generally speaking, a more universal approach to religion is emerging – a feeling that there is one God and we are all being drawn to Him in our different ways. Let us therefore resist being bound to ideas and images from past cultures which prevent us from being open to the 'now', and to what the Spirit is saying to us *now*, in our present situation. We would do well to learn from a holy Muslim who said:

> For thirty years I sought God, but when I looked carefully I saw that in reality God was the seeker and I was the sought.[5]

He had it the right way round: God the instigator, Man the co-operator. The unconscious yearning we have within, often not recognized for what it is, which is a feeling of 'exile' from our Source, will never leave us and, like 'The Hound of Heaven', He will pursue us down the years:

> I fled Him, down the nights and down the days;
> I fled Him, down the arches of the years;
> I fled Him, down the labyrinthine ways
> Of my own mind; and in the midst of tears
> I hid from Him, and under running laughter
>   Up vistaed hopes, I sped;
>   And shot, precipitated,
> Adown Titanic glooms of chasmed fears,
> From those strong feet that followed, followed after.[6]

Where do we go from here, you may ask? Maybe it is now time to recognize and release those historical facts which were suppressed in the centuries immediately following Christ's death, along with the thoughts suppressed within our own psyche. Maybe then all things will be made new. If Jesus were born into this world today, He would not be able to use the thinking of 2,000 years ago and construct His teaching within that mental climate. We have moved on in our understanding and are growing up, albeit slowly; so why does the Church try to keep us encapsulated in the thought and behaviour patterns of a bygone age? We all know that the machinery that goes to make up any large organization can get top-heavy, making progress well nigh impossible. Our plea is that those who are less encumbered should move freely and be allowed to acknowledge the truths that are emerging within their consciousness without being condemned as 'heretics'.

We read or hear a good deal about the 'New Age' and the New Age person, about leaving the Age of Pisces behind to enter the Age of Aquarius, and at first glance this may seem to have little to do with the Gospel story as we have understood it. Many of those who have put themselves under the 'New Age' banner have left behind the Church and its doctrines, unable to reconcile their understanding with the teaching they had received during religious education. They found that they had to be true to their inner feelings, and so felt it necessary to break away from the old order.

Throughout history it appears to have been necessary to have an extreme-sounding, overemphasized movement in order to formulate and draw attention to new ideas. Later, when the process has become established, the extreme and often bizarre views drop away, allowing the Truth within the seed thought to unfold in its own good time. It takes time for the irrelevant trappings to be shed and for a balanced perspective to be formed. If we take a fresh look at the Gospel story we shall find that Christ did in fact come to inaugurate the new order or New Age. It was in the setting of celebration – at the wedding at Cana – that the symbol of the marriage of God and man took place. Jesus Christ came to make a relationship possible between the Creator and his creatures. He actually said: 'Then the One sitting on the throne spoke: "Now I am making the whole of creation new".'[7] St Paul writes: 'For anyone who is in Christ, there is a new creation; the old creation has gone, and now the new one is here.'[8] And elsewhere he tells us that 'He has given us the qualifications to be the administrators of the new Covenant, which is not a covenant of written letters but of the Spirit.'[9] He also exhorts us to be 'free to serve in the new spiritual way and not the old way of a written law.'[10]

It is only now, 2,000 years later, that man is beginning to understand what this means when put into the context of his daily life. Christ told us that a new order was to arise after His death and Resurrection: 'I give you a new Commandment...'[11] and 'When all is made new and the Son of Man sits on his throne of glory...'[12] is what He said. Surely His self-chosen title, 'Son of Man', is an indication that He was the New Adam? He introduced a new humanity, a new way of being human; no longer was it to be self-centred but God-centred. He demonstrated this by becoming an empty vessel desiring only to be filled by the Spirit of God and by creating a new species, a new race of human beings with divine potential – 'sons of God'.

He also told us, 'All that I have is yours',[13] and yet we still do not claim our inheritance as 'heirs and therefore sons'.[14] We have still not broken through the barrier of our limited thought patterns and our minds remain entombed in the sepulchre of Easter Saturday. The stone of illusion is still waiting to be rolled away so that we can break through the barriers of finite consciousness, into that greater freedom of Reality. Then, with the 'mind of Christ', whose human consciousness already dwells in us, we shall be able to start to see things as they really are. We must lose our sense of imprisonment and, with the freedom that comes in the Spirit, allow ourselves to claim our inheritance as children of God.

I have found that when I have been able to accept the gifts that God is always offering to us, the whole of life has changed and taken on a different perspective. In my case, this did not happen in charismatic circles, it happened almost imperceptibly. One minute this deeper awareness was not there; the next it was a living Reality: something with which I felt completely at home. This gift enables one to see the depth and implications of one's sins and thus to judge oneself; one is not judged. One could never even begin to appreciate the fact of the existence of these gifts had one not first been given a part of His consciousness, which allows one to understand their nature and origin. By being partakers of His consciousness we can begin to 'see' and 'hear' in this other dimension, which is 'Reality, not merely an illusion'.

I believe the bridging of the old and the new order is now within sight. It entails a building onto and upwards from the old, for it is not so much a case of discovering something new as of rediscovering something old. And it will be no revolution, but more a synthesizing of thought which will take us to the next stage on the upward spiral of man's spiritual evolution: 'They will rebuild the ancient ruins, they will raise what has long lain waste, they will restore the ruined cities, all that has lain waste for ages past.'[15]

We only have to remember that the new Creation is already here; it is we who are not always in touch with it. And seeing all things made new is not a 'vision', but seeing things as they really are. We are touching the hem of his consciousness – God is offering us a part of His Consciousness. We now have to 'become' rather than just imitate and follow: not only be like Christ but let Christ 'be' in us so that we too become 'Christed', as he was.

I believe that the laity who must come into the open and air their views, and help others within the Church to articulate their feelings of loneliness and occasional despair that nothing in the Church seems to be moving forward in the right way. Changing the Liturgy and singing more joyous hymns may help, but such things barely scratch the surface. We have already spoken of the necessity of first putting our own house in order, yet we can at the same time share with one another the eternal Truths. In this sharing, 'when two or three are gathered together', it frequently happens that a closed door is set ajar and that a draught of the Holy Spirit is felt. If we have 'ears to hear and eyes to see', we may find the necessary direction and guidance that is needed for the moment. We can only live one day at a time, but let us not waste a single precious moment. Life is unstable the world over at present, and there is no time to lose or waste. We must now move on and look ahead to glimpse what is still to be revealed. The Holy Spirit moves us ever onwards: there can be no standing still in Creation.

The business of the Church, like our own, must remain unfinished in this earthly life, and the matter of who or what God is when stripped of our human conceptions must remain a mystery. Each of us who truly seeks God can, by turning within where His kingdom is to be found, receive from Him an answer corresponding to the extent of our openness and our awareness of spiritual matters. If nothing else, we soon realize that God is Life and that the whole of Creation is an expression of God.

In his book *Living the Infinite Way*, Joel Goldsmith tells how his direct experience of God revealed to him: 'That which I am seeking, I am', 'To me I already am; it already is' and 'To me, It [God], is no longer a concept, it is a revealed truth because of an experience that took place in my consciousness.'[16] No outer authority can bestow an experience of any kind; we can only be led so far and pointed in the direction of our goal. No amount of reading 'about' can give us that inner experience of God, our very own Life Source, which is to be found in the depths of our being. The only work we have to do is on ourselves. As members one of another, of the Body of Christ, we must make sure that we each become a whole, healthy 'cell'. It is in this way that the kingdom of heaven, which is not a place but an experience, will finally be found on earth and humanity, together with the whole of Creation, will find its resurrection into a fuller dimension.

We can play with words and hypotheses – even indulge in theological debates for as long as the mind can stand it – yet we can never reach an indisputable solution. Who dares declare that God can be defined with our finite minds? This being so, you may ask, 'Why bother to add to the confusion?' My reply is, if nothing else, to encourage others to think for themselves and discover that out of 'thinking' will come 'feeling', and out of 'feeling' a gradual realization of the truth about mankind, his life and his Creator. The truth is within, and we must learn to find it there, to wean ourselves from overdependence on external authority with its imposed 'beliefs'; for we are all in our different ways an expression of the One Mind.

10.
The Way Ahead

In looking at the way ahead we both feel a certain urgency in the air. We hope that the sharing of these several odysseys will help our fellow travellers to articulate thoughts that may be surfacing and will encourage them to take notice of their strong hunches. The more our intuitive aspect can be used, the more we shall learn to distinguish the true from the false and thus make good use of these inner promptings.

If these promptings have brought us to a dilemma, then we are aware that it is the same dilemma that has ever been the experience of those who have challenged the conventional wisdom, in whatever field. Always, there are the loyalties and the inertia that pull us back to the orthodoxy of the times; but always, to some, will come the call deep within to move with new thought forms, new levels of awareness beyond established areas of belief, beyond commonly accepted practices and codes. This will inevitably result in a lonely journey, yet it is a path that many have chosen before. In the past, each individual was called upon to walk alone, the emphasis having been on personal salvation; may it now be that we are entering an age when we shall tread it together— the age of the brotherhood of Man? Whether or not this is so, we know deep within ourselves that it is 'Hand in hand that we must go forward together.'[1] We cannot walk alone.

What we are finding, as we dare to share our insights with others, is that there is beginning to appear an almost formless community, not just throughout the British Isles but throughout the world; and that the link is at soul level. Nothing can stop it spreading. It is not sought in the first place, and it does not seem to originate in the minds of men. The members of this community are from varying cultures, backgrounds and levels of education. Some are living very hidden, humble lives, and go unrecognized by the world; others are publicly respected people giving great service as priests, doctors, psychotherapists, writers and so on. They are to be found in widely diverse spheres, and there is nothing 'elitist' about them except by 'their fruits ye shall know them'.

In the past it has often been the leaders of society who have heard the call and moved forward. What we feel we are expressing in this book are the views of ordinary lay people now seeking for their voice to be heard within the Church. For 2,000 years, theologians have held the pulpits and told us what to believe and how to behave before our God. When the layman has differed he has felt himself in error, saying apologetically: 'I am afraid I am not a churchgoer now. "Do unto others as you would be done by" is the only way I know.' Arguments over religious belief now leave us far behind. The God whose existence is the topic of theological debate is not the God whose presence in the world is, we feel, waiting to break through. The God of whom we write cannot be approached through intellect alone but from that still point where head and heart combine, permitting intuitive wisdom to break through.

In following this intuitive wisdom we are discovering what spiritual communion is; we have broken the 'sound barrier', as it were, and are beginning to learn what it means to be in tune with Cosmic Consciousness and the laws of the universe. Jesus was only able to teach up to the point of understanding reached by those who lived all those years ago, and He said: 'I still have many things to say to you but they would be too much for you now. But when the Spirit of truth comes he will lead you to the complete truth.'[2] As we glimpse a sense of this 'truth' we must move with it if we are to obey 'the spirit of the Law, not the letter of the Law'. This can lead us to the idea of the boundlessness of Infinity, and may frighten us.

It may seem that we are arguing for a formlessness and for a dismantling of the Church structures that have gone before. On the contrary, we believe that structure is important and that each of us must discover the institutional vehicle to which he feels drawn. What we do find is that while structure can contain, it should not confine. If we can be open to the movement of the Spirit then the structures may adapt easily to contain the new forms that emerge.

We recently both attended a Catholic Mass celebrated by a Jesuit priest. Only one of us, a Catholic, was able to take Communion as she normally did. It was a mixed congregation, and the priest suggested that those who were prevented from partaking by man-made limitations should make an inner spiritual 'Communion' in their own way. He felt inspired to say that he was convinced that the experience and blessing of Communion would be the same. The one who did not go forward to receive had no doubt that this occurred.

This experience of an inner spiritual communion should not surprise us, and indeed, should perhaps be part of our daily prayer life, for Jesus told us 'God is Spirit and they that worship Him must worship Him in spirit and in truth.'[3] If we pray at a deeper level, in silence, without using words, and with our fellow men of other faiths and denominations, then we are praying in the Spirit, where we are all one, all looking to the One God. It is at this level we shall ultimately find mankind coming together in spiritual brotherhood.

If we are to seek this brotherhood and follow the way as it opens up before us, we cannot know in advance what this may mean. We may be led in directions that cost us dearly in social and economic terms. Once values are turned on their heads and seen from the spiritual point of view, many of the criteria on which today we base our lives for the sake of expediency may well be overtaken by criteria of a different kind: people not money, food not weapons, recycling not destruction, love not coins. The inner way can lead us, this Spirit that is deep within. We may be entering the computer age, the post-industrial age, the space age, but we may also be entering the age of the Spirit, and the Holy Spirit always speaks within.

There now exists a movement based on the 'inner game' – the inner game of tennis, the inner game of skiing – and there is an inner game to everything we do. The rules of the game are that we follow the promptings that come to us within and not the codes and conditioning we have been taught. By following the inner game we may be releasing the potential within ourselves that can drive away the inhibitions imposed on us by our conditioning. Is not this release of potential what Christ was meaning when he asked, 'Wilt thou be made whole?' May not the wholeness of Man be close to what religion is all about?

We are very aware that throughout this book we have spoken in Christian terminology, for that is what is familiar to us, but we hope this does not give the impression that what we have said is out of reach for those who may not have shared our background. Recently we travelled to Turkey together and shared a week with friends who are Muslims.

Though Muslims in their background and form of worship, in their inner understanding of what is meant by God, they were truly at one with us. We are finding more and more that the inner path of each religion is the same. Up to now, each faith has enshrined its truth and passed it on, yet each has also become institutionalized, so that essential truths have been partly overlaid with man-made dogmas. As we seek and find an inner way in our own faith and come to acknowledge the oneness of humanity and the true brotherhood of man, so shall we recognize that we are all following the One Creator. The newly emerging universal awareness that we can be separated neither from our Source nor from each other will not mean that the way in which we worship will be uniform, for our different cultures and traditions are a built-in part of our inheritance. What it will mean is that we shall be able to see beyond the symbols and know truly that there can be no 'right' or 'wrong' way of worshipping, that the object of our rituals is far greater than the outward and visible signs. We sense a world religion somewhere beyond where we are now and feel that without setting up new structures we will find ourselves a part of a universal Church in which the divisions that we experience at present will dissolve.

Maybe now is the time for rigidities to dissolve and for a new openness to the Spirit to begin. The key to this is simple, for all of us can acknowledge our creative source, can find in the silence that 'still small voice' within and be aware of the Love with which we are constantly surrounded. Despite the discord and violence, and amidst the overturning of material values that the next few decades may bring, we need to find an inner centredness and serenity that will enable us to work with the 'God' force that is awakening in us and leading us on to build a new world. 'The whole creation eagerly waits for God's sons to be revealed', and it is vital that each one of us should take up our inheritance.[4] Our friends in Turkey were also aware of this challenge. The transforming power is within the grasp of us all if only we can find the courage and humility to move with it when it comes; for we have an idea that somehow *it* will come, though the form it will take can only be open to conjecture. We think again of the Baptism of Jesus, when the Spirit reached down from the Highest to ignite, in some mysterious way, the Christ Light within Him. Was then part of his mission to prepare the way for a 'Christing' of mankind? Was this preparation, started 2,000 years ago, to be the work of the Church? And if so, has the Church done its work, or is the business as yet unfinished? It has, if hearts of love are waiting to respond and if man has awoken sufficiently to discover who he truly is.

We pray 'Thy Kingdom come' – but have we yet prepared the way? This Kingdom of Love seems waiting to burst through each atom of the universe: the Christification of the planet of which Teilhard de Chardin spoke. At the core of all religions is an endeavour to prepare ourselves for this transforming power. We spend a great deal of time talking about it all and how it should be, and we write about it convincingly and at length, but the hardest thing of all is to live out what we know. There is only one way that we have found for this to come about, and that is for us to give time and space to allow 'it' to unfold from within, to spring from the root of our being – our divine spark. For this to happen we have to enter fully into the Greater Silence where contact is made with our Source or, as some have put it: 'We are plugged into the mains'. Then we become filled with the waters of Life itself, and from that point on it is not we ourselves who do anything; we merely allow the energy of Life itself to manifest in and through us. The greater the degree to which we allow this to happen, the purer are the channels that we become for God to be made manifest in man. Was not St Paul really saying the same thing when he said, 'I live, yet not I, but Christ lives in me'?[5]

Two visions seem to be moving together to build a new world. One is the Christ of the Gospels impelling us to go out into all the world and love our neighbours truly as ourselves. The other sees the Light shining within all men – the Christ – as an indwelling presence in us all. We feel it is important that these two visions can move together now, for the world faiths have the systems and the structures to spearhead a planetary-wide movement to a better world and the young have an intuitive knowing that the Light does indeed shine in all men. May it shine in us all and make all things new.

Epilogue

1.
It was said earlier that a book is inclined to take off on a course of its own, leaving its author to follow behind in a way that was not envisaged at the start. This can be quite a frustrating experience until one learns to be open and trustful enough to understand that, maybe, something is being asked of one, something which the writer could in no way achieve of his own accord.

In conclusion, I would like to say two things. The first is that on rereading what was written almost two years ago one finds that one's thinking has been enlarged and that in the light of more recent experience all that was previously understood takes on a deeper and broader perspective. It is always thus in life as we progress further on our journey.

When the author is in a negative frame of mind, there will be an urge to tear up everything that was written earlier as representing 'stale' thinking; when in a more positive state, there will be a desire to expand and elaborate on what has already been said and also to incorporate the fresh ideas that have formed in the interim period. Both these desires must be resisted: a new file had to be started for the 'second' book!

Through working on my own writing I have found confirmation of some of these ideas in other books, especially in the writings of Bede Griffiths, in particular, *The Marriage of East and West*.[1] Father Gerald O'Collins S J, in *The Second Journey: Spiritual Awareness and the Mid-Life Crisis*, has both helped me understand my own journey better and made it a less lonely one.[2] Father Gerard Hughes S J, in his book *In Search of a Way: Two Journeys of Discovery*, has enabled me to appreciate the depth there is in ordinary day to day encounters, if we can live a life of 'awareness'.[3] All that has been written in the aforesaid books has been put much more simply, clearly and profoundly than I could ever have put it, for I am no student of theology, no 'intellectual', not even a writer. I am only an 'ordinary' woman who has battled with the traumas of marriage and motherhood and been led, through these trials and sufferings, to look upwards and inwards a little more deeply and who has been granted the grace to be receptive to the truths and the wisdom revealed in prayer and meditation. I simply felt the call to put these thoughts and experiences onto paper. For whom? Maybe for one single soul who is, at this very moment, waiting to hear one of these thoughts articulated. I have found that to have one's inner feelings confirmed as echoes of one's own heart's longing is exciting. Also, this inward journey to realization is then made to seem less lonely.

Secondly, on rereading past work one sometimes has no recollection of ever having written it. I know my own limitations only too well, and I feel that I cannot always claim it as all my own work! Indeed, often at the time of writing, one is aware that thoughts are being impressed upon one either from somewhere deep within, or else from somewhere 'far beyond' – a place that has not yet been reached in one's consciousness, the boundaries of one's thought being still limited.

I write these final words on the island of Iona, a place to which I owe so much spiritually and inspirationally. The vision here is always less clouded, for the veil between the two worlds is indeed thin. Here, also, it is not difficult to lose oneself: to forget oneself and become totally absorbed in something, outside of and beyond, our small selves. Self-forgetfulness is a gift that belongs to childhood, and as we get older and have to battle with life as it is presented to us today, we lose the childlike ability to become totally absorbed in something other than ourselves, to become unself-conscious, lost in 'wonder, love and praise'. We must learn to recapture this gift and must be grateful for any means that makes this possible.

One day, maybe, the realization of man's destiny – the world's destiny – will be set free; and maybe this sacred isle, made holy by the prayers of St Columba and the Celtic saints, will be the place of this release, where the Uncreated Light will be able to break through and make all things new.

Ursula Burton

2.

When one comes to the end of writing a book such as this, one begins to think of those who may read it, and one imagines the friends and colleagues who may well wonder how someone offering insights on such issues could be so far from perfect and get into so many muddles in daily life! The answer might be that we are all on the path to perfection, whether unconsciously (rather like sleepwalkers) or in a relatively aware fashion. As we have said throughout the book, it is the times of quiet and stillness that help us to awaken and also to live in a way that is more in harmony with the Truth we discover. In earlier periods of my life, when I had young children, I managed to find the opportunity for quiet moments, especially while most of them were at school. The challenge now, I find, is how to remain 'in tune' – balanced and serene – despite the seeming necessity of 'filling each living minute with sixty seconds worth of distance run'. It is not easy to have perfect trust in the inner knowing, when apparent disasters loom all around. Kipling was right: we do need 'to treat those two impostors of triumph and disaster just the same'. There are frequent challenges that we all fail to meet, time and time again, yet mastery comes by slow degrees and we can eventually become detached from the ups and downs that confront us.

I think that somewhere there is a point within this 'detachment', as we loosen our hold on everything we cherish, that we will find ourselves in an oasis of steady calm. Within this space we find the dynamic which I would call the Christ, in a universal or cosmic sense; but as this term has become synonymous with Jesus of Nazareth, who so perfectly expressed the Christ, then it may be more helpful to use an expression such as 'Life', the creative principle which is the Source of all. This, for me, is the Son of God, the Second Person of the Trinity, expressed by all the great Masters of the race and most supremely of all by the One we call Jesus. As we let this 'Life' express itself in our lives, it will build bridges between ourselves and others, between our way of thinking and that of others. Thus, in some distant time we might find ourselves converging on the same point and know that we are in the same place at the same time.

In conclusion, I would like to offer a few of the ways that I have found daily life to take on a different quality since I began to see things in the 'new' way we have been describing. Mostly importantly, I think the discovery that we each have our own inner contact with 'the still small voice' – albeit hard to detect if one's emotions get out of control – brings an inner peace and assurance, that despite the seeming difficulties, one knows that a way ahead will always open up for us and that, as Shakespeare advised, 'There's nothing good or ill but thinking makes it so.' The inner knowing, like a piper deep within, can bring a greater sense of direction in one's life and a greater awareness of a pattern. There does seem to be a plan, and once one opens up to the synchronicity of events one accepts seeming coincidences as part of the pattern. It seems that the plan is unfolding through us – each one of us. Life, for me, has taken on a broader perspective, both in terms of time and dimension. A result is that I am increasingly aware that I should spend less time rushing around 'doing' and a little more time just 'being'. 'Let your light so shine before men.' We do not have to strive to shine it out ourselves; it will shine through us if only we can learn not to get in the way!

> There is a light that shines
> Beyond all things on earth
> Beyond us all, beyond the heavens,
> This is the light that shines in our heart.
>
> 'Creating a New World' from the *Chandogya Upanishad*

Janice Dolley

The authors hope that a wider discussion of the issues raised in this book will take place increasingly both inside and outside the Church. They feel that the 'New Age Christian' is one who is continuously open to the Truth, and that a free interchange of insights and understanding is an important part of this process. They would therefore be pleased to hear of the experiences, views and comments of others which can be sent to them via the publishers.

Notes

Chapter 1 Unfinished Business
1. Revelations 21.5
2. Kahil Gibran, *The Prophet*

Chapter 2 Ursula's Journey
1. Matthew 7.1, *Jerusalem Bible*
2. Matthew 6.6, *Jerusalem Bible*
3. John 14.12, *Jerusalem Bible*
4. Luke 17.21, *Jerusalem Bible*
5. John 16.15, *Jerusalem Bible*
6. Joel S. Goldsmith, *The Contemplative Life: A Guide for Personal Growth and Extended Awareness*, Citadel Press, Secaucus, N.J. 1963.
7. Matthew 7.7, *Jerusalem Bible*

Chapter 3 Janice's Journey
1. Matthew 22.37-39
2. Matthew 25.40
3. George Bernard Shaw, *St Joan*
4. Psalm 46.10
5. John 15.5
6. John 14.12
7. Matthew 5.17
8. William Shakespeare, *Hamlet*
9. John 4.14
10. David Spangler, *Revelation – Birth of a New Age*, Findhorn Publications
11. Helen Greaves, *The Testimony of Light*, World Fellowship Press Ltd.

Chapter 4 Journeys of Other Travellers on the Way
1. Keats, 'Ode on a Grecian Urn'
2. William Blake, 'Jerusalem', Preface to Chapter IV 'To the Christian'

3. *God Calling* by Two Listeners, edited by A. J. Russell, Arthur James, The Drift, Evesham, Worcs.
4. *God at Eventide*, as above

Chapter 5 My Dilemma in the Church
1. T. S. Eliot, *Four Quartets*
2. Matthew 5.44
3. Luke 12.31
4. Marilyn Ferguson, *The Aquarian Conspiracy: Personal and Social Transformation*, Routledge & Kegan Paul
5. *Ibid.*
6. Gerald Priestland, *Priestland's Progress*, Ariel Books
7. David Hay, *Inner Space*, Pelican
8. Peter Russell, *The Awakening Earth – Our Next Evolutionary Leap*, Routledge and Kegan Paul
9. Christopher Fry, *The Sleep of Prisoners*
10. Shakespeare: *Hamlet*
11. 'The Gospel of Thomas' 32, 19-33.5, quoted from *The Gnostic Gospels* by Elaine Pagels
12. *Ibid.* 37, 20-25
13. Bede Griffiths, *The Marriage of East and West*, Fount Paperbacks
14. *Ibid.*
15. Psalm 23.1
16. Revelations 3.20
17. Bronwen Astor, 'Praying for the Peace of the World', *The Times*, 15 January 1983
18. John 10.10

Chapter 6 The Role of the Church in the Next Decades
1. Luke 18.22
2. Alexander Pope, 'An Essay on Man' Epistle I 267-268
3. Alexander Solzhenitsyn, 'A Letter to the West'
4. *Love is the Way*, a collection of inspirations
5. John 17.21
6. Psalm 46.10
7. Wordsworth, *Sonnets, VIII*
8. Kahlil Gibran, *The Prophet*
9. UK Christian Handbook, Bible Society (Europe)
10. Kahlil Gibran, *The Prophet*
11. Archbishop of Canterbury, sermon given in St Paul's Cathedral, 26 July 1982
12. Proverbs 29.18

13. E. F. Schumacher, *A Guide for the Perplexed*, Johnathan Cape
14. Matthew 7.12
15. J. K. Galbraith, *The Age of Uncertainty*
16. King George VI, Christmas broadcast 1939, quoted from Minnie Louisa Haskins, 1875-1957

Chapter 7 Citizens of One World
1. Fritjof Capra, *The Tao of Physics*, Fontana
2. Exodus 3.14
3. John 8.58
4. *New Scientist*, 1 May 1982
5. Acts 17.28
6. Wordsworth, 'Ode on Intimations of Immortality'
7. Sri Aurobindo, *The Life Divine*
8. John 17.21
9. Romans 12.21 (R.S.V.)
10. A declared objective of New Humanity (see list of organizations)
11. Published as a card by World Unity Service, P.O. Box 41338, Craig Hall, Johannesburg 2024, South Africa
12. Brandt Commission 1983, *Common Crisis North South: Cooperation for World Recovery*, Pan
13. Kahlil Gibran, *The Prophet*
14. Robert Muller, Assistant Secretary General of the United Nations, speech to the Universal Peace Conference, Mount Abu, India, 14 February 1983
15. 'The Salutation of the Dawn', translated from the Sanskrit
16. Teilhard de Chardin, *Le Mileiu Divin*
17. *Ibid*
18. Mark 13.7
19. Luke 2.14
20. Alexander Solzhenitsyn, Templeton Address, 10 May 1983

Chapter 8 The Emergence of a New Consciousness
1. Winifred Rushforth, *Something is Happening: Spiritual Awareness and Depth Psychology in the New Age*, Turnstone Press Ltd., Wellingborough, 1981
2. Matthew 13.43, *Jerusalem Bible*
3. *Ibid.*
4. *The Myth of God Incarnate*, edited by Professor John Hick, S.C.M. Press Ltd., 1977
5. *Mahatma Gandhi: an Interpretation* by E. Stanley Jones. Published by Hodder & Stoughton, 1948
6. Mahatma Gandhi, *An Autobiography: The Story of my Experiments with Truth*, Beacon Press, Boston, 1957
7. John 10.30, *Jerusalem Bible*

8. Mark 10.18, *Jerusalem Bible*
9. John 14.28, *Jerusalem Bible*
10. John 14.12, *Jerusalem Bible*
11. *What Jesus means to Me*, compiled by R. K. Prabhu, Navajivan Publishing House, Amedabad, 1959
12. *The Myth of God Incarnate*, Preface
13. *Ibid.*, p.202
14. *Ibid.*, p.9
14a.*Ibid.*, p.6
15. *The Hidden History of Reincarnation: Historical Evidence in Support of the Edgar Cayce Readings,* edited by Noel Langley, A.R.E. Press, Virginia Beach, 1965
16. Galatians 6.7
17. *The Life of the Blessed Virgin Mary*, from the visions of Anne Catherine Emmerich, published by Burns & Oates Ltd., London, 1954
18. John 10.38
19. Elaine Pagels, *The Gnostic Gospels*, Weiderfeld and Nicolson, London, 1980
20. *Ibid.*
21. *Ibid.*, p.120
22. Matthew 6.6
23. Romans 8.17
24. Luke 22.42

Chapter 9 The New Creation
1. *The Prayers and Meditations of St Anselm*, translated by Sr Benedicta Ward, S.L.G., Penguin, 1973
2. Psalm 46.10
3. David Head, *He sent Leanness*, Epworth Press, London
4. Galatians 2.19
5. *The Wisdom of the Sufis*, edited by Kenneth Cragg, Sheldon Press, London
6. Francis Thompson, *The Hound of Heaven*, Burns & Oates, London
7. Revelations 21.5, *Jerusalem Bible*
8. 2 Corinthians 5.17, *Jerusalem Bible*
9. 2 Corinthians 3.6, *Jerusalem Bible*
10. Romans 7.6, *Jerusalem Bible*
11. John 13.34, *Jerusalem Bible*
12. Matthew 19.28, *Jerusalem Bible*
13. Luke 15.31, *Jerusalem Bible*
14. Galatians 4.7, *Jerusalem Bible*

15. Isaiah 61.4, *Jerusalem Bible*
16. Joel S. Goldsmith, *Living the Infinite Way*, p.56, George Allen & Unwin Ltd., 1976

Chapter 10   The Way Ahead
1. Pope John Paul II, Mass at Bellahouston, Glasgow, June 1982
2. John 16.12-13, *Jerusalem Bible*
3. John 4.24, *Jerusalem Bible*
4. Romans 8. 19, *Jerusalem Bible*
5. Galatians 2.20, *Jerusalem Bible*

Epilogue
1. Bede Griffiths, *The Marriage of East and West*, Collins, 1982
2. Gerald O'Collins, S. J., *The Second Journey: Spiritual Awareness and the Mid-Life Crisis*. Villa Books Ltd., Dublin
3. Gerard W. Hughes S.J., *In Search of a Way: Two Journeys of Discovery*. E. J. Dwyer, Rome and Sydney, 1978

Organizations and Publications

We are including a personal selection of some of the organizations and publications that we have found helpful in our quest for spiritual understanding. We apologise to the many associations we have omitted, particularly in related fields of conservation and ecology, the growth of human potential, holistic healing and education. There are many paths now offered to us whereby we can discover and grow to our spiritual maturity. We do not necessarily endorse everything that a particular association may teach and their inclusion in this list does not indicate that they would endorse all that we have written in this book.

The Anthroposophical Society 35 Park Road, London NW1 6XT: a centre for developing the work of Rudolf Steiner, Austrian philosopher, natural and spiritual scientist, whose teaching originated from a renewed vision of Christianity.

The Association for Promoting Retreats Church House, Newton Road, London W2 5LS: works in collaboration with the Roman Catholic National Retreat Movement and the Methodist Retreat Group. It aims to foster the growth of spiritual life by the practice of retreats, and to introduce retreats to those who do not know of them. It welcomes all Christians in sympathy with this aim into its membership.

The Axminster Light Centre 66 Willhayes Park, North Street, Axminster, Devon: a New Age teaching centre, receiving and publishing information from higher sources under the leadership of the Cosmic Christ. The main mission of the centre is to help in the spiritual re-education of humanity and prepare people for the coming changes.

Burrswood – The Dorothy Kerin Trust – Burswood, Groombridge, near Tunbridge Wells, Kent: founded by

Dorothy Kerin, a nursing home and Church of Christ the Healer, expressing between them a partnership of medicine and religion to 'heal the sick, comfort the sorrowing, and give faith to the faithless.' The work also includes hydrotherapy for disabled children, occasional retreats and seminars on the Ministry of Healing.

The Bridge Trust Wychwood, 20 The Chase, Reigate, Surrey: aims to build bridges between the old and the new. Based on a sense of the one spiritual source of all things and the underlying unity that this brings, it is an association for those who seek to build towards a future based on love, co-operation and goodwill and to translate concern for some of the issues facing us today into practical action. Runs a quarterly newsletter, conferences and other gatherings.

The Bridge Educational Trust 20 The Chase, Reigate, Surrey: an educational charity established by the Bridge Trust to encourage organic methods in farming and ecological understanding in all aspects of education. A partnership with a farm in Dorset offers an opportunity for the understanding of farming and conservation of wildlife and for peace and relaxation in the countryside.

Centre for Social Development Old Plaw Hatch House, Sharpthorne, West Sussex: is part of Emmerson College, Forest Row, West Sussex, and provides courses of varying lengths for people working with groups, individuals and organizations that cover many spheres of work in education, industry, government, etc. The main object of the training is to help people in the task of bringing about individual and social healing and development.

Centre Space Cookham Farm, Crockham Hill, Edenbridge, Kent: 'is an ecumenical consultancy and centre for the practice of spirituality. The aim is to explore the dimensions of contemplative Christianity, the dimensions of comparative spiritualities and the relationship and creative interaction between spirituality on the one hand and psychology, art/ crafts, ecology, politics, worship and culture on the other.'

The Christian Community 51 Queen Caroline Street, London W6: based on the ideas taught by Rudolf Steiner. 'The new upsurge of spiritual interest and awareness does not mean leaving Christianity behind, it means assisting in its re-birth.' The centre is concerned with Christian studies and ritual, that is to say the seven sacraments essential to Christianity in their new expression. It also offers a counselling service.

The Churches Fellowship for Psychical and Spiritual Studies St Mary Abchurch, Abchurch Lane, London EC4N 7BA: 'The fellowship is an ecumenical body of Christians, founded in 1953, for the study of the wider reaches of the paranormal and extrasensory perception in their relation to the Christian faith. The field of study includes psychical phenomena, mysticism, creative meditation and spiritual healing.'

The Elizabeth Bellhouse Foundation Coombe Castle, Elworthy, Taunton, Somerset: a charitable trust set up to study Christ's miracles in depth, with a view to the relief of suffering within the human, plant, micro-organism and mineral kingdoms. The ultimate aim being to assist world transformation. Its findings to date are summarized in *Measureless Healing* (£2.00 inc. p&p). The foundation issues a newsletter.

European Christian Industrial Movement Barrowdale, Stainton, *near* Dalton-in-Furness): 'The Bridge-builders', the aim of their work is 'to turn the hearts and minds of men to God so they may walk in his ways'. Groups meet regularly to consider issues of local and national importance.

The Francis Bacon Research Trust The Old Rectory, Alderminster, *near* Stratford-upon-Avon, Warwickshire CV37 8NY: 'Truth prints Goodness'. The trust offers conferences and seminars to those who would be 'builders of a new and truly charitable society with an improved and enlightened consciousness' to study the works of Francis Bacon. He 'envisaged the coming together of groups of men and women the world over, united with a fundamental love of learning and a common desire to discover and put into action all aspects of truth, in an endeavour to serve God and gradually to receive illumination uncovering the light within their hearts and growing by degrees towards the state of Christhood, as "Sons of God".' Friends of the trust receive newsletters and the Journal.

ORGANIZATIONS AND PUBLICATIONS 153

Friends House Euston Road, London NW1: for information on the Quakers for whom silence is a fundamental part of a prayer meeting and who also engage in many social concerns.

The Gatekeepers Trust 160 Maryland Road, London N22: founded to investigate the mysteries of the earth seen as a living spiritual organism and dedicated to the renewal of the earth by pilgrimage, ritual and illumination.

The Grail 125 Waxwell Lane, Pinner, Middlesex: is a lay society of Roman Catholic Christians, some of whose members live communally and run a conference centre. In addition to work for the deaf, for the distribution of its publications, for the animating of small groups, the Grail puts on conferences on silent meditation, prayer, the teaching of the English mystics, scripture and liturgy. It also has courses on pastoral counselling as well as prayer workshops.

Grass Roots 57 Dorchester Road, Lytchett Minster, Poole, Dorset, BH16 6JE: a bi-monthly journal published by the Post Green Community and committed to the renewal of the church and society. From the more charismatic end of the spectrum it shares signs of hope and faith in a struggling world.

Inigo Centre W Hewett S. J., Southwell House, 39 Fitzjohn's Avenue, London NW3 5JT: a new venture for the sharing of Ignation and allied insights and exercises, by providing workshops and resources for people of all or no religions and all walks of life; for people of deep experience or no experience in the areas offered – prayer, therapy, social initiative, adult initiation, renewal, formation, etc.

Interchange 25 The Carrions, Totnes, Devon: a quarterly journal on a shoe-string budget offering an exchange of positive ideas, caring attitudes and deepened experiences. The mood is one of hope for the future.

The Inter-Faith Association Shantock Hall, Bovingdon, Herts., HP3 0NG: promotes inter-faith dialogue and fellowship amongst Christians. There is an advisory panel consisting of leaders of the inter-faith world from amongst the Christian denominations and leaders of other faiths. There is an annual conference and membership covers *Insight*, published by the World Congress of Faiths, and the *Inter-Faith* newsletter.

Life-Style Movement Secretary: Mrs Margaret Smith, The Community, Little Gidding, Huntingdon, Cambs PE17 5RJ: 'offers a voluntary common discipline to those who are committed to a more equitable distribution of the Earth's resources among the members of the human family and to the conservation and development of these resources for our own and future generations' – 'We may live more simply that others may simply live.'

The National Centre for Christian Communities and Networks Westhill College, Selly Oak, Birmingham B29 6LL: offers a resources unit containing information on Christian groups in the UK, Associates have access to a directory with details of 400 Christian groups, communities and networks of all denominations, receive the magazine 'Community three times a year and information on courses, etc.'

New Humanity 51a York Mansions, Prince of Wales Drive, London SW11: a politico-spiritual journal, published bi-monthly, which speaks for the need to find a balance between the spiritual and material aspects of life and the new concepts required to create a better world structure; 'Neither Left nor Right but Uplifted Forward'.

The Ockenden Venture Guildford Road, Woking, Surrey: offers full-time care to refugee children at several centres in the UK and places emphasis on education as a prime factor in the development of global consciousness in a sense of individual responsibility in the needs of humanity as a whole.

The Omega Order and Trust Kent House, Camden Park, Tunbridge Wells, Kent: a modern religious order whose hallmark is 'Contemplation in Action'. 'It is concerned with "the new ecumenism" that is unity at the level of common spirituality whereby he who is truly centred in the heart is walking in "the Light of the World".' Cassette training courses are available and as well as conferences, a bi-monthly newsletter which focuses on the new consciousness in religion, science, medicine and the arts.

One Earth Findhorn Publications, The Park, Forres, IV36 0TZ, Scotland: a bi-monthly magazine featuring 'perspectives on the emerging new age consciousness and forms, news of groups and individuals building a harmonious planetary culture and sharings from the life and experience of the Findhorn community.'

Open Centres Newsletter Avils Farm, Lower Stanton, Chippenham, Wilts: bi-annual magazine that gives details, articles and news from a large number of 'Open Centres' and groups that are 'open to the truth through meditation, movement and healing'. Particularly helpful for those who would like to locate a centre in their own part of the country.

Piccadilly Press 197 Piccadilly, London W1: published monthly in association with St James's Piccadilly — 'a local community with a global vision'. Features articles on topical issues with a Christian perspective. It also offers news on events at St James's and elsewhere which range from music to healing, politics and prayer.

The Raja Yoga Centre 98 Tennyson Road, London NW6: Raja Yoga offers a combination of meditation and study towards the achievement of 'peace, happiness and a positive attitude on the mental level, which is reflected by our words, our actions, our relations with others and, ultimately, by our total environment.'

Resurgence Ford House, Hartland, Bideford, Devon: a journal which keeps people in touch with emergent ideas, trends and events that push the frontiers of social interaction further toward what is popularly termed the 'new age'. Subject matter ranges from economics, ecology, peace matters, medecint to health of the whole person and community.

Saint Beuno's Spiritual Exercises Centre St Beuno's, St Asaph, Tremeirchion, Clwyd, LL17 0AS: the main section of each course is a 30 day individually given retreat using the full Spiritual Exercises of St Ignatius of Loyola, founder of the Jesuit Order. These grew out of Ignatius' own spiritual experience and are a series of Scripture based, Christ-centred meditations and contemplations designed to help the retreatant's inner self to come alive. With the help of the retreat giver, the retreatant comes to know his/her own feelings and emotions, sifts the deep and genuine from the superficial and false and so comes to know God's will.

School of Economic Science 90 Queensgate, London SW7: regular evening groups on economics and philosophy are held termly in several centres. Economics is studied from the point of view of natural law, while in philosophy, students are introduced to the teachings of the great philosophies and religions. The experience of the practical value of these teachings to daily life is an important part of the work.

Schumacher Society *also* Ford House, Hartland, Bideford, Devon: distributes books and other literature and holds lectures that promote the ideas of Dr E. F. Shumacher, best known as the author of *Small is Beautiful*.

Science of Thought Review (Bosham House, Chichester, West Sussex PO18 8PJ: A monthly magazine devoted to the teaching of Applied Right Thinking with a large circulation worldwide. Founded by Henry T. Hamblin; editor – Brian Graham. The underlying theme of this helpful magazine is based on a greater understanding of the True Self and a practical approach to assist with dealing with the difficulties of life. Contains a wealth of interesting material at a very reasonable price.

Scientific and Medical Network Lake House, Ockley Near Dorking, Surrey: a group seeking to 'extend the framework of contemporary thought in science and medicine beyond the ideas at present considered orthodox taking into account the relevance of intuitive and spiritual insights.' Involved in a range of educational programmes.

Seniors Farmhouse Semley, Near Shaftesbury, Dorset: a centre, run in association with The Bridge Trust and linked with several other organizations. It offers a meeting place for those who 'in the face of the violence and acquitiveness of the material world see that there are no easy answers or options but that serious questioning of ourselves and the world requires a deep fundamental open-ness coupled with a dynamic affirmation of ways being based on co-operation, sharing and non-violence.' Seniors is the administrative centre of 'Prayer for Peace' which is offered by people of all paths at noon each day around the world thus creating a chain of global prayer and meditation for peace.

The Teilhard Centre: for the Future of Man. 23 Kensington Square, London, W8 5HN: 'This is an educational project to encourage study and application of the thought of Teilhard de Chardin and to develop it further. Its object is to make people increasingly aware of their responsibility for directing the future. Evolution has now reached a critical stage and there is growing recognition that we must build a system of values as a guide for decision making if world wide catastrophe is to be avoided.' Publish a journal and other literature and offer a wide variety of resource material.

Turning Point Spring Cottage, 9 New Road, Ironbridge, Telford, Salop TF8 7AU: an international network of people who share a common feeling that humankind is at a turning point. 'We see that old values, old lifestyles and an old system of society are breaking down and that new ones must be helped to break through.' Bi-annual newsletters include details of new initiatives in economics, health, education, agriculture, religion, third world, environment, peace, alternative technology, etc. Occasional meetings and publications.

The Unity Teaching and Healing Trust The Priory, Thornbury Holsworthy, Devon EX22 7DA: a centre in Devon which offers retreats for spiritual study and meditation and the holistic approach to healing through homeopathy and the dynamic power of prayer. A journal is published twice yearly.

Vita Florum Coombe Castle, Elworthy, Taunton, Somerset: a homeovitic transcreational healing energy that flows from creation through unfoldment and evolution to perfection and fulfilment, thus effectively strengthening and increasing the psyche's awareness of the indwelling Spirit. Very effective relief of physical and mental suffering has resulted for people and animals. Ailing plants recover and flourish. The soil's true fertility is enhanced by the increase of its micro flora and fauna. The use of *vita florum* provides experience of the Spirit's factual indwelling of all things.

White Eagle Lodge Newlands, Rake, Liss, Hants: a spiritual school developing the understanding of the Christ in the heart of man based on the teachings of White Eagle. Services of worship, healing and meditation; wide selection of books including vegetarian cookery, and bi-monthly magazine. There is also a London centre at 9a, St Mary Abbot's Place, Kensington, W8.

World Congress of Faiths 28 Powis Gardens, London W11: brings together the committed followers of the great living religions, as well as 'seekers', in an international movement of all who cherish spiritual values and who look upon our planet as one world. Publish *World Faiths Insight* and *Inter-faith News*. Arranges conferences, lectures, devotional weekends etc. Supports the World Conference of Religions for Peace and participates in the Week of Prayer for World Peace. Sponsors the Standing Conference on Inter-Faith Dialogue in Education. Links with local and international inter-faith groups.

World Goodwill Suite 54, 3 Whitehall Court, London SW1 A: an international movement working for the establishment of right human relations through the practical application of the principle of goodwill. Publications include a quarterly newsletter (no charge). Monthly public meetings – World Service Forum. World Goodwill, a service activity of the Lucis Trust, is an accredited non-governmental organization with the United Nations.

World Spiritual Council Pleshey Grange, Pleshey, Chelmsford: an international society of those who seek to bring into harmony all positive paths, in religion, in the arts and sciences, for the fulfilment of humanity. Publish *World Harmony* and organize conferences.

The Wrekin Trust Dove House, Little Birch, Herefordshire: offers a 'programme of short residential and day conferences concentrating on various aspects of spiritual knowledge and designed to stimulate exploration and awareness of the wonder and mystery of life and death.' The Wrekin Trust have been in the vanguard of spiritual adult education.

Index

Anseln, Archbishop of Canterbury, 128
Aquarian Conspiracy, The, 74
Attenborough, R., 116
Awakening Earth and Our Next Evolutionary Leap, The, 75
Aurobindo, Sri, 104

Bahai, 96
Bailey, Alice, 48
Beatles, The, 93
Blake, W., 88
Bonhoeffer, Dietrich, 65, 66, 68
Brahman, 102
Brandt Commission, 106
Brandt, Willy, 106
Buddhism, 38, 41, 43, 44, 49, 60, 91, 96, 120

Cairo visitations, 128
Capra, Fritjof, 101
Cayce, Edgar, 119
Christian Science, 60
Cloud of Unknowing, 61
Columba, St, 87, 142
Columbus, C., 76
Confucius, 87, 106, 120
Constantine, 87
Copernicus, 74

Dark Ages, the, 87
Darwin, C., 74
de Chardin, Teilhard, 17, 27, 88, 108, 139
Descartes, R., 88
Dharmadaya, 102
Doors of Perception, The, 55
Dorothy Kerin Centre, 20
Dream Game, The, 57

Ecumenical Congress of
   Constantinople, 22
   Fifth, 119
Exploring Inner Space, 75

Faraday, Anne, 57
Fatima apparitions, 127
Ferguson, Marilyn, 74

Galileo, 74
Gandhi, M., 116-7, 118
Garabandal apparitions, 127
George VI, 99
Gibran, Kahlil, 107
Glaszewski, Father, 65
Goldsmith, Joel, 133
Gnostics, 123, 124
God Calling, 70
Greaves, Helen, 35
Griffiths, Father Bede, 81, 141
Guide for the Perplexed, A, 94
Guild of Health, 61
Guild of St Raphael, 61
Gurdjieff, G., 57

Hamlet, 32
Hay, David, 75
Hick, John, 118
Hinduism, 39, 41, 43, 44, 56, 96, 102, 117
Hughes, Gerald, 141
Hunas, 17
Huxley, Aldous, 55

In Search of a Way: Two Journeys of Discovery, 141
Imitation of Christ, The, 61
intuition, 13-15, 36
Islam, 39, 41, 43, 56, 95, 96, 102

INDEX

Jainism, 96
Joan of Arc, 28, 74
John Paul II, Pope, 64-5
Jones, E. Stanley, 116
Judaism, 32, 43, 96
Jung, C., 17, 57, 111, 112, 120, 124

King, Martin Luther, 83
Kingdom of God is Within You, The, 103
Kipling, R., 143
Knights Templars, 87
Krishna, 38, 39

Lennon, John, 77
Letters and Papers from Prison, 65
Life of our Blessed Lady, The, 121
Living the Infinite Way, 133
Lourdes, 127
Loyola, St Ignatius, 112

Man and His Symbols, 57
Mandala Symbolism, 57
Marriage of East and West, The, 81, 141
Maryamana, 121
Maya, 30
Muller, Robert, 107
Myth of God Incarnate, The, 115, 118, 120

Nag Hammadi, 80, 123
New Age, 13, 28, 42, 49, 52, 53, 54, 63, 66, 67, 68, 95, 101, 103, 104, 130, 131

O'Collins, Gerald, 141
Open University, 91
Origen, 60, 119

Pagels, Elaine, 123
Paul, St, 17, 59, 112, 122, 139
Pentecostal Church, 26
Priestland, Gerald, 75
Priestland's Progress, 75
Prophet, The, 107
Pythagoras, 87

Quaker church, 26

Raja Yoga, 40

Rama, 38
Renaissance, the, 88
Runcie, R., (Archbishop of Canterbury), 93
Rushforth, Winnifred, 111, 114
Russell, Peter, 75

Sandford, Agnes, 19
Schumacher, E. F., 94
Science of Thought Review, 69
Second Journey : Spiritual Awareness and the Mid-Life Crisis, The, 141
Shakespeare, 27, 144
Sikhism, 96
Siva, 81
Socrates, 106
Solomon, King, 23
Solzhenitsyn, Alexander, 88, 109
Something is Happening, 111
Spielberg, Steven, 93
Sufism, 26, 56, 87
Swedenborg, E., 60

Tao of Physics, The, 101
Tao, the, 102
Taoism, 96
Temple, Archbishop, 61
Teresa, Mother, 33, 58, 59
Teresa, St, 61
Testimony of Light, The, 35
Theosophy, 60
Thoreau, Henry David, 36
Tolstoy, Leo, 103

Van der Post, Laurens, 107
Vatican Council, Second, 121
von Durkheim, Graf, 57

Wordsworth, 27, 103
Way of Transformation – Daily life as Spiritual Exercise, The, 57
White Eagle, 26
Wiles, Maurice, 118
Wrekin Trust, 103

Young, Frances, 115, 120

Zoroastrianism, 96

PAUL LEVIN

CONSTRUCTION CONTRACT CLAIMS, CHANGES & DISPUTE RESOLUTION

SECOND EDITION

ASCE PRESS

American Society of Civil Engineers
1801 Alexander Bell Drive
Reston, VA 20191-4400

Abstract: This thorough and comprehensive update of the highly successful 1977 edition by the author is intended to serve as a handbook for those involved in construction contracting and in the prevention, preparation, management, and resolution of construction claims and change orders. The general guidelines and legal principles provided in this book were shaped by the outcome of federal and heavy construction cases and will be of value to those in the private sector, local governments, and commercial construction as well. This book seeks to merge principles of construction law with practical advice to aid those involved in the construction claims process. Contractors, engineers, owners, and construction managers will all find this book to be a useful guide, reference, and training manual.

Library of Congress Cataloging-in-Publication Data

Levin, Paul, 1946–
    Construction contract claims, changes, and dispute resolution / by Paul Levin.
    p.   cm.
    Rev. ed. of: Claims and changes. 1978.
    Includes bibliographical references and index.
    ISBN 0-7844-0276-0
    1. Construction contracts—United States. 2. Dispute resolution (Law)—United States.   I. Levin, Paul, 1946–   Claims and changes. II. Title.
KF902.L48 1998
692'.8—DC21
97-28354
CIP

Any statements expressed in these materials are those of the individual authors and do not necessarily represent the views of ASCE, which takes no responsibility for any statement made herein. No reference made in this publication to any specific method, product, process or service constitutes or implies an endorsement, recommendation, or warranty thereof by ASCE. The materials are for general information only and do not represent a standard of ASCE, nor are they intended as a reference in purchase specifications, contracts, regulations, statutes, or any other legal document. ASCE makes no representation or warranty of any kind, whether express or implied, concerning the accuracy, completeness, suitability, or utility of any information, apparatus, product, or process discussed in this publication, and assumes no liability therefore. This information should not be used without first securing competent advice with respect to its suitability for any general or specific application. Anyone utilizing this information assumes all liability arising from such use, including but not limited to infringement of any patent or patents.

Photocopies. Authorization to photocopy material for internal or personal use under circumstances not falling within the fair use provisions of the Copyright Act is granted by ASCE to libraries and other users registered with the Copyright Clearance Center (CCC) Transactional Reporting Service. Requests for special permission or bulk copying should be addressed to Permissions & Copyright Dept., ASCE.

Copyright © 1998 by the American Society of Civil Engineers,
All Rights Reserved.
Library of Congress Catalog Card No: 97-28354
ISBN 0-7844-0276-0
Manufactured in the United States of America.

Previous edition: Claims and Changes: Handbook for Construction Contract Management, by Paul Levin. Copyright 1978 WPL Associates, Inc.
The masculine pronoun has been used to denote both the male and female gender.

FOREWORD

As I noted in the foreword to Paul Levin's original book, published in 1978, the construction industry has long needed a practical day-by-day guide to the proper administration of contract claims and change orders. This 1998 edition—larger, more complete and more sophisticated—continues to serve this purpose well.

Claims management, changes, and dispute resolution have become more sophisticated in the past 20 years despite the fact that the basic principles of construction law have changed very little. Today, however, the emphasis on early claim identification, analysis, and management is more important to the contracting community than ever.

As a construction lawyer for nearly 40 years, and as National Chairman of the Section of Public Contract Law of the American Bar Association during 1976–1977, I have had ample opportunity to observe the best and the worst of contract claim administration. Without fail, it is the inexpert contractor, the administrator unskilled in the ways of change order processing, who leaves the arena financially dissatisfied and perhaps mortally wounded. A similar comment can be made for owner representatives. On the other hand, he who understands the process can benefit from it—sometimes very handsomely. In short, this is a process that must be understood by all who participate in it.

Paul Levin's book is written for both the busy project staff and for the more experienced claims engineer. It represents a significant education step for the contracting community, and explains complicated concepts briefly, clearly, and in the language of the construction industry. I commend it to your attention and use.

Roy S. Mitchell
January 1998

ACKNOWLEDGMENT

The writer is grateful to the individuals whose efforts contributed so much to make the original book possible in 1978, especially James Baumgarner and J.D. Kidd. In writing this updated book, I thank profoundly my contributing editors, Bruce Jervis, Esq., editor of *Construction Claims Monthly,* as well as Randall C. Allen, Esq., and Dorothy E. Terrell, Esq., of the firm of Smith, Pachter, McWhortor & D'Ambrosio, P.L.C. of Vienna, Virginia. In addition, I am grateful to those individuals at the Barrington Consulting Group who assisted in the review process. I also wish to thank my son Jonathan for his help with the appendices.

Paul Levin

PREFACE

This work is intended to serve as a handbook for those engaged in construction contracting and involved with, or in a position to influence, the prevention, preparation, management, and resolution of construction claims and change orders. Shaped by the outcome of federal and heavy construction cases, the general guidelines and legal principles should be of value, and apply, to those involved in private-sector, local-government, and commercial construction as well. Interpretations of the law contained in this handbook are solely those of the writer and are not intended to serve as legal advice.

Originally written in 1978, this book sought to merge principles of construction law with practical advice to aid those involved in the construction claims process. While originally directed toward contractors, a significant number of engineers, owners, and construction managers purchased the book as a project guidebook, reference, and training manual.

Four printings, 9,000 copies, and 20 years later, repeated requests to purchase the long out-of-print book led to an effort to update and enhance it—this volume being the resulting product. To both market more effectively to the more expanded audience, and to meet with the popularity of the claims subject in *Civil Engineering* magazine, ASCE invited the writer to submit a proposal to publish it under the ASCE Book Division. The writer is both honored and flattered.

I have sought the assistance of Bruce Jervis, the founding editor of *Construction Claims Monthly*, published since 1979, and Randall C. Allen, an attorney whose invaluable experience and advice in construction claims and dispute resolution worldwide since 1972 have kept me always well informed, to make sure this update was accurate, correct, and complete.

In the past 20 years, the principles of construction law have changed very little. The major focus is for all the parties involved—engineers, architects, owners and contractors—to be aware of these principles and to seek to direct their efforts to reduce or eliminate the factors that give rise to claims, as well as to put in place the procedures for expeditious and fair resolution of those claims that will be inevitable. As in the original volume, this update of *Claims and Changes* attempts to continue in this tradition of straightforward, simple approaches.

For more information on claims, documentation tools, recent cases, resources and links to construction/claims-related resources, please visit the Construction Contract Claims website at www.wpl.net.

CONTENTS

FOREWORD iii

ACKNOWLEDGEMENT iv

PREFACE v

1. INTRODUCTION 1

    1-1. Claims Background 1
    1-2. Definition of a Claim 2
    1-3. Purpose of Book 2
    1-4. Public Contracts (Heavy Construction) 3
    1-5. Private Contracts (Commercial and Residential) 4
    1-6. Beyond the Contract—Principles of Construction Law 4
    1-7. Policies and Procedures for Administration 5
        1-7a. Necessity of Procedures for Administrative Relief 5
        1-7b. Basic Procedures for Claims and Change Order Administration 5
        1-7c. Active Claims Policy 5
        1-7d. Active Claims Program 6
        1-7e. Procedural Roadblocks and How to Overcome Them 6
    1-8. Review of Chapters 6
    1-9. Owners, Designers, and Their Representatives 7

2. IDENTIFICATION AND NOTIFICATION 8

    2-1. Claims Consciousness 8
    2-2. Early Identification 8
    2-3. Identification of Claims and Change Orders 9
        2-3a. Importance of Identification 9
        2-3b. First Requirement of Identification—Knowledge of Contract Documents 9
        2-3c. Frame of Reference 9
        2-3d. Communications 10
        2-3e. Second Requirement of Identification—Familiarity with Legal Concepts and Rights 10
        2-3f. The Changes Clause 11
        2-3g. Warning Signs of Claim Situations 13

2-4. Notification of Claims and Change Orders 14
2-5. Notification—Time Requirements 14
    2-5a. Federal Clauses 14
    2-5b. Private Clauses 15
2-6. Late Notice 16
2-7. Failure to Notify 17
2-8. Notification—Problems of Owners 17
2-9. Federal Contracts and the Contract Disputes Act 18
    2-9a. Request for Final Decision, Claims Certification 18
    2-9b. Notice Requirements for Appeal of Decision 20
    2-9c. Failure to Request Decision or Certify Claim 20
    2-9d. Appeal of Board Decision 20
    2-9e. Additional Notes on Claims Certification 21
2-10. Conclusion 21

3. DIFFERING SITE CONDITIONS 22

3-1. Introduction 22
3-2. Differing Site Conditions Clause 22
3-3. Type One Conditions—Examples 23
3-4. Type Two Conditions—Examples 24
3-5. Man-Made Conditions—Previous Construction 25
3-6. Forces of Nature 26
3-7. Site Investigation 26
    3-7a. Duty to Investigate: Reasonable Investigation 26
    3-7b. Disclaimers for Differing Site Conditions 27
    3-7c. Representations of Conditions Must Be Specifically
           Incorporated in Specifications 29
    3-7d. Inadequate Investigation 30
    3-7e. Site Investigation Requirements 30
3-8. Summary and Checklist 31

4. INTERPRETATION AND REQUIREMENTS OF CONTRACT SPECIFICATIONS 32

4-1. Introduction 32
4-2. Rules of Contract Interpretation 32
    4-2a. Background 32
    4-2b. Reasonableness 33
    4-2c. Read the Contract as a Whole 34
    4-2d. Language 34
    4-2e. Custom or Usage 35
    4-2f. Parol Evidence Rule 36

	4-2g. "Against the Drafter"	36
	4-2h. Conduct	37
4-3.	Defective Specifications	39
	4-3a. Introduction	39
	4-3b. Suitability of Designated Methods or Materials	40
	4-3c. Possibility and Practicality	41
	4-3d. Cardinal Changes	41
	4-3e. Disclosure of Knowledge	41
	4-3f. Cost and Notification Aspects	42
4-4.	Duty to Seek Clarification	43
	4-4a. Obligation to Notify Owner of Errors or Discrepancies	43
	4-4b. Zone of Reasonableness	44
	4-4c. Two-Step Test	45
	4-4d. "Not Part of Contract"	46
4-5.	Duty to Inform	46
4-6.	Duty to Proceed	47
4-7.	Inspection: Duty to Inspect	48
	4-7a. Improper Rejection	48
	4-7b. Improper Acceptance	49
4-8.	Conclusion	50

5. DELAYS AND ACCELERATIONS 51

5-1.	Introduction	51
5-2.	Delays—Excusability and Compensability	51
5-3.	Noncompensable Delays	52
5-4.	Nonexcusable Delays	53
5-5.	Compensable Time Extensions	53
5-6.	Compensable Delays	54
5-7.	Unreasonable Delays	56
5-8.	Delays—Site Access	56
5-9.	Concurrent Delays	58
5-10.	Proving Delay and Delay Costs	59
	5-10a. Disruption, Loss of Efficiency, and Loss of Learning Curve	59
	5-10b. Out-of-Sequence Work	59
	5-10c. Ripple Effect	59
	5-10d. Delays Due to Differing Site Conditions	60
5-11.	No Damage for Delay Clauses	61
5-12.	Three Types of Acceleration	61
5-13.	Constructive Acceleration	61
	5-13a. Directive Not Required	61
	5-13b. Notice, Request for Time Extension	62

5-13c. Explicit Denial of Time Extension Not Required 62
5-13d. Identification 63
5-14. Proving Delays, Time Extensions, and Acceleration 64
5-15. Acceleration Costs 64
5-16. Conclusion 65

6. RECORDS AND DOCUMENTATION 66

6-1. Introduction 66
6-2. Types of Records 66
6-3. Time Cards 67
6-4. Cost Account System 67
6-5. Production Rates 68
6-6. Material Receipts 68
6-7. Schedules 68
6-8. Cash Flows 68
6-9. Correspondence and Transmittal Logs 69
6-10. Computer (Cost) Reports 69
6-11. Daily Reports 70
6-12. Photographs 70
6-13. Special Forms for Claims and Change Order Records 71
6-14. Monthly Claims Review 72
6-15. Conclusion 73

7. USE OF PROJECT SCHEDULES AND THE CRITICAL PATH METHOD IN CLAIMS 74

7-1. Introduction 74
    7-1a. Description of CPM 74
    7-1b. Obstacles to Use of CPM for Construction Scheduling 75
7-2. Use of CPM in Claims Analysis 76
7-3. Pitfalls to Avoid in CPM Claims Analysis 77
7-4. Construction of As-Planned Schedule 79
    7-4a. Essential Elements in Constructing the Schedule 79
    7-4b. Additional Considerations of Schedule Preparation 80
7-5. Float 81
7-6. Float—Early Completion 81
7-7. Concurrent Delay 84
7-8. Voluntary versus Constructive Acceleration 84
7-9. Schedule Analysis Techniques for Claims Support 85
    7-9a. Impacted As-Planned Analysis 85
    7-9b. Fragnet (Windows, Chronological Impact) 85
    7-9c. Time Impact Analysis 86

	7-9d. Collapsed As-Built ("But For")	87
	7-9e. Comparison Chart of CPM Analysis Methods	87
	7-9f. Other Methods	89
7-10.	Scheduling Expert's Analysis	89
7-11.	Conclusion	89

8. SUBCONTRACTORS AND SUPPLIERS 90

8-1.	Introduction	90
8-2.	General Contractor's Performance	90
8-3.	Contractor-Subcontractor Relationship	91
8-4.	Subcontractor-Owner Claims	91
8-5.	Suppliers	92
	8-5a. Delays, Drawing Approvals	92
	8-5b. Supplier Purchase Orders	92
	8-5c. Proprietary Specifications—Contractor's Right to Substitute	93
	8-5d. Supplier Schedules	94
8-6.	Documentation of General Contractor Subcontractor/Supplier Transactions	94
8-7.	Other Contractor-Subcontractor Issues	95
	8-7a. Severin Doctrine	95
	8-7b. Miller Act	95
	8-7c. Sponsoring Subcontractor Claims	96
8-8.	Subcontractor-Specific Claims Publications	96
8-9.	AGC/ASA/ASC Standard Form Contract	97
8-10.	Conclusion	99

9. PRICING 100

9-1.	Introduction	100
9-2.	The Two Types of Pricing	100
	9-2a. Description of Forward Pricing and Postpricing	100
	9-2b. Forward Pricing Is Typically Preferred	101
	9-2c. Dealing with Risk in Forward Pricing	102
	9-2d. Postpricing	102
9-3.	Total Cost	102
	9-3a. Total Cost and Modified Total Cost	102
	9-3b. Last Resort	103
	9-3c. Four Conditions for Total Cost Claim	104
9-4.	Cost Analysis	104
	9-4a. Actual Cost	105
	9-4b. Reasonable Costs Developed from Existing Job Data	105
	9-4c. Estimating Reasonable Cost	105

9-5. The Proposal—Request for Equitable Adjustment 106
    9-5a. General Pricing Philosophy 106
    9-5b. Pricing Elements and Details 106
    9-5c. Production Rates 107
    9-5d. Overhead and Profit 108
        9-5d.1. Project Overhead Rates 108
        9-5d.2. Overhead on Large Claims 109
        9-5d.3. Home Office Overhead—Eichleay Formula 110
        9-5d.4. Profit 111
9-6. Use of Forms 112
9-7. Material Quantities and Prices 112
9-8. Impact and Inefficiency Costs 113
    9-8a. How Impact Costs Are Incurred 113
    9-8b. Specific, Identifiable Extra Work 114
    9-8c. Pricing Inefficiency and Loss of Productivity 114
        9-8c.1. Disruption 115
        9-8c.2. Crowding 115
        9-8c.3. Increasing the Size of Crews 116
        9-8c.4. Increasing Shift and/or Days Worked
                per Week 116
    9-8d. Material and Equipment Costs 116
9-9. Other Issues of Claims Pricing 117
    9-9a. Interest Costs 117
    9-9b. Legal Fees, Change Orders, and Claim Preparation
         Costs 118
    9-9c. Use of Expert Opinions 119
    9-9d. Critical Path Method Submissions for Payment
         Purposes 119
    9-9e. Federal Cost Principles 119
9-10. Conclusion 120

10. NEGOTIATIONS **121**

10-1. Introduction 121
10-2. Preparation and Knowledge 122
10-3. Forward Pricing Claims 122
10-4. Preparation for Negotiation Meeting 123
10-5. Tactics—Control of the Meeting 124
10-6. Tactics—Large Claims 125
10-7. Other Negotiation Tactics 126
10-8. Other Negotiation Considerations 126
10-9. Authority to Negotiate 127
10-10. Conclusion 127

11. DISPUTES AVOIDANCE, RESOLUTION, AND ALTERNATIVE DISPUTE RESOLUTION 128

11-1. Introduction 128
11-2. Disputes Avoidance 128
11-3. Partnering 129
    11-3a. Partnering Defined 129
    11-3b. History of Partnering 129
    11-3c. Elements of Success 129
    11-3d. Obstacles to Partnering 130
        11-3d.1. Tradition of Construction 131
        11-3d.2. Past Dealings and Nature of the Parties 131
    11-3e. Results of Partnering 132
11-4. Dispute Review Boards 132
    11-4a. Dispute Review Boards Defined 132
    11-4b. DRB Procedures 133
    11-4c. DRB Costs 134
    11-4d. DRB Effectiveness and Success 134
        11-4d.1. Quick Resolution of Disputes and Reduction of Unresolved Claims 134
        11-4d.2. High Resolution Rate 135
        11-4d.3. DRB Cost-Effectiveness 135
    11-4e. International Applications 136
    11-4f. Other Considerations of DRB Procedures 136
    11-4g. DRB Summary 136
11-5. Escrow Bid Documents 137
11-6. Geotechnical Design Summary Report 137
11-7. Arbitration 138
11-8. Mediation 139
11-9. Other ADR Methods 140
    11-9a. Minitrials 140
    11-9b. MedArb 141
    11-9c. Summary Trials before the Boards of Contract Appeals 141
    11-9d. Hybrids of Mediation 141
11-10. Alternative Dispute Resolution Act and the Federal ADR Experience 141
11-11. Formal Administrative and Judicial Dispute Resolution 142
    11-11a. Federal Contracts 143
    11-11b. Private Contracts and State and Local Public Contracts 144
    11-11c. Mechanics' Liens 144
11-12. Conclusion 144

12. TERMINATION 145

12-1. Introduction 145
12-2. Federal Clauses 145
    12-2a. Termination for Default 146
        12-2a.1. What to Do When You Receive a Notice of
                Default Termination 146
        12-2a.2. Damages Owed by Contractor 147
    12-2b. Termination for Convenience 147
        12-2b.1. What to Do When You Receive a Notice of
                Termination for Convenience 148
        12-2b.2. Constructive Termination 148
        12-2b.3. Termination for Convenience versus
                Change 148
    12-2c. Notice of Termination 149
12-3. Private Clauses 149
    12-3a. Termination for Cause 149
    12-3b. Suspension for Convenience 150
    12-3c. Termination by Contractor 150
        12-3c.1. After 30-Day Work Stoppage 150
        12-3c.2. After 60-Day Work Stoppage 150
        12-3d.3. Proposed Revisions to A201 150
12-4. Conclusion 151

13. CONCLUSION 152

13-1. The Claims, Changes, and Dispute Resolution Process 152
13-2. Roles of Construction Team 152
    13-2a. Contractor's Role 154
    13-2b. Designer's Role 154
    13-2c. Owner's and Owner's Representatives' Roles 154
13-3. Role of Alternative Dispute Resolution 154
13-4. Legal Considerations 155
13-5. Use of Experts 156
13-6. Claims Consciousness 156

APPENDICES 159

1. Contract Disputes Act of 1978/FAR 33.2 159
2. Relevant FAR Clauses—Subparts 52 and 33 164
3. AIA A201 186
4. EJCDC Selected Clauses (1910-8) 192
5. Site Investigations Report Form 203

6. Restatement of Contracts	205
7. Overtime Statistic References	206
8. Daily Production Report Form	207
9. Change Order Initiation Form	208
10. Change Order Status Report	211
11. Schedule Cover Letter	212
12. ACG/ASA/ASC Selected Clauses	213
13. Flat Rate System	220
14. Pricing Formats	222
15. Pricing Checklist	223
16. Productivity Charts	224
Construction Operations Learning	224
Chart	224
Crowding Loss Curve	225
Efficiency Loss	225
Composite Effects of Crew Overloading	226
Unproductive Labor at Crew Overloading	226
BLS #917	227
Cumulative Effect on Overtime	228
17. Cost Principles—F.A.R. Clauses	229
18. ASBCA ADR Sample Forms	238
19. DART Declaration	245
20. Index to Legal Citations	247

BIBLIOGRAPHY/REFERENCES 251

INDEX 253

CHAPTER 1

INTRODUCTION

1-1. CLAIMS BACKGROUND

Claims and change orders have often been linked with cost overruns, mismanaged jobs, legal entanglements, and alleged spurious practices on the part of some contractors. Admittedly, claims and change orders suggest to most laymen and owners a costly, nonproductive aspect of the construction process. This is a misconception, as claims and change orders are an integral part of the construction process, and good claims administration principles are as important as good engineering, safety, and business principles.

Claims and change orders are the administrative processes required to handle construction events that take place where the contract leaves off—changed conditions, design changes, defective specifications, quantity variations, delays, disruptions, and accelerations—and the successful resolution of the resulting disputes produced by these events.

In the last 30 years, as construction projects became larger and more complex, the volume of disputes and litigation grew substantially.

> One may speculate as to the reasons, but it is evident that some of the factors influencing the serious and substantial increase in the number of claims for additional compensation is the complexity of the projects now being undertaken, the price structure of the industry, which does not permit the absorption of the unanticipated additional cost by the contractor, and the superlegalistic approach taken by many owners and contractors. It is not an unusual philosophy of some owners that once a contract is let and the price

determined, all further financial risks or exposure should fall on either the contractor or architect. The limitation on claims today is fixed only by the limitation of ingenuity of those engaged in the construction industry, whether they be contractors, architects, engineers, or lawyers.[1]

Attitudes about claims that prevailed 20 years ago, reflected in the previous quote, have given way to more enlightened concepts where the contracting parties work toward mutual resolution of disputes. Even successful projects have claims. As you read through this book, you will come to think of claims as standard operating procedures, and this understanding will help you formulate the proper outlook, approach, and procedures for dealing with them. The key to a successful project is the successful resolution of contract disputes without resorting to litigation.

1-2. DEFINITION OF A CLAIM

In the last 15 years or so, a "claim" has gained formal recognition by various agencies and organizations. In 1980, a claim was defined by the federal government as "a written demand or written assertion by one of the contracting parties seeking, as a matter of right, the payment of money in sum certain, the adjustment or interpretation of contract terms, or other relief arising under or related to a given contract."[2]

The 1987 edition of the American Institute of Architects (AIA) standard form construction contract, General Conditions (AIA A201-1987¶4.3.1) added, "A claim is a demand or assertion by one of the parties seeking, as a matter of right, adjustment or interpretation of contract terms, payment of money, extension of time or other relief with respect to the terms of the Contract." [See Appendix 3 for entire AIA A201 section 4.3 "Claims and Disputes" and 4.4 "Resolution of Claims and Disputes."]

1-3. PURPOSE OF BOOK

The purpose of this book is to describe the general nature of claim problems encountered on construction projects and to serve as a guide for effective claims management and dispute resolution. It covers most pertinent topics that might be anticipated on the typical construction project, without being so detailed or so broad as to be meaningless or burdensome. This

---

[1] Leslie A. Hynes (1971). "Construction Law." *Contractors Management Handbook*, ed. J. J. O'Brien and R. G. Zilly, eds., McGraw-Hill, New York, N.Y., 22–28.

[2] Policy Letter No. 80-3 (1980). Office of Federal Procurement Policy, 45 Fed. Reg. 31,035 (May 9); **FAR ¶33,201 and 52.233-1**. (See appendix 1 & 2, respectively.)

book should help members of the construction team feel comfortable with claims and change orders and how to approach new situations encountered on the job. It does not attempt to give specific answers to all claim situations, and it is not intended to make the contractors completely self-sufficient in the resolution of claims. When legal assistance or expert help is needed, it should be sought.

This is also designed to provide the construction project staff with a frame of reference with which to understand and administer construction claims and change orders. Since the change order problem is such an integral part of the construction process, it is imperative that each member of the construction project staff have a full understanding of the legal concepts and administrative workings of changes and claims. This includes the architect, engineer, owner, owner's representative, and/or the construction manager. It is necessary to insure the project receives equitable adjustments without creating financial burdens for the contractor and owner. Finally, the contractor and owner should pursue and resolve changes early and accurately to insure successful construction and avoid expensive litigation occurring at the end of the project. To this end, the chapter on alternative dispute resolution should be of particular importance.

1-4. PUBLIC CONTRACTS (HEAVY CONSTRUCTION)

Most of the topics covered in this book originate from problems encountered during performance of public (government) contracts that have produced claims in the past. Many resulted in Board of Contract Appeals and/or U.S. Court of Federal Claims[3] trials, the decisions having established an extensive body of law concerning public construction contracts. This body of law largely involves Federal Acquisition Regulation (FAR) provisions, which provide uniform policies and procedures for acquisitions by executive agencies of the federal government as well as federally funded public projects such as the Washington Metropolitan Area Transit Authority. These provisions also serve as a model for many state and local government construction contracts.

Many FAR clauses are derived from those included in the old standard form 23-A for government construction contracts, and are included in Appendix 2. Of particular importance is the Changes clause (FAR ¶52.243-4), which provides the vehicle for which most equitable adjustments are made for changes to the contract.

---

[3]This court has undergone a few name changes in recent years. Previous names include U.S. Court of Claims and the U.S. Claims Court.

1-5. PRIVATE CONTRACTS (COMMERCIAL AND RESIDENTIAL)

While geared toward public contracts and the heavy construction industry, the principles and features of this book can also be applied to private construction. Indeed, it is the body of decisions handed down from the federal courts and boards of contract appeals that has shaped construction law, with the subsequent development of related clauses in both public and private contracts. However, private construction contracts vary from state to state and from owner to owner. Each owner and contractor tries to draw up contracts to suit its own respective interest. Familiarity with, and understanding of the terms and conditions of, each new contract is essential before signing so that each party is fully aware of its obligations and risks.

The private contractor or construction manager should be familiar with the standardized contract forms that must be signed and he should study very carefully any changes or variations encountered on new contracts. In using this book, the nongovernment construction manager should reconcile the general principles of personal contract procedures with the similarities of public contracts explained here. Where private contracts do not have sophisticated claims machinery found in the standardized government contracts, contract changes must be handled in a manner suitable to the instant contract. When a claims situation arises, the private contractor—perhaps upon the advice of an attorney—will have to analyze the particular problem and determine whether it is compensable under a specific clause or under the implied terms of the contract.

1-6. BEYOND THE CONTRACT—PRINCIPLES OF CONSTRUCTION LAW

Interpretation and resolution of contract disputes is not limited to the contract documents. Trade custom and practice has significant meaning in how contractors prepare and carry out the plans and specifications. There are implied obligations, such as the adequacy and sufficiency of the specifications, the duty to plan and coordinate the work of multiple contractors, the duty to cooperate in the various construction processes, and specific past dealings of the parties. Together, these concepts form the current body of construction law we know today.

The body of construction law and practices, informally referred to as the "principles of construction law," are well established and have changed little in the past 20 years. This book introduces the rights, customs, and practices that comprise these principles. Such tenants as "one party shall not hinder or delay the progress of another," the various types of delays, concerns over two types of differing site conditions, and rules of contract interpretation are revisited frequently during the progress of a construction

INTRODUCTION

contract. A working familiarity with these principles underlies successful administration of the construction process.

1-7. POLICIES AND PROCEDURES FOR ADMINISTRATION

1-7a. Necessity of Procedures for Administrative Relief

The constraints of cost, time, and the environment leave little room for perfect contract documents or perfect construction conditions. The contractor is committed to build the project within the constraints of budget, the contract documents, and good construction practices. Any variance from these constraints will cause variations in time and cost, and as such, remedies are sought through contract claims and change orders. Changes in contract time or cost must be instituted through formal contract modifications, which are the end result of claims and change orders.

1-7b. Basic Procedures for Claims and Change Order Administration

For self-protection and to maximize the chances of adequate and profitable recovery in claims and change orders, it is imperative that the contractor have sound, systematic policies and procedures for the administration of all claims and change order situations. The basic procedures for claim and change order administration are

- Contract knowledge—ability to recognize and identify changes
- Notification
- Systematic and accurate documentation
- Analysis of time and cost impacts
- Pricing
- Negotiation
- Dispute resolution and settlement

1-7c. Active Claims Policy

Some contractors avoid an active and aggressive policy for claims and change order administration. This is due in part to the history of construction contracts and the public record for litigation and costly overruns. This should not be seen as a deterrent, but rather should signal the importance of claims administration. It is the contractor's contractual and legal right to pursue the recovery of increased costs attributed to valid claims and change orders. It is the naive contractor who wishfully attempts to establish better relations with the engineer or owner by downplaying claims and change order problems. This contractor only creates a false sense of security, neither recognizing the owner's need to be informed nor allowing for discontinuities due to personnel changes, and therefore often contributes to costly litigation.

1-7d. Active Claims Program

An active program of claims and change order identification and notification is the only way the owner can be made aware of adverse or potentially adverse job conditions. It is necessary to advise the owner of the potential magnitude of cost and time effects early enough to secure adequate funds and make appropriate and timely adjustments, which the owner otherwise would not, or could not, do alone. The owner will respect the contractor's efforts to keep the job organized and to isolate changed conditions and difficulties encountered. This is especially valuable when the owner participates in effecting remedies. Ample notification gives the owner the opportunity to take proper steps and institute special procedures. It also forces the owner to commit any interpretations early rather than after the work is complete. Thus, the owner need not resort to defensive tactics, and the contractor is spared unfavorable surprises later. Organized procedures form the backbone of a strong construction company and for a successful claims and change order program.

1-7e. Procedural Roadblocks and How to Overcome Them

Contractor laxity toward claims administration policies until the job is well under way or complete creates untold problems. Lack of experience in the processing of claims, lack of awareness of claim situations, and lack of knowledge of legal and contractual rights are also common problems. These work to make it difficult for the contractor to develop the habit of including good claims administration with other procedures. This book brings together much of the contemporary information on the subject and highlights the important elements of each topic. It develops a set of basic procedures and policies to serve as a ready reference for the construction manager. This will enable the construction manager to successfully administer the claims on projects even though he may not be a claims expert or not want to hire a claims engineer for the project.

1-8. REVIEW OF CHAPTERS

Chapter 2 discusses the "hows and whys" of identifying claims and notifying the owner of all potential problems. One of the most important chapters, chapter 2 is paramount to avoid losing one's right to submit a claim as well as to establish the foundation for ultimate proof and recovery.

Chapters 3, 4, and 5 review the several areas of construction contract difficulties most often encountered: differing site conditions, contract specifications and interpretations, and delays and accelerations. Increased knowledge of these topics substantially enhances the identification process.

Chapter 6 describes the types of job records necessary for claim substantiation and introduces special records for claims administration. Ultimately, the success of many claims depends on the sufficiency and usefulness of project documentation. Project scheduling (critical path method), its impact on the job, its importance in claims and change orders, and its use as a valuable tool for pricing and negotiations, is developed in chapter 7.

Chapter 8 reviews the special problems for suppliers and subcontractors. Chapter 9 discusses techniques and methods of preparing and pricing claims. Negotiation goals and techniques rounds out the handbook's coverage of day-to-day claims management in chapter 10.

Chapter 11 covers the topic of how disputes are resolved when they cannot be negotiated by the parties. This includes formal procedures of litigation before arbitration panels, courts, and boards of contract appeals, as well as the increasingly important use of alternative dispute resolution methods. This chapter is intended to promote a *decrease* in expensive claims litigation costs through the increased use of mediation, partnering, dispute resolution boards, and other methods. Chapter 12 goes in-depth into the details of termination—what you need to be aware of in the event your contract is terminated, or, if you're an owner, considerations necessary before terminating a contractor.

1-9. OWNERS, DESIGNERS, AND THEIR REPRESENTATIVES

While this handbook originated as a guide for the construction contract manager, it should be of substantial benefit to other members of the construction effort, including

- **Project owners**—those individuals representing both public agencies and private owners
- **Designers**—the engineers and architects retained to prepare the contract drawings and specifications
- **Owner's representatives**—the construction managers and resident engineers retained to represent the project owner's interests during construction

Honesty and candor between the owner and the contractor is necessary for progressive construction management. Any information that furthers such understandings while reducing adversarial attitudes will improve project performance.

CHAPTER 2

IDENTIFICATION AND NOTIFICATION

2-1. CLAIMS CONSCIOUSNESS

"Claims consciousness," or active familiarity with, and awareness of, potential claim situations is a prerequisite to successful project management. This does not mean the contractor should seek every possible opportunity to earn extra revenue. It does mean the contractor should be aware of the potential risks associated with claims and that one of his highest priorities should be proper management of these risks. Proper claims management begins with identification of a claim. The contractor must be able to recognize and identify a claim situation when it first develops, not after it has become a controversy. Identification goes hand-in-hand with notification. Most public and private contracts contain clauses requiring notification of differing site conditions, changes, and delays within a stated period of time before equitable adjustments can be pursued.

2-2. EARLY IDENTIFICATION

Prompt identification and notification is imperative in order to comply with contractual requirements (see section 2-5b). If the contractor does not recognize a situation, or waits too long to take actions, any and all rights to claim can be lost. Late notification, however is not necessarily fatal to a claim, as will be explained in section 2-7. Early identification is also important for the following reasons:

IDENTIFICATION AND NOTIFICATION

1. It enables the owner to verify, confirm, and possibly remedy the situation at the earliest opportunity.
2. Sometimes new designs, new material or equipment, or different construction methods may be required by a changed condition. It is to the mutual benefit of all parties to spot and solve time-consuming and costly problems as early as possible. Even though equitable adjustments are ultimately made, it is to the contractor's benefit to complete his work and move out as soon as possible, which implies making every effort to expedite the resolution of all changes and claims situations.
3. Early identification allows the contractor adequate time to study the problems, analyze different proposal and notification options, and best prepare for claims that might prove troublesome.

2-3. IDENTIFICATION OF CLAIMS AND CHANGE ORDERS

2-3a. Importance of Identification

Identification of a claims situation is the first and the most important phase of the entire claims process. One cannot remedy a problem unless it is known to exist. Very often, identification is automatic, such as a change order from the owner or a directive from the engineer. Most claims situations, however, arise out of subtle differences in field conditions, from job-site delays or as a result of differences of contract interpretation. In these and in all other instances, a claim situation must be recognized and identified as soon as it occurs.

2-3b. First Requirement of Identification—
Knowledge of Contract Documents

The construction project staff must have a good working knowledge of the contract documents. This includes the project manager, the project engineer, the general superintendent, and the engineering support staff. Familiarity with pertinent technical and general terms is essential for project personnel to recognize their contract rights and duties. If these key personnel have a thorough and detailed picture of the entire job, they will be in the best position to recognize claims and change order situations as soon as they occur, it is very important to be able to anticipate the flow of work and to predict potential problems.

2-3c. Frame of Reference

To help recognize problems that are not always obvious, there must be a frame of reference to measure job performance. With the specifications as a general plan, and with the contractor's detailed engineering and scheduling activities, job management has a standard by which to compare the actual work. Cost reports also are a good indicator of the relative progress of the work. When measurements indicate that work items are not progressing as planned, the manager should try to determine if design problems, adverse job conditions, or other outside factors are contributing to the delay. At this point, superintendents and foremen should be queried. These field personnel may not be cognizant of the conditions promised by the specifications and may be plugging away to overcome unnecessary obstacles, often at extra expense and needless frustration.

2-3d. Communications

Communication of ideas—and problems—is essential for efficient production and effective management. Day-to-day communication of supervisory personnel with foremen and management must be supplemented by routine management observation of field operations. The project staff must be knowledgeable about expected field conditions and be aware of actual conditions that differ from those expected; soil types, interference of structures, other contractors, traffic, weather, and labor composition are likely to be sources of changed conditions. This observation (and communication) philosophy is abetted by requiring general foremen, supervisors, superintendents, and labor foremen (if possible) to note unusual items on a designated spot on their time cards and daily diaries. "If he fails to record extra work circumstances, the very fact that nothing was included in a report which specifically provides for the reporting of extra work may raise a damaging inference that no extra work in fact occurred."[1]

2-3e. Second Requirement of Identification—
Familiarity with Legal Concepts and Rights

The second requirement of identification is that the project staff have a working familiarity with the legal concepts and rights that will affect the outcome of potential claim situations. Chapters 3, 4, and 5 discuss the salient features of current legal views and attempt to provide an overview of the processes of boards and courts in dealing with claim issues. With a firm background in these legal precepts, the contract manager is in a position to sense and appreciate the significance of events that may lead to later problems.

---

[1]Overton A. Currie and Luther P. House, Jr. (1968). "Preparing Construction Claims for Settlement," *Briefing Papers #68–5*, 1 Briefing Papers Collection, 350, Washington, D.C. 1–10.

2-3f. The Changes Clause

As noted in chapter 1, the contractual vehicle for seeking price and schedule adjustments largely depends on the specific contract in question. Some specialized contract clauses appearing in federal procurement standard forms and other sophisticated contracts are discussed separately in ensuing chapters. For instance, concepts such as differing site conditions, suspensions of work, and acceleration are addressed in detail.

Section 2-4g. provides a list of circumstances that should alert the project manager that a claim situation exists. Unless one of the specialized clauses is involved, the contractor will most frequently be seeking cost reimbursements and time extensions via a Changes or Extra Work clause. The contractor must be continually vigilant for circumstances that will expressly or constructively activate such a clause. The problems and suggestions discussed in following chapters are intended to delineate the action the contractor should take when those circumstances are encountered. Effective project management requires that the contractor keep open the right to cost reimbursement and schedule adjustments via the Changes or Extra Work clause. Thus, skillful notification procedures, record keeping, claim pricing, and negotiations—topics discussed in subsequent chapters—are important to assure the contractor that these clauses are used most advantageously.

Reproduced below is Changes clause 52.243-4 of the Federal Acquisition Regulation (FAR).[2] The flexibility of the four enumerated change categories—which are not, incidentally, exclusive—demonstrates the vast importance of such a clause. It should be noted that subparagraph (b) contemplates the concept that the courts have characterized as "constructive changes." That is, the contractor is given the benefit of the equitable adjustment policy even in the absence of a formal change order issued by the owner. Again, close adherence to the notice requirements is mandatory. This clause, or a similar provision in private construction contracts, is the primary vehicle for adjustments in contract price and time. Its importance and proper implementation cannot be overemphasized.

52.243-4 CHANGES (AUG 1987)

(a) The Contracting Officer may, at any time, without notice to the sureties, if any, by written order designated or indicated to be a change order, make changes in the work within the general scope of the contract, including changes—

  (i) in the specifications (including drawings and designs);
  (ii) in the method or manner of performance of the work;

---

[2] Formerly Article 3 of Standard Form 23-A.

(iii) in the Government-furnished facilities, equipment, materials, services, or site; or
(iv) directing acceleration in the performance of the work.

(b) Any other written order or an oral order (which terms as used in this paragraph (b) shall include direction, instruction, interpretation or determination) from the Contracting Officer that causes a change shall be treated as a change order under this clause; *provided* that the Contractor gives the Contracting Officer written notice stating (1) the date, circumstances, and source of the order and (2) that the Contractor regards the order as a change order.

(c) Except as provided in this clause, no order, statement, or conduct of the Contracting Officer shall be treated as a change under this clause or entitle the Contractor to an equitable adjustment.

(d) If any change under this clause causes an increase or decrease in the Contractor's cost of, or the time required for, the performance of any part of the work under this contract, whether or not changed by any order, the Contracting Officer shall make an equitable adjustment and modify the contract in writing. However, except for an adjustment based on defective specifications, no adjustment for any change under paragraph (b) above shall be made for any costs incurred more than 20 days before the Contractor gives written notice as required. In the case of defective specifications for which the Government is responsible, the equitable adjustment shall include any increased cost reasonably incurred by the Contractor in attempting to comply with such defective specifications.

(e) The Contractor must assert its right to an adjustment under this clause within 30 days after (1) receipt of a written change order under paragraph (a) of this clause or (2) the furnishing of a written notice under paragraph (b) of this clause, by submitting to the Contracting Officer a written statement describing the general nature and amount of proposal, unless this period is extended by the Government. The statement of proposal for adjustment may be included in the notice under paragraph (b) above.

(f) No proposal by the Contractor for an equitable adjustment shall be allowed if asserted after final payment under this contract.

In many contracts, such a clause is the only vehicle for price adjustment. In any contract, project management must be intimately familiar with each and every requirement of the changes clause. Study it and know both when

IDENTIFICATION AND NOTIFICATION

and how to use it—the failure to do so can mean the difference between a profitable contract and a financial disaster.

2-3g. Warning Signs of Claim Situations

A list of the general circumstances that typically cause claims and change orders is printed below. This list summarizes different types and categories of claims and change orders and can be used as a ready reference. These administrative aids form a foundation for proper claims engineering and serve to keep the contractor out of trouble and free to concentrate on his larger role: construction of the job. The circumstances are as follows:

1. Additional work not specified in the contract documents
2. Work different from that specified
3. Work in a particular manner or method that varies from that originally anticipated (from implied conditions or interpretation of specifications)
4. Work resulting from contract drawings or specifications that have been changed, amended, revised, amplified, or clarified
5. Unanticipated work that results from insufficient details in the plans and specifications
6. Work required to be performed in one particular method when specifications allows two or more methods
7. Work out of sequence
8. Stopped, disrupted, or interrupted work; wholly or partially; directly or indirectly
9. Joint occupancy
10. Owner furnishing equipment late, in poor condition, or not suitable for the intended use
11. Accelerated performance in any way, to regain schedule, to add men or materials, or to work overtime or extra shifts
12. Following any new, different, or shorter schedule
13. Relocating existing work because of lack of coordination, information, or other factors
14. "Differing" site conditions
15. Differences in contract interpretation
16. Defective specifications
17. Delays from the owner's acts or failure to act
18. Unwarranted work rejection
19. Increased inspection requirements, tests or quality control program
20. Owner's failure to disclose information
21. Strikes
22. Forces of nature

2-4. NOTIFICATION OF CLAIMS AND CHANGE ORDERS

Identification of claims must be followed by notification. The owner or a representative must be formally notified of a claim or change order if the contractor intends to seek equitable adjustments for additional time or costs. The obvious purpose of notification clauses, such as those noted in the beginning of this chapter, is to insure that both parties have on record the dates and facts that initiate a claims situation, and to protect their respective rights. Notification allows both parties to verify conditions, to assemble facts, and to resolve disputes while the items are fresh in their minds. When encountering differing site conditions as well as errors or omissions on drawings, the contractor should stop work on that portion of work until a satisfactory response is obtained from the owner. Continued work on the affected portion could result in a contractor's obligation to correct at his own expense any defective work already completed. In giving notice, the contractor should always stress his urgency to resolve a dispute and should request acknowledgment of the situation.

2-5. NOTIFICATION—TIME REQUIREMENTS

2-5a. Federal Clauses

The following time requirements for notification are taken from the FAR (emphasis added):

52.243-4 (d) Changes
The Contracting Officer shall make an equitable adjustment and modify the contract in writing. However, except for an adjustment based on defective specifications, no adjustment for any change . . . shall be allowed for any costs incurred more than *20 days before* the Contractor gives written notice.

52.243-4 (e) Changes
The Contractor must assert its right to an adjustment under this clause *within 30 days* after (1) receipt of a written change order . . . or (2) the furnishing of a written notice . . . by submitting to the Contracting Officer a written statement describing the general nature and amount of proposal.

52.-236-2 (a) Differing Site Conditions
The Contractor shall promptly, and *before the conditions are disturbed*, give a written notice to the Contracting Officer.

52.249-10 (b)(2) Default

The Contractor, *within 10 days* from the beginning of any delay . . . notifies the Contracting Officer in writing of the causes of delay.

52.242-14 (c) Suspension of Work

A claim under this clause shall not be allowed (1) for any costs incurred *more than 20 days* before the Contractor shall have notified the Contracting Officer in writing of the act or failure to act.

The above clauses are reproduced in their entirety in appendix 2.

2-5b. Private Clauses

The American Institute of Architects A201 General Conditions Section 4.3 provides

4.3.2 Time Limit on Claims

Claims by either party must be made within 21 days after occurrence of the event giving rise to such Claim or within 21 days after the claimant first recognizes the condition giving rise to the Claim, whichever is later.

4.3.4 Claims for Concealed or Unknown Conditions

If conditions are encountered. . . .then notice by the observing party shall be given to the other party promptly before conditions are disturbed and in no event later than 21 days after first observance of the conditions.

4.3.7.1 Claims for Additional Time

If the Contractor wishes to make Claim for an increase in the Contract Time, written notice as provided herein shall be given. The Contractor's Claim shall include an estimate of cost and of probable effect of delay on progress of the Work. In the case of a continuing delay, only one Claim is necessary.

Note section 4.3.8.1 specifies an *estimate* of cost must be included with the claim. The 21-day time limit expressed in 4.3.3 applies to this subsection as well. The above clauses are reproduced in their entirety in appendix 3.

Finally, the clauses from the Engineers' Joint Contract Documents Committee General Conditions, No. 1910-8, provides

Article 10.05 Claims and Disputes

Notice: Written notice stating the general nature of each Claim, dispute, or other matter shall be delivered by the claimant to ENGINEER and the other party to the Contract promptly (but in no event later than 30 days) after the start of the event giving rise thereto. Notice of the amount or extent of the Claim, dispute, or other mattter with supporting data shall be delivered to the ENGINEER and the other party to the Contract within 60 days after the start of such event (unless ENGINEER allows additional time for claimant to submit additional or more accurate data in support of such Claim, dispute, or other matter). A Claim for an adjustment in Contract Price shall be prepared in accordance with the provisions of paragraph 12.01B. A Claim for an adjustment in Contract Time shall be prepared in accordance with the provisions of paragraph 12.02B.

Relevant EJCDC clauses are reproduced in appendix 4.

2-6. LATE NOTICE

Although failure to give notice, or timely notice, may defeat a legitimate claim, a large body of case law has waived the notice clause for the following reasons:

1. The owner was aware of the situation.
2. The owner was not prejudiced by the late notice.
3. The contractor was not immediately aware of the facts.

If late notice is filed, and the owner is not prejudiced by such late notice, the courts tend to recognize these claims as long as absence of prejudice is established. The contractor should give notice as soon as possible after identifying a problem, even if the notice is late or informal. In one case where informal notice was given during contract performance, but the formal claim was submitted after final payment, the court found that "What is necessary ... is that the contractor reasonably manifest to the government its present intention to seek recovery of money based on a claim of legal right under the contract as a result of the alleged constructive change."[3] Consideration of a claim is not barred if "the contracting officer knew or was chargeable

---

[3]*Missouri Research Lab Inc.,* ASBCA 12355, 69-1 BCA ¶ 7762.

IDENTIFICATION AND NOTIFICATION 17

with knowledge that appellant had asserted a legal right to additional money despite its failure to file a formal claim."[4]

Critical path schedule submittals, inspector diaries, and meeting minutes have all served as valid notice in demonstrating that the owner was aware of a situation and waiving the requirement of a more formal notice. In one case, an inspector was aware of a situation but considered it normal. The contractor considered it a changed condition but no constructive notice was found since the contractor did not call specific attention to the condition he had considered abnormal. The court ruled the government was "undoubtedly prejudiced" by this failure to give notice. The court did not bar the claim because investigation and defense of the claim was still possible, and the government (had it been given adequate notice) would unlikely have ordered alternate action (more expedient or economical construction, for example). The contractor, however, bears an increasing burden of proof, according to the court, roughly equivalent to the prejudice caused the government by lack of timely notice.[5]

2-7. FAILURE TO NOTIFY

Failure to notify the owner of problems or potential problems can put the burden of responsibility on the contractor for extra costs or damages. This is not restricted to change order items only, but may also include general job conditions that may adversely affect the owner's property or plant. "If the contractor is knowledgeable in the field where the plans are faulty, it is his duty to warn the owner for whom he is erecting the structures."[6]

2-8. NOTIFICATION—PROBLEMS OF OWNERS

It is not uncommon in large projects for owners and engineers to be understaffed or bogged down in daily affairs so that claims and change order problems are overlooked. Owners and engineers should therefore settle active claims and change orders, otherwise lost records and hazy memories will result, and extraneous negotiation sessions at the project's end will be necessary to resolve unsettled items. Negotiations under these circumstances are the least productive and provide the least monetary return. Notifi-

---

[4]*Machinery Associates, Inc.*, ASBCA 14510, 72-2 BCA ¶ 9476; also see *Appeal of The Little Susitna Co.*, PS BCA No. 2216 (May 24, 1990). (Contractor alerted the government to a site condition problem even though the contractor did not provide formal notice.)

[5]*C. H. Leavell & Co.*, ASBCA 16099, 72-2 BCA ¶ 9694.

[6]*Co-Operative C. Store Builders, Inc. v. Arcadia Foods, Inc.* 291 So. 2d 403 (La. App. 1974); also see *D'Annunzio Brothers, Inc. v. New Jersey Transit Corp.*, 586 A.2d 301 (N.J. Super. A.D. 1991). (Contractor was aware of a woefully inadequate quantity estimate.)

cation and follow-up are simply a matter of obligations and protection of rights. Changes are just too costly to leave unattended in the hands of the owner and his representatives without follow-up to insure that they are not bogged down because of red tape, understaffing, unmotivated personnel, or lack of funds.

If a claim or change order is denied or rejected by the owner, then the contractor must re-evaluate his position and take further action as necessary, including collecting additional documentation, seeking legal assistance, filing a formal appeal, or combining the claim with another claim depending on the value and substance of the work in question. The contractor should keep a running record of all actions on each changed item and periodically take action on those items that remain unsettled. This identification, notification, and follow-up should be a formal operating procedure, backed up by a complete and detailed set of job records.

2-9. FEDERAL CONTRACTS AND THE CONTRACT DISPUTES ACT

For federal contracts, the Contract Disputes Act of 1978 (and revisions through 1995) (CDA) provides formal appeals procedures for claims denied by the government. This act includes various time requirements for the government to respond to claims, for the contractor to appeal, and for subsequent agency or court actions (see Figure 2.1). The various provisions of the CDA have been incorporated into the FAR (see appendix 1).

2-9a. Request for Final Decision, Claims Certification

In order for procedures under this act to take effect, a "final" decision must first be rendered by the "contracting officer."[7] For claims under $50,000, a decision must be rendered within 60 days of the request. For claims over $50,000, the contracting officer shall, within 60 days, issue a decision or notify the contractor of when the decision will be issued. Additionally, for claims over $50,000, "the contractor must certify that the claim is made in good faith, that the supporting data are accurate and complete to the best of his knowledge and belief, and that the amount requested accurately reflects the contract adjustment for which the contractor believes the government is liable."

If no decision is rendered within the time period required and an extension is not requested, it is deemed to be denied by the contracting officer.

---

[7]Contractors are now required by the Federal Streamlining Act of 1994 to submit claims to the contracting officer within six years "after accrual of the claim."

IDENTIFICATION AND NOTIFICATION

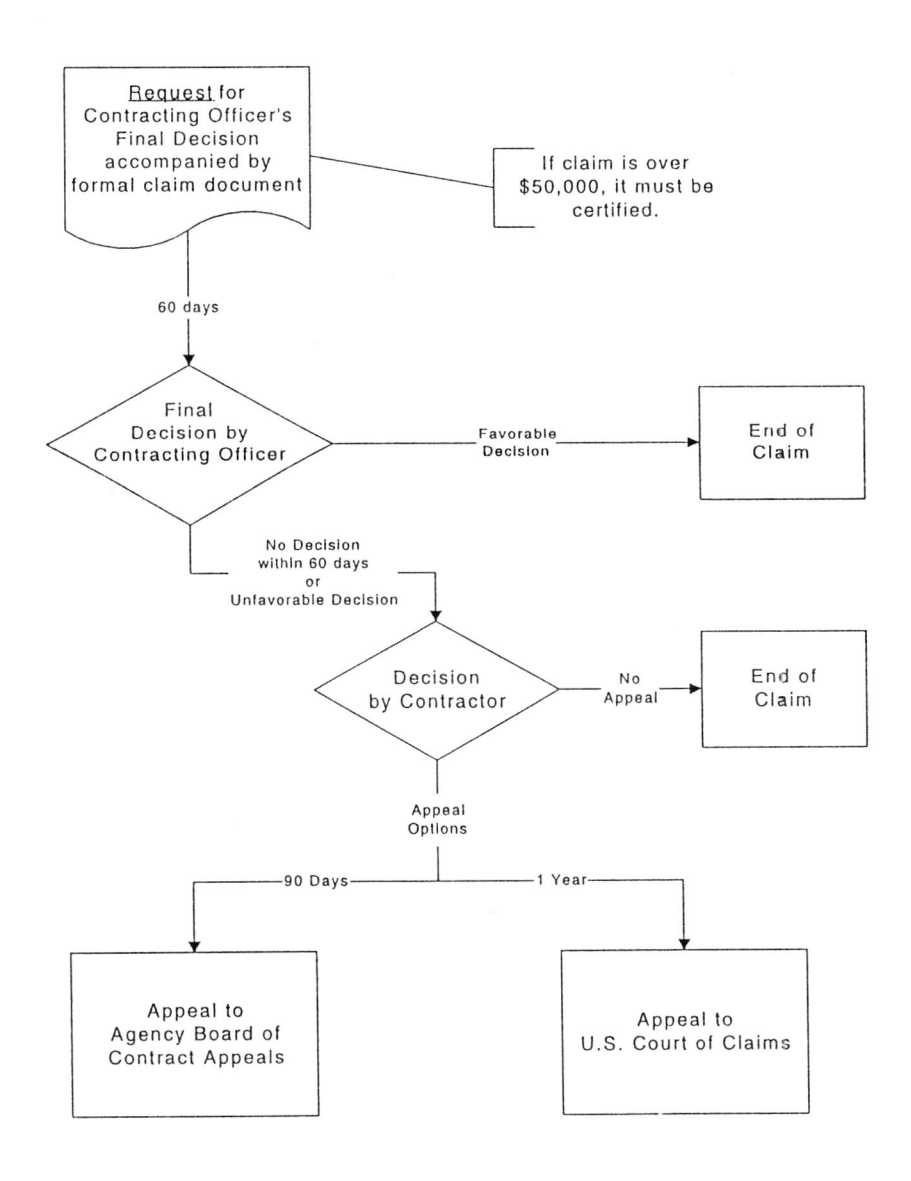

FIG. 2-1 Contract Disputes Act Flow Chart

2-9b. Notice Requirements for Appeal of Decision

Once a final decision has been issued, the contractor may, within 90 days of the decision (or 60 days from the request if no decision is rendered[8]), appeal the decision to an agency board of contract appeals, or, within 1 year, bring an action directly in the United States Court of Claims.

2-9c. Failure to Request Decision or Certify Claim

Failure to clearly request a decision from the contracting officer, failure to certify claims over $50,000, and other procedural deficiencies can result in dismissal of a Disputes Act suit or request for agency decision.

To minimize the chance that a claim will be dismissed for procedural reasons, be sure that the request for a final decision

1. Is addressed to the contracting officer
2. States that the issue is a claim
3. References prior submission(s) to the contracting officer's representative(s)
4. States that the claimed issues are in dispute
5. States that efforts to resolve the issue are at an impasse
6. If over $50,000, is certified by an authorized representative of the contractor

2-9d. Appeal of Board Decision

For disputes of $50,000 or less, the contractor can elect for an accelerated appeals procedure which shall be resolved (by an agency board), whenever possible, within 180 days from the date the contractor elects to use the procedure.

Decisions of the board are final, except that an appeal may be made, by either party, to the United States Court of Claims within 120 days from the date of receipt of a copy of the board decision. In most cases, this is the last step in the judicial process, with the Supreme Court of the United States being the final step—rare is the construction case that goes to the Supreme Court.

Until litigation in a court has commenced, the contracting officer has the authority to settle a dispute throughout the entire administrative appeals process.

---

[8]*Lakeview Construction Co. v. U.S.*, 21 Cl. Ct. 269 (1990); letters sent to Resident Officer in Charge of Construction more than 60 days prior to suit; although evidence shows contracting officer received the claim, the suit was dismissed since it was filed within 60 days of receipt by the contracting officer.

2-9e. Additional Notes on Claims Certification

It is still critical the contractor take all precautions to properly certify the claim and follow to the letter the CDA notification requirements. This includes being satisfied with claims, and the content therein, submitted on the behalf of its subcontractors. It is not necessary to verify or agree with each and every detail in a subcontractor's claim, but to be confident the claim is grounded in basis and in fact.

The following language, taken directly from the CDA, must be used in certification:

> I certify that the claim is made in good faith; that the supporting data are accurate and complete to the best of my knowledge and belief; that the amount requested accurately reflects the contract adjustment for which the contractor believes the Government is liable; and that I am duly authorized to certify the claim on behalf of the contractor.

Although most contractors will require the subcontractor to certify its claim, the general contractor cannot rely on the subcontractor's certification and the general contractor must itself certify the claim. The general contractor's certification cannot substitute the word "subcontractor" in the above paragraph[9]

2-10. CONCLUSION

The contractor must be aware of claims and change order situations; be fully conversant with, and appreciative of, the specifications, give prompt notice of potential problems, and maintain a good set of records. With this foundation, the "claims conscious" contractor will possess the basic elements of a solid claims management program.

---

[9]*Century Construction Company v. U.S.*, 22 Cl.Ct. 63 (1990). (General contractor did not properly certify subcontractor's claim); also see *United States v. Turner Construction Co.*, 827 F.2d (Fed. Cir. 1987).

CHAPTER 3

DIFFERING SITE CONDITIONS

3-1. INTRODUCTION

Differing site conditions are usually thought to be subsurface physical conditions such as geological configurations, water levels, or suitability of soils that differ from those promised or implied by the contract documents. Indeed, the differing site conditions clause is most often invoked for subsurface conditions. However, differing site conditions can also include manmade site conditions from previous or concurrent construction activities. This chapter reviews various types of differing site conditions and discusses the requirements of the site investigation.

3-2. DIFFERING SITE CONDITIONS CLAUSE

The "differing site conditions" clause of the Federal Acquisition Regulation (FAR) [¶52.236-2 (Appendix 2)] classifies such conditions into two types. Type one conditions are "sub-surface or latent physical conditions at the site differing materially from those indicated in this contract." Latent conditions include natural or man-made conditions that are hidden from normal investigations. The substantiation of a type one claim is accomplished by demonstrating that the conditions actually encountered differ from those expected, as indicated by the plans and specifications.

Type two conditions are "unknown physical conditions at the site of an unusual nature, which differ materially from those ordinarily encountered and generally recognized as inhering in work of the character provided for in the contract." The key words here are "unknown," "unusual," and "differing materially." To substantiate a type two claim, the contractor must demonstrate that the conditions encountered could not be reasonably anticipated at the time of bid. In the absence of a specific clause contemplating differing site conditions, the problems described below would typically be processed as claims through the traditional changes clause.

The American Institute of Architects (AIA) A201, "Claims for Concealed or Unknown Conditions" (¶4.3.4) uses almost identical language. The EJCDC[1] contains more extensive language in its Differing Subsurface or Physical Conditions [¶4.03] but includes similar wording—"3. differs materially from that shown or indicated in the Contract Documents; or 4. Is of an unusual nature, and differs materially from conditions ordinarily encountered and generally recognized as inherent in work of the character provided for in the Contract Documents." (See Appendix 4).

In any event, read your contract carefully to make sure it contains a differing site conditions clause. In a case involving an AIA contract with a deleted concealed conditions clause, the contractor was barred from recovery for larger foundations encountered and for subsurface soil problems.

3-3. TYPE ONE CONDITIONS—EXAMPLES

In discussions of subsurface conditions, attorney Paul E. McNulty has compiled a list of typical examples of type one conditions that have been the subject of court or board (U.S Armed Services Board of Contract Appeals) decisions (McNulty 1975). He aptly illustrates a wide range of problems that can be encountered by the contractor:

1. The presence of rock or boulders in an excavation area where none were shown or indicated or the existence of such rock at materially different elevations than had been indicated in the data available to bidders
2. The presence of permafrost or subsurface water where none had been indicated by the contract documents
3. The encountering of loose, soft material at a location or elevation where the boring data indicated the existence of sound rock
4. Physical differences in the behavior characteristics and workability of soils encountered as contrasted with the type of soils indicated by the borings, even though the soils encountered could be utilized with additional effort for the intended contract purpose

---

[1] *Standard General Conditions of the Construction Contract* (1996), prepared by Engineers' Joint Contract Documents Committee. Issued and published jointly by National Society of Professional Engineers (NSPE), Consulting Engineers Council, ASCE, and the Construction Specifications Institute.

5. The failure of designated borrow pits or quarry sites to produce the required materials entirely or in sufficient quantities without excessive waste or unusable materials beyond that reasonably anticipated from the prebid data
6. The presence of rock debris or other subsurface obstructions in substantially greater quantities than shown in the bid documents
7. The existence of a subfloor not shown on the drawings that had to be removed under a contract to renovate a building
8. The encountering of ground water at a higher elevation, or in quantities in excess of those indicated or reasonably anticipated from the data available to bidders
9. The encountering of rock materially harder or tougher to excavate or drill and blast than was expected from information available prior to bidding
10. The presence of a higher moisture content in soils to be compacted than was anticipated from the contract data
11. Ground contour elevations at the site that differed from those shown on the drawings, and, accordingly, required greater quantities of excavation or fill ("latent condition")
12. The existence of numerous taxiway crossovers that had to be removed to perform the contract work, but that were not disclosed on the drawings, having security regulations that prevented the contractor from making an adequate prebid site investigation ("latent condition").[2]

3-4. TYPE TWO CONDITIONS—EXAMPLES

McNulty also describes the examples that can be encountered in type two conditions:

1. The unexpected and highly corrosive nature of ground water at the site, which resulted in extensive damage to the contractor's dewatering equipment
2. Excessive hydrostatic pressure encountered in the laying of a pipe line, which could not have been anticipated at the time of bidding
3. Jet fuel that flooded manholes because of an unknown blockage in an airport drainage system and caused damage to underground transmission cable installed by the contractor

[2]Paul E. McNulty "Changed Conditions and Misrepresentation Under Government Construction Contracts," Government Contracts Monograph No. 3 (Published by the Government Contracts Program, the George Washington University, 1975), pp. 21 & 22.

DIFFERING SITE CONDITIONS

4. The presence of caked material that was not revealed by a site inspection of heating ducts to be cleaned under the contract
5. An unknown and unanticipated oily substance that prevented adherence of polyvinyl chloride that the contract required be applied to the roof
6. Failure of rock from an approved borrow pit to fracture in the manner expected for production of contract aggregate.[3]

3-5. MAN-MADE CONDITIONS—PREVIOUS CONSTRUCTION

Previous structures in the vicinity of new construction that are either misrepresented or not represented at all on the contract drawings could cause considerable problems to the contractor. Such conditions fall within the scope intended by the "differing site conditions" clause and are usually treated as such. In a recent Board of Contract Appeals case, the Board ruled that a brick and mortar sewer differed materially from the brick and concrete sewer indicated on the contract drawings. The contractor expected a brick and concrete sewer to be a brick sewer cradled in concrete. It would not have required a special support system when tunneling under, according to the contractor's interpretation of the specification. Finding the sewer unable to withstand the tunneling operation, the contractor was forced to replace that portion over the tunnel. The Board ruled that the actual sewer uncovered differed materially from that represented by the specifications, and the contractor was entitled to an equitable adjustment in contract price, Furthermore, the Board said that references in the specifications to the as-built drawings of the sewer did not bind the contractor to review these drawings, because the "Physical Data" section of the contract clearly provided that the drawings were "not intended as representations or warranties and were not part of the contract."[4]

In another case,[5] a "stage two" contractor relied on the conditions indicated by the specifications rather than the conditions being created by the stage one contractor, who was working prior to the bid opening date. The conditions were found to be "different." The U.S. Court of Appeals, which reviewed the case, ruled that an owner implies a warranty when a contractor

---

[3]Ibid, pp. 23 & 24.

[4]*American Structures, Inc. & Mining Equipment Manufacturing Cooperation*, ENGBCA 3408 75-1 BCA ¶11,283; also see *Green Construction Co. v. Kansas Power & Light Co.*, 1 F.3d 1005 (10th Cir. 1993) (Contract effectively disclaimed the owner's responsibility for the accuracy of site condition information.)

[5]*Moorhead Construction Co., Inc. v. City of Grand Forks*, 508 F. 2d 1008 (8th Circuit, 1975); also see *Appeal of Minter Roofing Co., Inc.*, ASBCA No. 31137 (Aug. 24, 1989). (The government's prior jacking of buildings caused them to be seriously out of plumb, but that had not been indicated in the contract documents.)

is forced to base its price and schedule on certain specified site conditions. The court held that if the site does not meet the specifications at the time construction is scheduled to begin, the contractor is entitled to recover its total additional cost under the changed conditions clause.

A more specific example of this situation was frequently encountered on the construction of the Washington, D.C. subway. The drawings for the structural sections were thought to accurately describe conditions that would be found by the follow-on contractors (such as trackwork), even though the as-built sections were known to be outside the specified tolerances. In the trackwork case, the elevations and slope of the concrete inverts were clearly spelled out in the specifications, but by site investigation these inverts were found to be outside the tolerances. The contractor, however, prepared his bid on the basis of the contract drawings, and did not include costs associated with extra work to meet the as-built inverts. During performance of the contract, the trackwork contractor claimed, and received, all additional costs, including impact, for the work necessary to compensate for the out-of-spec inverts. One obvious rationale behind this ruling is that the contractor might reasonably expect the owner to require the stage one contractor to correct all deficiencies before the follow-on contractors are prepared to perform their work.

3-6. FORCES OF NATURE

Forces of nature generally do not qualify as a differing site condition in that they create physical changes after award of the contract. There are exceptions, however, including marginal or inadequate job conditions that invite unforeseen changes due to adverse weather. For example, when a roadway built for construction use became a quagmire due to an early thaw, unusual capillary action and questionable drainage, the court held the extra maintenance expenditures to be an unforeseen (unusual) condition.[6] In another case where inadequate drainage contributed to a quagmire condition created by rain, the court affirmed that the contractor was entitled to an equitable adjustment for changed conditions.[7]

3-7. SITE INVESTIGATION

3-7a. Duty to Investigate: Reasonable Investigation

In general, site investigations are based on observance of the apparent surface conditions. Bidders do not usually have access to make detailed

---

[6]*John A. Johnson Contracting Co. v. U.S.* 132 Ct. Cl. 645, (1955).
[7]*Phillips Construction Co. v. U.S.,* 184 Ct. Cl. 249, (1968); also see *Appeal of Peterson Construction Co., Inc.,* ASBCA No. 44197 (Nov. 12, 1992). (Ground water exceeded the quantity indicated in the contract, complicating dewatering activities. This was a differing site condition.)

studies of these surface features, let alone subsurface features. Even with access, time and money present a major obstacle to detailed study and further exploration. However, it is still the bidder's duty to investigate the site, in order to be familiar with local conditions and to allow for a bid adjustment following any unusual findings. The owner, however, is responsible for allowing a reasonable period of time and access so that the bidders can make the investigation described by the invitation to bid. The following comments by McNulty (1975) emphasize these and other salient points:

> When the Government has made express representations in the contract documents which cannot be readily verified, the contractor is generally entitled to rely upon the same, and is not required to make an independent study or to conduct his own tests to determine the accuracy of such representations.
>
> In this same regard, in making a site investigation, the bidder is only charged with the knowledge that a reasonably intelligent and experienced contractor would acquire from such an investigation and will not necessarily be expected to reach the same conclusions that a geologist or other specialized expert might formulate from the same data. Nor is the prospective bidder obligated to seek out experts to determine the validity of the contract indications.
>
> It should also be emphasized, with respect to the obligation imposed upon the contractor under the "Site Investigation" clause, that where such an investigation would not have alerted the contractor to the conditions actually encountered, the failure to make such an investigation prior to bidding will not deprive the contractor of his right to relief under the "Differing Site Conditions" clause. . . .
>
> Similarly, relief under the clause will not be precluded where it is shown that the contractor was denied the chance to make a meaningful site investigation before bidding. The burden of clearly establishing that he was denied the opportunity to make such an investigation rests upon the contractor.[8]

3-7b. Disclaimers for Differing Site Conditions

The site investigation clause of the FAR states that "The government assumes no responsibility for any conclusions or interpretation made by the contractor based on the information made available by the government. Nor does the Government assume responsibility for any understanding reached or representation made concerning conditions which can affect the work by any of its officers or agents before the execution of this contract, unless that

[8]McNulty, pp. 28 & 29.

understanding or representation is expressly stated in the contract." (See Appendix 2, ¶52.236-3 for complete clause). There are occasions when the government, or owner, will use such a clause to deny a differing site conditions claim on the premise that the site conditions were not misrepresented. It is, therefore, important to be familiar with the requirements for investigation, the effect of contract disclaimers for differing site conditions, and the warranty (express or implied) of existing conditions. Particularly in private construction, the courts have generally denied differing site conditions claims when there existed

1. An absence of positive misrepresentation upon which the contractor reasonably relied
2. A clause in the contract that clearly relieves the owner of extra costs resulting from differing site conditions
3. An opportunity to conduct a site investigation and to inspect the plans and specifications before submitting a bid.[9]

The state courts later eased up on this view of the differing site conditions clause. This was apparent in *Metropolitan Sewerage Commission v. R. W. Construction, Inc.*, where, after studying the drawings and making a site investigation, the contractor made reasonable conclusions in his interpretations and expectations. The owner maintained that water problems encountered could have been anticipated from information in the contract and that there was neither misrepresentation nor a changed condition. The Wisconsin Supreme Court, however, in addition to finding that the water problem was not indicated in the contract, stated that the contractor should be held to a standard of reasonableness in drawing his conclusions: "that which any reasonable contractor should have anticipated is derived from a blend of his past experience, the customs and insights shared generally by contractors in the area, and the information conveyed by the contract."[10]

In federal contracts, discussed in section 3-2, misrepresentation is not a requirement for a differing site conditions claim (type one). A type two differing site condition would address the situation found in the Wisconsin case above, but since the contract did not contain such a clause, the owner maintained that absence of such a clause made the contractor liable for all site conditions that could possibly have been encountered.

Of further interest in this contract is that the court concluded that the

---

[9]John S. Martel and Bruce R. MacLeod, "Defenses in Construction Litigation" in *Construction Contracts*, 1976, ed. Jotham D. Pierce, Jr. (New York: Practising Law Institute, 1976).

[10]*Metropolitan Sewerage Commission v. R.W. Construction, Inc.*, 241 N.W 2d 371, (1976); also see *Weeks Dredging and Contracting, Inc. v. United States*, 13 Cl. CT. 193 (1987). (Contractor drew unreasonable conclusions from the soil boring logs.)

existence of changed conditions was *confirmed* by increased cost to do the work. The two factors involved in this conclusion are (1) that the contractor hired to complete the work was paid substantially more for the same work; and (2) a contractor who had a subcontract to perform a portion of the work with the first contractor was paid substantially more for the same work under the second contract.

On the other hand, in another case, extra work did not confirm differing site conditions where the government's approval of a claimed highly inefficient dredging method added $11 million to the contractor's cost.[1]

3-7c. Representations of Conditions Must Be Specifically Incorporated in Specifications

As illustrated by the brick and concrete sewer case, soil reports, boring data, as-built drawings, and other items referenced in the contract specification do not bind the contractor, unless specifically incorporated as part of the contract. The data is made available for the contractor's information only and is not intended as representations or warranties. It should be noted, however, that regardless of disclaimers or other limiting language, a project owner will be liable if it withholds from a contractor information that is not available from other sources.[12]

Another example of referenced specification issues were found in the Washington Metropolitan Area Transit Authority project contract clauses that read, "Information and data referred to below are furnished for the Contractor's information and for whatever use the Contractor may find therefor. The subsurface and other physical data such as those mentioned herein and contained in the Contract Documents, or otherwise made available to the Contractor by the Authority, are not intended as representations or warranties. It is expressly understood that the Authority will not be responsible for the completeness or accuracy thereof nor for any deductions, interpretations or conclusions drawn therefrom."[13] The board pointed out that in view of the strong disclaimers on the accuracy of the information and that the referenced information was not expressly "contained in the Contract Documents," the contractor was under no obligation to seek out and examine the information. It would have been a simple matter for the owner to have made the information part of the contract.[14]

This does not alleviate the contractor from seeking clarification where subsurface conditions might be ambiguous. In *Delcon Construction v. U.S.*[15]

---

[11]*Hydromar Corp. v. U.S.*, 25 Cl.Ct.555 (1992).
[12] *P. T. & L. Construction Co. v. State of New Jersey, Department of Transportation*, 5-31 A.2d 1330 (N.J. 1987).
[13]*Gordon H. Ball, Inc.* ENGBCA No. 3563, 78-1 BCA.
[14]Ibid.
[15]*Delcon Construction v. U.S.*, 27 Fed. Cl. 634 (1993).

the Postal Service provided boring logs, for information only, that indicated the presence or rock, but nothing else in the contract documents either confirmed or denied whether rock excavation was part of the contract. In this case, the court found that the bid documents "contained a patent ambiguity as to whether the contract required rock excavation, that the plaintiff had a duty to clarify the ambiguity, and that the plaintiff's inquiry failed adequately to fulfill that duty. Therefore, the risk of misinterpreting the contract requirements falls on the plaintiff."[16]

3-7d. Inadequate Investigation

In preparing a bid, the contractor assumes the responsibility of making an adequate investigation of the site, and failure to do so will not excuse extra costs incurred in overcoming the adverse conditions encountered. In a case involving the repainting of existing bridges, the contractor did not notice the peeling of existing paint. When the contractor sued for the additional cost to remove the peeling paint, the court rejected his claim because of the failure to notice the paint condition, even though the contract did not specifically address removal of peeling paint. "The company here explicitly assumed the responsibility for examining the bridge and determining the subsurface conditions. This duty cannot be excused simply because the company's visual inspection proved to be inadequate."[17]

3-7e. Site Investigation Requirements

The contractor should approach the site investigation as if already awarded the contract and as if it were the first week of the project. Every bit of information that will influence planning and performance of the contract should be recorded. These records should include sketches and photographs of the jobsite. Ideally, the principals who will be involved in managing, as well as estimating, the project should participate in the site investigation. Appendix 5 contains a "Site Investigation Report" form for heavy construction. This outline lists information to obtain or check when conducting a site investigation.

The importance of the site investigation should not be treated lightly. In addition to aiding the contractor in preparing a bid and planning the work, the site investigation (and bid estimate) can play a crucial role in claims situations. For example, the bid estimate work method and price are sometimes used as a standard of reference to compare changed conditions and

---

[16]Ibid.
[17]*Commonwealth of Pennsylvania DOT v. Mitchell's Structural Steel Painting Co.*, 336A2-913 Commonwealth Court of Pennsylvania (1975); also see *Green Construction Co. v. Department of Transportation*, 643 A.2d 1129 (Pa.Cmwlth. 1994). (Contractor's inadequate prebid site inspection caused the contractor to underestimate the difficulty of the work.)

DIFFERING SITE CONDITIONS 31

actual cost. If the bid estimate work method was not followed by the contractor, it may invalidate its use as representative of the contractor's "reasonable" cost.

3-8. SUMMARY AND CHECKLIST

When a situation is encountered that appears to represent a differing site condition, the contractor should ask himself the following:

1. What was the recognized and usual physical condition of the site?
2. What physical condition was actually encountered?
3. Did it differ from known and usual?
4. If so, did it cause an increase in the cost or time of performance, that is, did it differ materially?

A further reference for trying to determine if a disputed condition has a reasonable basis for claim is the checklist reprinted here from the July 1976 issue of "*Construction Methods and Equipment*"[18]:

1. All that is necessary to apply the clause is enough information to impress or lull a reasonable bidder into not expecting the actual conditions.
2. Contractors need not make a scientific and skeptical analysis of the conditions in preparing bids.
3. Broad admonitory and exculpatory clauses will not restrict application of a changed conditions clause.
4. Design features may indicate expected conditions.
5. Design changes may confirm a changed condition.

---

[18]Reprinted from *Construction Methods and Equipment*, July 1976, Copyright McGraw-Hill Incorporated. All rights reserved.

CHAPTER 4

INTERPRETATION AND REQUIREMENTS OF CONTRACT SPECIFICATIONS

4-1. INTRODUCTION

Several aspects of contract problem areas are frequently responsible for claims and change order situations, including contract interpretation, defective specifications, duty to seek clarification, duty to inform, duty to proceed, and inspection and duty to inspect. All of these items are encompassed by the Changes clause of the Federal Acquisition Regulation (FAR) and generally are addressed by a changes clause in private construction contracts.

These problems arise from different interpretations of contract provisions, different experiences in method or manner of construction procedures and divergent objectives sought by the owner and contractor. Of course, the objective of the contractor and the owner is to have a structure erected in a workman-like manner and at a reasonable price, but the size and complexity of today's construction projects hardly leave time or space to pin down all details. Each contractor and each owner will probably interpret any given situation differently. However, over a period of time, these situations have evolved into standard interpretations as the situations have been repeatedly encountered. This chapter attempts to review and illustrate some of the methods used to settle these contract interpretation issues.

4-2. RULES OF CONTRACT INTERPRETATION

4-2a. Background

Over the years, a set of rules has been developed to assist in the interpretation of construction contracts. These rules have frequently been used by the Contract Appeals Board and the courts as guidelines for developing sound, consistent judgment on interpretation problems. These rules, published by the American Law Institute in Restatement of the Law of Contracts[1] (1932) are shown in Appendix 6. The salient features of these references bear examination.

4-2b. Reasonableness

The basic principle underlying contract interpretation is that of reasonableness. Are the interpretations given by the parties to the contract reasonable? If so, is one interpretation more reasonable? A number of interpretations can be given to each specification, and the task is to decide if there is a singular, more predominant interpretation of a specification or if several viable interpretations might be acceptable. A specification might be intended to have a restricted meaning, but unless that meaning is clearly expressed, the other party to the contract cannot readily infer the single interpretation the contract is supposed to express. The most reasonable meaning under the circumstances at hand will govern the interpretation of the contract. "A government contractor cannot properly be required to exercise clairvoyance in determining its contractual responsibilities. The crucial question is 'what plaintiff would have understood as a reasonable construction contractor,' not what the drafter of the contract terms subjectively intended."[2]

The boards and courts will "seek the meaning that would be attached to the language by a reasonably intelligent bidder . . . who would be expected to have the technical and trade knowledge of his industry and know how to read and interpret technical engineering specifications and perform construction work in accordance with such specifications."[3]

If, when preparing a bid, the contractor finds and resolves an ambiguity in accordance with her own reasonable interpretation prior to bid time, the boards (ASBCA) will uphold this interpretation if the contract is not otherwise sufficiently clear.[4]

> Long years of practical experience and vast technical resources too often bear nothing more fruitful than poor draftsmanship or *contrived* analysis. In any event, the language of a contract must be afforded the meaning derived from the contract by a reasonably

---

[1]*Restatement of the Law of Contracts*, Copyright 1932 by The American Law Institute. Reprinted with the permission of the American Law Institute. §§ 235 & 236.

[2]*Corbetta Construction Co. v. U.S.*, 198 Ct. Cl. 712 (1972).

[3]*Blount Brothers Corporation*, NASA BCA 865-29, 67-2 BCA ¶6562; also see *Appeal of Pool & Canfield, Inc.*, ASBCA No. 4-3399 (March 4, 1992). (Contractor's interpretation of drawing lines depicting conduit was consistent with industry practice.)

[4]*Blake Construction Co., Inc.*, GSBCA 1345, 65-1 BCA ¶4624.

intelligent person acquainted with the contemporary circumstances. . . . The unexpressed, subjective, unilateral intent of one party is insufficient to bind the other contracting party, especially when the latter reasonably believes otherwise.[5]

4-2c. Read the Contract as a Whole

If a reasonable interpretation cannot be derived from a specification on its own merit, then assistance must be sought from other sources, preferably from within the contract documents. The third rule [Primary Rule (c)] of the Restatement of Contracts is that the contract must be read as a whole. This rule requires that the contractor does not take an interpretation out of context in one part of the specification when that specification is modified or clarified in another part of the contract. Also, if a *part* of a specification is interpreted in such a fashion that its inclusion in the contract would render it meaningless, chances are that interpretation would itself be meaningless. If different parts of the specifications can be read in more than one way, and one way causes more conflicts than the other, then the reader of the contract should "interpret the provisions of a contract as coordinate, not contradictory," and should "seek to find concord, rather than discord."[6]

4-2d. Language

The first two rules [Primary Rules (a) & (b)] of the Restatement of Contracts state that language will be given its ordinary meaning and that technical terms will be given their technical meanings unless otherwise stated in the contract or indicated by the usage of the term in the contract. Does a close reading of the contract document give a reasonable and clear expression of the meaning and intent of the specification?

> Our ultimate goal is always to give full force and effect to the expressed or implied intentions of the contracting parties, if such can be discerned . . . and only by defining the contract terms clearly, simply, and in accordance with commonly accepted usage, can this paramount obligation be judiciously discharged. . . . We will not, as (contractor) has attempted to do . . . ascribe a meaning to the language . . . which is neither stated, expressly or by implication . . .[7]

---

[5]*Firestone Tire & Rubber Co. v. U.S.*, 195 Ct. Cl. 21 (1971); also see *Department of Transportation v. Semanderes*, 5-31 A.2d 815 (Pa.Cmwlth. 1987). (Contractor's interpretation of a latently ambiguous specification was more reasonable than the owner's interpretation.)

[6]*Unicon Management Corp. v. U.S.*, 179 Ct. Cl. 534 (1967).

[7]*Massachusetts Port Authority v. U.S.*, 197 Ct. Cl. 721 (1972).

In trying to determine the meaning of a term or provision, the contractor should try to ascertain its meaning by gaining support from other terms or other provisions in the specifications. The Court of Claims established this concept-giving meaning to all words rather than reading a term in isolation in the well-known case of *Hol-Gar Manufacturing*

> ... The intention of the parties must be gathered from the whole instrument ... Also, an interpretation which gives a reasonable meaning to all parts of an instrument will be preferred to one which leaves a portion of it useless, inexplicable, inoperative, void, insignificant, meaningless, or superfluous; nor should any provision be construed as being in conflict with another unless no other reasonable interpretation is possible ...[8]

If a contractor can gather sufficient and reasonable meaning from one part of the contract, he is not expected to look elsewhere and in unlikely parts of the contract to determine if there might be alternative meanings. Thus, this rule of interpretation was not held against a contractor who reasonably inferred information on one sheet of plans as sufficient for bid takeoff and did not have to seek further clarification on other drawings.[9]

Additionally, it is common for contracts to address the possibility of internal discrepancies, stating, for instance, that in the event of a conflict the specifications will govern the drawings. Contractors are entitled to rely on these clauses when interpreting the contract documents.[10]

4-2e. Custom or Usage

Trade custom or usage can be used to ascribe meaning to words if it appears that such meaning was the intent of the contract, whether or not the ordinary meaning is ambiguous

> For the principle is now established in this court (and almost every other court) that in order that the intention of the parties may prevail, the language of a contract is to be given effect according to its trade meaning, notwithstanding that in its ordinary meaning

---

[8]*Hol-Gar Manufacturing Corp. v. U.S.*, 169 Ct. Cl. 384 (1965); also see *Appeal of Fort Mechanical, Inc.*, GSBCA No. 6350 (July 18, 1983). (Contractor could not simply ignore a drawing scale when interpreting the contract documents.) Also *Hills Materials Co. v. Rice*, 982 F.2d 514 (Fed. Cir. 1992) (Change in OSHA slope requirement compensable because specific reference to specific OSHA regulation ... "issued" superseded the more general terms in the Permits and Responsibilities clause, which placed responsibility with the contractor for compliance with changed regulations.)
[9]*Jarbet Co.*, ASBCA 14554, 72-1 BCA ¶9379.
[10]*Appeal of Hull-Hazard, Inc.*, ASBCA No. 34645 (June 29, 1990).

it is ambiguous. That is to say that trade usage or custom may show that language which appears on its face to be perfectly clear and unambiguous has, in fact, a meaning different from its ordinary meaning.[11]

In *W. G. Connell Co. v. U.S.*, the Court of Claims explicitly allows that trade usage and custom may always explain or define contract language

> Moreover, evidence of trade usage and custom may always explain or define, as distinguished from vary or contradict, contract language . . . evidence of trade usage still must be taken into consideration, since it supplies a meaning to that phrase which is not disclosed from a casual reading thereof. Even in the absence of ambiguity, contract language must be given that meaning which would be derived from the contract by a reasonably intelligent person acquainted with the contemporaneous circumstances.[12]

4-2f. Parol Evidence Rule

The Parol Evidence Rule [Restatement of Contracts Primary Rule (d)] provides that oral agreements cannot be used to vary, contradict, or add to the terms of a written agreement. However, the rule does not exclude evidence offered for the purpose of interpreting and giving meaning to those terms, "If, therefore, the written specifications are deemed to be ambiguous or unclear . . . the oral negotiations are admissible to help clear up the uncertainty."[13] "Facts and circumstances antecedent to and contemporaneous with the making of contracts can be considered in the interpretation of the contract provisions."[14]

4-2g. "Against the Drafter"

When both parties to the contract have reasonable interpretations of terms of the specification, and when there is still some ambiguity as to the intent of the terms, the boards and courts will rule against the drafter of the document [Restatement of Contracts Secondary Rule (c)]

> Where the government draws specifications which are fairly susceptible of a certain construction and the contractor actually and reasonably so construes them, justice and equality require that

---

[11]*Gholson, Byars and Holmes Construction Co. v. U.S.*, 173 Ct. Cl. 374 (1965).
[12]*W. G. Cornell Co. v. U.S.*, 179 Ct. Cl. 651 (1967); also see *Appeal of Santa Fe, Inc.*, VABCA No. 2167 (Dec. 18, 1986). (In the absence of an express contract requirement to the contrary, contractor was entitled to rely on standard industry performance practices.)
[13]*Sylvania Electric Products, Inc. v. U.S.*, 198 CT. Cl. 106 (1972).
[14]*Gibbs v. U.S.*, 175 Ct. Cl. 411 (1966).

INTERPRETATION AND REQUIREMENTS OF CONTRACT SPECIFICATIONS

that construction be adopted. Where one of the parties to a contract draws the document and uses therein language which is susceptible of more than one meaning, and the intention of the parties does not otherwise appear, that meaning will be given the document which is more favorable to the party who did not draw it. This rule is especially applicable to government contracts where the contractor has nothing to say as to its provisions. This rule usually works to the advantage of the contractor since the government almost always is the drafter of the contract language.[15]

Ambiguity does not have to be proven

To prevail . . . it is not essential that (contractor) demonstrate his position to be the only justifiable or reasonable one. A specification susceptible to more than one interpretation found to be consistent with the contract's language and the parties' objectively ascertainable intentions, becomes convincing proof of an ambiguity; the burden of that ambiguity falls solely upon the party who drew the specifications.[16]

4-2h. Conduct

Restatement of Contracts Primary Rule (e) deals with the conduct of the parties' actions as lending weight or new meaning to a contract interpretation. Conduct can be established by prior course of dealings, actions on other contracts, and conduct of the parties during the performance of the instant contract

The importance of a prior course of dealing reaches its zenith in instances where the experience on past contracts is allowed to substantially modify or, perhaps, contradict the plain language of the contract. In *L.W. Foster Sportswear Co. v. U.S.*, the contractor had never been able to meet the strict requirements of the specifications and had, under a series of prior contracts, received certain necessary deviations. The Court of Claims held that the contractor was entitled to rely on its understanding of what would be acceptable even though there were slight differences in the inspection

---

[15]*Peter Kiewit Sons' Co. v. U.S.*, 109 Ct. Cl. 517 (1947).
[16]*George Bennett v. U.S.*, 178 Ct. Cl.; also see *Department of Transportation v. Mosites Construction Co.*, 494 A.2d 41 (Pa.Cmwlth. 1985). (Ambiguous payment schedule construed against the project owner that drafted it.)

standards in the instant contract and even though the procuring agency had changed.[17]

The contractor can essentially rely on his own previous dealings with identical contracts as establishing an interpretation. However, when relying on similar work being performed by other contractors, it must be shown that the other parties were aware and accepting of the situation. If the other contracts had specific circumstances peculiar to those contracts or if the interpretations underlying those prior contracts were unknown to the contracting officer of the current contract, then the rule of conduct may not apply. In other words, what may hold for one contractor and owner on a contract may not apply to a similar contract between another contractor and owner.

The conduct of the parties during performance of the contract will usually establish a precedent of contract interpretation for disputes which later arise from the specification requirement. In *Maxwell Dynamometer Co. v. U.S.*, the Court of Claims stated that the government was bound by the interpretation adopted by the contractor when, after the government became aware of the interpretation, its contract representatives said nothing

> Either of two conclusions can be reached from the government's actions. One is that the government's officials at these tests interpreted the contract in the same manner as (the contractor) and though the contract required that speed be measured from the power roller, the Clayton dynamometer at Newport notwithstanding. Since great weight is given to the practical interpretation of a contract by the parties to it before the contract becomes the subject of controversy, if such is the case, then it reinforces (contractor's) interpretation of the specifications. . . . The other conclusion is that the representatives of the Government were aware (that contractor) was reading the contract specifications more stringently than required, but that they said nothing, possibly in the hope that (contractor) would be able to meet this more demanding standard. Such action is unconscionable and would not serve to defeat (contractor's interpretation).[18]

If an interpretation of an element of work is to be disputed, it should be done as soon as it is recognized or becomes known. If a contractor is performing work under one interpretation, then decides that a new interpreta-

---

[17]C. Stanley Dees and Gilbert J. Ginsburg "Contract Interpretation and Defective Specifications," *Government Contracts Monograph No. 4* (Published by the Government Contracts Program, the George Washington University, 1975), pp. 16 & 17.

[18]*Maxwell Dynometer Co. v. U.S.*, 181 Ct. Cl. 607 (1967).

INTERPRETATION AND REQUIREMENTS OF CONTRACT SPECIFICATIONS

tion is more correct and wants to claim extra costs of performing the original work, he may be denied such extra costs. "The interpretation of a contract by the parties to it, before the contract becomes a subject of controversy, is deemed by the court to be of great, if not controlling weight. It is a canon of contract construction that the interpretation placed by the parties on a contract during its performance is demonstrative of their intentions."[19]

4-3. DEFECTIVE SPECIFICATIONS

4-3a. Introduction

The existing body of law dealing with defective specifications finds its origin in the landmark case of *U.S. v. Spearin*. This decision established the precedent that, where the government issues detailed specifications, the government implies a warranty that the finished product will perform as required. The case states, " . . . if the contractor is bound to build according to plans and specifications prepared by the owner, the contractor will not be responsible for the consequences of defects in the plans and specifications."[20]

Although the government sometimes rightfully puts the contractor on notice of potential errors in the specifications, the government cannot necessarily avoid liability through the use of exculpatory language. For example, the common requirement for the contractor to verify all dimensions and conditions prior to submission of bid does not require the contractor to verify accuracy and to interpret every possible error

> Contractors are businessmen usually pressed for time and consciously seeking to underbid competitors. Consequently they estimate only those costs which they feel the contract terms will permit the government to insist upon in the way of performance. They are not expected to ferret out hidden ambiguities or errors in the bid documents and are protected if they innocently construe in their own favor an ambiguity equally susceptible to another construction or overlook an error."[21]

The realm of defective specifications, in addition to obvious cases of design defects, encompasses suitability or availability of designated materials, practicality or possibility of performances, and duty to disclose knowl-

---

[19]*Max Drill, Inc. v. U.S.*, 192 Ct. Cl. 608 (1970).
[20]*U.S. v. Spearin*, 248 U.S. 132 (1918).
[21]*Bromley Contracting Co.*, ASBCA 14884, 72-1 BCA ¶ 9252; also see *Appeal of Harrison Western/Franki-Denys, Inc.*, ENGBCA No. 552-3 (Nov. 22, 1991). (Contractor was not required to detect a latent error in a drawing note.)

edge or information pertinent to the performance of the contract. These aspects of defective specifications are discussed briefly in the following three sections.

4-3b. Suitability of Designated Methods or Materials

While the owner is obligated generally to ascertain the availability of specified materials, the contractor carries the primary responsibility in this area. In preparing a bid, the prudent contractor must assure himself of the commercial availability of the materials. For instance, an owner issuing specifications calling for 500 tons of welded rail may know that the steel mills are in full production and be confident that his needs can be filled at published steel prices. He may not, however, realize that the welding plants are two years behind in their orders. The contractor who has neither qualified his bid accordingly nor established his own on-site welding capacity will have assumed the risks of the consequences of resulting material shortages.

The owner's obligation is stronger, however, when specifying performance of designated materials. That is, in specifying a material or its approved equal, the owner is implying a warranty that the material will perform and that it is reasonably available. In a case where a designated supplier would not sell to the contractor, the Court of Claims found the contractor not liable for failure to secure the material

> Where the government issues an invitation for a procurement item containing a component which is given a purchase description consisting of a brand name product manufactured by a designated company or its 'approved substantial equal.' . . . It was improper for the government to cast this burden of advance ascertainment upon bidders without explicitly warning them of the questionable availability or physical makeup of the component."[22]

Similar to this situation is the specification that describes and clearly allows several alternative methods or materials and the method or material chosen fails to perform. The implied warranty to perform if the specifications are followed (*Spearin v. U.S.*) applies to all the alternatives and the contractor should recover additional costs due to such failures.[23]

Design deficiencies aren't always clear cut with obvious causes and effects. Sometime the end products are usable, but extra costs were still incurred. In *Neal & Co. v. U.S.*, extra allowable costs were incurred to overcome bonding problems of steel plates to concrete in precast panels.

---

[22]*Aerodex, Inc. v. U.S.*, 189 Ct. Cl. 344 (1969).
[23]Ralph C. Nash, Mr., *Government Contract Changes* (Federal Publications, Inc., Washington, D.C., 1975), p. 275.

INTERPRETATION AND REQUIREMENTS OF CONTRACT SPECIFICATIONS 41

The extra costs included hiring of a design consultant to monitor the extra work as well as the extra work in loading, unloading, and installation planning of the panels.[24]

4-3c. Possibility and Practicality

The Restatement of Contracts defines impossibility to mean "not only strict impossibility but impracticability because of extreme and unreasonable difficulty, expense, injury or loss involved."[25] However, performance will not be excused simply because the work is more difficult or expensive than anticipated: "The law excuses performance (or, in the case of government contracts, grants relief through a change order) where the attendant costs of performance bespeak commercial senselessness, it does not grant relief merely because performance cannot be achieved under the most economical means. . . . The Government does not, when it directs the method of manufacture, warrant that its method can be pursued without difficulty or other unanticipated problems. The warranty, properly construed, promises only that performance is possible and within the state of the art."[26]

4-3d. Cardinal Changes

Related to impossibility and/or impracticability is the concept of a cardinal change. Where a change or changes made by an owner is so extensive or of such magnitude as to be outside the scope of the original contract, the owner has made such a change. The contractor may refuse to perform the work and would be permitted to abandon the project. Conversely, the contractor may elect to complete under protest and recover fair and reasonable costs for performing the changed work.[27]

Cardinal changes may arise from changes in quantity, or from changes in the means or methods of performing the work. A cardinal change does not have to be a single change or several massive changes, but can be the result of many minor changes.

4-3e. Disclosure of Knowledge

Withholding knowledge of information that might adversely affect contract performance may be held as a defective specification. Failure to disclose inaccuracies about contract provisions, access dates, degree of other work, and interference that might be expected can cause otherwise unexpected additional costs for the contractor. However, if the contractor has

---

[24]*Neal & Co. vs. U.S.*, 19 Cl. Ct. 463 (1990).

[25]*Restatement of the Law of Contracts*, § 454.

[26]*Natus Corporation v. U.S.*, 178 Ct. Cl. 1 (1967); also see *Appeal of Centex Construction Co., Inc.*, ASBCA No. 29323 (Sept. 30, 1985). (Contractor was required to devise construction techniques that would meet a difficult design.)

[27]*Saddler vs. U.S.*, 287 F.2d 411 (Ct. Cl. 1961).

access to the same information, then knowledge is also imparted to the contractor.

The question of disclosure of knowledge is intertwined with problems of what the knowledge is, who has the knowledge, and the common availability of certain types of information. Basically, if knowledge is readily available to both owner and contractor, then one party cannot be responsible for having withheld knowledge from the other. If one party, however, has superior knowledge of pertinent information that might affect performance, he is obligated to make known such information, as established in the case of *Helene Curtis Industries*:[28]

> The Government violates its contractual obligations if it permits the contractor to bid for a project and subsequently undertake a course of action in pursuance thereof which the Government knows to be defective, provided that the Government possesses knowledge which is vital to the successful completion of the contract, and provided further that it is unreasonable to expect the contractor to obtain that vital information from any other accessible source (Curtis rule). Of course, the corollary of the Curtis rule is that the Government is under no duty to volunteer information in its files if the contractor can reasonably be expected to seek and obtain the facts elsewhere.[29]

4-3f. Cost and Notification Aspects

There are two significant features attendant to defective specification claims. The first is that the contractor is entitled to receive equitable adjustments for cost incurred from the inception of the claim (20-day notice limitation does not apply), and the second is that the equitable adjustment shall include any and all increased costs incurred in attempting to comply with the defective specifications. The boards and courts have given liberal consideration to costs in defective specification claims including delay costs. This interpretation is based on the government's obligation to insure the adequacy and accuracy of the specifications it has drafted and the owner's obligation to not hinder the performance of the contractor. This is explicitly stated in the case of *Laburnum Construction Company v. U.S.*

> There is a condition implied in every construction contract that neither party will do anything to hinder the performance of the other party. If faulty specifications prevent completion of the con-

---

[28]*Helene Curtis Industries, Inc. v. U.S.*, 160 Ct. Cl. 437 (1963).
[29]*H.N. Bailey & Associates v. U.S.*, 196 Ct. Cl. 166 (1971); also see *Uhley v. Tapio Construction Co., Inc.*, 573 So.2d 391 (Fla.App. 1991). (Contractor had an obligation to confirm benchmark elevations in the field.)

INTERPRETATION AND REQUIREMENTS OF CONTRACT SPECIFICATIONS

tract, the contractor is entitled to recover damages for the (government's) breach of its implied warranty. Those damages extend to the costs incurred by reason of the idleness resulting from the mistakes in the plans. The (government) cannot, by errors in the specifications, cause delay in (contractor's) completion of the work and then compensate (contractor) merely by extending its performance time *and by* payment of any added direct cost occasioned by changes to correct those errors.[30]

The significance of this case is that the contractor is entitled to all costs as a result of the defective specifications, and avoids the application, by the owner, of the right to reasonably delay the job while he issues a change. It therefore behooves the contractor to claim for delays associated with the change issuance as an action incurring out of a defective specification, rather than as a routine change to the contract.

4-4. DUTY TO SEEK CLARIFICATION

4-4a. Obligation to Notify Owner of Errors or Discrepancies

The burden to inform the other party of pertinent information rests on both the contractor and the owner. The contractor, because of his superior experience with construction methods, is under obligation to notify the owner of glaring errors or discrepancies found both before and after bid. This obligation was stated as a rule of law in *Beacon Construction. Co. v. U.S.*

> The bidder who is on notice of an incipient problem cannot rely on the principle that ambiguities in contracts written by the government are held against the drafter. The bidder is under an affirmative obligation . . . to call attention to an obvious omission in a specification, and make certain that the omission was deliberate, if he intends to take advantage of it. . . . If the bidder fails to resort to the remedy proffered by the Government, a patent and glaring discrepancy should be taken against him in interpreting the contract. We do not mean to rule that under such contract provisions, the contractor must at his peril remove any possible ambiguity prior to bidding: what we do hold is that, when he is presented with an obvious omission, inconsistency, or discrepancy of signifi-

---

[30]*Laburnum Construction Corp. v. U.S.*, 163 Ct. Cl. 339 (1963). [Also see *Appeal of Oneida Construction Co., Inc./David Boland, Inc., Joint Venture*, ASBCA No. 44194 (Oct. 6, 1994). (Government's defective specifications hindered the contractor's progress.)]

cance, he must consult the Government's representatives if he intends to bridge the crevasse in his own favor.[31]

4-4b. Zone of Reasonableness

This rule of law in *Beacon* is more clearly affirmed in *WPC Enterprises v. U.S.*, which now stands as the prevailing test of the application of the rule. Thus

> If some substantive provision of a government-drawn agreement is fairly susceptible of a certain construction and the contractor actually and reasonably so construes it, in the course of bidding or performance, that is the interpretation which will be adopted. . . . Although the potential contractor may have some duty to inquire about a major patent discrepancy, or obvious omission, or a drastic conflict in provisions . . . he is not normally required (absent a clear warning in the contract) to seek clarification of any and all ambiguities, doubts, or possible differences in interpretations.[32]

That is, to quote *WPC* further, the contractor does not have to seek clarification if its interpretation falls within a "zone of reasonableness"

> The Government, as the author, has to shoulder the major task of seeing that within the zone of reasonableness the words of agreement communicate the proper notions—as well as the main risk of a failure to carry that responsibility.

If the contractor has questions about interpretation or allowable procedures that will have a major impact on his construction methods, he should ask questions before his bid rather than gamble that his assumptions are correct. He has to weigh the reasonableness of his interpretation against the expressed or apparent intent of the contract.

In a recent case before the U.S. Court of Claims, the contractor based its construction method on a diagram included in the bid documents, which is designated as "schematic and for the purpose of estimating only." When, after the award, the government directed the contractor to proceed in accordance with the method in the specification, the contractor sued for increased costs over a method he thought he was free to propose by his reading of the

---

[31] *Beacon Construction Co. v. U.S.*, 161 Ct. Cl. 1 (1963). [Also see *Appeal of Sherman Construction Corp.*, VABCA No. 1942 (Dec. 13, 1984). (Contractor had a duty to seek clarification of conflicting contract provisions.)]

[32] *WPC Enterprises, Inc. v. U.S.*, 163 Ct. Cl. 1 (1963). [Also see *Appeal of Bruce-Anderson Co., Inc.*, ASBCA No. 29411 (Aug. 1, 1988). (Contractor had no duty to discover or seek clarification of a latently restrictive specification.)]

contract. The court, without ruling whose interpretation was correct, stated that there was a patent ambiguity that the contractor should have sought to clarify. In denying the contractor's claim, the court concluded

> The rule that a contractor, before bidding, should attempt to have the government resolve a patent ambiguity is a major device of preventative hygiene; it is designed to avoid just such post-award disputes as this by encouraging contractors to seek clarification before anyone is legally bound.[33]

4-4c. Two-Step Test

In *Gaston & Associates v. U.S.*,[34] the court stated the Corp of Engineer's requirement for separate inspectors for three separate buildings and its refusal to allow the superintendent to also serve as quality control manager was neither clearly specified nor the sole reasonable interpretation of the contract, and the government, as the drafter of the specification, bore responsibility for its misinterpretation. In its decision, the court pointed out that neither party submitted credible evidence of prevailing industry practice as to the quality control manager's simultaneous performance of additional duties. The contractor supported his argument that the government was capable of clarifying its intention by pointing out similar clauses (and clearly more specific) that existed in the Corp's own "Guide Specification" manual. In ruling that "the government cannot make a contractor the insurer of all government mistakes,"[35] the court applied the two-step test established in *Mountain Home Contractors*:

- First Test: Discrepancy must *not* be glaring, substantial and patent.
- Second test: The contractor's interpretation was reasonable.

These two steps were first enounced in *Blount Bros Const. Co.* The first test, like in *Beacon*, provides that the contractor is "obligated to bring to the Government's attention major discrepancies or errors which they detect in the specification or drawings, or else fail to do so at their peril."[36] Note that in *Mountain Home Contractors*, the court noted the fact that the cost of the disputed item was less than half of 1% of the total contract price, hence not substantial.

The second step declared in *Blount* is that contractors "are protected if they innocently construe in their own favor an ambiguity equally susceptible

---

[33]*S. O. G. of Arkansas v. U.S.*, Ct. Cl. 546 F 2d 367 (Dec. 15, 1976).
[34]*Gaston & Associates v. U.S.*, 27 Fed Cl. 243 (1992).
[35]*Mountain Home Contractors v. U.S.*, 192 Ct.Cl.16, 425 F.2d 1264.
[36]*Blount Bros. Const. Co.* 171 Ct.Cl. 478, 496, 346 F.2d 962,973 (1965).

to another construction for as in *Peter Kiewit Sons' Co. v. U.S.*, 109 Ct. Cl 390, 418 (1947), the basic precept is that ambiguities in contracts drawn by the government are construed against the drafter."[37]

4-4d. "Not Part of Contract"

To summarize the discussions of this section along with those of section 3-7, Site Investigations, information that is provided "for information only" and is not expressly contained as part of the contract documents can be used by the contractor, but not relied on. However, if such information raises clear questions or obvious conflicts, it may raise a duty to inquire. If references to "for information only" doesn't say "not part of contract," it may raise even more of a duty to inquire.

4-5. DUTY TO INFORM

There is also an obligation on both parties to a contract to inform each other of possible problems that may prevent or seriously hinder performance, "If the contractor knows or should know of circumstances indicating that the plans are bound to lead to failure, he has a duty to inform the owner (regardless of the owner's personal expertise)."[38] Likewise, the owner has a duty to disclose all pertinent information relevant to successful completion of the contract

> The government possessing vital information which it was aware the bidders needed but would not have, could not properly let them flounder on their own. Although it is not a fiduciary toward its contractors, the government, where the balance of knowledge is so clearly on its side, can no more betray a contractor into a ruinous course of action by silence than by the written or spoken word.[39]

Types of information withheld by the owner that might affect a contractor's performance that have been ruled the basis of changed conditions in the past, are

1. Discrepancies in the work done on the project by a prior contractor
2. Performance of an item in prior tests
3. The possibility that only the specified item in an "or equal" spec would meet the government's requirements

[37]Ibid. @ 496, 497.
[38]*Lewis v. Anchorage Asphalt Paving Co.*, F. 2d 1188 (Alaska 1975).
[39]*Helene Curtis Industries, Inc. v. U.S.*, 160 Ct. Cl. 437 (1963).

INTERPRETATION AND REQUIREMENTS OF CONTRACT SPECIFICATIONS 47

4. Full information of the performance of a specified subcontractor
5. Problems inherent in a contract specification
6. Conditions of a building on which work was to be done
7. Technical information indicating that the technique proposed by the contractor would be unsuccessful
8. Other Government contracts to be awarded at the site of construction.[40]

Proof that the information was withheld does not insure the contractor that an equitable adjustment will be made. The contractor must show that the availability of the information would have affected his performance or bid. The New York Supreme Court found that the state had a duty to disclose all available boring tests and subsurface information in the area of a project. The contractor claimed his bid would have been higher had he had access to all available information. However, the court rejected the claim because the contractor had failed to submit satisfactory evidence to establish the specific effect that more complete information might have had on his bid and how the bid would have differed.[41]

4-6. DUTY TO PROCEED

The contractor's duty to proceed is usually obligatory. The contractor should be extremely cautious and seek legal advice before even considering stopping work for any cause. Perhaps the only situation where the contractor can cease work is a situation in which he is unable to obtain clear direction on a course of action. It becomes incumbent on the owner (government) to provide clarification or direction when the contractor has failed in his performance, has requested clarification or direction, and has made good faith efforts to meet the specifications.

> In our view any period of performance is tolled by the negotiations which were never concluded due to the failure of (the government) to furnish a decision in the dispute over the modified specifications. We think (contractor) was entitled to withhold performance until the matter was settled. In his termination notice the contracting officer denied that (contractor) had excusable cause for non-performance based on defective specifications. We do not think it necessary to determine whether the specifications were defective. (Contractor) contended they were defective and (the

---

[40]Nash, p. 313.
[41]*A. S. Wikstrom, Inc. v. State*, N.Y. Supreme Court, App. Div. (April 8, 1976).

government) entered into negotiations to modify them. Until these negotiations were completed and a decision made as to the form of the modified specifications, (contractor) had no duty to proceed with performance.[42]

The contractor's duty to proceed is clearly spelled out in the Disputes clause of government contracts: "Pending final decision of a dispute thereunder, the contractor shall proceed diligently with the performance of the contract and in accordance with the contracting officer's decision" [see Appendix 2, 52.233-1(i)]. Even if the contractor's interpretation of a dispute is correct and a time extension is imminent, the contractor is still obligated to perform. In *American Dredging v. U.S.* the board and contracting officer were justified in finding that the contractor "had not and would not, as it was contractually obligated to do, diligently proceed with the work pending resolution of the changed condition dispute."[43]

4-7. INSPECTION: DUTY TO INSPECT

Overinspection and untimely inspection can cause changed conditions or delays. If the engineer or owner imposes a higher level of performance than required by the specifications, the contractor is entitled to an equitable adjustment. Sometimes overzealous inspectors require installation and placement tolerances of materials and equipment much tighter than is customarily followed by the crafts. The different material institutes (e.g., American Concrete Institute, American Reinforcing Steel Institute) set tolerances for manufacturing and installation of their products. The crafts usually try to adhere to these tolerances, but some variances are expected that are beyond the worker's control and are not harmful. Unless an installation is structurally unsound or the appearance is clearly beyond the reasonable intent of the specifications, additional costs to maintain tighter control or make corrections may be cause for an equitable adjustment.

4-7a. Improper Rejection

The owner has a right to set tight specifications so long as they are clear and not impossible. However, where costs are incurred due to rejection of the work for improper interpretation of the specifications by the inspector, an equitable adjustment may be due. In the case of *Granite Construction*

---

[42]*Monitor Plastics Co.*, ASBCA 11 187, 67-2 BCA ¶6408.
[43]*American Dredging Co.*, ENGBCA Nos. 2920 et al. 72-1 BCA ¶9316. *American Dredging Co. v. U.S.*, 207 Ct. Cl. 1010 (1977); also see *Appeal of Gaudelli Brothers, Inc.*, GSBCA No. 7123 (March 5, 1984). (Default termination was proper where a contractor refused to proceed with the work until an agreement had been reached on the price of a change order.)

Company, the owner rejected concrete on the assertion that it did not meet porosity and durability criteria not mentioned in the specification. The board found "that the concrete in question was improperly rejected on a basis not specified in the contract."[44] The contractor, therefore, was entitled to an equitable adjustment for the demolition and replacement of the concrete.

4-7b. Improper Acceptance

If the government is aware that the contractor is deviating from the specifications in an unacceptable manner, it has a duty to so inform the contractor. In *Hydrospace Electronics & Instrument Corp.* (ASBCA 17922, 74-2 BCA ¶10682), "the government was aware that (the contractor) was deviating from the contract requirement for stainless steel in a manner that was determined to be patently unacceptable. In our opinion the government, under these circumstances, had a duty to inform (the contractor) of its erroneous course of action in a timely manner and the (contractor) is entitled to recover for the consequences of the government's failure to do so."[45] However, this case is an exception and the wise contractor will not rely on the owner's inspection program.

In the above example, the government was initially quiet about the improper work. In another case, the engineer specifically authorized improperly changed material and subsequently approved improper application of the materials, relieving the contractor of a suit for unworkman-like installation.[46]

Untimely inspection, inconsistent inspection, changed inspection systems, and increased paperwork requirements have all been held as constructive changes causing unnecessary interference with the contractor's work. Test requirements in excess of that required by the specifications, (e.g., increased frequency, different types of tests) are constructive changes, even if such tests show the work to be defective. Untimely inspection that delays the contractor may be considered a delay under the Suspension of Work clause (if the contract has such a clause).

However, the contractor cannot rely on inspection by the owner to absolve himself of any responsibility for defects that might have been observed by better inspection methods. In a case in which a derrick collapsed because the contractor used undersized bolts, the court rejected the contractor's contention that the bolts were a patent defect that should have been discovered by the government under its right to inspect: "Just because the material was subject to inspection and test did not impose upon the government the duty to conduct all-inclusive tests. The right to inspect does not

---

[44]*Granite Construction Co.* (ENGBCA No. 3561, 76-1 ¶11,748).
[45]*Hydrospace Electronics & Instrument Corp.*, ASBCA 17922, 74-2 BCA ¶10682.
[46]*Bechtold Paving, Inc. v. City of Kenmore*, 446 N.W.2d (N.D. 1989).

imply a duty to inspect. . . . It did not place any duty on the government to conduct such tests at the risk of assuming responsibility for the deficiencies which it might have discovered."[47]

4-8. CONCLUSION

Specification-related issues certainly rank as one of the leading causes of extra costs, delay, and disruption on construction projects. Putting together a complete set of contract drawings and specifications is not a simple task. It requires the coordination of several design disciplines, keeping current, and familiar with, the availability of building materials, keeping up with building technology, fitting a structure into a confined construction site, keeping up with the ever-changing needs of the construction owner, and, finally, meeting established budgets. Errors, omissions, miscues, and misunderstanding are to be expected to some degree, and dealing with these in the fairest way possible is the intent of the established rules of contract interpretation. Owners should spend the money necessary to get the best set of specifications possible. Designers should put in that extra effort to minimize errors and omissions, and contractors should show their interest in improved constructability by notifying owners of ambiguities or foreseeable problems in the contract documents.

---

[47]*Kammer Construction Co. v. U.S.*, 203 Ct. Cl. 182 (1973); also see *Appeal of Kelley Control Systems, Inc.*, VABCA No. 2,337 (July 24, 1987). (An interim inspection and approval did not relieve the contractor of the duty to conform to the specifications.)

CHAPTER 5

DELAYS AND ACCELERATIONS

5-1. INTRODUCTION

Delays, disruptions, and accelerations share a reputation with differing site conditions as the most recurring causes of contract problems. Strikes, adverse weather, third parties, contractor errors, change orders, and owner-directed suspensions—all can cause delay. These delays can be a few hours, or extend several years, and they almost always cause additional direct and indirect costs. Closely associated with delays are accelerations, for very often contractors must accelerate their work in order to make up for time lost to delays. We first look at the broad range of situations encompassed in the delay concept, how they are incurred, their effects and what to do about them. At the close of the chapter we discuss acceleration and the attendant conditions that can affect the success or failure of acceleration claims.

5-2. DELAYS—EXCUSABILITY AND COMPENSABILITY

Delays to the progress of a construction job fall into two basic classes—*excusable* and *nonexcusable*. Nonexcusable delays are those that are within the control of the contractor, are the result of the contractor's actions, or are due to the failure of the contractor to anticipate expected conditions, such as increased lost work days during the winter.

Excusable delays, or delays that are beyond the control of the contractor, entitle the contractor to extensions of contract time (unless specifically stated otherwise in the contract). Or, the contractor can be considered to have constructively accelerated if the time extensions are due but not granted. Furthermore, the contractor cannot be terminated for default or assessed liquidated damages for excusable delays.

Contract time extensions for excusable delays are either noncompensable or compensable. *Noncompensable delays*, or sometimes more familiarly known as excusable delays, are delays to the completion of the work arising from conditions beyond the control and without the fault or negligence of the contractor or owner. *Compensable delays* are delays, suspensions, or interruptions to all or part of the contract by an act or failure to act by the owner. The distinction between a noncompensable and compensable delay, aside from the preceding definitions, is that for a compensable delay, the contractor is entitled to an adjustment for any increase in cost to the performance of the contract.

5-3. NONCOMPENSABLE DELAYS

Noncompensable time extensions are provided for in the Federal Acquisition Regulations (FAR) *Default*[1] provision ¶52.249.10 (see Appendix 2) and similar provisions in the AIA A201 Standard Form Contract (1997, ¶8.3.1) (see Appendix 3) and Engineers' Joint Contract Documents Committee (EJCDC) Standard General Conditions (1996, Article 12.03 see Appendix 4). The FAR clause states that the contractor will not be terminated nor charged with damages for delays arising from "causes beyond the control and without the fault or negligence of the contractor." These include but are not restricted to

- Acts of God
- Acts of the public enemy
- Acts of the Government in its contractual capacity
- Acts of another contractor in the performance of a contract with the government
- Fires
- Floods
- Epidemics
- Quarantine restrictions
- Strikes
- Freight embargoes
- Unusually severe weather
- Delays of subcontractors or suppliers at any tier arising from causes other than normal weather beyond the control and without the fault or negligence of both the Contractor and such sub-contractors or suppliers

---

[1] Formerly "Termination for Default—Damages for Delay—Time Extensions" clause of the Standard Form 23-A.

5-4. NONEXCUSABLE DELAYS

Nonexcusable delays are delays to the performance of the work for which the contractor is entitled to neither time extensions nor extra costs. This includes delays that are directly caused by and/or the result of the contractor's, his subcontractors', and/or suppliers' actions; or due to external, foreseeable factors such as weather. For example, delays attributable to underestimates of production rates, inadequate scheduling or management, construction mistakes, equipment breakdowns or just plain bad luck.

Other examples of nonexcusable delays include

- Ordinary and usual weather conditions
- Delays to start-up and mobilization activities
- Failure to procure permits in a timely fashion
- Failure to plan activities in anticipation of, and to avoid, bad weather
- Failure to manage, coordinate, and schedule the project
- Lack of adequate working capital for purchase of supplies and/or equipment
- Delays in submission of shop drawings
- Delays in purchase, fabrication, and/or delivery of materials
- Poor workmanship, causing rework or delaying follow-on work
- Delays by subcontractors
- Ordinary and foreseeable weather conditions

Such delays are not only burdensome in terms of increased overhead and direct costs, but may result in the contractor's termination for default or the assessment of liquidated damages. The contractor's number one priority, and contractual obligation, to the extent that it is under his control, is to keep the project on schedule.

5-5. COMPENSABLE TIME EXTENSIONS

In government contracts, compensable time extensions can arise from either (1) the Changes and Differing Site Conditions clauses; or (2) the Suspension of Work clause. When a time extension is granted under the first case, the contractor is entitled to direct costs of the change or changed condition plus indirect costs (overhead) and profit for the extended period. However the indirect cost is limited by the pricing requirements of the contract. Some contracts may allow overhead at a fixed percentage of the direct cost[2] while others allow all overhead attributable, and traceable, to the change.

---

[2]*Sante Fe Engineers, Inc. v. U.S.*, 801 F.2d 379 (Fed. Cir. 1986); see also *Reliance Insurance Company v. U.S.*, 20 Cl. Ct. 715 (1990).

A time extension granted under the Changes or Differing Site Conditions clauses is not considered a delay or suspension of work as defined by the Suspension of Work clause in government contracts. Contract modifications for change orders that included time extensions fall into this category. Time extensions due to delays and suspensions are considered compensable delays and are discussed in the next section.

5-6. COMPENSABLE DELAYS

Compensable delays are delays to the performance of the contract and are governed generally by the Suspension of Work clause, which provides for an equitable adjustment to the contract (excluding profit). "If the performance of all or any part of the work is, for an unreasonable period of time, suspended, delayed, or interrupted (1) by an act of the Contracting Officer in the administration of this contract, or (2) by the Contracting Officer's failure to act within the time specified in this contract (or within a reasonable time if not specified)" (see Appendix 2-52.242.14 for entire clause).

Similar provisions in the AIA A201 Standard Form Contract (1987, ¶8.3) and EJCDC Standard General Conditions (1996, Article 12) also provide for recovery of costs. AIA A201, ¶8.3.3 states, "This Paragraph 8.3 does not preclude recovery of damages for delay by either party under other provisions of the Contract Document." (See Appendix 3.) The EJCDC ¶12.06 Delay Damages states "B. Nothing in this paragraph 12.06 bars a change in Contract Price pursuant to this Article 12 to compensate CONTRACTOR due to delay, interference, or disruption directly attributable to actions or inactions of OWNER or anyone for whom OWNER is responsible." (See Appendix 4.)

Such delays are not restricted simply to stop orders issued by the owner or directives to work on a different schedule or sequence. The owner is liable for his actions and inactions that result in unreasonably delaying or disrupting the contractor. According to the seminar textbook published by scheduling expert A. James Waldron

> There is an implied obligation on the part of the owner not to delay, interfere with or hinder the contractor's performance of his contract, Thus, liability for delays and interferences, and the additional costs arising therefrom, has been imposed upon the government or owner in situations where the owner:
>
> a. Fails to properly and timely perform certain work which necessarily precedes the work of the contractor;
> b. Interferes with the contractor's schedule and orders him to

proceed under conditions (e.g., inclement weather) which he felt precluded his satisfactory performance;
c. Supplies erroneous information, not patently or obviously erroneous, which misleads and disrupts the contractor in his performance;
d. Fails to disclose information necessary to satisfactory performance, or to provide models necessary for the contractor's performance;
e. Fails to provide timely inspections of completed work;
f. Improperly assumes the direction or execution of field operations, which are the responsibility of the contractor;
g. Requires the contractor to perform by one particular method when the contract does not specify any particular method;
h. Acts in an arbitrary or unreasonable manner; or
i. Otherwise unreasonably delays the contractor, that is, causes delays which could reasonably have been avoided.[3]

Furthermore, the Waldron textbook says

The owner has an implied obligation to cooperate with the contractor in the performance of his work. This includes the affirmative duty to do whatever is necessary to enable the contractor to perform his contractual obligations. An owner has been held to have breached this warranty in situations where he has:

a. Failed to provide timely inspection of completed work;
b. Failed to provide inspectors for field tests conducted in accordance with contract requirements;
c. Failed to approve of required shop or production drawings within a reasonable time; and
d. Failed to approve change orders within a reasonable time, for errors or omissions in specifications found by the contractor. Thus, in a case where the contractor's sequence of operations was "completely dislocated" and increased time and expense were incurred because the Government failed to act within a reasonable time on his request for a change order to correct deficient specifications, the Government was held to have breached its implied duty to cooperate and recovery was permitted for the additional costs.[4]

---

[3]Waldron, James A., Publisher, *The Legal Implications of a Project Schedule* (Haddonfield, N.J., 1974), pp. III-86–III-87.
[4]Ibid.

5-7. UNREASONABLE DELAYS

In issuing changes and making decisions, it is not unreasonable for the owner to consume a short period of time to process the change or to assure himself of the correctness of the decision. The contractor should expect some periods of time where he might halt work in a specific area while changes are being made, just as he expects bad weather, holidays, absenteeism, and strikes. However, the extent of each change can be expected *not* to be for an unreasonable amount of time. In the appeal of *Royal Painting Co., Inc.*, the Board said that "it did not consider it unreasonable for (the contractor) to have sought an authoritative decision on the point (in question) and to delay its work on the specified area pending a decision. . . . (However) it was unreasonable for the government to take eight days to furnish its decision. One day appears to have been enough time under the circumstances."[5]

Since the Suspension of Work clause provides for a contract adjustment for "any increase in the cost of performance of this contract (excluding profit) necessarily caused by the unreasonable suspension, delay or interruption," the contractor must show that he did incur a delay and that the delay was unreasonable. However, when the contractor experiences delay resulting from changes that are necessitated by defective plans and specifications, he would not have "to prove the delay unreasonable, since all delay due to defective or erroneous specifications are per se unreasonable and hence compensable.[6]

5-8. DELAYS—SITE ACCESS

Site availability has often been a source of contention in construction contracts, the issue centering around the owner's knowledge of, and responsibility for, the readiness of the site for construction. It is commonly recognized that delay in access to the jobsite is an excusable delay (under the FAR Default clause), even if the contractor can make an educated guess that the site won't be ready in time when the job is bid. Time and again, however, the contractor tries to claim for extra cost on a Suspension of Work claim, despite contract provisions that provide otherwise. This situation usually results from dependency on a prior contractor to finish his work, and contract disclaimers that the owner will not be responsible for the prior contractor's late performance. As in the *Gilbane Building Co.* case[7], the court

---

[5]*Royal Painting Co., Inc.*, ASBCA 20034, 75-1 BCA ¶11,311; also see *Appeal of M.I.T. Alaska*, PSBCA No. 1348 (Sept. 3, 1986). (A one-week suspension of work was reasonable under the circumstances, but a second week became compensable.)

[6]*Chaney & James Construction Company v. U.S.*, 190 Ct. Cl. 699 (1970).

[7]*Gilbane Building Co. v. U.S.*, 166 Ct. Cl. 347 (1964); also see *Appeal of H. A. Kaufman Co.*, GSBCA No. 10687 (Dec. 20, 1990). (Government expressly disclaimed obligation to provide unimpeded site access.)

relieved the government of fault for such late performance and subsequent delayed access, pointing out that

1. The contract did not warrant the availability of the site.
2. Although the contract contained a representation that the site would be available on a certain date, other provisions in the contract and specifications show that there was a possibility the site might not be available on the date specified.
3. The contract expressly provided that delays caused by acts of another contractor in the performance of a contract with the government would entitle the contractor to an extension of time only.

When the owner does specifically guarantee that the site will be available, his fault (and liability for extra costs) is limited to the extent that (1) the owner was at fault for the prior contractor's delay; or (2) the owner had clear knowledge the site would not be available.

An example of the first case is the Court of Claims case of *Koppers/Clough*, where the court found that: "The mere existence of past delay does not automatically yield a presumption of future delay, or deny that the past delay will be made up by acceleration in the future. Nor would the openness of the existing delay negate a representation that the government had not been and would not in the future be at fault."[8] The significance of this case occurs where the contract promised the availability of a pier for a materials unloading site, and, although it was apparently going to be incomplete at the time specified, the contractor relied on the representations by the contract documents that it would be ready and available for use on a certain date specified in the contract. The court goes further to limiting the government's liability for the extra costs due to the site's unavailability to only the portion of the pier construction delay due to the government fault, and not the portion beyond the government's control.

A more recent case, involving the owner's prior *knowledge* of the lack of access to the jobsite is the *Head* case before the Board of Contract Appeals. The board, in ruling that suspension of work had occurred, stated that the owner's "Issuance of a notice to proceed . . . before the necessary authority and clearances were in hand as premature and imprudent. . . . [The owner] is chargeable with the knowledge that such clearances were required and cannot now be permitted to escape the consequences of its own neglect in obtaining those clearances."[9]

---

[8]*Koppers/Clough, a Joint Venture v. U.S.*, 201 Ct. Cl. 344 (1973).
[9]*Head Construction Company* ENG BCA 3537, 77-1 BCA ¶12,226; also see *J. A. Tobin Construction Co. v. State Highway, Commission of Missouri*, 680 S.W.2d 183 (Mo.App. 1984). (Owner issued notice to proceed without first relocating utility lines.)

What we have in both the above cases is sometimes more commonly known as a "third party" delay. In most cases, if the delay can be reasonably foreseen by the contractor, and it is without the fault or negligence of the owner, it is not considered a suspension of work but is considered to be an excusable delay. If, however, the reason for the third party delay is for the owner's advantage and convenience in administering the project, or within the owner's control, it may be considered a constructive suspension of work.[10] This principle may be applied not only to initial access delays, but to delays during the course of the project as well.

5-9. CONCURRENT DELAYS

The FAR Suspension of Work clause (¶52.242-14) states that "no adjustment shall be made under this clause for any suspension, delay, or interruption to the extent that performance would have been so suspended, delayed, or interrupted by any other cause, including the fault or negligence of the contractor." This clause, along with the provisions for time extensions in the Default clause, leads to the "concurrent delay" position now recognized by most boards and courts. This position provides for the offsetting effect of a delay suffered by a contractor (due to the owner) by the amount of delay that would have been incurred anyway by the contractor during the same period. For example, if an owner issues a stop work order for a five-week period for the processing of a change order, and during that five-week period the contractor incurs a three-week strike, the owner is only liable for suspension costs for the two weeks of effective delay that was solely the owner's responsibility. Note, it must still be shown that the job would have concurrently incurred three weeks of delay due to the strike, absent the five-week stop order.

The reverse also holds. That is, the contractor cannot be assessed liquidated damages for late completion if during all or part of the period, events took place that would also have delayed the contract and that were beyond the control of the contractor. For example, a contractor has to stop work on a critical item while waiting for material that had been delivered late (clearly within the contractor's control). After the third week, a strike occurred that lasted for four more weeks. The contractor subsequently finished the job 10 weeks late but can only be assessed liquidated damages for six of the 10 weeks, even though the start and finish of the delay period was due to the

---

[10] *John A. Johnson & Sons v. U.S., (12* CCF ¶81,196), 180 Ct. Cl. 969 990; also see *Appeal of C & C Plumbing and Heating,* ASBCA No. 44270 (July 29, 1994). (Government's failure to coordinate with separate asbestos abatement contractor resulted in a constructive suspension of work.)

DELAYS AND ACCELERATIONS   59

contractor's actions. In another case, (Driscoll 1971),[11] a cabling contractor was denied original site access while the prime contractor completed certain work. When the government found that the cable did not arrive until several weeks after the initial suspension was lifted, the contractor was granted a time extension only, as it was aware that a concurrent delay was in effect. Concurrent delays are discussed further in Chapter 7. Project Schedules and the Critical Path Method (CPM).

5-10. PROVING DELAY AND DELAY COSTS

5-10a. Disruption, Loss of Efficiency, and Loss of Learning Curve

Costs of delays and disruptions must be traced directly to the claimed delays in a clear cause and effect relationship. Delay costs, such as loss of efficiency due to stop and go situations, rescheduling, and disruption to learning curves are allowable as long as the extra costs can be clearly shown to have resulted from the delay. In *Bliss*,[12] while the court recognized learning curve costs, the contractor did not establish a causal connection between the changes and the amount claimed as learning curve effect. Disruptions to learning curves are valid claimable items but difficult to prove. The contractor should demonstrate that the repetitive nature of the task has been diminished, preventing increased productivity.

5.-10b. Out-of-Sequence Work

In addition to proving delays, critical path method (CPM) schedules can be effectively used to demonstrate the repetitive nature of the work requirements as well as the impact any change has had on the planned sequence of operations. In some cases, such as production interruptions or variations due to a defective specification, "The boards and courts have recognized that when new techniques are required because of design deficiencies, and the contractor cannot follow the sequences originally contemplated, then the extra costs resulting from a loss of expected learning curve are compensable."[13]

5-10c. Ripple Effect

It is not infrequent that, on a job with many changes, the contractor, at the end of the job, is in a loss position and submits claims for the total impact of the changes. Such claims are usually denied because the impacts and delays are not traceable to specific causes. In denying one such claim for the

---

[11]Thomas J. Driscoll, "Claims," in *Contractors Management Handbook* ed. James J. O'Brien and R. G. Zilly (New York, McGraw-Hill, 1971), p. 16-6.
[12]*E. W. Bliss Co.*, ASBCA 9489, 68-1 BCA ¶6906.
[13]*Hicks Corp.*, ASBCA 10760, 66-1 BCA ¶5469.

"ripple effect" of a large number of change orders, the board said, "The appellant's contention that the number of change orders had an adverse effect without showing what the impact was fails for lack of proof."[14]

The contractor can recover for additional *direct costs* of changes, such as ripple effect not apparent during negotiations of change orders, as long as he has specifically reserved his rights to do so.[15] But the contractor cannot claim additional indirect costs not provided for in the contract (also *Briscoe*).[16] In *C.A. Fielland*,[17] the contractor attempted to recover overhead costs under the Suspension of Work clause by arguing that time extensions granted by the government (under the Changes clause) were in effect delays or suspensions of work caused by the government. In denying the claim, the court said that the contractor "has not cited any case where a contractor has been paid for materials, labor, the applicable percentages, and granted time extensions for performance of a change order pursuant to the (Changes) clause . . . and then further reimbursed for delay costs under . . . (the Suspension of Work clause)."[18] (See section 5-5.)

5-10d. Delays Due to Differing Site Conditions

Where delays are incurred due to differing site conditions, extra costs, time, *and* profit can be recovered. In an excavation contract, where the government's 41% underestimate of unclassified excavation delayed the contract 138 days, the U.S. Claims Court held the contractor was entitled to compensation, above and beyond payment received for the modified unit price negotiated to cover the extra quantities.[19] This case is interesting as it additionally illustrates the following occurrences:

- Extra work pushing follow-on work into winter weather delays
- A contract being completed within the original time period plus noncompensable time extension for weather (e.g., the contractor successfully demonstrated early completion would have been achieved but for the government delay)
- The court not being impressed by improper and unsupported CPM analysis

---

[14]*Harrod & Williams, Inc.*, DOT BCA 72-10, 73-2 BCA ¶10,266; also see *Vanlar Construction, Inc. v. County of Los Angeles*, 217 Cal.Rptr. 53 (Cal.App. 1985). (Change order language waived contractors right to recover indirect impact costs allegedly resulting from 81 change orders.)

[15]*Frank Briscoe Company, Inc.*, GSBCA 3330, 72-2 BCA ¶9714; also see *Appeal of Hibbitts Construction Co., Inc.*, ASBCA No. 37070 (Jan. 4, 1990). (Parties never discussed or considered indirect costs, so a general release did not waive the contractor's right to claim those costs.)

[16]Ibid.

[17]*C.A. Fielland, Inc.* GSBCA 2903, 71-1 BCA ¶8734.

[18]Ibid.

[19]*Weaver-Bailey Contractors, Inc. v. U.S.*, 19 Cl.Ct. 474 (1990).

DELAYS AND ACCELERATIONS

5-11. NO DAMAGE FOR DELAY CLAUSES

A no damage for delay clause specifies that the contractor is not entitled to any compensation for delays caused by the owner. They are generally enforceable but usually fail in the face of defective specifications, interference, disruption, and other unreasonable and/or unforeseeable events, but are still used in some private construction contracts. Enforcement varies from state to state.

5-12. THREE TYPES OF ACCELERATION

Acceleration is an action taken by the contractor in order to speed up the progress on a job to accomplish early completion or to make up for lost time. The contractor can accelerate (1) voluntarily; (2) constructively; or (3) pursuant to a directive by the owner.

Voluntary and directed acceleration are fairly obvious. The contractor, at his own initiative, makes efforts to overcome his own delays and/or to complete activities earlier than planned. Directed, or ordered, acceleration occurs when the owner explicitly directs the contractor to accelerate the work. In all cases of acceleration, the contractor makes a reasonable attempt to accelerate and incurs additional expenses.

Constructive acceleration is acceleration of activities by the contractor to finish the job according to the planned schedule where excusable delays have occurred but no time extensions have been granted.

5-13. CONSTRUCTIVE ACCELERATION

5-13a. Directive Not Required

It is not necessary for the owner to direct the contractor to accelerate. Constructive acceleration occurs when the contractor is *induced* by the actions of the owner to complete the work in accordance with schedules not updated to include all time extensions for excusable delays. This doctrine is stated in *Continental Consolidated Corporation v. U.S.*:

> The absence of a written directive to accelerate is not fatal to a claim of constructive change based on acceleration. The principle enunciated is that government actions which require the contractor to complete in accordance with a progress schedule not updated to include all claims for excusable delays then outstanding

is a constructive change for which the contractor is entitled to an equitable adjustment under . . . the contract."[20]

5-13b. Notice, Request for Time Extension

In the *Continental* case the court also pointed out that the contractor did not have to file a formal claim for the time extension but only that the owner has to have "actual or constructive knowledge of the delay.[21] However, because the owner may not know of a delay, the contractor should be certain to notify the owner not only of all delays, but of any action on the owner's part that the contractor considers an acceleration order. By such action, the owner will be warned of the extra costs and have a chance to take alternative action, as well as to document the fact that the contractor is not doing the accelerated work voluntarily. A request for information concerning acceleration cannot be treated as a request to accelerate, as established by *A. Teichert & Son*, "A request that appellant submit a plan how lost time can be regained or further loss of time avoided . . . was not an order by the contracting officer or his representative to accelerate the work."[22]

Surrounding circumstances, however, can occasionally transform a request to a directive. In a case where the resident engineer requested the prime contractor to speed up its work, the government claimed that the contractor voluntarily complied because it was in the mutual interest of both parties not to extend the work into winter. Not so, said the board, "We are unable to see any difference between a request and an order under the circumstances. The initiative came from the government for the government's convenience. It makes no difference whether (the contractor) complied willingly or unwillingly, or whether or not it also benefited from the compliance."[23]

5-13c. Explicit Denial of Time Extension Not Required

As stated earlier, the clear cut case of constructive acceleration exists where a time extension is requested by the contractor and refused by the owner, who requests the contractor to adhere to the original schedule. However, failure to request the time extensions and/or failure of the owner to

---

[20]*Continental Consolidated Corp.*, Ct. Cl., 214–69, 17 CCF ¶81,1137; also see *Mobil Chemical Co. v. Blount Brothers Corp.*, 809 F.2d 1175 (5th Cir. 1987). (Project owner and construction manager share liability for directing trade contractors to add crews and work overtime.)
[21]Ibid.
[22]*A. Teichert & Son, Inc.*, ASBCA 10265, et. al., 68-2 BCA ¶1175; also see *Appeal of Donald R. Stewart & Associates*, AGBCA No. 89-222-1 (Jan. 16, 1992). (A government directive to stay on schedule did not give rise to a claim for constructive acceleration.)
[23]*Hyde Construction Co.*, ASBCA 8393, 1963 BCA ¶3911.

DELAYS AND ACCELERATIONS

deny the requested time extensions will not necessarily defeat a claim for constructive acceleration. In the *Electronic and Missile Facilities*[24] decision, the board recognized an acceleration claim, not on the owner's refusal to act on the time extension request, but on the owner's actions, which impelled the contractor to accelerate the work (no formal requests to adhere to the original schedule or to accelerate had been issued). In *Sylvania Electric Products, Inc.* the board said that the contractor "should not be barred from . . . adjustment . . . merely because of the absence, technically, of an outright request and refusal for prime contract time extension."[25]

It is also important to note here that in a constructive acceleration situation, a claim for equitable adjustment for additional moneys will not be defeated where an original request for time extension was rejected but later granted (subsequent to the intervening accelerated effort).[26] For example, in a disputed constructive acceleration situation where a contractor was entitled to a 200-day time extension but finished the contract 150 days late, there were 50 days of time recovered through constructive acceleration.

5-13d. Identification

Cuneo and Ackerly have listed the following guidelines to use in determining whether or not an accelerated effort was undertaken for the owner's benefit and with his participation:

1. Knowledge on the part of the government (either constructive or actual) that excusable delays have occurred
2. Government activities that urge, importune, or implicitly require the contractor to speed up work
3. Knowledge on the part of both parties that completion dates are firm
4. The existence (and promptness) of notifications to the contracting officer that excusable delays have been incurred and requests for schedule extensions will be based thereon
5. Government delays in responding to the notice and requests mentioned in item 4 and denials of those requests
6. The existence of numerous or extensive changes to the contract work without concurrent extensions of time for performance.[27]

---

[24]*Electronic & Missile Facilities*, ASBCA 9031, 1964 BCA ¶4338.

[25]*Sylvania Electric Products, Inc.*, ASBCA 11206, 67-2 BCA ¶6428.

[26]*Brock & Blevins Co. v. U.S.*, 170 Ct. Cl. 52 (1965); also see *Appeal of Blake Construction Co., Inc.*, ASBCA No. 39937 (July 24, 1990). (Failure to grant an appropriate time extension was a constructive acceleration of the schedule.)

[27]Gilbert A. Cuneo and Robert L. Ackerly "Acceleration." *Government Contracts Monograph No. 9* (Published by the Government Contracts Program, the George Washington University, 1975), pp. 62, 63.

More simply put, constructive acceleration occurs when

1. Excusable delays occur that (would have) entitled the contractor to time extensions.
2. The owner was notified of the delay and a time extension was requested.
3. The owner failed or refused to grant the time extension and required completion by original completion dates.

5-14. PROVING DELAYS, TIME EXTENSIONS, AND ACCELERATION

Schedule analysis is the method of choice in proving delays and requesting time extensions, and is routinely recognized by boards and courts. Schedules should be accurate, complete, and regularly updated.

In government contracts, ongoing schedule analysis is used to measure contractor performance and to determine when time extensions and/or acceleration are required. In the Schedules for Construction Contracts clause, "If the Contractor falls behind the approved schedule, the Contractor shall take steps necessary to improve its progress, including those that may be required by the Contracting Officer, without additional cost to the Government. In this circumstance, the Contracting Officer may require the Contractor to increase the number of shifts, overtime operation, days of work, and/or the amount of construction plant, and to submit for approval any supplementary schedule or schedules in chart form as the Contracting Officer deems necessary to demonstrate how the approved rate of progress will be regained."[28] Detailed methodology for schedule analysis is discussed in chapter 7.

5-15. ACCELERATION COSTS

Pricing of acceleration claims follows the same general pattern used to price delay claims as discussed earlier in this chapter, that is, determining the additional direct and indirect costs incurred or to be incurred over the performance period, including resequencing, rescheduling, and other impacts that arise out of the accelerated effort. The type of costs most peculiar to acceleration claims are

1. Additional labor, equipment, material (purchase and/or delivery), supervision, and overhead
2. Reduced efficiency due to increased manpower

---

[28]FAR 52.236-15 (b.)

DELAYS AND ACCELERATIONS 65

3. Disruption of schedules designed for optimum equipment, manpower, and overhead utilization
4. Overtime (and accompanying inefficiencies) and premium time
5. Stacking of trades

Inefficiency costs are computed by comparison of unit costs with acceleration to unit costs without acceleration, One method sometimes used to price inefficiencies, especially for forward priced claims, is by implementing statistical data such as that published by the Bureau of Labor Statistics. Appendix 7 lists several references on overtime effects, including a chart from the Bureau of Labor Statistics report 917, which shows various efficiency losses for different combinations of overtime hours.

5-16. CONCLUSION

Delays and suspensions produce extra costs on a job. Many delay and suspension problems, although real, are ambiguous and difficult to isolate, clarify, and quantify. But any construction supervisor who is thoroughly familiar with the project using a CPM and other job planning data can effectively outline the causes and results of delays and their accompanying costs. These kinds of data are helpful at the notification stage and are imperative in the proposal and negotiation stages. On large jobs, multiple delays of minor and major proportions are commonplace, and the resultant costs can rapidly grow over budget. The temptation is to ignore the minor items and to figure them as relatively insignificant. If the contractor desires not to send notice on each and every item he encounters, he should still keep accurate and detailed records, and, in some situations, combine them periodically into larger, more substantial claims. Additionally, when the contractor considers an acceleration effort, either voluntary or directed, he should accelerate only those items of work that are critical to contract completion.

CHAPTER 6

RECORDS AND DOCUMENTATION

6-1. INTRODUCTION

Records and documentation play probably the most significant role in the successful settlement of contract claims. The daily events and details of the job must be documented to substantiate claims and prove damages. Facts must be recorded and preserved. Armed with a carefully prepared claims package of facts and figures, the contractor can support his position and propel negotiations toward a favorable settlement.

But all too often, contractors do not keep good records. Procedures may be set up properly and files may be stuffed with documents, but frequently the details of daily events are inadequate or not readily accessible, if available at all. This is understandable, as most construction personnel are more concerned with doing work than with keeping records, but it is also potentially damaging. Conversely, the owner or its representative, having more time available for administrative tasks, is more likely to keep records and to be better prepared to defend against claims.

6-2. TYPES OF RECORDS

The different types of records that should be kept in the daily conduct of business include time cards, payrolls, material receipts, purchase orders, invoices, cash flows, quantity takeoffs, correspondence, forecasts, schedules, and computer cost reports. Maintaining good records is not only plain good business, it is an absolute necessity when it comes time to price changes and claims. How can one price changed work if the cost of doing contract work is unknown? It is very important to keep accurate records of costs for equipment, overhead, direct cost items, and work orders. The more closely one keeps direct costs associated with specific work items, the easier

RECORDS AND DOCUMENTATION 67

it is to use such information and the more valid it becomes. If the contractor combines too many costs into one account, the data become meaningless.

6-3. TIME CARDS

The time card, which usually serves as the basis for the job payroll, is the basic document for recording hourly progress of job labor and equipment. It establishes where individuals worked and what they did on any given day. It establishes the number of hours worked overtime and documents when two or more items of work were performed on any given day. Additionally, the time card can be used to record daily production for each item worked. The time card also serves as a means for the foreman to record daily occurrences, such as unusual site conditions, weather, delays, accidents, safety aspects, subcontractor problems, and other current or potential problems. Time cards are usually prepared at the foreman level and then later reviewed by supervisory and administrative personnel.

6-4. COST ACCOUNT SYSTEM

The job cost account system, which serves as the basis for cost coding of time cards, should follow the original estimate. That is, assuming the estimate was made in sufficient detail, the cost coding breakdown should bear some resemblance in format to the system used in the bid estimate. Bad bids excluded, this method is a good gauge to compare job progress with budget and additionally serves as a basis of comparison for claims. Because the bid estimate is only an estimate, contracting agencies are hesitant to use the bid estimate as a base for evaluating extra costs, but under extreme circumstances it may be the only reasonable method available. With delays, suspensions, and accelerations, very intricate analyses of efficiency rates, overhead, and equipment costs must be prepared before contracting agencies or jurisdictional bodies will award equitable adjustments. Such awards are usually based on one of the following methods of comparison of costs:

1. Actual cost to perform compared to the original bid estimated cost to perform
2. Actual cost to perform compared to a "reasonable" estimated cost to perform
3. Actual cost to perform compared to actual cost of identical work performed under normal conditions

Keeping these methods in mind, the contractor will want to establish a record- and cost-keeping program that allows ready implementation of any or all of these methods.

6-5. PRODUCTION RATES

To demonstrate actual costs it is not enough to produce unit costs or production rates from computer reports. Contracting agencies require detailed documentation that show actual crew sizes and equipment. The valid documentation of production rates and job progress, as well as a descriptive narrative showing cause/effect relationships between changed conditions and extra costs, also are needed. So it is very important to have detailed and accurate records as well as production rates. When a contractor's records prove he was capable of pouring 250 cubic yards of concrete daily, this data will work wonders when he must claim extra costs to show that, due to a changed condition, he could only pour 100 cubic yards, or that it took triple the resources to achieve these production rates to counter the effect of a changed condition.

6-6. MATERIAL RECEIPTS

It is important to have detailed records of all material transactions. The contractor must be able to prove that he made timely procurement of permanent materials and equipment as well as temporary construction materials, that he kept inventory of materials, and that he took all steps within his control to keep material delays to a minimum, thus avoiding unnecessary delays and potential price escalations. These material records, including purchase orders and invoices, are required to verify escalation costs and are necessary to establish proof that the contractor did not cause delays due to failure to have material on time. These records also serve as the basis on which escalation determinations are made and the amounts that will be allowed.

6-7. SCHEDULES

Scheduling techniques such as the critical path method are often routinely required in many of today's contracts. The primary value of schedules for claims use is as a tool to prove or disprove job schedule changes and delays. The importance and techniques of schedules is fully discussed in chapter 7.

6-8. CASH FLOWS

When the project is in the bidding or planning stage the contractor will chart projected cash flows for the purpose of computing his financing needs. The revenues and costs expended are tied in with the contractor's scheduled progress, balancing (unbalancing) of bid items, and the restraints of the

RECORDS AND DOCUMENTATION

contract schedule. Financing costs are real, and when related to changes in the job cash flow due to unreasonable owner delay, they may be recovered when properly documented and verified (for example-interest paid to a bank).[1]

6-9. CORRESPONDENCE AND TRANSMITTAL LOGS

It is a good idea for the contractor to keep up-to-date logs of all correspondence and drawing transmittals. The logs should have a brief description of the contents of each piece of correspondence or transmittal. This allows the contractor easy access to a specific item and the opportunity to pinpoint quickly items that are lagging in response or need action. The logs also can serve as references when preparing new correspondence. Logs come in most handy, however, when the contractor must show a sequence of events and demonstrate how actions (or inactions) on the part of the owner played a significant part in a delay or changed condition. This information is, of course, in the contractor's files and can be researched when needed for further detail. But the speed and convenience of having the information summarized in a log pays off when the contractor must periodically prod the owner to process shop drawings, approvals, change orders, and claims on a prompt basis.

6-10. COMPUTER (COST) REPORTS

Computerization of job cost records, especially on large projects, is essential if the contractor is to have a quick and thorough measure of the progress of his efforts and costs. Depending on the format, computer reports may or may not be used to substantiate records, but the real value for claims is to provide the contractor with a large volume of statistical data. The contractor can use this data in preparing a claim and in determining the best approach to take in computing the cost of the claim. Computer printouts can quickly show, for example, when the best unit costs have been achieved, the highest volumes achieved, and the maximum overhead spent. By studying the costs and patterns from the computer reports, the contractor can select the information best suited to benefit a claim and then concentrate effort in that area. Computer printouts also make it easier to compile data on work-hours and wage rates when there are labor escalation dollars involved.

---

[1]See *Keco Industries, Inc.*, ASBCA 15181, 15,547, 72-1 ¶ 9576; *Keco Industries, Inc.*, ASBCA 15131, 72-1 ¶ 9262, and *Sun Electric Corporation*, ASBCA 13031, 70-2 ¶ 8371; also see *Servidone Construction Corp. v. U.S.*, 931 F.2d 860 (Fed.Cir. 1991). (Contractor entitled to recover interest paid on funds borrowed to perform changed work where there was proper documentation and segregation of the funds.)

The information in the computer, however, must be accurate to be of any use for gauging progress or processing claims.

6-11. DAILY REPORTS

Daily reports, including diaries, production records, and general job progress reports, are the most important records available to document events or demonstrate adverse job conditions. Michael S. Simon, a New York attorney and author of legal reviews for *Engineering News-Record*, says, "I need to know what happened, when it happened, why it happened, who caused it to happen, and what we did about it. I need to know all of this on a daily basis. As your legal counsel, I must say that no single document is more important than your daily reports. The reports are often crucial to the outcome in negotiations or in court. Write true and complete daily reports. No one expects a job without problems. It's essential to write down all the facts that exist."[2]

Supervisors, superintendents, project engineers, and project managers should keep daily diaries, recording such information as where they worked, what and how much done, instructions from inspectors, visitors to job, unusual conditions, work done by subcontractors, delays encountered, and extra work. The project engineer or project manager should receive a copy of all diaries for compilation into one daily summary report, in case of claims as well as to keep himself informed of important events in the field.

In addition to their value as an information source for upper management, daily production records are very important for claims as they lend credibility to the statistics in computer reports. The costs that go into the computer via time cards and invoices should be recorded against production accomplished contemporaneously in order to generate accurate unit costs for the work done. It is usually advisable to devise special reporting procedures and forms to insure that production is recorded daily and accurately. One example of such a form is that used to record track-work production on rapid transit rail systems, shown in Appendix 8. Also shown in Appendix 8 is a copy of a form used to demonstrate the disruptive effect of extra work and interference on the track-work contractor for the project. This form was used to compile excerpts of problems from the different diaries of the supervisors and the project engineer. It helps greatly to substantiate the cost effects of reduced efficiency on the project.

6-12. PHOTOGRAPHS

Photographs provide one of the best, if not *the* best, record of job progress. It is never more true than in construction that one picture is worth

[2]Michael S. Simon, "The Importance of Proper Daily Reports," *Constructor*, December, 1976 (Washington, D C., Associated General Contractors of America), p. 16.

RECORDS AND DOCUMENTATION 71

a thousand words. The contractor should endeavor to regularly take pictures, with dates and captions, of representative samples of job progress, preferably each week. The photographs should be kept in albums and the negatives safely stored. Such photographs will frequently assist in substantiating events as well as help describe construction activities to those not familiar with the project.

In a claims situation, photographs can be used to verify the existence of prior or changed conditions, to describe characteristics of the worksite under different conditions, and to present a factual recording of methods and equipment employed to accomplish different items of work. Pictures can also be used to show cause and effect relationships of changes as well as to demonstrate the type of extra costs involved. For example, a picture can show how an added structure to a contract caused the necessity of rerouting access roads to another portion of the job through other contractor operations and a swampy area not originally anticipated (and not shown on the contract drawings).

A number of recent developments in photography and computers can aid in the preservation of events during the progress of the job. These include

- **Video cameras**—inexpensive handheld video cameras can be used to record job progress and easily allow spoken narrative describing highlights of the photography sessions. There are also devices that allow transfer of both video clips or single "frames" into personal computer databases.
- **Digital photography**—use of digital cameras to transfer still photos directly from the camera to a computer. Some digital cameras will also capture voice descriptions. Both conventional and digital cameras are capable of stamping time and date on the photos.
- **Scanners**—inexpensive devices for personal computers allow scanning of documents and photos into computer databases or word processing documents.

All of these technological developments, properly used, can help create a fully documented photographic history of the project. Use of such histories will greatly aid in eliminating disagreements of facts concerning past events, allowing the parties to focus on entitlement and pricing issues.

6-13. SPECIAL FORMS FOR CLAIMS AND CHANGE ORDER RECORDS

The contractor should have a change order initiation form (COI) for each change or potential claim encountered, and should immediately complete the form upon observance of the change or claim situation. The COI should be used to record all important historical events of the change order, including pertinent dates—the date each situation is observed, date of information requests, dates work is performed, date notice is given, and date(s) of negotiations. The COI also indicates the nature of the claim and type of extra work performed, potential costs and impacts, evaluation of effect on subcontractors, pertinent points on negotiations and conditions of settlement, and any other information relevant to the change order. (A sample COI form is included in Appendix 9.) It is important to have an accurate history of each change so as to successfully resolve each change order in the face of fading memories, changing personnel, and an increasing pile of job administrative records.

A separate file should be kept for each change, with a copy of the initiation form, pertinent correspondence, associated invoices and time cards, memos-to-file, and any other items relevant to the change order or claim. It is also advisable to keep a separate folder exclusively for copies of all initiation forms. This will serve as a handy reference when making periodic reviews of the status of job claims and change orders.

In order to keep the owner informed of the status of unresolved change orders, a claims & change order monthly status report should be submitted. The purpose of such a report is to show the owner/engineer which items are still in progress, which are awaiting the engineer's action, which are ready to be negotiated, and which are negotiated and awaiting formal modification. (A sample of this form is included in Appendix 10 along with a sample cover letter.)

Graphs and charts also come in handy in analyzing and substantiating claims. Cash-flow charts, partial payment charts, contract work-hour charts, productivity measurement charts, extra work order work-hour charts, and job progress charts (actual versus planned) are some of the more common charts that have proven valuable. Such charts, usually plotted against time, serve as indicators of overall job impact of the disruptive effect of suspensions, accelerations, and multiple change orders. These charts and the data behind them can be especially useful in obtaining interim payments for suspensions or accelerations, as they have a strong visual impact in showing the detrimental effects of such actions.

6-14. MONTHLY CLAIMS REVIEW

In addition to updating charts each month and making a change order status report, the contractor should endeavor to have a formal review session of all these items to see if any actions have been overlooked or if additional actions need to be taken. One example of such a formal monthly program is as follows:

RECORDS AND DOCUMENTATION

1. Review daily diaries and daily production reports.
2. Analyze monthly cost reports.
3. Prepare monthly summary of impact. Identity causative factors and their effect on overall contract work, and make a rough estimate of costs.
4. Prepare a monthly graph of overall job progress in terms of cost and labor to reflect the inefficiencies that have occurred.
5. Review and make a summary of change orders to determine their effect on progress and costs.
6. Study all major sources of delay and inefficiencies to determine the difference in cost of actual work versus original estimate.
7. Consolidate all of the above and file monthly in loose-leaf form.

The loose-leaf document described in item 7 serves as a useful reference during the job as well as at project completion. Not only for claims purposes, but as a quick lookup for other aspects of the project, the summary of monthly claims can be useful for evaluation and support of impact claims.

One should not wait until the end of the project, however, to file impact claims, but should try to file them as they are incurred, or at least give notice of the potential claims. The above loose-leaf catalogue would then become useful for absolving liquidated damages or for filing an overall impact claim of any loose ends that slipped by during the course of the project. It must be emphasized, though, that this is a last-resort procedure. It is preferable to file and settle all claims as they are incurred, but the above program should still help to keep the claims situation current and under control.

6-15. CONCLUSION

The importance of documentation cannot be overemphasized. The better the documentation, the less costly it will be to prepare claims, and the better the chance of more timely and favorable settlements. It's that simple.

CHAPTER 7

USE OF PROJECT SCHEDULES AND THE CRITICAL PATH METHOD IN CLAIMS

7-1. INTRODUCTION

It is customary for a contractor to create, whether contractually required or not, some type of progress schedule that defines how the job will be performed, as well as submit regular updates to measure actual progress and reaffirm established completion dates. Schedules can be in the form of bar charts, flowcharts or critical path method (CPM) network diagrams. During actual performance of the job, other schedules can come into play, such as short-interval or look-ahead schedules, which break larger, overall project schedules into more detailed tasks for immediately upcoming phases of work. In all these cases, schedules are used to plan the work, and later on, are analyzed to determine responsibility for delays encountered on the project. Since CPM analysis is frequently used, and often specified as a means, to substantiate delay and acceleration claims, this chapter discusses considerations regarding use of CPM schedules to analyze time-related claims and changes.

7-1a. Description of CPM

The CPM is a planning and scheduling method that often employs a graphically plotted network diagram, similar to a flowchart, to show all job operations in the logical fashion necessary for orderly completion. Engineering author Richard H. Clough best summarizes what the network diagram does and its advantages: "The network diagram portrays, in simple and direct form, the complex time relationships and constraints among the various segments of a project. It has the tremendous advantage of easily accommodating modifications, refinements, and corrections." According to Clough, the network diagram provides the project manager with the following invaluable time-control devices:

1. A means to predict with reasonable accuracy the time required for overall project completion
2. Identification of those activities whose expedient execution is crucial to timely project completion (called critical activities, hence the name of the method)
3. A guide for project shortening when the completion date must be advanced
4. A basis for the scheduling of subcontractors and material deliveries to the jobsite
5. A basis for balanced scheduling of manpower and construction equipment on the project
6. Rapid evaluation of alternative construction methods
7. A convenient vehicle for progress reporting and recording
8. A basis for evaluating the time effects of construction changes and delays.[1]

Prior to 1980, the use of critical path scheduling was by either contracting with a service bureau or through use of in-house data processing capabilities of companies large enough to retain the computer hardware, software, and support knowledge required to run the programs. This created a situation whereby jobsite personnel worked, or attempted to work, with schedules that had been updated once a month at best, and, more often than not, updated only to satisfy contract requirements.

With the advent of the personal computer, desktop critical path scheduling programs became available at reasonable cost and slowly became utilized by more contractors as an interactive scheduling tool. Today, there are a number of easy-to-use scheduling programs available. Many more contracts today require the use of a critical path schedule, and some contracts require them for calculating the contractor's monthly progress payments. Using the CPM software's capability for cost loading activities, the earned value of the work complete is computed based on the percentage completion of activities performed in the period.

7-1b. Obstacles to Use of CPM for Construction Scheduling

Contractors have historically resisted CPMs, not because they find fault with the theory, but because of numerous administrative problems. First, it

---

[1]Richard H. Clough, *Construction Project Management* (New York, John Wiley & Sons, Inc., 1972), pp. 7–8.

forces the contractor to study operations in detail, with careful planning and sequencing of work. The contractor must, in a very short period at the beginning of the job, plan his construction methods for a job that may have taken two years to design and will take three years to build. Second, since the CPM is a logical sequence, and since it details task durations, obvious errors can be easily spotted. Aside from embarrassing the contractor, these errors tend to create artificial obstacles to realistic problem solving or constructive actions. Third, a written schedule puts the contractor's operations "on the line" for all to see, and what was composed as an "estimated" schedule becomes a tool or weapon for self-serving purposes of all involved—owners, subcontractors, suppliers, corporation managers, and government officials. The project manager may feel a proposed schedule is an irrevocable commitment.

Other potential obstacles to CPM scheduling that arise on a recurring basis are as follows:

- It is a lot of work to prepare a good CPM and a lot of work to maintain it (i.e., keep it up to date) in the dynamic, ever-changing world of a construction project (where sequence changes are being made on a daily or even hourly basis).
- The front line (i.e., field superintendents/general foreman) tends to be more comfortable with simpler forms of scheduling (i.e., they don't understand the CPM).
- Different people have different ideas as to how to approach the work—and these different opinions have to be confronted/reconciled in order to prepare a CPM schedule.

While these apparent concerns may be valid, the benefits of CPM scheduling most often far outweigh these obstacles. In some cases, these issues can be addressed with such actions as additional resources, training, and/or the use of a simplified or alternative schedules made specifically for the use of field personnel.

7-2. USE OF CPM IN CLAIMS ANALYSIS

A CPM schedule can provide an effective tool for demonstrating schedule cause and effect relationships. CPMs are especially helpful for determining project impact arising from time-related problems, such as delays, suspensions, or accelerations. Changes that add (or delete) work and differing site conditions may also have a time impact on the contract. To best analyze the effect of such situations, the CPM is the most often used tool to measure the relative impact of different time factors on project completion. The use of CPMs has long been accepted by the boards and courts, so long as

- The schedules have been established as reasonable and accurate.
- The schedule has been updated and maintained during construction in accordance with the specifications.
- The analysis is employed in an accurate and consistent manner in accordance with acceptable scheduling theory, including adjustments for contractor-caused and concurrent delays.
- A cause and effect relationship between actual events and delays to the job is shown.

It is difficult to counter the graphic display of delays on a CPM diagram. Once a delay is plotted on the CPM, its impact can be seen on all subsequent activities. At this point, the cost and time impacts resulting from a change order, suspension, delay, or disruption can be determined. Additionally, CPM updates may, in some cases, fulfill notice requirements. However, they should not be substituted for the submission of formal notices specified by the contract. Note, although graphic display of the CPM schedules is preferred, it is not always necessary or practical, such as in projects with large numbers of activities or using scheduling programs that do not have graphical plotting capabilities. In such cases, the information necessary must be obtained from printed reports and can still, if necessary, be displayed on hand-drawn summary charts.

The basic methodology of CPM analysis is to show the impact of delay by comparing actual performance (as-built) to a baseline schedule (as-planned). In-depth analysis of CPM schedules involves considerations of "float," concurrent delay, acceleration, and early completion. These issues and the various methods of CPM analysis are discussed in the following sections.

7-3. PITFALLS TO AVOID IN CPM CLAIMS ANALYSIS

Abnormal weather, change orders, delays, strikes, and other job impacts should be plotted on the CPM, adjustments made, and claims or notices subsequently filed as necessary. Failure to prepare or update the CPM properly during construction of the job can be cause to invalidate its use in substantiating a claim. In rejecting one contractor's claim, the Board noted, "The work sequence shown was not used in estimating and bidding the job since the original chart from which the two exhibits were derived was not in existence until . . . the end of the project. Also, as the contractor's project manager admits, the sequence shown on the critical path charts was not followed in performing the contract work."[2] Additionally, a clear relation of

---

[2]*Chaney & James Co. v. U.S.*, 190 Ct. Cl. 699 (1970); also see *Titan Pacific Construction Corp. v. U.S.*, 17 Cl. Ct. 630 (1989). (An as-planned CPM schedule was not conclusive regarding delay impact because the contractor failed to follow the schedule during construction.)

the CPM presentation to the job is "the single most important factor in determining the acceptability of the contractor's CPM-based claim."[3] To summarize factors that have been used to discredit CPM presentations in claims, Waldron in his seminar textbook has compiled the following important highlights from several relevant cases:

1. The network was not used either in the preparation of the bid or in the management of the project. Failure to use the CPM in executing the work pursuant to contract requirements may give rise to a claim for breach of express or implied warranties. The fact that the system was not used or implemented will not prevent the claimant from using a CPM analysis to compare the originally approved schedule with an 'as built' chart to support his breach claim or to support a delay or disruption claim. This assumes, of course, that documentation is available to support the analysis. Frequently, such data is not available when the system was ignored during performance.
2. The diagram and network analysis were prepared specifically for use in the presentation of the claim before the board or court and had no real relevance to the actual scheduling employed.
3. The contractor's expert witness could only testify that the presentation 'appeared logical' and 'looked right,' since he had not made a detailed analysis of all relevant job records or other documentation, nor had he made a site inspection before or after the project was complete. It is absolutely necessary to have a fully competent expert witness who will not only review all of the relevant records and make a detailed and independent analysis, but who also can make a convincing presentation at trial.
4. The contractor offered no evidence to support his claim that the key activity was critical to job progress or on the critical path.
5. The original network contained numerous mathematical errors, or failed to consider foreseeable weather or labor conditions, for this proper adjustment was not made in the analysis.[4]

---

[3] Wickwire and Smith, 1974, p. 13. [Also see *Appeal of Titan Mountain States Construction Corp.*, ASBCA No. 2-3095 (Feb. 21, 1985). (CPM consultant's work product was not persuasive because it did not address the cause and effect of delay in the field.)]

[4] A. James Waldron, Publisher, *The Legal Implications of a Project Schedule*, (Haddonfield, N.J., Waldron Enterprises, 1974), pp. XIII-3 and XIII-4.

PROJECT SCHEDULES AND CPM IN CLAIMS

These points illustrate what is to be avoided when preparing a claim that relies on CPM scheduling. The contractor should also submit to the owner, along with the CPM schedule, a transmittal letter that very specifically notes the flexibility and limited responsibility provisions of the schedule. Appendix 11 contains an example of a cover letter that illustrates this approach.

7-4. CONSTRUCTION OF AS-PLANNED SCHEDULE

7-4a. Essential Elements in Constructing the Schedule

While it is not the intent of this book to explain the detail and mechanics of CPM scheduling, there are a few considerations worth keeping in mind when constructing the original, or "as-planned," schedule. As discussed above, the as-planned schedule represents the contractor's original plan for constructing the job, and may later serve as a baseline to determine the effects of delays. Essential elements of constructing the schedule, in addition to adherence to the contract completion dates and a method to measure progress, include

1. Performing a detailed/comprehensive review of contract drawings and specifications
2. Getting your subcontractors involved
3. Getting "buy-in" from your jobsite management personnel (i.e., the people who will actually be doing the work)
4. Getting "buy-in" from the owner
5. Organizing breakdown of activities so that responsibilities can be clearly defined
6. Enlisting the support of a qualified scheduler
7. Selecting an appropriate level of detail
8. Constructing the original schedule in accordance with the milestone dates in the contract documents
9. If possible, using the resource loading capabilities of your scheduling software to evaluate the manning of the job
10. Drawing up the schedule as realistically as possible
11. Formulating a method of measuring progress.[5] If progress cannot be measured and compared to the CPM, then the CPM may becomes useless.

[5]Note, concerning this last item, pay quantities may be useful in that they represent an agreement between the owner and the contractor on work completed. Thus, when it comes time to discuss progress of work at any given date on the CPM, agreed quantities would reduce disagreements on measuring progress. Some contracts require progress payments to be based on CPM updates. However, some contractors may find use of pay quantities distracts from the CPM's intended purpose as a planning and scheduling tool.

7-4b. Additional Considerations of Schedule Preparation

There is no single, correct way to perform a project. However, as long as a contractor uses sound judgment and reasonable assumptions in laying out a schedule, such schedules can be considered reasonable. According to Wickwire and Smith (1974, p. 5), "CPM schedules are necessarily grounded in pragmatic considerations which govern all activity in the real world of construction. They must therefore be evaluated in light of certain basic principles which affect major construction projects." Wickwire and Smith further examine some of these pragmatic considerations:

1. A CPM is only as good as the information on which it is based. There was a tendency during the early days of CPM to view this scheduling device as a guarantee that the project would be built on schedule. Contractors have learned through experience that fallacious logic or duration estimates will not be transformed into correct logic or estimates simply because they are contained in a CPM computer printout.
2. On most building construction, the work sequence of the various trades occurs over and over again throughout the project. Further, since follow-on trades do not wait for the initial trades to complete their work for the entire building prior to commencing the follow-on work, different areas of the project are at different stages of completion within the sequence of work.
3. On most major construction projects there are essential installations that must receive extra attention even when these installations are not reflected on the critical path. For example, from experience a contractor may know that certain key systems (i.e., major mechanical piping and ductwork; switch-gear; bus duct; and primary electrical feeders) present substantial obstacles to the completion of construction due to the complexity and magnitude of the installations. In addition, the contractor may know that these systems constitute a condition precedent to the work of follow-on trades in significant portions of the project. In these circumstances, the contractor knows that more attention may be required for these installations than for certain work on the critical path due to the substantial variables in the time required for making these key installations and the possible disruptive effect to the project if the installation of the key systems is extensively delayed.
4. Timely completion of most projects requires the establishment of flow and momentum. The speed of the installation of various trades is substantially affected by the rhythm of a project. When a smooth flow of the work is scheduled or established, the

PROJECT SCHEDULES AND CPM IN CLAIMS

majority of the activities will probably be very close to the critical path (in terms of float time) since these activities closely precede or follow the activities on the critical path.

Wickwire and Smith conclude that "the examples of pragmatic considerations discussed above point out that the contractor must exercise good judgment in interpreting the information revealed on a CPM schedule. A contractor must temper a CPM schedule in light of its construction experience."[6]

7-5. FLOAT

Float, in simple terms, is the time period between scheduled early finish and late finish of an activity in the CPM schedule. Allocation of float time has often been a source of controversy in disputes involving delays, suspensions, and change orders. At issue is the right to use available float time—does it belong to the contractor or to the owner? If the contractor is able to finish early, is he still obligated to be available through the contract completion date to perform change orders affecting activities that have float (either during performance or after completion of the original contract work)? If the contractor has a 15-day float period, for example, and experiences two sequential 10-day delays (one 10-day delay his own fault and the other due to the owner) is the contractor entitled to a five-day contract extension?

Those questions are often answered by determining which party used the float first. In other words, the float belongs to neither party but is for the use of both parties[7]. If the owner orders a 10-day suspension of an activity, the contractor is still on schedule and has five days float left on that activity. Subsequently, the contractor falls behind in his work by 10 days, finishes the contract five days late but is not granted a contract extension. Why? Because at the time the suspension occurred, the overall contract completion date was not affected. If the contractor, however, was 10 days late on the item before the suspension occurred (and had only five days float on the item), he would then be entitled to a five-day contract extension.

7-6. FLOAT—EARLY COMPLETION

A controversial situation on the use of float occurs when the contractor is able to, or intends to, finish early—before the specified contract completion

---

[6] Jon M. Wickwire and Richard F. Smith, "The Use of Critical Path Method Techniques in Contract Claims," *Public Contract Law Journal I* (October, 1974): pp. 5–7.

[7] The nonexclusive use of float time is explicitly stated in various scheduling specifications, such as the Corp of Engineers' NAS Section, ER 1-1-11 and the Washington Metropolitan Area Transit Authority's Appendix F. The most recent version of the NAS specification has omitted this clause.

date. The owner feels that since the contract gives him the right to issue change orders, it allows him to use any available time (float) during the contract performance period, and thus requires the contractor to perform changes right up to the contract completion date. While the boards and courts have not been uniform in their treatment of this issue, the trend now leans toward the contractor's right to finish early. The following comments supporting this position are taken from the *Construction Contract Negotiating Guide*

> An interesting problem occurs when the government attempts to take advantage of positive slack (that is, the contractor's lead on schedule) built up by the contractor. Assume that through diligence, luck, or unnecessarily long completion time, or perhaps a combination of these, the contractor will be able to finish his work and leave the job site thirty days before the specified contract completion date. Assume additionally that the government wishes to make certain modifications that will require an additional thirty days to complete. Is the contractor, in this case entitled to a time extension, and, more important, to additional overhead?
>
> The answer to the question appears to be yes. By the terms of the contract the contractor has obligated himself merely to complete the work for a fixed price by a given date, not to remain on the jobsite until a given date. Under the aforementioned assumption, he would fulfill his contract obligation thirty days prior to the outside completion date. Now the government changes the obligation by adding work, but can it expropriate the positive slack without payment? This is really an attempt to recoup cost savings the contractor may have accrued (since time is worth money) under a firm fixed price contract. In brief, the contractor has a valid argument. Of course, the 'ahead-of-schedule' condition is negotiable and he may agree to do the added work by the original completion time, provided the price is fair and reasonable. But a fair and reasonable price must include compensation for the increase in indirect cost incurred, plus profit on those costs. Some contractors are willing to accept modifications that require additional costs for extended overhead but that cannot be evaluated because of insufficient information necessary to determine the amount of time extension required.[8]

Another example of the preceding situation was ruled upon in the Weaver-Bailey.[9] In this case, the U.S. Claims Court ruled the contractor

---

[8] U.S. Dept. of the Army, Office of the Chief of Engineers, *Construction Contract Negotiating Guide*, (1974 Edition), p. B-17.
[9] *Weaver-Bailey Contractors, Inc. v. U.S.*, 19 Cl.Ct. 474 (1990).

would have been able to finish early but for the government-caused delay, and therefore awarded it compensation for delay, despite the fact that the contractor's original schedule did not show early completion. In other words, the Board ruled that the owner did not have the right to use available float if the owner's action delayed performance of the contractor's work. It is instructive to take a closer look at why the contractor did not show early completion on its progress chart

> As to why Weaver-Bailey submitted proposed construction progress charts utilizing all of the time allotted in the contract, Mr. Stephenson [project manager for Weaver-Bailey] explained that there is no incentive for a contractor to submit projections reflecting an early completion date. The government bases its progress payments on the amount of work completed each month, relative to the contractor's proposed progress charts. A contractor which submits proposed progress charts using all of the time in the contract, and which demonstrates that work is moving along ahead of schedule, will receive full and timely progress payments. If such a contractor falls behind its true intended schedule, i.e., its accelerated schedule, it will still receive full and timely progress payments, so long as it does not fall behind the progress schedule which it submitted to the government.
>
> On the other hand, if a contractor which intended to finish early reflected such an intention in its proposed progress charts, it would have to meet that accelerated schedule in order to receive full and timely progress payments; any slowdown might deprive the contractor of such payments, even if the contractor is performing efficiently enough to finish within the time allotted in the contract. In short, a contractor cannot lose when it projects that it will use all of the time allowed, but it can be hurt by projecting early completion. Additionally, Mr. Stephenson and others testified that they were told by government representatives to fill out the proposed progress charts using all of the allotted time. The government did not challenge this testimony, either or cross-examination or on direct examination of a government witness.[10]

Although this makes reasonable sense, it should not be taken as a hard and fast rule. In Weaver-Bailey, it was clear from the sequence of events the government's action delayed the contractor's performance. This situation may not always be clear. Generally, if either party intends at any time to avail itself of float time, or to change its schedule, to complete early for

[10]Ibid.

example, it would be best to notify the other party as soon as possible of its intentions. Such notification would eliminate ambiguities and give the other party an opportunity to react or adjust its own schedules and intentions. As is discussed in the next section, there are a variety of approaches to schedule analysis in an area that continues to evolve.

7-7. CONCURRENT DELAY

Many disputes on delay boil down to issues of concurrent delay. As mentioned in section 5-9, concurrent delays by the contractor can convert a compensable delay to an excusable, noncompensable one. The most frequent approach adapted by owners in defense of delay claims is to show the existence of concurrent delays. In any event, the best approach for contractors to avoid being tripped up by concurrent delays is to assess as realistically as possible the effect of delays as they are incurred.

First, the contractor obviously should avoid causing any delays, and most often will take steps to counter such delays and/or make up lost time. This can be done by acceleration and/or making sequence changes for future work. Second, until a thorough analysis of a delay is performed, one should not assume a delaying event will automatically delay project completion. For example, although most construction clauses provide that the contractor is entitled to a contract extension for strikes, the occurrence of a strike does not automatically imply a delay. Rather than automatically request a time extension at the end of a delay, a thorough CPM analysis should be performed to see if the strike actually delayed project performance. However, the contractor should still serve notice of the event.

7-8. VOLUNTARY VERSUS CONSTRUCTIVE ACCELERATION

The contractor can choose to make up for delays on his own by acceleration or by performing critical items of work concurrently. In so doing, he is entitled to the time saved by his efforts. If the contractor expedites his work without a directive or condition of constructive acceleration the work will be considered voluntary.

As discussed in chapter 5, the contractor is not required to accelerate unless directed to do so by the owner, or so as to adhere to original schedule requirements when excusable delays have been encountered, but time extensions not granted (constructive acceleration). The contractor should be careful to show on his schedule where activities and logic changes are for constructive acceleration efforts as opposed to those that are for its own acceleration purposes (make up for contractor delays; attempts at early completion).

PROJECT SCHEDULES AND CPM IN CLAIMS

7-9. SCHEDULE ANALYSIS TECHNIQUES FOR CLAIMS SUPPORT

There are several basic methods of CPM-based schedule analyses commonly used in analysis of delays. The methodology selected will be dependent on such factors as whether or not a computerized CPM was used *and* updated during the course of construction, the number and extent of delays encountered, and past rulings by the board or court that will hear disputes of the particular owner or agency responsible for the project. These methods are

1. Impacted as-planned
2. Fragnet ("windows, chronological impact")
3. Time impact analysis
4. Collapsed as-built ("but for")

These different approaches differ with respect to interpretations regarding float utilization, the appropriate baseline to be used for measuring delay, and the treatment of concurrent delays. Consequently they may yield different results when applied to the same set of facts. There are other types of analyses used from time to time, which are typically a variation of the above four methods.

7-9a. Impacted As-Planned Analysis

This method takes the original as-planned schedule as the baseline and inserts owner-caused changes/delays to compute the resulting impacted as-planned schedule and a new contract completion date(s). The difference between the impacted completion date and the original as-planned completion date represents the total amount of excusable delay. Although this method is often used because of its simplicity, it has been consistently rejected by courts and boards.

The main disadvantage of this method is it takes into account neither contractor-caused delays nor other conditions affecting the work during project performance. Obvious variations of this method would be to include all excusable delays (not just owner-caused) and/or contractor-caused delays. Even with the inclusion of these other delays, this method still does not account for actual performance conditions, such as actual versus planned productivity rates or changes in sequence of the work.

7-9b. Fragnet (Windows, Chronological Impact)

This method starts out using an updated schedule at the point the impact first occurred as the baseline. A fragnet, or subnetwork, representing the changes or delaying activities, is then inserted into the CPM. After adjusting the schedule of the balance of the project for any logic changes, such as for delay-mitigating activities, an impacted schedule is generated with the new contract completion date. The difference between completion date of the impacted schedule and the completion date of the baseline schedule represents the net delay of the impact.

Additionally, the effect of the changes on unchanged activities should be analyzed. As specified in the *Modification Impact Evaluation Guide*, questions such as the following must be answered[11]

1. Has any activity been moved from where the contractor had it scheduled into a season where normal weather is more unfavorable or makes it impractical to do this type of work?
2. Are there now more activities in progress at a given time than indicated by the schedule before revision?
3. Have any activities slipped to the extent that significant phases of the work, such as closing in a building for winter, providing necessary utilities, completing an access road, building a coffer dam, etc., will not be accomplished before some overriding factor (winter, high water stages, unavailability of site) prevent it, thus making it necessary to defer a portion of the work until the next favorable season?

The duration of the impacted activities should be adjusted to reflect the time now realistically required for their accomplishment and the schedule recalculated. This may result in further slippage of the final completion date.[12]

This method is one of the preferred methods to use during performance of the work, as opposed to an after-the-job analysis, and in essence, is a forward-priced change order. The *Modification Impact Evaluation Guide*, section 3-3, describes this method in detail and specifies its preferred use as the basis for developing impact cost estimates.[13] However, the burden of performing a detailed analysis and risk assessment may not seem too advantageous to the busy project staff already steeped in the day-to-day activities of running the job.

7-9c. Time Impact Analysis

Time impact analysis is one of the methods more frequently used for after-the-fact analysis of project delays. This method takes a series of snapshots, or windows, at various periods throughout the job, typically at the end

---

[11]*Modification Impact Evaluation Guide*, EP 415–1-3, U. S. Dept. of the Army, Office of the Chief of Engineers, 1979, p. 3–6.
[12]Ibid, p. 3–7.
[13]Ibid. p. 3–5.

of an impacting event. Using existing as-planned information, adjustments are made to the remaining schedule, such as logic changes to mitigate the impacts, and a new adjusted schedule is computed. The difference between the completion date of the new adjusted as-built schedule and the prior baseline becomes the amount of time the project is delayed.

The new adjusted schedule also becomes the baseline for the next period to be analyzed. As each window is analyzed, the various category of delays are tallied, that is, contractor-caused, owner-caused, and excusable noncompensable. After stepping through the complete series, the final extended completion date is determined along with the various categories of delay, which can be used for calculating impact costs. Typically, impact costs would be calculated at the time of the impact, as the level of delay costs will vary from period to period.

Depending on how the method is applied, it may or may not take into account concurrent or "near-critical" delays. Some scheduling experts only look at the longest delaying activity (controlling impact) in a given window.

7-9d. Collapsed As-Built ("But For")

Another method frequently used is the "but for" schedule, which we'll call here the "collapsed" as-built. This method starts off with an accurate as-built CPM schedule as the baseline. All impacts are identified in the schedule at the time of occurrence so they can be easily removed ("collapsed out") and the schedule recalculated. The various owner-caused changes and delay activities are removed to determine what the completion date would have been "but for" the owner actions. The same analysis can be performed with removal of owner-caused plus excusable noncompensable delays to determine the total time extension for which the contractor is entitled.

Similar considerations as observed above must be applied to the collapsed as-built method. The as-built schedule should be accurate, and some adjustments may be necessary for changes in schedule logic resulting from the encountered impacts. As in the previous method, float time may have been created and appropriated by the delays.

7-9e. Comparison Chart of CPM Analysis Methods

In general, for any of these methods to work well, it is imperative that the as-planned schedules (where used) be reasonable, and that both as-planned and updated schedules are free of logic errors, omissions, or inaccurate estimates of activity durations. It may sometimes be necessary to make corrections to the as-planned schedule(s) before its use as a baseline. Appropriate logic changes must also be made to the as-built schedules to reflect actual changes in sequence of the work, whether initiated by the contractor

Type of Schedule Analysis	Point of Reference	(Delay = Schedule B minus Schedule A)	
		Schedule A	Schedule B
Impacted As-Planned	"Day 1"	Original As-Planned Schedule	Impacted As-Planned Schedule
Fragnet Approach	Start of Impact	Contemporaneous Schedule at start of impact	Schedule A with fragnet inserted
Time Impact Analysis	Conclusion of Impact	Schedule update at conclusion of prior impact	Schedule update through conclusion of impact
Collapsed As-Built	Conclusion of Project	Collapsed As-Built Schedule	As-Built Schedule

FIG. 7-1 Comparison Chart of CPM Delay Analysis Methods

or the owner. Shown in Figure 7.1 is a summary level comparison of the four primary CPM delay analysis methods.

7-9f. Other Methods

Other methods sometimes used for schedule analysis are essentially variations of the four methods described above. Typically, these variations will substitute either the original as-planned and/or as-built with an alternate schedule. The alternative schedule may reflect assumptions or considerations not originally included. The substitutions may be intended to show hypothetical situations such as how an activity "should have been" done or "would have been" planned, for example.

7-10. SCHEDULING EXPERT'S ANALYSIS

Schedule analysis can become extremely tedious for both simple and complex projects, depending on the detail of the CPM network, number of activities, reasonableness of the original as-planned schedule, and accuracy of the as-built schedule. The outcome of disputed claims that end up in litigation will often turn on the thorough analysis of reputable scheduling experts.

PROJECT SCHEDULES AND CPM IN CLAIMS 89

The ability for the scheduling expert to perform an analysis is highly dependent on the availability of project documentation and personnel. It is absolutely crucial that all project documentation be retained and accessible, especially diaries/logs kept by foremen, superintendents, and other project personnel.

7-11. CONCLUSION

The contractor should consider the compilation and use of CPM scheduling techniques as a valuable tool and not just a nuisance contract requirement. The as-planned CPM should be constructed realistically and accurately, and the schedule should be updated on a regular basis to reflect actual events, durations, and start and stop times. The schedule clauses should also be read carefully because each contract may demand different scheduling and update requirements of the contractor. Finally, the boards and courts have become sophisticated in the understanding of CPM scheduling theory and will look for the underlying proof of cause and effect relationships before relying on the schedule analysis presentations provided by the parties.

CHAPTER 8

SUBCONTRACTORS AND SUPPLIERS

8-1. INTRODUCTION

Subcontractors have a dual problem—guarding their interests against the general contractor as well as the owner. Unfortunately, general contractors sometimes rank subcontractors on the lower half of their list of priorities. Subcontractor work items are often placed off the critical path, and the general contractor will alter subcontractor schedules to suit his convenience. This is to be expected to a degree, and both the general contractor and the subcontractor should try to keep this flexibility within reasonable limits. Participation by subcontractors, particularly major subcontractors, in drawing up the critical path method (CPM) is helpful in planning realistic schedules and establishing contingency plans. Planning and execution of the job should be accomplished so that the general contractor does not delay the subcontractor and vice versa, as the courts have noted, "The provision of the subcontract giving the defendant (general contractor) the right to direct the sequence or general progress of work does not release it from liability for delay. It implies an obligation on the part of the general contractor to keep the work in such a state of forwardness as to enable the subcontractor to perform within a limited time."[1]

8-2. GENERAL CONTRACTOR'S PERFORMANCE

The general contractor must be very careful to act as a two-way conduit between the subcontractor and the owner, for the general contractor can be

---

[1] *J.J. Brown Co. v. J.L. Simmons Co.*, 2 111. App. 2d. 132,118 N.W. 2d 781 (1954); also see *Unis v. JTS Constructors/Managers, Inc.*, 541 So.2d 278 (La.App. 1989). (Contractor had an implied obligation to avoid hindering or delaying its subcontractors.)

SUBCONTRACTORS AND SUPPLIERS 91

held responsible for any delays he causes by not taking appropriate action in processing directives, changes, or claims. Good relations with the subcontractor go a long way toward enhancing mutual reinforcement in claim situations. The general contractor must also be careful about submitting delay claims that may be rejected by the owner as a contractor delay, thereby giving the subcontractor cause to claim against the general contractor. This can be a tricky situation unless addressed properly in the subcontract or astutely handled by good relations between the subcontractor and the general contractor. For obvious protective reasons, all contact and correspondence between the subcontractor and the general contractor should be well documented.

8-3. CONTRACTOR-S[UBCONTRACTOR REL]ATIONSHIP

By having the subcon[tractor set] up the CPM schedule, in updating the sched[ule in coordin]ation meetings, the general contractor create[s an atmosphere] . Such cooperation works toward mutual re[solution as we]ll as the elimination of scheduling conflicts [that m]ight result in claims [if th]e contractor does not indicate his intention [to participate in] CPM formulation or coordination meeting[s. By dis]e the initiative by encouraging the general [contractor, if the gener]al contractor still offers no cooperation, the [subcontractor w]ith his work as best he can, with frequent n[otices] of what his work schedules and intentions [are and what delays he m]ay have as a result of the lack of planning or [coordination by] the general contractor.

8-4. SUBCON[TRACTOR-OWNER RELATIONSHIP]

Very often on [a project, directives are] made or changes issued that affect only the s[ubcontractor. Since there i]s no privity of contract between the owne[r and subcontractor, the gene]ral contractor will often let the matter be h[andled directly between the tw]o, acting only as an official go-between fo[r the record. While this pr]actice, although common, is not always in [the general contractor's best in]terest. The general contractor should attempt to p[articipate in subcontra]ctor-owner problems to protect his own interests and also to ma[ke sure the su]bcontractor is acting to resolve these problems expeditiously. The general contractor does not want his contract adversely affected because of unresolved subcontractor problems.

In one case involving the three parties, the general contractor's final contract completion was withheld on a project for two years, including a $50,000 retention by the owner. The owner would not accept a steamline built by the utility subcontractor because the line had developed leaking ball joints. After more than five years of claims, counterclaims, fact finding meetings, studies, and negotiations, the issue was finally resolved two years after contract completion, at which time contract retention was released. Had the general contractor sought to bring pressure on the subcontractor (and the owner) to take action on the problem when it first surfaced, delayed closing of the contract would not have occurred. The contractor would have had his retention money two years earlier, the subcontractor would have received a better settlement, the owner would have had a better system, and many wasted hours by all parties would have been saved.

Often, too, subcontractors may not be as experienced or adept as the general contractor at handling such problems and will benefit by the general contractor's assistance. So it is important to keep after both subcontractors and owners to resolve these problems as early as possible.

8-5. SUPPLIERS

8-5a. Delays, Drawing Approvals

Suppliers can pose a variety of problems for the general contractor—poor quality, improper material, late production, or damage in transit. Since shop drawings are involved, it is important that the contractor allow sufficient time for approval of drawings, and that he maintain accurate records of all transactions and transmittals involving the supplier. Contract delay caused by a supplier can possibly be excused when it is shown to be beyond his control, as a result of strikes, unavailability of materials, or mechanical breakdowns. Delayed approval of drawings by the owner can also contribute to contract delays, and may result in excusable and compensable delay.

8-5b. Supplier Purchase Orders

The contractor should do everything possible to avoid supplier problems by writing explicit purchase orders (with appropriate lead times), keeping adequate inventory of parts and supplies, and actively monitoring the supplier's activities. Of course, when writing purchase orders and accepting supplier acknowledgments, the contractor wants to be sure the agreement will be governed by terms and conditions favorable to the contractor. Thus, acknowledgments and other documents received from the supplier should be scrutinized to insure they do not create terms that are inconsistent with the purchase order.

Particularly at issue is the disclaimer of express and implied warranties. Express warranties are representations made in published specifications, sales catalogues, and other promotions. Even though not a part of, and not required by, the specification between the owner and contractor, the owner may rely on these representations and attempt to enforce them against the contractor and/or the supplier. Any attempt by a supplier to limit or disclaim prior express warranties is cause for concern.

An implied warranty is a warranty that exists when a seller is aware of the intended use of his product and the product is suitable for that particular purpose. Sellers may disclaim implied warranties, particularly for consequential damages, offering only to replace the defective product. This does not relieve the contractor of potentially costly obligations to the owner if the product fails to perform properly.

For these reasons, contractors must be extremely cautious about the acceptance of supplier terms, conditions, and qualifications contained in purchase order acknowledgments. The best defense here is to notify suppliers in writing of any objections to preprinted clauses or acknowledgment exceptions, as well as the intent to rely on express representations by the supplier. These actions may lead to the battle of the forms, each party trying to have its own terms prevail. Since contractor-supplier purchase orders are a frequent subject of litigation, the contractor is well advised to consult legal counsel before drawing up purchase orders or accepting acknowledgments that offer the potential to affect the outcome of the job.

8-5c. Proprietary Specifications—Contractor's Right to Substitute

On private construction contracts, owners have a right to specify and insist on proprietary specifications. The situation is different on public contracts and may lead to a number of different issues, as described in the March 1992 issue of *Construction Claims Monthly*[2]:

> On publicly funded construction contracts, statutes and regulations generally limit the use of proprietary specifications. The contract may call for a particular brand and model, but the contract usually authorizes the substitution of "equal" products. The policy behind this is two-fold. Public project owners need to avoid even the appearance of favoritism toward particular manufacturers or suppliers. It is also believed that by maintaining the maximum degree of open competition, the taxpaying public will benefit from lower prices.
>
> A substitute product is "equal" to the specified product if it is substantially equivalent to the "salient characteristics" listed in the contract. Salient characteristics are usually performance capabilities and the alternative product need only be functionally equivalent to the brand name product. But if the salient characteristics

---

[2]"Proprietary Specifications," Bruce Jervis, Esq., *Construction Claims Monthly*, March 1992 (Published by Business Publishers, Inc., Silver Spring, MD).

are of a precise design nature, the substitute product must conform exactly. *Matter of Cohu, Inc.,* Comp. Gen. No. B-199551 (1982). When reasonably necessary to meet the owner's legitimate needs, even aesthetic factors can be stated as salient characteristics.

Once the salient characteristics of the specified proprietary product have been stipulated, it is those characteristics, not the project owner's subjective judgment, which determine whether a proposed alternative product is equal. *Appeal of R.R. Mongeau Engineers, Inc.,* ASBCA No. 29341 (April 14, 1987). And once the owner's engineer or other representative has approved a product as possessing the salient characteristics of the specified product, the owner is bound by that determination. *E.A. Berman Company v. City of Marlborough,* 419 N.E.2nd 319 (Mass. App. 1981).

If the specifications fail to authorize the use of substitute products or fail to list the salient characteristics of the proprietary product, they may be considered defective. *Matter of R.R. Mongeau Engineers, Inc.,* Comp. Gen. No. B-218356 (July 8, 1985). Courts and administrative boards are also hostile toward specifications which are not overtly proprietary, but are drafted or interpreted in such a manner that only one product can possibly comply. *Waldinger Corp. v. CRS Group Engineers, Inc.,* 775 F.2d 781 (7th Cir. 1985); *Appeal of Bruce-Anderson, Co., Inc.,* ASBCA No. 29411 (Aug. 1, 1988).

8-5d. Supplier Schedules

Suppliers (and subcontractors) should be aware of where they fit in the CPM schedule and should be obligated to show their own schedules for accomplishing work. These schedules should contain check points for monitoring supplier activities and the supplier should produce periodic updates or status reports. It is the contractor's responsibility to secure materials and thus do everything possible to satisfy himself that he is taking all reasonable steps to meet this obligation and not imperil the project.

8-6. DOCUMENTATION OF GENERAL CONTRACTOR SUBCONTRACTOR/SUPPLIER TRANSACTIONS

For claims arising from contractor-supplier problems, detailed records are very beneficial for tracing delays due to working or shop drawings, difficulties with design, production problems, and nonresponsive activities by the owner or engineer. Contract documents usually specify the length of time to be expected for drawing approvals, but whether they do or do not, the contractor has a right to expect approvals within a reasonable length of time as the particular situation warrants. Often enough, there are contributory delays by both the owner (or his representative) and the contractor (or subcontractor). However, by showing through documented evidence that the owner contributed to an overall delay, that portion and possibly the entire delay period could be held the responsibility of the owner.

8-7. OTHER CONTRACTOR-SUBCONTRACTOR ISSUES

8-7a. Severin Doctrine

Another transaction requiring careful scrutiny is the handling of contract modifications and subcontract change orders. The general contractor does not want to create liability by improperly signing off a modification with one party while it remains unsettled with the other. For example, a subcontract change order or modification should not be signed by the general contractor until the same change order or modification has been executed between the general contractor and owner.

If the general contractor has a claim against the owner for delays or other actions that involve a subcontractor, the owner is not liable to pay additional costs to the general contractor if the general contractor is not in turn obligated to pay the subcontractor these damages. This situation might occur when a general contractor is able to convince a subcontractor to sign off for little or no extra costs for outstanding claims in order to close out a subcontract. Known as the Severin Doctrine:[3] the Court of Claims in a breach of contract case ruled that if the prime contractor is not liable to a subcontractor for damages (for delay) caused by the government, then the prime contractor has suffered no damages that he can collect from the government. The subcontractor wants to be sure he has a subcontract clause that establishes an obligation to him for all sums collectable by the prime contractor from the owner for actions by the owner that affect the subcontractor's work. Likewise, any final payment to a subcontractor by the general contractor should leave open any active claims of the subcontractor that are being processed through the general contractor against the owner. As noted above, this should be done in a manner whereby the general contractor's obligation to the subcontractor is limited to the amount that the general contractor actually receives from the owner for the subcontractor's benefit.

8-7b. Miller Act

Subcontractors and suppliers should be familiar with the Miller Act, which requires contractors on federal projects to post a surety bond to guarantee payment to all persons supplying labor and material to the contractor. The Miller Act protects subcontractors and suppliers because they have no

---

[3]*Severin v. U.S.*, 99 Ct. Cl. No. 435 (1943).

lien rights on federal projects. In a recent case involving the Hirshhorn Museum, in Washington, D.C., a U.S. District Court ruled that "under the Miller Act a subcontractor may recover from the prime contractor's surety for delay costs for labor or materials furnished and used in the prosecution of the contracted work, where the subcontractor did not cause or contribute to the delay."[4] The court noted that it made no difference whether the government or the general contractor was responsible for the delay. The court also noted that it did not matter whether the costs expended were part of the original contract or for changed work; if the costs for labor and material were in fact expended, then the surety is liable (if the general contractor does not pay).

8-7c. Sponsoring Subcontractor Claims

A number of years ago, before a subcontractor claim could be pursued against the owner, the subcontractor had to first prevail against the contractor, who in turn would then pursue relief against the owner. Sponsoring agreements have been implemented to overcome these obstacles.

On private construction contracts, some states will require an admitted liability of the prime contractor to the subcontractor before a court will hear the dispute. Other states will not require that a liability preexist, but some courts may insist that the subcontractor has not waived its rights against the prime. These issues are intended to prevent the prime from irresponsibly passing through claims that are unsubstantiated in fact or in cost support. Absent appropriate sponsorship agreements, a sub must first submit its claim against the prime.

On federal projects, it is not necessary that the prime has admitted liability to the sub, only that the claims are properly certified and correct, as specified in the Contracts Disputes Act.

8-8. SUBCONTRACTOR-SPECIFIC CLAIMS PUBLICATIONS

While the information contained in this book is applicable to subcontractors and general contractors alike, subcontractors are urged to check with their trade association for resources specific for their needs. Examples of some useful publications include those from the American Subcontractor Association[5]:

---

[4]*U.S. for the Use & Benefit of Leonardo Mariana v. Piracci Construction Co., Inc.*, 405 F. Supp. 904 (District of Columbia, 1975); also see *U.S. for the Use and Benefit of Superior Insulation Co., Inc. v. Robert E. McKee, Inc.*, 702 F.Supp. 1298 (N.D.Tex. 1988). (Subcontractor recovered delay damages from Miller Act payment surety where the damages were characterized as the increased cost of labor and material furnished to the project.)

[5]American Subcontractors Association, Alexandria VA. (703)684–3450.

SUBCONTRACTORS AND SUPPLIERS

- *Partnering for Peace, Principle and Profitability*
- *Protecting Your Profitability Through Project Documentation*
- *Contract Changes and Claims Manual for Subcontractor Project Managers, Estimators and Supervisors*
- *Succeeding at Contract Changes and Claims*

one from the National Electrical Contractor's Association[6]:

- *Guide to Electrical Contractors' Claims Management* (Vols. 1, 2 and 3)

and one from the Mechanical Contractors Association of America[7]:

- *Change Orders - Overtime - Productivity*

8-9. AGC/ASA/ASC STANDARD FORM CONTRACT

Developed through the joint efforts of the Associated General Contractors of America (AGC), the American Subcontractors Association, Inc. (ASA), and the Associated Specialty Contractors (ASC),[8] a standard form Construction Subcontract[9] was published in June 1994 to achieve two primary goals:

- Provide more efficient, timely, and economical construction for the mutual benefit of owners, architect/engineers, contractors, subcontractors, and suppliers
- Create equitable and ethical relations between general contractors and subcontractors

Intended to be generally compatible with AIA A201, this document attempts to elevate the two-way exchange of information and responsibilities of the contractor and subcontractor to a more productive and fair level.

While it is beyond the scope of this book to evaluate these clauses in detail, it is worth noting the new contract contains clauses dealing with

---

[6]National Electrical Contractors Association, Washington, DC (301)675–3110.
[7]Mechanical Contractors Association of America, Inc., Rockville, MD (301)869–5800.
[8]The ASC is an umbrella organization composed of the following groups: Mason Contractors Association of America, Mechanical Contractors Association of America, National Association of Plumbing-Heating-Cooling Contractors, National Electrical Contractors Association, National Insulation and Abatement Contractors Association, National Roofing Contractors Association, Painting and Decorating Contractors of America, Sheet Metal and Air Conditioning Contractors' National Association.
[9]AGC Document No. 640/ASA Document No. 4100/ASC Form No. 52.

many of the topics discussed herein. The following clauses are worth noting (See Appendix 12 for complete text of these articles):

Article 6—Performance of Work. Article 6.2, Schedule of Work, specifies that the (general) contractor shall prepare the schedule with any scheduling information provided by the subcontractor and in consultation with the subcontractor. Both parties shall be bound by the schedule and subsequent changes made by the contractor, who has the right to make changes to time, order, and priority in the various portions of the work.

Article 7—Subcontract Interpretation. Article 7.1, Inconsistencies and Omissions, states it "shall be the duty of the Subcontractor to so notify the Contractor in writing within three (3) working days of the Subcontractor's discovery thereof." Article 7.4, Attorneys' Fees, states the prevailing party shall be entitled to reasonable attorneys' fees to institute suit or demand arbitration to enforce the contract provisions.

Article 8—Contractor's Obligations.

Article 9—Subcontractor's Obligations.

Article 13—Changes, Claims and Delays. Article 13.2, Claims, differentiates between claims relating to the owner and claims relating to the contractor. Notification requirements relating to the owner shall be consistent with the contractor's contract provisions with the owner, but in sufficient time for the contractor to make such claims against the owner (13.2.2). Additionally, the subcontractor can pursue claims against the owner in the name of the contractor (13.2.2). Claims relating to the contractor require seven calendar days notice (13.2.3). Time extensions shall be provided for excusable delays (13.3.1). Liquidated damages may be proportionally assessed against the subcontractor by the contractor (13.2.2).

Article 14—Payment. Article 14.1.2, Copy of a Payment Request, says the contractor will provide the subcontractor, on request, a copy of the contractor's application for payment reflecting amounts approved and/or paid for the subcontractor work performed to date.

Article 15—Dispute Resolution. Article 15.1, Initial Dispute Resolution, recommends mediation before requesting arbitration. Article 15.3, Stay of Proceedings and Consolidation, addresses issues involving disputes with third parties and joint proceedings. Additionally, the contractor may consolidate arbitration with other subcontractors involving a common question of fact or law.

Article 16—Recourse by Contractor. Contains various clauses related to termination or suspension of work by either the owner or the contractor. It attempts to address issues of representation of the subcontractor by the contractor in dealing with the owner for various remedies.

8-10. CONCLUSION

Much has been said in this chapter about the need for good contractor-subcontractor relations. This cannot be overemphasized. Cooperation and good relations will help the contractor and subcontractor reduce the number of overall job problems and increase the chances of success for the project. Formal industry efforts, such as the use of fairer subcontract agreements described above and the implementation of partnering, discussed in chapter 11, are welcome actions for improvement of contractor-subcontractor relations.

CHAPTER 9

PRICING

9-1. INTRODUCTION

The purpose of pricing a claim is to give the owner a substantive description and detail of the extra costs incurred or to be incurred due to a contract change. The owner or his representative must have this detailed cost description in order to understand, negotiate, and justify extra contract costs.

Pricing of claims is divided into two types: forward pricing—where the price is negotiated before the work is done; and postpricing—pricing during or after performance of the work (e.g., actual costs). In either case, the pricing elements of the claim itself are the same, and include direct cost of performing the changed work, impact and/or delayed performance costs, and markups. There are no magic approaches or secret formulas for the successful pricing of claims. What is important is that the various pricing elements be carefully calculated and substantiated.

9-2. THE TWO TYPES OF PRICING

9-2a. Description of Forward Pricing and Postpricing

Forward pricing establishes a firm fixed price before the work is done, so the owner knows exactly how much a change will cost. This puts the bulk of the responsibility and risk of the new work on the contractor. The owner wants to negotiate a fair and reasonable price with the contractor, including time and compensation for foreseeable risks. This is a very practical approach for both parties as it allows the work to be incorporated into the contract with a firm price and (usually) schedule for the owner, provides a method of payment for the contractor, and resolves any issues of risk—typically born by the contractor.

Postpricing is used during performance of the work, for example, force accounting (payment based on records of actual work-hours and equipment use), or after the work is complete. Postpricing is used when a firm price cannot be reached before performance or when the nature and extent of the changed or added work is unknown.

In either case, it is important for the contractor to be aware of all costs to properly prepare proposals and ensure a fair return. The contractor will not receive any more than those costs which can be documented and justified to the owner. The theory that the contractor "makes out" on claims is a gross misconception. Owners are making it increasingly more difficult to recover anything more than actual costs plus a very small profit. Contracting bodies are using detailed profit and overhead computations, open ended negotiations, audits, and delayed payments to enable them to minimize the expense of claims and changes.

9-2b. Forward Pricing Is Typically Preferred

The U.S. Army Corps of Engineers, in its *Modification Impact Evaluation Guide*[1] emphasizes the importance of agreeing on price/time terms *before* allowing the contractor to proceed on modification work, "The attitude that the urgency for reaching a settlement no longer exists once the NTP [notice to proceed] has been issued is self-defeating. For many reasons, it is advantageous to the contractor to delay final settlement of all modifications until the work is finished." The *Guide* gives the following reasons:

1. The contractor can be less cost-conscious in doing the work.
2. Some of the risks contractually assigned to the contractor are shifted to the Corps of Engineers.
3. The contractor will have actual cost data with which to confront the Corps of Engineers. (Actual cost under this circumstance does not necessarily represent reasonable cost.)"[2]

The guide notes advantages to the Corps for forward pricing, but goes on to say, "A major benefit of settling modifications before performance is that it encourages prompt revision of the progress schedule, thus maintaining accurate knowledge of the sequencing of the remaining work, the final contract price, and the final completion date. The schedule then remains a realistic tool for determining the impact of changes on the contractor's

---

[1] U.S. Dept. of the Army, Office of the Chief of Engineers, *Modification Impact Evaluation Guide*, (1979 Edition), p. 3–4.
[2] Ibid.

operations. An up-to-date CPM schedule is a prerequisite to forecasting the presence and extent of impact."[3]

9-2c. Dealing with Risk in Forward Pricing

Because the contractor bears the bulk of the risks, the approach to forward pricing should be conservative and "pessimistic." It is important that a "worst case" condition be assumed when estimating costs, and everything affected or potentially affected by the change be included. The owner will not accept undefined contingencies in the price proposals and, often, the owner/engineer will not go out of his way to inform the contractor of all cost implications the change order might have on the project. After all, no one knows the costs better than the contractor himself.

A change order price proposal should include everything, within reason, that could be affected directly or indirectly by the change. This includes the effect on contract work not directly changed by the change order but nevertheless made more difficult or costly to perform. Claims for impact on "unchanged" work are recognized by the standard Changes clause for government contracts (see section 2-4f.). In estimating a new job, ideal conditions, worst conditions, or conditions somewhere between can be assumed when preparing the bid. In forward pricing, the worst conditions expected should be assumed—to serve as a contingency for the risks to be taken. That is, the contractor should list all possible risks and base his price on those that are more substantial and probable. Where substantial risks are identifiable, but unlikely and/or difficult to quantify, they should be explicitly excluded from the change proposal.

In the event there is reason to believe a change order will affect unchanged work, but cannot be either (1) discerned; (2) accurately estimated; or (3) negotiated, the contractor should expressly reserve the right to claim such cost, and time extensions, at a later date.

9-2d. Postpricing

In postpricing, the risks have been incurred and the added costs known. The difficulty is identifying and isolating all the changes and their attendant costs, such as impact costs. The contractor must have good cost records, with adequate descriptions of work performed. Thus, after a determination of which work was affected by a change, the contractor will be able to identify and price all the costs associated with the changed work.

9-3. TOTAL COST

9-3a. Total Cost and Modified Total Cost

Sometimes used on large claims where impact is significantly incurred throughout the project or certain phases of the project, and such impact is

[3]Ibid, p. 3–5.

difficult to identify and measure, a total cost, or modified total cost, approach may be taken to price the claim. Total cost is simply the actual total cost less the base bid cost and less the cost of change orders already paid. Instead of the bid cost, the modified total cost, or should cost, uses what original contract work should have cost (unimpacted cost) as the base cost and/or what the actual cost should have been rather than the actual cost. Either way, the difference between the two costs represents a measure of the resulting impact cost. This unimpacted baseline cost, or "reasonable" cost, can be established several different ways. These include

1. **Bid cost**—the costs as bid by the contractor if determined to be reasonable
2. **Actual cost data**—if identical work was performed on the same job, or another job of a similar nature, where the work was performed unimpaired by the change
3. **Reasonable estimate**—a new estimate of the work compiled using methods, crew size, and equipment based on the contractor's experience with the actual job conditions. The contractor recomputes what his costs would reasonably have been had changes not been encountered.

The use of the bid cost, although convenient, is generally unacceptable for representing the "reasonable" cost. The possibility of the estimator's unfamiliarity with local conditions, misjudgment of escalation, eagerness to get a job, unbalanced bids, or errors and omissions in the rush to complete the estimate before bid time, as well as owners' traditional mistrust of the contractor's bid amount, are all factors that tend to make bid estimates unacceptable. However, there are a few cases where the bid cost has been used to determine equitable adjustments in conjunction with total cost claims.

9-3b. Last Resort

Total cost claims result from a job that is so affected that the only feasible way of pricing the costs of the impact is to deduct from the actual cost the contractor's bid price (or reasonable cost). This method is less popular for computing adjustments because it is difficult to prove the owner's liability for the extra costs and the reasonableness of the bid costs

> Costs must be tied into fault on defendant's (owner's) part. A schedule of verified costs . . . is not proof of damages but only the starting point from which they can be proved. . . . Such a schedule verified by the defendant is not an admission of anything but the accuracy of the statement reflecting the contents of books and

records examined and the allocations and computations based thereon. Plaintiff's one witness who testified about costs only verified that they were incurred on the job. . . . That did not prove the defendant's responsibility for those costs nor their reasonableness.[4]

However, we have used this method under proper safe-guards where there is no other alternative since we recognized that the lack of certainty as to the amount of damages should not preclude recovery. . . . In cases (where) the fact of government responsibility for damages was clearly established the question was how to compute reasonable damages where no other method was available.[5]

9-3c. Four Conditions for Total Cost Claim

In WRB Corp. v. U.S., the Court of Claims has summarized the four conditions that should be present before consideration of a total cost approach can be taken on a claim settlement. They are that

1. The nature of the particular losses makes it impossible or highly impracticable to determine them with a reasonable degree of accuracy.
2. The contractor's bid or estimate was realistic.
3. The contractor's actual costs were reasonable.
4. The contractor was not responsible for the added expense.[6]

When the contractor's bid price is determined to contain inaccuracies, a modified total cost method can be employed, which substitutes a reasonable bid for the contractor's actual bid.[7]

9-4. COST ANALYSIS

Several types of analysis can be used to estimate what the work should have cost, absent impacts, including actual cost and estimates of reasonable costs.

---

[4] *River Construction Corp. v. U.S.*, 159 Ct. Cl. 254 (1962); also see *Appeal of Griffin and Dickvon*, AGBCA No. 74-104-4 (Dec. 4, 1985). (Contractor could not use total cost method to quantify claim because contractor failed to show that cost increase was caused solely by drawing errors.)

[5] *Hedin Construction Co. v. U.S.*, 171 Ct. Cl. 70 (1965).

[6] *WRB Corp. v. U.S.*, 183 Ct. Cl. 409 (1968); also see *Servidone Construction Corp. v. U.S.*, 931 F.2d 860 (Fed.Cir. 1991). (Contractor allowed to use the total cost method because all four conditions for its use were met.)

[7] *Servidone Construction Corp. v. U.S.*, 931 F.2d 860 (Fed.Cir. 1991). Affirming on appeal of 19 Cl.Ct.346 (1990).

9-4a. Actual Cost

In many instances of contracts affected by changes, each operation or item of work is not impacted completely from beginning to end. An item of work may begin as planned, only to undergo differing site conditions that have an adverse affect on the remainder of the operation. The actual unit prices for the work before or after an impacted period can be used to represent what the contractor would have experienced for the complete operation. The process of identifying a period of unimpacted work to serve as a baseline is sometime known as the measured mile approach.

However, such factors as high start-up costs, learning curve effects, future escalations, and weather may be necessary to adjust the experienced cost to reflect a realistic average for the entire item.

9-4b. Reasonable Costs Developed from Existing Job Data

Unit costs pulled from a computer report alone cannot be expected to prove factual evidence of cost. Unit costs vary widely depending on quantities recorded, material purchases made (and recorded), size of crews used, and types of equipment deployed for a particular period. The actual crews, equipment, and materials used should be described in the claim as well as the production achieved for the same period. The method used to record production should also be stated or demonstrated to support the unit costs that are being developed as the reasonable cost to perform an item of work. It is very important to show that such cost is "reasonable," or a representative average. If an ideal cost is shown, with ideal work conditions, the owner will not recognize those figures as representative. Reasonable unit costs must demonstrate normal inefficiency, typical weather conditions, and normal amounts of overtime that would be expected over the course of the job without any effects of impact due to changes.

9-4c. Estimating Reasonable Cost

If reasonable costs cannot be developed from historical data, they should be estimated as accurately as possible based on what the contractor thinks would have actually been incurred. The bid can be used as a guide or as supportive data for the reasonable estimate. Or, if the contractor has experience with similar work on other projects, he can use those cost experiences to help establish reasonable costs.

The contractor's experience and records of the work actually performed, even though impacted, can serve as a valuable reference in establishing how he would have done the work, that is, types of crews, equipment, methods, and material used. Both estimating aids will greatly help the contractor to compute reasonable costs. The same holds true for production and production rates, because both are instrumental in supporting costs. Of course, if the change being priced is a forward pricing change order, the contractor has less solid data to work with, but any existing historical data already accumulated can serve as a guideline.

9-5. THE PROPOSAL—REQUEST FOR EQUITABLE ADJUSTMENT

9-5a. General Pricing Philosophy

Claims typically begin with the submission of a change order proposal, or request for equitable adjustment (REA). In pricing claims, it is advisable for the contractor to keep in mind the goal of maintaining credibility with the owner. Pricing data should be clear, accurate, and concise.

Proposals should be in sufficient detail to permit an analysis of all material, labor, equipment, subcontracts, overhead costs, and profit, and should cover all work involved in the modification, whether such work was deleted, added, or changed. The contractor should strive to have the proposal prepared in an orderly, understandable, and contractually accurate manner to minimize analysis delays and to prevent unnecessary misinterpretations of the claim documents. Nothing is more counterproductive and disheartening than to invest a lot of time, money, and effort on a claim, only to have it rejected or returned because it is incorrect or unacceptable for analysis.

In government contracts, the best opportunity to settle disputed claims is with the contracting officer. The claim should be fully documented and cite relevant regulations and case law. This should be presented to the contracting officer as if he knew nothing about the cause of the claim, since it may be reviewed by persons unfamiliar with the case or may ultimately end up in court. The supporting data should be complete so the contracting officer will be able to justify to any superiors that an equitable adjustment would be fair and reasonable.

A thorough and complete claim document is absolutely essential, not only to support the validity of the claim but also to demonstrate at first glance that it is a well prepared case for the contractor.

9-5b. Pricing Elements and Details

The basic elements of the change order/claim proposal include

- Summary
  Entitlement, amount
  Time extension
  Reference to contract clauses and/or contract disputes act
- Narrative
  Facts
  Entitlement
- Schedule analysis, if applicable

- Pricing
    - Direct costs
        - Labor
        - Equipment
        - Permanent materials
        - Job materials
    - Impact costs
        - Impacts on other activities
        - Delay costs (standby time, escalation)
        - Acceleration costs (overtime premium, disruption)
        - Lost productivity (disruption) costs
    - Markups
        - Jobsite overhead
        - Home office overhead
        - Profit
        - Bond

In forward pricing, the most convenient and acceptable method of pricing is to estimate production rates for the changed work, show crew compositions and crew hours required to perform the changed work, and determine the type of equipment and equipment hours needed to support the crews. Material costs should be listed separately and substantiated with quotes, invoices, or price lists. For postpricing, names and dates of people and equipment can be listed, summarized, and submitted. Copies of time cards are usually not required, so long as they are available for verification. On force account change orders, the work is documented and verified on a daily basis by both the owner and the contractor. Where possible, preagreed equipment rates, unit costs and/or crew rates should be established early in the project. This will expedite the negotiation and processing of individual changes.

9-5c. Production Rates

In computing production rates for forward-priced changes and to establish a reasonable cost, it is important to consider all the factors that might possibly increase or decrease the computed rate. The size of the crews and the production rates are the two most important items affecting the value of the work to be performed. The *Construction Contract Negotiating Guide* (1974, p. 4–8) recommends including all possible factors that will influence production rates, including

1. Relative experience, capability, and morale of workers
2. Size and complexity of the job
3. Climatic and topographic conditions

4. Degree of mechanization
5. Quality of the job supervision
6. Existing labor-management agreements and/or trades practices
7. Learning curve—function of size, type of work, amount of interruptions, and nonrepetitive tasks.[8]

The *Guide* also says

> The complex interplay of factors affecting work rates tends to produce more than the usual amount of doubt and disagreement, and increases the danger of substantial contingency allowances. To offset the advantage that uncertainty always gives the contractor, the negotiator must bring all his analytical skill and experience to bear on the work rate problem. This is particularly important since contractor-subcontractor direct labor is commonly the single largest dollar item in Government construction. Thus a relatively small 'cushion' in a contractor's work rate estimate, perhaps as small as 2% of the total estimate cost, may double or even triple the contractor's profit margin.[9]

9-5d. Overhead and Profit

In addition to the direct costs of performing extra work, a contractor is entitled to a reasonable allowance for overhead and profit, typically in the form of fixed percentage markups. These markups are either specified in the original contract or agreed in writing by the parties after the contract has been signed. Combined rates for overhead and profit may be specified, such as 15% for overhead and profit sometimes used in Veteran Administration contracts. More often, separate percentage markups are used, including two overhead elements—jobsite overhead and home office overhead.

9-5d.1. Project overhead rates. Computation of overhead poses special problems because it is difficult to isolate the extra elements of costs due to contract changes. Overhead costs are not allocated to different items of work like direct costs, but are lumped into a series of overhead accounts that are theoretically spread out over the entire project. Thus, when performing a change order, the additional overhead costs that accompany the change are inseparable from the routine overhead costs. The time relationship of overhead costs as well as the impact of costs that do not manifest themselves immediately, if ever, are two additional problems in determining full overhead costs of each change.

---

[8]U.S. Dept. of the Army, Office of the Chief of Engineers, *Construction Contract Negotiating Guide*, (1974 Edition), p. 4–8.
[9]Ibid, p. 4–9.

PRICING

Therefore, overhead is often estimated on a percentage basis. Some contracts provide fixed percentage markups for overhead, profit, and subcontracts under a changes and/or pricing clause, thus avoiding the problem of computing actual additional overhead costs for each change order. However, the suspension of work clauses under those contracts, as well as the changes and pricing clauses under current federal contracts, require a showing of all the elements of overhead, and a computation of profit on a weighted factor basis.

Overhead costs include two elements: (1) fixed costs; and (2) variable costs. Fixed costs are those that remain essentially unchanged over time or volume of work, for example, the rental of an office trailer. Variable costs change with volume of work and passage of time, for example, utility costs. A greater use of water or electricity brings higher monthly bills.

Since many overhead costs appear to be fixed, owners are very reluctant to pay additional overhead costs without convincing documentation. This is a legitimate concern, except that it is very difficult to identify and prove overhead costs that are hidden or do not show up until later in the job. These include the wear and tear on fixed assets and human resources, diversion of supplies or equipment that must later be replaced, and decreased attention to contract work due to increased attention that the changes require. Contract overhead is often spread thin at the outset in order to keep down costs, and changes can create significant demands on the contractor's limited resources. Any means by which the contractor can identify and quantify such items are helpful in substantiating and recovering overhead costs.

On contracts that do not contain fixed percentage markups, it is usually advantageous to negotiate a supplemental agreement to the contract to permit fixed markups for minor changes. This saves both the owner and contractor the time-consuming tasks of computing and analyzing overhead costs for each and every change order. An example of a fixed rate percentage system is the "Flat Rate System for Changes under $15,000" once used on the Washington Metro subway system (see Appendix 13).

9-5d.2. Overhead on large claims. On major claims, there are several means of computing overhead costs, and the one offering the most reasonable result should be selected. The first method is similar to that discussed: applying percentages based on cost experience, or the original bid percentage, to the direct costs claimed. Second is the "total cost" method, where the bid overhead (plus any overhead received on other change orders) is deducted from the total actual overhead (during the period in question). A third method, which amounts to a modified "total cost," is to take the total actual overhead and deduct the "reasonable" overhead. Reasonable overhead can be computed any number of ways. The simplest method is to take a percentage of the direct costs that would have been incurred had there been no change or delay.

For use in claims where delayed performance or suspended work is incurred, the contractor can compute an average daily rate for project overhead. This rate is then multiplied by the number of days of delay or suspension experienced to arrive at the overhead cost for the affected period.

Finally, a fifth method is to identify, isolate, and include as a direct cost of the claim any items normally included in overhead accounts but that have been added for the purpose of administration of, and therefore are, clearly attributable to, the specific claim or change order. For example, an additional supervisor, bookkeeper, or engineer required strictly because of the change would not be fairly compensated in the normal percentage markup. With this last method, the basic overhead for the change is computed on a percentage basis.

9-5d.3. Home office overhead—Eichleay formula. In addition to project overhead, contractors incur home office expenses that serve all projects, such as rent, telephone, home office salaries, taxes, payroll and bookkeeping expenses, and insurance. As such, these overhead expenses are an indirect expense that benefit all projects and must be allocated to all projects on a shared basis. For the purpose of routine change orders, a fixed percentage markup is often negotiated, as described above, that is added to direct costs along with project overhead and profit.

For delay claims, a formula has evolved that computes home office overhead on a daily rate basis. Recognized by the boards and courts, the Eichleay formula[10] has become accepted as a method to measure and reimburse the contractor for overhead costs when a delay or suspension has stopped the revenue flow that would have been used to cover the delayed project's portion of the home office overhead. This formula assumes that almost all overhead is fixed and evenly distributed across all projects. The formula computes the daily amount of overhead to be applied to each day of delay incurred as follows:

(a) $\dfrac{\text{Contract Billings}}{\text{Total Billings for Contract Period}} \times \text{Total Overhead for Contract Period} = \text{Overhead Allocable to the Contract}$

(b) $\dfrac{\text{Allocable Overhead}}{\text{Days of Performance}} = \text{Daily Contract Overhead}$

(c) $\text{Daily Contract Overhead} \times \text{Days of Delay} = \text{Amount claimed (Total Added Overhead)}$

---

[10]*Eichleay Company,* ASBCA ¶ 5183, 60–2 BCA ¶ 2688.

In recent years, the federal courts have carefully defined the circumstances under which the Eichleay formula must be allowed. The formula must be allowed when there is a distinct period of government-caused suspension or delay of work that has an impact on the absorption of the contractor's fixed home office overhead expenses.[11] If the suspension or delay is of an uncertain duration, forcing the contractor to stand by at the jobsite, it is presumed that the contractor was prevented from obtaining replacement work that could have absorbed the home office overhead.[12]

These rulings recognize that when a contractor bids a fixed amount for a construction contract with a stipulated performance period, the contractor reasonably expects that contract to absorb a certain portion of the contractor's fixed home office expenses. To the extent performance is delayed or suspended and cash flow is reduced, the contractor experiences an underabsorption of home office overhead.

Although there may be other methods of computing home office overhead, Eichleay is clearly the formula of choice, as ruled in 1994 by the Federal Circuit Court

> Because it is impossible to determine the amount of unabsorbed overhead caused by the delay of any particular contract, and because the *Eichleay* formula provides an equitable method of compensating a contractor for unabsorbed overhead without costing taxpayers more than they should pay, we hold that the *Eichleay* formula is the exclusive means for compensating a contractor for unabsorbed overhead when it otherwise meets the *Eichleay* prerequisites.[13]

Even though other methods have been accepted in the past and are fully described in the *Audit Guidance Delay and Disruption Claims*[14] guidebook, unless and until such time other formulas are accepted again by the Federal Circuit Court, use the Eichleay formula.

9-5d.4. Profit. Contractors are entitled to a reasonable profit on extra work. As mentioned earlier, profit is a fixed percentage amount to be added to the direct cost of changed work. The percentage amount may be specified in the contract, otherwise it must be negotiated between the owner and the

---

[11]*Capital Electric Co. v. U.S.*, 729 F.2d 743 (Fed.Cir. 1984).
[12]*Interstate General Government Contractors, Inc. v. West*, 12 F.3d 1053 (Fed.Cir. 1993).
[13]*Wickham Contracting Co., Inc. v. Fischer*, 12 F.3d 1574 (Fed.Cir. 1994).
[14]*Audit Guidance Delay and Disruption Claims*, Defense Contract Audit Agency, 1988, p. 9–13. Note, this pamphlet was formally canceled on July 11, 1994 and no longer represents DCAA's policies on the audit of claims. As of Oct. 15, 1996, guidance on claims is provided in CAM 12-500-800.

contractor. Some contracts will provide a formula for the contractor to use to calculate the profit on a "weighted" basis, using such factors as risk, complexity, and size of the change.

Profit on claims made under suspension of work clauses is not allowable. The contractor should be careful when choosing the clause under which he submits his claims, for delays originating from differing site conditions or defective specifications do qualify for profit markup.

9-6. USE OF FORMS

When pricing change orders, the use of forms aids the preparation of proposals and improves organization of records. This also establishes the contractor's line of thought for the negotiation that is sure to follow. Since good preparation is the single most important item required for successful negotiations, well-organized proposals and supporting data are essential for establishing a strong bargaining position. Standardized forms aid cost computations and reduce the chances of duplications and omissions. They also allow for adjustability when computing alternate proposal methods. When negotiating, standardized forms facilitate recalculation of proposal totals as adjustments are made. Knowing how adjustments of specific negotiated items are going to affect the total price is an important element of negotiations, and the quicker the contractor can say yes or no to an adjustment, the quicker a settlement will be reached.

Pricing of proposals is an art similar to estimating contracts, and one becomes more adept with experience. Each change order may contain variables, so there is no single standard format or procedure to be used for all changes. Appendix 14 contains examples of simplified pricing formats that have been used on large public construction projects for both small and large change orders. This form shows how the data was summarized and how markups were applied. It should be noted that the application and use of standard forms was acceptable to the owners, and that the forms served as the basis for settlement of many changes.

9-7. MATERIAL QUANTITIES AND PRICES

When estimating material costs for change orders, the same considerations normally given to material takeoff and pricing apply. Since changes involve purchasing of small quantities with increased handling, more attention should be paid to pricing to ensure all costs are considered. "In estimating quantities, an allowance must be made for loss due to waste, spoilage, scrap, pilferage . . . and should always be evaluated in the light of the specific job conditions. Allowance should be kept to a minimum by the require-

PRICING 113

ment for reasonable and adequate care."[15] Sources for material prices include quotations, published price lists, records, handbooks, and published indices. The U.S. Army cites a number of factors that should be taken into account when pricing materials, including

1. Purchasing practice—higher prices of a reliable supplier
2. Salvagability of job material and excess purchases
3. Odd lot sizes cost more
4. Quantity discounts not applicable or not able to be taken
5. Cash discounts not applicable or not able to be taken
6. Transportation and handling costs (special deliveries)
7. Inspection and testing costs
8. Taxes and duties
9. Escalation
10. Storage[16]

Pricing varies with the estimator's experience and judgment. Most contractors have general guidelines for preparing bids, and the claims estimator can base the price procedure on a personal estimating system. The price theories and approaches discussed in this chapter are intended to be compatible with any estimating system. Appendix 15 contains a pricing checklist for the estimator for computing allowable costs due to claims and change orders.

The estimator should add to this list any additional items from prior experience. The contractor's list of job cost accounts can serve as an additional reference, particularly for detailing overhead costs.

9-8. IMPACT AND INEFFICIENCY COSTS

9-8a. How Impact Costs Are Incurred

Under the Changes clause, the cost of performing unchanged work can be included in the equitable adjustment only if such cost is affected by the performance of the change, "If so, those increased costs of performing the unchanged work which are directly attributable to and which flow from the change are properly compensable under the change order."[17] Examples of impact on unchanged work due to a change order are

[15]See Note 8, p. 4–2.
[16]Ibid, p. 4–3.
[17]*Bruno Law & Richard Marlink, Trustees v. U.S.*, 195 Ct. Cl. 370 (1971); also see *Appeal of Batteast Construction Co., Inc.*, ASBCA No. 35818 (Dec. 31, 1991). (Contractor compensated because a directed change in the mortar mix specification resulted in lost labor productivity for masonry work.)

- Changes in sequence of work
- Changes in the manner and method planned to do the work
- Use of different types or capacity equipment
- Disruption to planned continuity of work
- Additional mobilizations and demobilizations
- Increased congestion of work areas
- Overtime or premium time incurred to overcome delays caused by the above.

9-8b. Specific, Identifiable Extra Work

To compute the effect of changes on unchanged work, it is necessary to show specifically what increased costs are incurred, or to show what the actual cost was compared to what the work would have cost without the change order. With smaller change orders, it is easier to show the added cost of an item of work. For example, costs increase if an item took three shifts to complete where it normally would have taken two shifts; or, since a bigger crane was needed to perform the change order work, the same bigger and more expensive crane was used to perform contract work, or its access was blocked on one side of the project due to added work. In such cases, it is simply a matter of computing the additional hours of equipment and labor used or planned to be used as well as additional materials that will be needed. With larger delay, or disruption or acceleration claims, the pricing of impact becomes more complex.

9-8c. Pricing Inefficiency and Loss of Productivity

Unfortunately, most impact costs are not as easily identified and quantified as the examples in the previous section. Inefficiency and lost productivity costs can often be identified and directly traced to the change, including

- Restricted access
- Larger crews
- Different crew makeup
- Hiring of additional, less well-trained workers
- Loss of trained workers (due to delays or negative working conditions)
- Loss of morale
- Stacking of trades (unplanned, concurrent work by two or more trades)
- Overcrowding
- Out-of-sequence work
- Stop and go operations
- Piecemeal work
- Rework

- Standby
- Loss of learning curve gains
- Working in different environmental conditions (winter weather)

One can compute inefficiency factors by comparing productivity of work performed under actual impacted conditions versus work rates achieved under normal working conditions. In addition, generalized industry rates can be used to substantiate and supplement calculated factors. The *Modification Impact Evaluation Guide*[18], was written specifically to assist U.S. Army Corps. of Engineer personnel to identify, evaluate, and estimate costs arising from impact on unchanged work. It discusses issues of disruption, crowding, and acceleration, including examples of calculating costs using productivity charts as well as detailed examples of network schedule analysis. The *Impact Guide* productivity loss calculations include

- Disruption
- Crowding
- Increasing the size of crews
- Increasing shift and/or days worked per week

9-8c.1. Disruption. Loss of job rhythm, stop-and-go work, repetitive setup, adjustments to new tasks, and loss of learning curve opportunity all impact productivity. The basic principle of all learning curve studies is that efficiency increases as an individual or team repeats an operation over and over. The *Impact Guide* presents a method to quantify such disruption costs by using a theoretical productivity scale.

Assuming a skilled construction worker can reach maximum productivity after one eight-hour shift, the theoretical productivity scale shows the different losses of "getting up to speed" when shifting from one task to another. If shifting to an activity that a person doesn't normally do, such as an ironworker switching from work with structural steel to reinforcing steel, the first eight hours of work would be considered at starting from a 0 starting point, with the result of a four-hour loss of efficiency. Shifting to a similar item of work, such as a carpenter switching from wall forms to column forms, or shifting the same type of work from one location to another, might result in a 90% starting factor, which translates to a 0.8-hour productivity loss. (See the construction operations learning chart, Figures 4-1a. and 4-1b. in Appendix 16.)

9-8c.2. Crowding. According to the *Impact Guide*, lowered productivity can result from scheduling more workers than can normally function effectively into a limited working space. To quantify such resulting loss

[18]See Note 1, p. 4–6 to 4–11.

of productivity, a crowding factor is calculated and the percentage loss is developed from a crowding loss curve. For example, if an activity that takes three workers is shifted into a period of time where 15 workers are already performing work activities, a 20% crowding factor (3/15) has been incurred. According to the crowding loss curve, the 20% crowding factor translates to an 8% loss of labor efficiency (Appendix 16, Figure 4-2).

9-8c.3. Increasing the size of crews. As more workers are added to the optimum crew, each new worker will increase crew productivity less than the previously added worker. The optimum crew size for a project or activity represents a balance between an acceptable rate of progress and the maximum return from the labor dollars invested. Increasing crew size above optimum can usually produce a higher rate of progress, but at a higher unit cost. The composite overloading chart provided by the *Impact Guide* summarizes the effects of such impact, including percentage increase in productivity, percentage efficiency loss, and total crew unproductive labor cost (Appendix 16, Figure 4-3a).

9-8c.4. Increasing shift and/or days worked per week. Working more than eight hours per day or more than five days per week introduces premium pay rates and efficiency losses. The efficiency losses result from a slower pace by workers, fatigue from longer hours, working in conditions of less light in the later hours of the day, and traffic, disruption, and loss of coordination with workers not working the same overtime who leave the jobsite. The *Impact Guide* includes an efficiency loss chart for various configurations. (See Appendix 16, Figure 4-4. Also see Appendix 7 in the Bureau of Labor Statistics' *Report 917* and the Business Round Table's *Productivity Loss Due to Overtime.*)

9-8d. Material and Equipment Costs

Material and equipment costs for unchanged work can also be affected by delays and impacts. Possible increased material costs can be incurred through

- Escalation due to price increases or inflation
- Loss of discounts
- Disruption to suppliers' planning, production, and/or delivery schedules
- Additional handling, storage, and damage replacement costs
- Obsolescence

Possible equipment increases include

- Standby and storage costs
- Idle time
- Additional demobilization and mobilization costs

PRICING 117

- Increased wear and tear due to different working conditions
- Loss of efficiency, disruption, and longer hours to accomplish the same work
- Equipment unable to be used on other jobs or tasks
- Loss of use of equipment planned to be obtained from other jobs but now having to be purchased or leased from other sources (at higher rates)

9-9. OTHER ISSUES OF CLAIMS PRICING

9-9a. Interest Costs

A contractor is responsible for providing the capital required to perform a construction contract. If the project owner expands the scope of work and increases the contract price, however, the contractor may be able to recover the cost of borrowing money necessary to perform the additional work.[19] This assumes the contract does not contain a clause that specifically disallows interest. To collect interest, if allowed, the contractor must segregate the loan proceeds in a separate account and the funds used solely for performance of the change order work.[20]

If the contractor does not borrow money to perform change order work, but uses its available equity capital, there can be no recovery for imputed interest, or the "cost" of this capital.[21]

From the collective readings of these and other cases, it can be concluded that four factors must be met for interest costs to be allowed:

1. The work must be directed by the owner.
2. The funds must have actually been borrowed.
3. The borrowed funds must be segregated in a separate account.
4. The borrowed funds must have been used only for the changed work.

On federal construction contracts, interest on claims is allowable from the date that (1) the contracting officer receives the claim (certified if required); or (2) payment otherwise would be due, if that date is later, until the date of payment.[22] Simple interest for such claims is paid at rates fixed by the Secretary of the Treasury as provided in the Contract Disputes Act.

---

[19]*Joseph Bell v. United States*, 404 F.2d 975 (Fed.Cir. 1969).
[20]*Appeal of J.W. Bateson Co., Inc.*, VABCA No. 1148 (Dec. 4, 1985).
[21]*Gevyn Construction Corp. v. U.S.*, 827 F.2d 752 (Fed.Cir. 1987).
[22]*Interest on Claims*, F.A.R. 33.208.

9-9b. Legal Fees, Change Orders, and Claim Preparation Costs

The costs of preparing routine change orders are typically considered incidental to contract performance and included as part of the overhead markup added to the price of the change order. One situation where change order preparation costs may be allowed is when the owner *requests* a price for a change order but then never issues the change order.[23]

On private and nonfederal contracts, legal fees are typically not allowed on claims unless specifically provided for in the contract. Similarly, on federal contracts, costs of legal, accounting, and consulting services, and related costs, incurred in the connection with "the prosecution of claims or appeals against the Federal Government" are unallowable."[24] In other words, once a claim has met the definition as described in the Federal Acquisition Regulation (FAR), further costs to pursue the case are unallowed.

However, there are situations where the fees of outside consultants have been allowed: "In contrast to the cases where recovery was disallowed, these consultant services were provided at a time when both sides were amenable to a contract modification and were actively negotiating a price adjustment. The efforts therefore provided a direct benefit to the contract and were not merely the preparation of a claim."[25] Also

> The line between costs that are incidental to contract administration and costs that are incidental to prosecution of a claim is rather indistinct. . . . The negotiation process often involves requests for information by [the owner] and inevitably this exchange of information involves costs for the contractor. These costs are contract administration costs, which should be allowable since this negotiation process benefits the owner, regardless of whether a settlement is finally reached or whether litigation eventually occurs, because the availability of the process increases the likelihood of settlement without litigation."[26]

Another situation that may provide recovery of legal fees is the Equal Access to Justice Act (EAJA). The EAJA provides that appeal costs of an adverse contracting officer's decision can be recovered under the following conditions:

---

[23]*Appeal of Tele-Sentry Security, Inc.*, GSBCA No. 7037 (May 7, 1984); see also *Appeal of Kirk Brothers Mechanical Contractors, Inc.*, ASBCA No. 35771 (June 29, 1992).
[24]F.A.R. 31.205–47.
[25]Recovery of Change Order Administration Costs, *Construction Claims Monthly*, Sept. 1996.
[26]*Bill Strong Enterprises, Inc., v. Shannon*, 49 F.3d 15431 (Fed.Cir. 1995).

PRICING

1. The business has a net worth of not more than $7 million and no more than 500 employees.
2. The contractor was the "prevailing party" in the appeal.
3. The government's position in response to either the initial claim or the appeal was not "substantially justified."

The EAJA provides for a maximum hourly rate of legal fees, plus paralegal and consulting fees not exceeding rates paid for comparable services by the federal government. Certain preparation costs, expert witness fees, and expenses are also recoverable. Only those expenses incurred after the contracting officer's decision are allowed by the EAJA.

9-9c. Use of Expert Opinions

The use of experts for large claims may be an expense well spent. Scheduling experts should be used when the claim involves delays, acceleration, and attendant impact. A good consultant will make an objective analysis of the situation, one that can stand up under oath during testimony, and will help the respective parties make more reasoned judgments on the validity of time and costs. An outside expert may find the value of an impact vastly higher or lower than the contractor's assessment, and if called in during occurrence of the change, the expert can assist the contractor in finding ways to mitigate the effects of the change. If incurred in the interest of preparation of change order proposals, such costs may occasionally be allowed as described in the previous section.

9-9d. Critical Path Method Submissions for Payment Purposes

Many projects require an updated critical path method schedule to either determine or accompany monthly progress payment requests. Although accepted during the course of the job for payment purposes, if the quantities and percent complete are not accurate, they will not be accepted in court for the purpose of schedule analysis. Conversely, if accurate, these submissions will help support baseline production rates used in claims.

9-9e. Federal Cost Principles

A set of cost principles has been developed by the federal government to assist in the negotiation of government contracts and contract modifications. Section 31.000 of the FAR reads: "This part contains cost principles and procedures for (a) the pricing of contracts, subcontracts, and modifications to contracts and subcontracts whenever cost analysis is performed (see 15.805–3) and (b) the determination, negotiation, or allowance of costs when required by a contract clause."

These principles may be used as a guide, but the contractor should include those costs that he feels are justified and allowable. Appendix 17 contains portions of FAR sections 31.1 and 31.2, and a list of the various cost classifications contained in section 31.2. Of particular interest here are the several opening paragraphs of section 31.201 to 31.203, which discuss "Determining allowability," "Determining reasonableness," "Determining allocability," "Direct costs," and "Indirect costs."

9-10. CONCLUSION

Once entitlement is settled, the amount of the equitable adjustment is essentially a matter of proof of costs. Good records and a thorough understanding of the items of work are more than half the effort in pricing a claim. Assembly of the information, organization of the data, and performance of necessary calculations then follow easily. Since this supporting data are essential for successful negotiations and are subject to audit on larger claims, the contractor is well advised to prepare accurate and complete price proposals.

CHAPTER 10

NEGOTIATIONS

10-1. INTRODUCTION

Negotiation is an art, and negotiation in construction is a high form of that art, since it requires the deliberate application of techniques and strategies aimed at a specific goal: the equitable adjustment of an impacted contract based on time and cost. On small changes, the difference in an engineer's (owner's) estimate and those of the contractor are often resolved through the simple verification of prices and computations. Of course, if the engineer's estimate is higher than that of the contractor, the owner is likely to settle for the contractor's price without negotiation.

As the dollar or time magnitude of a contract change increases, the likelihood of negotiation is greater and, concurrently, the gap between the engineer's and contractor's estimates is likely to widen. At this point the negotiating parties enter the picture, and politics, as well as engineering, come into play. In fact, negotiation is sometimes considered a relief from the normal administration of the contract, for it offers both parties the opportunity to break away from the daily administrative pressures of the contract. Innovation and personality now come into play.

Each side has particular advantages and disadvantages. The contractor knows his costs exactly, can adjust prices for maximum revenue, and can accept or reject a settlement as he so chooses. The owner's representative, the engineer, has a strong advantage in that he holds the purse strings. Although there is an obligation to reach a settlement, the engineer is bound by procurement rules, regulations, and approvals by superiors. He is often caught between trying to keep the contractor content and his superiors happy. Former Secretary of State Henry Kissinger said that each party to a negotiation has certain requirements and goals—and the art of negotiation is finding out what the other party's goals are and satisfying them. The successful contractor and negotiator is the one that knows how to achieve this goal quickly. Since the contractor has a larger degree of freedom in making his proposal and accepting a settlement, he has a tremendous asset in setting the pace and direction of the negotiations.

10-2. PREPARATION AND KNOWLEDGE

Adequate preparation and familiarity with the job are the two most important items required of the successful negotiator. He can be more aggressive and is less likely to end up floundering for defensive comments when confronted with what would otherwise be unfamiliar questions. The contractor wants to take the offensive and be as aggressive as possible. Such an attitude, along with firm knowledge of the work, can be very persuasive and influential

> The successful negotiation of price demands careful and complete preparation. Negotiation without adequate preparation invites failure. . . . Spending sufficient time and effort on analyzing the proposal, gathering pertinent pricing and other data, and formulating a definitive and defensible negotiation position will serve the negotiator better than any repertoire of bargaining table techniques. Adequate preparation enables the negotiator to negotiate with strength—to take and hold the initiative throughout the negotiation conference and to meet any contingency with confidence, self-respect, and integrity of position.[1]

10-3. FORWARD PRICING CLAIMS

When negotiating forward pricing changes, well-prepared estimates serve as a solid foundation from which to bargain. "The successful negotiator will have well thought-out logic to support his pricing theory and will present data showing that the theory was an accurate predictor of costs in past cases. This combination of concrete factual data and sound pricing logic is the essential ingredient of a strong negotiating position. A second principle is that there is greater strength in an affirmative position than in a negative one."[2]

---

[1] U.S. Department of the Army, Office of the Chief of Engineers, *Construction Contract Negotiating Guide*, (1974 Edition), p 8–1.
[2] Ralph C. Nash, Jr., *Government Contract Changes* (Federal Publication, Inc. , Washington, D.C., 1975), p. 480.

In preparing the claim, include everything that appears justified. If, in the owner's opinion, an item is not justified and the owner convincingly explains why, it will not be allowed. However, if entitlement to an item is not clear cut or the cost not clearly unallowable, the owner may concur with the item. At other times, these marginal items may influence leniency toward other sections of the claim or be used as a tradeoff. At worst, concession of questionable items will have a favorable psychological effect in that the owner will have won some battles and will be more inclined to concede other issues.

Additionally, owners should not try to prescribe how contractors should perform and schedule the work, otherwise, they will become responsible for all resulting risks and costs. The *Construction Contract Negotiating Guide* specifically warns of this in discussion of imposing scheduling restraints

> The government assumes additional work can be performed within existing time restraints and without additional resources by performing the work on a concurrent basis. . . . [The] government may *suggest* that by concurrency techniques, the contractor could and should have been able to make up some of the delay. However, the contractor is under no contractual compulsion to do this. The government is at a serious disadvantage in this type of negotiation [time changes]. Insistence that the contractor accept the government's schedule approach and price may open the way for the contractor to argue that the government is prescribing a method of construction and thereby relieving the contractor of all technical and time responsibility. In combination with the contractor's sole-source position, this argument quickly exposes the weakness of the government bargaining leverage. If the government has been so imprudent as to indicate that there is also a rigid time requirement, the contractor need do little more than sit back and wait for his price terms to be met.[3]

10-4. PREPARATION FOR NEGOTIATION MEETING

Before going into the negotiation meeting, it is important to establish a strategy, the framework from which the topics to be negotiated will be approached. The following points are stressed by the *Construction Contract Negotiating Guide*

---

[3]See Note 1, p. B-16.

1. Establish objectives and how they might be obtained

    a. Which objectives cannot be compromised under any circumstances
    b. Which can be compromised and to which extent
    c. Which ones are expected to be compromised or dropped totally (pie-in-the-sky)

2. Anticipate position of your opponent

    a. Is there competition for forward priced changes (can another contractor be given the work)?
    b. How bad is the need for the work?
    c. Is there time pressure for an agreed price?
    d. Are there any regulatory, legal, political, and/or public pressure aspects that might affect an agreement?

3. Strategies should be flexible (Plan alternate strategies in case the primary strategy has to be abandoned.)[4]

Proper preparation also means assembling all necessary data and documents that may be required to support the contractor's position in the negotiation sessions. Most of this data probably is already included in the claim document, but additional substantiation that might be of assistance—comparison charts, for example—should be brought along to the meeting.

10-5. TACTICS—CONTROL OF THE MEETING

The contractor wants to control the tone, pace, and atmosphere of negotiations by choosing which items to discuss first, taking the heat off items that are not going well, accepting certain decisions, and knowing when to compromise. Some claims are better negotiated by discussing the strongest sections first, to be reassured that no flaws or surprises will be sprung later to alter the rest of the claim. At other times, weaker portions should be discussed first to explore the attitude of the opposition. Keeping the opposition off balance is an active negotiation tactic that can be used to achieve optimum results. If the owner wants to begin discussions, he should be allowed to talk so long as his attitude is cooperative and the contractor is comfortable with the direction pursued.

Remember, the owner is also trying to maintain control of negotiations.

---

[4]Dept. of the Army, p. 8 3.

To control communication, the chief negotiator should avoid the defensive stance and keep the negotiating team members quiet: "An astute contractor might trick the team members into contradicting each other, or a team member might say something that would upset the team's planned strategy."[5] Control of communications can be maintained by diplomacy and tact. Be punctual, cordial, tolerant, and patient. Use clear, simple language and keep distractions to a minimum.

The contractor should try to maintain the pace of the meeting. The items within a claim can usually be arranged in any number of different logical sequences, so the contractor has a legitimate reason to request changes in topics. When negotiating large and difficult claims, it pays to be deliberate, and to plan and execute alternative strategies and tactics

> "Most contractors realize that, in negotiation, the less specific knowledge the government representatives possess, the more easily their judgment can be influenced. Consequently, during a negotiation the contractor will pass over a vulnerable point by presenting an abundance of information on the point, seemingly with good intentions, but actually with the aim of misdirecting the negotiators thinking or by making sweeping generalizations that, in themselves are true, but which are not decisive for the point at hand"[6]

The government negotiator will consistently ask questions of the contractor and make requests for details in order to control the meeting, find loopholes, and encourage the contractor to make concessions.

10-6. TACTICS—LARGE CLAIMS

In large claims, the amounts claimed are usually negotiated item by item. Early in negotiations, the contractor should ascertain the owner's position on all items, without making commitments, to get an idea where he stands on an overall basis. He should then study the differences to see where more work can be accomplished, and how much work might be needed to get the settlement closer to an acceptable amount. After strengthening his position with additional data, the contractor is ready for a second negotiating session. This time the contractor should make an all-out effort to achieve his goal and begin to make compromises on individual items. At the conclusion of the second session, the contractor should be approaching his goal and should attempt an overall settlement. If a satisfactory compromise cannot be

---
[5]Ibid, p. 8–5.
[6]Ibid, p. 8–9.

reached, the negotiation sequence must be repeated until either an agreement or impasse is reached.

Even though all points are not won, a strong position is important and should be maintained

> The Contracting Officer's decision will be made in the context of many factors, Sometimes these factors—although very human and understandable—are totally improper, and their consideration is contrary to his legal duty. Generally he will be favorable to your cause only to the extent you persuade him that you have a case strong enough to obtain, on appeal to a contract appeals board, a greater recovery than you are willing to settle for at his level[7].

Leave some bargaining room and expect some give and take. Initially, the contractor should request more than he expects to recover. No matter how justified his position, it is the naive contractor who is not prepared to bargain. What it ultimately boils down to is the strength of his position: "Within certain limits, at least, negotiation is a matter of 'horse trading.' The extent to which the negotiator or the contractor makes concessions without getting anything in return depends upon the relative bargaining positions of the parties."[8]

10-7. OTHER NEGOTIATION TACTICS

Sometimes "bargaining table" tactics are necessary to change the pace of a meeting. Take the adversary out to lunch, create a less tense environment. As a last resort, use politics. That is, go over a negotiator's head to any superiors who might be able to loosen things up, when justified.

If an item has to be conceded, do it graciously and with a sense of humor. Likewise, if a position is firm, don't back off. Never take a hard position from which you might retreat. If a lowest offer is tendered with the understanding that an appeal will be filed should that offer be rejected, then stick to that position.

There is a time and place for bargaining tactics, and they should be used with care and discretion.

10-8. OTHER NEGOTIATION CONSIDERATIONS

Getting the owner to the negotiation table can be a chore in itself. It is important not to give the owner any excuse to delay the negotiations. The

---

[7]Overton A. Currie and Luther P. House, Jr. "Preparing Construction Claims for Settlement, "Briefing Papers #68-5, 1 Briefing Papers Collection 347, 353.

[8]Dept. of the Army, p. 8–12.

proposal should be as complete as possible and submitted as early as possible. Meet with the owner and negotiate a timetable for submission of the proposal and commencement of negotiations. Failure to negotiate can be a cause for breach of contract, so the contractor should stay on top of the owner to be sure he comes to the negotiation table. With involved negotiations, the contractor should demand a schedule to insure that discussions remain continuous until a settlement is reached. Loss of momentum will do more harm than good when negotiating.

10-9. AUTHORITY TO NEGOTIATE

The contractor should seek the owner's assurance that his negotiator has full authority and will stick with the negotiation without unnecessary interruptions. The contractor should also confirm that the owner will participate or monitor the negotiations so that the whole effort will not be rejected or tossed back for renegotiation at a later date.

Detailed records of the negotiations must be kept, including dates of all meetings canceled or rescheduled. Meeting minutes should be dated and contain the names of all participants, the start-stop times, and as much detail as possible of the business that transpired in the meeting. Offers and counteroffers should be confirmed in writing by both parties. The method and schedule of payment should also be firmly established.

10-10. CONCLUSION

Negotiations should be fair and honest. In the long run, it behooves all concerned to attempt to negotiate equitable adjustments, for it keeps alive a spirit of cooperation and mutual respect. Sometimes it is difficult to reach agreements in the face of valid differences of opinion, the mass of government procurement rules, and the maze of legal precedents that influence owners today. If, after earnest attempts, an agreement cannot be reached and the contractor believes his position is correct, he should propose an alternative dispute resolution method. If this fails, the choices remaining are to implement the contract's "disputes" mechanism or take the matter to court, whichever procedure is appropriate under the contract in question. The government contractor, except in the case of a breach, must of course, exhaust administrative remedies before seeking judicial relief.

CHAPTER 11

DISPUTES AVOIDANCE, RESOLUTION, AND ALTERNATIVE DISPUTE RESOLUTION

11-1. INTRODUCTION

Until the late 1980s, traditional dispute resolution involved formal administrative appeal processes, litigation, arbitration, and, to a limited extent, mediation. With parallel pioneering efforts of various public agencies and trade associations, several alternative dispute resolution (ADR) concepts were developed to help avoid and resolve disputes without resorting to the more traditional, time-consuming, and expensive litigation-type processes. This chapter introduces these still-evolving, but important, ADR procedures as well as reviews the traditional dispute resolution paths and their recent developments.

11-2. DISPUTES AVOIDANCE

In addition to minimizing and avoiding disputes by practicing sound contract administration, discussed in earlier chapters, contractors and owners alike can now take advantage of new practices developed within the construction industry in recent years. Several programs and concepts have evolved to resolve claims on a relatively informal basis through early cooperative intervention. These programs include

- Partnering
- Dispute review boards
- Escrow bid documents
- Geotechnical design summary reports

11-3. PARTNERING

11-3a. Partnering Defined

Partnering, quite simply, is the establishment of a team approach for mutually beneficial resolution of the ongoing difficulties and problems that typically arise on a construction project. The Associated General Contractors characterize the partnering process as "attempts to establish working relationships among the parties through a mutually-developed formal strategy of commitment and communications. It attempts to create an environment where trust and teamwork prevent disputes, foster a cooperative bond to everyone's benefit, and facilitate the completion of a successful project."[1] A more useful way of looking at partnering is to see it as a way for the owner, designer, and contractor to maintain regular communication and cooperative efforts. It provides an alternative to the adversarial pattern that often exists where each party crafts all communication and correspondences in ways to establish and protects one's own position to the exclusion of all others.

Partnering is a voluntary process and primarily consists of workshops, meetings, and the occasional use of facilitators to help the parties establish working relationships where project problems can be discussed and resolved in a nonadversarial atmosphere.

11-3b. History of Partnering

Partnering's roots in public construction began in 1988 with the efforts of Larry Bodine, Commander of the Mobile (Ala.) District of the U.S. Army Corps of Engineers[2], later named the director of the Arizona Department of Transportation (ADOT). Since then, partnering has been successfully implemented to varying degrees by the Corps and other state and federal agencies, but most notably by ADOT. ADOT has implemented the partnering process on an agency-wide basis and is frequently cited in articles and case studies in the construction trade press.

11-3c. Elements of Success

The basic elements of partnering include principles and procedures designed to bring together the different layers of management to work together

---

[1] *Partnering—A Concept for Success* p. 1 (Sept. 1991).

[2] Thomas R. Warne, *Partnering for Success*, American Society of Civil Engineers, 1994, p. III.

as a team. The elements include the following activities and concepts, which lend structure to the partnering process:

- The **preconstruction workshop** is a one to two day meeting between key management and jobsite personnel representing the owner, contractor, designer, major subcontractors and suppliers, and other key stakeholders, such as local agencies or community groups. The two primary objectives of the initial workshop are intended to (1) build teams to work with different issues that are expected during the project; and (2) to develop a project charter.
- The **project charter** is a document to be signed by all at the workshop that defines the goals and objectives of the partnering effort. These goals are more than simply to complete the project on schedule and budget. They comprise specific and measurable tasks, such as no lost-time accidents, good community relationships, and development of efficient construction procedures to solve major job challenges.
- The **commitment of top management** is essential to the success of partnering. Top management of all the parties has to believe in the concept and stand behind commitments it has delegated, or empowered, to the field staff to resolve jobsite issues.
- **Empowerment** is the delegation of authority and responsibility to the lowest possible levels in an organization. This allows the various team members to meet, discuss, and resolve problems in a timely and efficient manner. The partnering process provides noncontentious procedures for escalating issues to higher levels in the event the parties cannot reach agreements within certain timeframes.
- **Partnership maintenance**, comprised of ongoing partnership meetings, follow-up workshops, close-out workshops and end-of-job rewards and recognition, are essential for keeping the partnership on task and properly evaluating its effectiveness.

These elements, properly implemented and practiced, have proven to foster less adversarial construction projects with more timely completion, reduced costs, and less claims.

11-3d. Obstacles to Partnering

It seems counterintuitive that the parties to a construction contract, with such diverse interests, could work together in a team atmosphere. If one looks at the past history and nature of construction, it is easy to see why.

Perhaps a review of these obstacles to partnering will allow one to more reasonably assess the trade-offs and benefits of partnering.

11-3d.1. Tradition of construction. Most obstacles to partnering lie in the history and nature of the construction process. Construction has been traditionally characterized as the realm of rough and tough individuals using raw nerve, brute force, and commanding presence to move earth, steel, and concrete to build the subways, dams, and skyscrapers of the world. To some of these highly independent individuals, who travel the world to construct projects under which they have full control, participating in group partnering activities is both foreign and incongruous.

11-3d.2. Past dealings and nature of the parties. The three main parties to a construction contract—owner, designer, and contractor—represent completely diverse entities, each with their own role and personality.

The owner is the provider of the project and the source of funds and typically the most passive and removed party of the process. The owner has established a budget and wants an end product. Not interested in the details, and often inexperienced with the complexity and risks of the construction process, the owner neither wants to be involved in day-to-day problems nor wants to spend extra money. The owner wants the end product on time and on budget.

The designer is the architect or engineer responsible for designing the project and putting together the plans and specifications for its successful execution. The designer typically works under a negotiated fixed-fee or cost-plus basis and works under typical white-collar office conditions of a normal workweek in a controlled environment.

The contractor is the party responsible for executing the plans and specifications in order to build the project. Construction is often seasonal, and within seasons, deals with varying degrees of daylight hours, diverse weather conditions, and unpredictable factors such as unexpected site conditions and external economic conditions. Contractors frequently must travel to where the work is, work with unknown local manpower and resources, and deal with unknown local utility and regulatory agencies. Construction is often fast paced, time is of the essence, and the contractor prefers to be at the jobsite building the project. Under the aforementioned constraints, contractor employees often work long hours under demanding conditions. Both companies and their employees undertake this extra work and risk in return for larger financial rewards and the enhanced satisfaction of successful job completion.

It's easy to see how the ideological differences among the parties, along with the potential for coordination conflicts in both scheduling and participation levels, can make it difficult to implement partnering efforts. Nevertheless, once employed, partnering efforts can overcome these difficulties and provide multiple benefits to the construction project and its members.

11-3e. Results of Partnering

Studies conducted by the successful participants in numerous partnered projects have consistently cited favorable tangible results[3]:

- An increase in projects completed on or ahead of schedule
- Improved contract administration procedures
- A reduction in claims
- A reduction in owner's engineering and administrative expenses (5 to 15% or more)
- Increased value engineering

Partnering can create a real sense of teamwork and productive use of time. The energies and creative efforts of the parties is put to better use in value engineering and mutually beneficial schedule improvements rather than writing letters and being involved in contentious and emotional claims endeavors. For both the owner and the contractor, the necessity of employees having to divert energies from new and future project to returning to old projects for claims preparation, depositions, litigation support, and trials is extremely disruptive, draining, and counterproductive.

To learn more about the details of partnering efforts, *Partnering for Success*, by Thomas R. Warne, is strongly recommended.[4] Also check with major trade associations, such as Associated Builders and Contractors and the Associated General Contractors for publications they may have.

11-4. DISPUTE REVIEW BOARDS

11-4a. Dispute Review Boards Defined

Dispute review boards (DRBs) are the least intrusive and often the most effective[5] of the ADR procedures for reducing claims as well as providing a timely procedure to resolve claims quickly. A DRB typically comprises three members, selected jointly by the contractor and owner, to monitor the progress of construction and provide recommended resolutions to disputes that are brought before it. The members are typically familiar with the type of construction involved, are respected in the industry, and approach their responsibilities with neutrality and impartiality.[6]

---

[3]Ibid, p. 58.
[4]Ibid, Available from ASCE Press, 1-800-548-2723.
[5]As discussed in this section, this statement can be said to apply at least to heavy and highway construction, but is not necessarily universal. A 1996 Associated General Contractors survey found "perceived effectiveness" of various ADR procedures to be led by partnering, followed by mediation, early neutral evaluation, binding arbitration, nonbinding arbitration, and dispute review boards, in that order. *Constructor*, Jan. 1997, p. 55.
[6]Matyas et al. (1995). *Construction Dispute Review Board Manual*, McGraw Hill Construction Series, 1995, p. xi.

DISPUTES AVOIDANCE, RESOLUTION, AND ADR

A DRB was first used in the early 1970s with the Eisenhower Tunnel second bore in Colorado, followed by occasional additional use until the mid-1980s. Since then, DRB use has expanded heavily and is now frequently used by the Caltrans L.A. Metro, Massachusetts Highway Department, Washington D.C. Metro, Toronto Transit Commission, San Francisco Metro (BART), and Maine DOT. The Colorado and Washington state DOTs, the two pioneers of DRB, continue to use DRBs extensively. International use is also in place, as discussed further below.

11-4b. DRB Procedures

The DRB board members are usually selected at the outset of a project, and visit the jobsite on a periodic basis (typically quarterly), keeping current with job activities and developments through progress reports and relevant documentation, and they are available to meet and hear disputes on an as-needed, as-requested basis. The contemporaneous familiarity with the project puts the board in the unique position of being able to make quick, informed, and reasonable recommendations to resolve disputes at early stages.

The first two members of the board are typically selected by the contractor and the owner, with each member being approved by the other party. These two members then select a third person, a chairperson, who must also be approved by the contractor and owner.

The board should hold its first meeting as soon as possible after the work begins. Frequency of subsequent visits depends on activity levels at the jobsite, but one meeting every three to four months appears to be appropriate for the more active phases of the project. In addition to routine visits, special, private meetings and hearings are held, at locations selected by the board members themselves.

As soon as a dispute becomes unresolvable at the job level, the board will arrange a hearing. Position papers will be provided to the board from each of the parties, accompanied by any supporting documentation, jointly prepared by the parties. The DRB hearing is typically held at the jobsite and is relatively informal. Witnesses, experts, and other resources that might provide the board with any information helpful to the board in making a decision can be used in the hearings. Note, either party can request a DRB hearing at any time.

As soon as possible after the conclusion of the hearing, the board will make a recommendation in writing that clearly describes its reasoning in reaching its decision. Although desirable, unanimous decisions are not required for a recommendation. The board may be asked to render a recommendation on entitlement, quantum, or both. The DRB's recommendations are nonbinding, but are usually admissible as evidence in later arbitration or litigation. Some owners are writing in their specifications that DRB recommendations are not admissable, detracting from the effectiveness of the entire DRB process.

The DRB procedures, costs, and related issues should be concisely spelled out in a DRB clause in the contract documents. A guide specification for a DRB clause is contained in the *Construction Dispute Review Board Manual* by McGraw-Hill.[7]

11-4c. DRB Costs

DRB costs include the administrative efforts of selecting the board, the costs of the DRB members' time, travel, and expenses for the periodic site visits, and the costs of additional trips and related expenses for board hearings beyond those that might take place during a periodic visit. Board members will often be paid a fixed monthly retainer fee to compensate each member for maintaining availability, for time spent reviewing documents at home, communications, clerical work, and other nontravel expenses. Other expenses include the administrative costs of distributing progress reports and documentation to the board members. The contractor and owner share the DRB costs equally.

11-4d. DRB Effectiveness and Success

11-4d.1. Quick resolution of disputes and reduction of unresolved claims. It has been found that the mere existence of the DRB tends to foster an environment that encourages the parties to avoid the promotion of frivolous disputes, to resolve most disputes at the project level, and to only involve the DRB in the few disputes that have reached an impasse. This is due to several factors:

- Members of the board are impartial, technically proficient, project-knowledgeable, and mutually selected. The board members are respected by the parties, which discourages both parties from the possible loss of credibility by bringing forth minor or nonmeritous claims.
- Improvement in relationships of parties by creating an atmosphere of communications and trust. Knowing that disputes are going to be resolved expeditiously and fairly, the parties are more willing to be more communicative and work toward a common goal, that is, settle disputes themselves whenever possible.
- A DRB is simple, straightforward, fair, and efficient. The board's familiarity with the particular project, its availability, and the knowledge it will act quickly and fairly tends to reduce opportunities for posturing and vacillation by the parties. Because boards typically

---

[7]Ibid, Appendix C.

hear only a single dispute at a time, the aggregation of claims is reduced.

In sum, the existence of a DRB makes resolution of claims a top priority and reduces to a minimum the list of unresolved disputes, allowing the parties to maintain their focus on construction of the project.

11-4d.2. High resolution rate. Plain and simple, DRBs have almost a 100% success rate for resolving construction disputes. "DRBs have been successfully utilized on projects costing as little as $6 million. Over 300 disputes have been heard and resolved on almost 200 projects worth over $10 billion. To date, no courtroom adjudication is known to have resulted from DRB projects."[8]

In those instances where a DRB was not able to resolve a dispute, the parties typically went on to negotiate the disputes themselves. Reiterating points mentioned above, this is due to the DRB members' knowledge and experience with

1. The design and construction issues germane to the project
2. The interpretation and application of contract documents
3. The process of dispute resolution
4. The specific design and construction for the project.[9]

Since both parties have agreed to the board members and the process in advance of any dispute, the parties are normally favorably predisposed to DRB proceedings.[10]

11-4d.3. DRB cost-effectiveness. For multimillion-dollar projects, DRBs are extremely cost effective because

- The DRB's existence encourages quick settlement of most claims and changes, reducing overall administrative costs and the nonproductive time of maintaining and pursuing open-change order lists. In this regard, its considered a money and time saver, as well as a prevention cost, since it prevents many claims from escalating into disputes.
- The disputes that do end up in front of the board cost far less in a DRB hearing then they would in arbitration, litigation, or board of appeal hearings.

---
[8]Ibid, p. xii.
[9]Ibid, p. 26.
[10]Ibid.

In the *Construction Dispute Review Board Manual*, a review of case histories indicates that the total direct costs of DRBs generally are considerably less than 0.5% of the final contract price.[11]

11-4e. International Applications

The movement toward DRB use has been implemented on international projects. A number of groups have become involved in this movement to promote the use of a neutral party to resolved disputes, including the World Bank, the U.K Institution of Civil Engineers, the Engineering Advancement Association of Japan, the International Chamber of Commerce, the Fédération Internationale des Ingénieurs Conseils, and the U.N. Commission on International Trade Law.[12] Efforts by these organizations include drafting and promoting DRB clauses for use on international projects.

11-4f. Other Considerations of DRB Procedures

A DRB is still a voluntary and nonbinding method of settling disputes. DRB specifications should be written to neither interfere nor hinder the parties' traditional dispute resolution methods in the event a DRB recommendation is not satisfactory to both parties. For example, time taken for attempted DRB resolution should not penalize either party in regard to notice provisions of claims, requests for contracting officer's decision, or requests for an appeal.

The DRB process of settling disputes is compatible with the partnering process, described above. The state of Washington (and others appear to be following suit) has taken steps to incorporate both partnering and DRB into the same projects.

Smaller projects that cannot afford full-time three-panel boards should consider a single-person board or seek the assistance of persons in the local area that can function as a board without the expense of a travel budget. Other alternatives include use of a multiproject, multicontract, or some sort of standing DRB that may be set up by sponsoring trade associations.

11-4g. DRB Summary

The importance of DRBs for settling disputes can not be overemphasized. Their usefulness and success is grounded in the overall concept of an "in place" jobsite panel to render quick and fair recommendations to resolve disputes before they become disruptive and contentious. In summary, the elements of a DRB include

---

[11] Ibid, p. 7.
[12] Ibid, p. 67.

- Creation of a panel of three board members, knowledgeable of the type of construction, at the beginning of the project
- An initial meeting at the start of construction before any disputes have developed, followed by periodic jobsite visits, along with regular written updates on job progress
- Encouragement of the parties to resolve disputes without board hearings
- Hearings at the request of either party when disputes cannot be negotiated at the jobsite level
- Written recommendation by the board as soon as possible after a hearing

This is not a complex process and DRB use should be used whenever possible on construction projects.

11-5. ESCROW BID DOCUMENTS

This is a relatively new concept often used in conjunction with DRBs and/or partnering, but does not have to be. Escrow bid documents (EBDs) is the process whereby the contractor's worksheets and backup used to bid the project are put in escrow for future use, primarily in negotiating change order prices and for settlement of disputes, claims, and other controversies. They are not be used for preaward evaluation of the contractor's methods or to assess the contractor's qualifications. The information therein is considered trade secrets and its confidentiality is to be protected as such.

The writer has no exposure to use of EBDs and offers no strong opinion one way or the other. It could lead to administrative disputes on the organization, readability, and structure of bid documents, and more often than not would probably be used against the contractor. No matter how secure the escrow process is, it seems like unnecessary exposure of the material.

11-6. GEOTECHNICAL DESIGN SUMMARY REPORT

Another new concept, also usually used in conjunction with DRBs and/or partnering, is the geotechnical design summary report, more frequently referred to as a geotechnical baseline report (GBR). An essential part of underground construction projects, the GBR goes a few steps further than traditional site-survey and boring logs. It represents the designer's interpretations of subsurface conditions and their impact on design and construction.

The GBR provides a more definable baseline of subsurface conditions for determining whether actual conditions encountered are materially different or not. It removes the uncertainty of how the subsurface conditions should be interpreted and what could be expected by a reasonably prudent contractor.

Along with the designer's description and interpretation of the anticipated subsurface conditions, the anticipated behavior of the ground consistent with the specified or most likely used construction methods is also described. Such factors as slope stability, dewatering methods, pumping quantity estimates, well spacing, and so forth should be engineered and provided as part of the GBR.[13]

The GBR has enjoyed significant success on numerous tunneling projects in reducing differing site condition claims and/or resolution at the contracting officer level. Its success rate is founded in eliminating the uncertainties surrounding a mere presentation of a subsurface survey or boring logs, with the owner taking a more proactive responsibility for the thoroughness of the conditions and the interpretation of the conditions by engineers and designers.

11-7. ARBITRATION

Because of the high cost of formal dispute resolution through litigation in state and federal courts, arbitration has been a popular form of alternative dispute resolution in nonfederal construction contracts for several decades. The American Arbitration Association (AAA) has promulgated a special set of arbitration procedural rules (construction industry rules) and maintains a nationwide panel of potential arbitrators. In response to criticism that arbitration of construction disputes has not always proven to be as quick and economical as originally intended, the AAA revamped their rules in 1996 to address these concerns. Three "tracks" of procedures based on the size of the claim are now available: regular track ($50,000–$1,000,000), fast track (less than $50,000), and complex, (claims of at least $1,000,000).

The fast track system is intended to resolve smaller claims within 60 days and includes accelerated procedures for appointing arbitrators and holding preliminary conferences. New claims and counterclaims are not permitted, discovery is virtually eliminated, and claims of less than $10,000 are resolved without a hearing by the arbitrators' review of documents. Hearings of one day are permitted for claims exceeding $10,000, and awards must be issued within seven days after the completion of the hearing. Fast track arbitrators are compensated at a per-case rate, and nonrefundable filing fees are between $500 and $750.

Under the new regular track system for midsize claims, arbitrators are given expanded authority to manage the arbitration process to expedite

---

[13]Guidelines and practices for writing a GBR are available in Randall J. Essex. *Geotechnical Baseline Reports for Underground Construction* (American Society of Civil Engineers, New York, 1997).

resolution of the dispute. Arbitrators have the authority to "direct" the discovery process, permit new claims and counterclaims, hold preliminary conferences, consider preliminary motions and rulings, and request or reject certain offers of proof. In addition to monetary awards, arbitrators have the authority to grant equitable relief such as specific performance, reformation, or recission, and they have limited authority to make modifications where an award contains technical or clerical errors. Filing fees for regular track cases range from $1,250 to $5,000.

The large complex track system is mandatory for claims in excess of $1 million and allows the parties the option to choose either one or three arbitrators. Where the parties agree to conduct a preliminary hearing, the rules set forth a detailed list of issues to be considered, including statements of claims and issues, stipulations as to uncontested facts, the extent of discovery and document exchange, witness identification, hearing schedules, stenographic recording of the proceedings, and the use of mediation or other dispute resolution techniques. The complex track rules permit the arbitrators to limit the discovery process and generally control the proceedings in order to expedite a speedy resolution of the dispute, and in certain circumstances to assign attorneys fees as part of the award. The nonrefundable filing fee for complex track cases up to $5 million is $7,000, and the fee is negotiated for claims over $5 million.

The AAA is also in the process of revising rules under all three tracks relating to the qualifications of arbitrators. Planned changes include requirements that potential arbitrators have a minimum of 10 years experience, be approved by regional construction advisory committees, and undergo mandatory training for initial qualification and retraining every three years.

An advantage of arbitration over formal litigation is the use of presumably knowledgeable individuals as arbitrators, generally contractors, design professionals, or attorneys experienced in construction law.

The key distinction between arbitration and mediation, discussed below, is that the arbitrators make a decision on the dispute that, is most instances absent agreement to the contrary, will have the same force and effect as a judgment entered by a court. Arbitration awards are seldom appealable, however, and once entered the dispute is generally concluded. In response to a generally held notion that arbitrators tend to issue "compromise" awards, some parties have engaged in "baseball" arbitration in which the arbitrator is required to issue a "winner take all" award selecting the entire claim position of one party or the other.

11-8. MEDIATION

Mediation has gained considerable and well-deserved popularity in recent years as a form of ADR. In a typical mediation, the parties select a mediator whose role it is to assist the parties in reaching a mutually satisfactory resolution of the dispute. As such, the mediator does *not* render a decision. Instead, he or she assists the parties in assessing their respective risks and finding areas for compromise.

Generally, the parties are free to fashion their own mediation rules, and doing so represents the first of hopefully several agreements leading to ultimate resolution of the dispute. The keys to successful mediation are joint commitment to "solving" a mutual problem as opposed to "beating" the opponent and a willingness to proceed in a nonadversarial mode with a genuine view toward reaching a compromise.

A typical mediation model involves some or all of the following steps:

1. exchange of written position papers, furnished also to the mediator
2. formal presentations of each party's facts and arguments in joint sessions, usually without cross-examination, but with an opportunity for questions and answers
3. caucus sessions in which the mediator meets privately with each party and shuttles between them attempting to find common ground, assisting in risk assessment, and expediting the movement of the parties toward compromise

The AAA maintains a panel of qualified mediators, as do several private mediation services. Key to a successful mediation is the selection of a mediator with construction and litigation experience, the ability to correctly and persuasively discuss weaknesses in the parties positions, and the ability to maintain the parties' confidence in his or her objectivity and advice.

Mediation is occasionally required by contract, including A1A 201A (1997 Edition), but frequently entered voluntarily by the parties after a dispute has been identified and routine negotiations have failed. It is most likely to be successful when each party recognizes some responsibility for the problem, each is familiar with and wishes to avoid the high cost and time-consuming nature of litigation, and when there is a mutual desire to maintain an ongoing business relationship. By addressing the dispute as a joint business problem requiring compromise, the parties are frequently able to reach a mutually acceptable settlement and do so in a manner preserving future commercial dealings.

11-9. OTHER ADR METHODS

11-9a. Minitrials

Variations on the typical mediation model have also gained in popularity in recent years. "Mini-trials" involve making rather formal presentations

DISPUTES AVOIDANCE, RESOLUTION, AND ADR

to a board or panel of senior management or executives from the respective parties.

A neutral individual selected by the parties may also sit on the panel. After argument and perhaps the testimony of witnesses, the panel attempts to reach a negotiated settlement. The procedure is designed to put the decision makers in the position of judges of the dispute rather than combatants. As with all forms of ADR, the parties are free to fashion their own rules and variations on the basic format. As with conventional mediation, the parties remain in control of the situation and have not surrendered decision making to a third party.

11-9b. MedArb

Another common ADR method is the hybrid proceeding known as Med-Arb. The parties' selected mediator first attempts to facilitate resolution through standard mediation techniques. If this fails, however, the parties can authorize the same individual to issue a decision, in the manner of an arbitrator, which will be either binding or nonbinding as the parties have decided.

11-9c. Summary Trials before the Boards of Contract Appeals

A summary trial is a less formal, expedited trial held before a judge or hearing examiner. The rules of evidence and procedures are relaxed and the trial session is short lived. Decisions are final, nonappealable, and do not set precedents.

11-9d. Hybrids of Mediation

Settlement judge, nonbinding arbitration, fact-finding, early neutral evaluation, and other related concepts all come under the category of nonbinding, advisory procedures. A third party is involved to assess the case, provide opinions, and assist the parties in reaching an agreement.

11-10. ALTERNATIVE DISPUTE RESOLUTION ACT AND THE FEDERAL ADR EXPERIENCE

The federal agencies have embraced mediation and other Administrative Dispute Resolution Act (ADRA) techniques in recent years with very positive results. The ADRA of 1990[14] encourages voluntary use of ADR techniques in federal contract disputes. The FAR now contains implementing regulations encouraging agencies to use ADR to the "maximum extent practicable."[15]

---

[14]P.L. 104-320, 110 Stat. 3870 (Oct. 19, 1996).
[15]FAR 33.204.

The agency board of contract appeals have adopted rules permitting and facilitating ADR procedures prior to formal administrative proceedings.

ADR is being used with increasing frequency and success as a method of resolving disputes with the federal government. In an October 1996 survey conducted by Judge Martin J. Harty of the Armed Services Board of Contract Appeals (ASBCA),[16] the boards collectively received ADR requests covering 169 appeals in fiscal year 1996. Binding ADR (summary trial) and nonbinding ADR (settlement judge and minitrials) have been the methods typically used. The ASBCA's experience with the 42 ADR requests it received is that nine out of 10 ADR proceedings result in an agreement that resolves the dispute.[17]

The October report identified cases particularly suitable for ADR as

1. Small dollar cases, particularly where litigation costs would seriously erode any award
2. Non-complex cases with relatively clear-cut factual or legal issues
3. Cases where only quantum is in dispute
4. Large, factually complex claims where both parties recognize some liability.[18]

In commenting on cases that do not settle but should, the most frequently cited reasons are

1. Emotional involvement preventing realistic assessment of case
2. Lack of preparation by one or both of the parties
3. Breakdown in communication due to personality conflicts.[19]

Copies of the ASBCA's full description of the methods it uses, along with sample agreements, are found in Appendix 18.

11-11. FORMAL ADMINISTRATIVE AND JUDICIAL DISPUTE RESOLUTION

The least desirable method of dispute resolution is generally litigation or administrative proceedings on federal (and some state) contracts. It is the

---

[16]Federal Contract Reports, Vol. 66, Nov. 15, 1996, 525–530.

[17]Report of transactions and proceedings of the Armed Services Board of Contract Appeals for the fiscal year ending Sept. 30, 1996. This report also notes that number of appeals docketed decreased 35% from a high of 1,712 in 1992 to 1,105 in 1996.

[18]See Note 16, p. 527.

[19]See Note 16, p. 530.

DISPUTES AVOIDANCE, RESOLUTION, AND ADR 143

time-consuming nature, the attendant expenses, and adversarial nature of these approaches that have fostered the tremendous support in recent years for the ADR techniques discussed above.

11-11a. Federal Contracts

The initial steps of pursuing a claim into formal dispute resolution on federal construction contracts were discussed in chapter 2. The strict certification rules, unforgiving time limits, and procedural technicalities involved in appealing the contracting officer's final decision on a claim require extremely careful attention by the contractor. A detailed examination of such legal matters is beyond the scope of this handbook, and contractors proceeding with claims beyond the contracting officer's level are well advised to seek legal advice from qualified attorneys.

A few of the major pitfalls and a general outline of the process is as follows:

> Contractors are now required by the Federal Streamlining Act of 1994 to submit claims to the contracting officer within six years "after the accrual of the claim." The government is required to submit any claims against the contractor within the same period.
>
> As noted in chapter 2, a failure to certify a claim in excess of $100,000 will result in a dismissal of an appeal. Mere errors in the required certification language can be corrected without penalty prior to the issuance of a final judgment by a board or court. Further, the contracting officer is required to advise the contractor of any alleged defects in certification within 60 days of receipt of the claim.
>
> A contractor disagreeing with the contracting officer's final decision may appeal that decision to either the board of contract appeals of the federal agency or to the U.S. Court of Federal Claims. The time limits for initiating such appeals differ. A notice of appeal to an agency board of contract appeals must be filed within 90 days of the contractor's receipt of the contracting officer's final decision. Alternatively, the contractor has one year to commence an action at the U.S. Court of Federal Claims.
>
> These time limits are strictly enforced and contractors must not wait until the eleventh hour to take the necessary steps. Appeals to the agency boards are commenced by filing a brief notice of appeal with the appropriate board, with a copy furnished to the contracting officer. Proceedings at the U.S. Court of Federal Claims begin more formally with the filing of a detailed complaint.

Several federal statutes, including the Contract Disputes Act, impose a variety of penalties on contractors submitting false claims.[20] Penalties include fines, imprisonment, claim forfeiture, and reimbursement of the government's costs of investigation. Contractors are strongly advised to avoid making any false representations concerning claims and to carefully examine all claims for accuracy and adequate support.

11-11b. Private Contracts and State and Local Public Contracts

Absent contract provisions or a subsequent agreement to proceed with a form of ADR, resolution of disputes on private contracts and public contracts at the state or local level will require litigation before state or federal courts. As with federal contract formal dispute resolution, these proceedings involve compliance with various statutes and rules requiring advice of counsel.

States also impose statutes of limitations for lawsuits involving written contracts. Under these legislated limitation requirements, lawsuits must be filed within a specified number of years—varying from state to state—after the "cause of action accrues." This is generally marked from the date the contractor knew or should have known of the basis for the claim.

11-11c. Mechanics' Liens

On private contracts, the contractor will typically have an alternative or parallel remedy in the form of a mechanics lien filed and perfected in strict accordance with the state's statutory scheme for such liens. In some states it is necessary to file a notice of lien before the work is commenced. Further, under most state mechanics' lien statutes, the time periods for filing and perfecting such liens are extremely short and are strictly enforced. Again, the assistance of an attorney and at least a general familiarity with the lien laws in the state where your construction contract is being performed is critical.

11-12. CONCLUSION

Disputes that cannot be resolved often result in ongoing nonproductive downtime for the parties to the contract. ADR procedures provide viable alternatives to costly litigation and help projects get back on track quickly and productively.

---

[20] E.g., 18 U.S.C.§287, 18 U.S.C. §1001, 41 U.S.C. §604.

CHAPTER 12

TERMINATION

12-1. INTRODUCTION

A party terminates a contract when it stops performing before the contract is completed. Generally, if there is no excuse for the failure to perform, the termination is considered a breach of contract and the breaching party is liable for common law damages. However, construction projects are usually complex and often unpredictable. Contingencies may arise requiring the owner or the contractor to change plans and terminate the contract earlier than originally anticipated. The "common law" scenario allows no flexibility for such contingencies and results in a breach of contract if either party terminates. When certain termination clauses are included in the contract, the responsibilities and obligations of the parties can be modified to allow for much needed flexibility in the contracting process.

This chapter summarizes the "termination for default" and "termination for convenience" clauses specified in the Federal Acquisition Regulation (FAR). In addition, termination provisions included in private standard form contracts are discussed and compared to the federal clauses.

12-2. FEDERAL CLAUSES

The FAR requires the use of specific termination clauses in all construction contracts. (See, generally, FAR 49.501) Specifically, the FAR authorizes the government to terminate a construction contract

a) For default (FAR 52.249-10)
b) For the convenience of the government (FAR 52.249-2)

12-2a. Termination for Default

Termination for default is a drastic action by the government for a contractor's inexcusable breach of obligation. A default termination on a contractor's record may result in a finding of "nonresponsibility" and hinder his ability to compete on future federal contracts. A default termination may also lead to the contractor's suspension or debarment.

The FAR permits the government to terminate a construction contract for default in four general circumstances. First, the government may terminate for default when the contractor fails to complete the work within the time specified in the contract. Second, when the contractor fails to make progress and endangers the contract, the government can terminate for default without waiting until the contract completion date. This generally occurs when it is obvious that the contract will not be completed on a timely basis because of the contractor's demonstrated lack of diligence.

A third ground for default termination occurs when the contractor fails to perform any other material provision of the contract, for instance, furnishing a required bond. Finally, the government may default terminate a contractor whose conduct represents an "anticipatory repudiation," that is, an expression by words or actions that the contractor is unable or unwilling to perform the contract.

The government's power to terminate a contract for default is discretionary and will not be enforced when against equity and good conscience. Although not required by the FAR in construction contracts, government agencies frequently issue a written notice ("cure notice") that a default termination is being considered and request that the contractor show cause why the contract should not be terminated. The government must consider a number of broad factors when deciding whether to terminate a contract for default [see FAR 49.402–3(f)]. The factors include the terms of the contract, applicable laws and regulations, the contractor's specific failure and excuses for failure, the availability of obtaining the work from other sources, the urgency of the government's need for the work, the contractor's ability to repay advances and progress payments, and the essentiality of the contractor in other government contracts.

12-2a.1. What to do when you receive a notice of default termination. A number of recognized defenses against an actual or anticipated default termination are available to a contractor. These defenses include

> a) **Excusable default.** This must be due to an unforeseeable cause "beyond the control and without the fault or negligence" of the contractor. (Examples include: acts of God or a public enemy, acts of the government or another government contractor, fire, flood, epidemic, quarantine, strikes, freight embargoes, unusually severe weather, and unforeseeable delays of subcontractors

or suppliers that are beyond the control and without the fault or negligence of the contractor, subcontractor or supplier.) In fixed-price construction contracts, the contractor must notify the government in writing of the causes of the delay within 10 days from the beginning of the delay [FAR 52.249–10(b)(1) and (2)]

b) **Government waiver.** This occurs when the government, by clear, decisive conduct, gives the contractor encouragement to proceed, and the contractor relies on this conduct and continues performing the contract. (Example: government waives a completion schedule without setting a new one.)

c) **Government failure to pay.**

d) **Defective specifications.** Making performance impossible

e) **Bad faith by the government.** Usually in making its decision to terminate for default.

These defenses are available to a contractor in two instances. First, they should be asserted by the contractor in an attempt to persuade the government not to issue the default termination in these situations when the government issues a cure notice. Second, once a default termination is issued, the contractor should assert these arguments on appeal to have the termination converted to a termination for convenience.

A contract will not be terminated for default if the government determines that the contractor's actions are excusable. If termination is in the government's interest, however, the contract may still be terminated for convenience, which is a result more favorable to the contractor.

12-2a.2. Damages owed by contractor. A contractor terminated for default is liable for certain specified damages. First, the contractor must pay the government's excess reprocurement costs, which are the additional costs incurred by the government in completing the work with a different contractor. When the government can prove it was injured, the contractor will also be liable for "common law" damages, the foreseeable damages directly resulting from the contractor's breach, including administrative costs.

12-2b. Termination for Convenience

The Termination for Convenience clause gives the government the unilateral right to terminate a contract before it is completed without regard to the contractor's performance and without being considered in breach. Once unique to federal government contracts, variations on the federal model are now appearing in local government and private contracts as well. The convenience termination clause immunizes the government from liability for certain breach of contract damages, such as anticipatory profits, that would be otherwise available in a private contract.

A contract can be terminated for convenience whenever it is in the government's best interest. If the government no longer needs the services for which it has contracted, the government may terminate the contract for convenience if in the government's best interest. This gives the government very wide discretion, and imposes the difficult burden of proving government bad faith or abuse of discretion on a contractor attempting to defeat a convenience termination. The government would likely be considered acting in bad faith, for example, for using a termination for convenience to suspend or debar a contractor without complying with due process requirements, or using a termination for convenience to obtain a better price when the circumstances were known to the government before award.

12-2b.1. What to do when you receive a notice of termination for convenience. Absent abuse of discretion or bad faith by the government, there are no defenses to a termination for convenience. Once a contractor receives a notice of termination for convenience, he is required to

1. Stop work
2. Place no additional subcontracts or orders
3. Terminate and settle all subcontracts and assign government all rights under the terminated subcontracts
4. Transfer title and deliver to government all work in process and completed work, supplies, and materials
5. Complete performance of the work not terminated
6. Take any action that may be necessary for the protection and preservation of the work
7. Submit a termination settlement proposal to the government within one year of the termination date unless the contracting officer agrees in writing to an extension. The FAR specifies in considerable detail the cost categories allowable in the contractor's settlement proposal.

12-2b.2. Constructive termination. When the government stops the contractor's performance for reasons that are later found to be invalid, such as by mistakenly calling the contract illegal or by erroneously canceling the contract the government is not considered in breach. Rather, the government's "breach" is "retroactively justified" and is considered a constructive termination for convenience.[1]

12-2b.3. Termination for convenience versus change. When the government deletes a portion of the contract, it can do so as either a deductive change or as a termination for convenience. This distinction is significant to

---

[1]*Maxima Corporation v. U.S.*, 847 F.2d 1549, 1553 (Fed Cir. 1988); *G.C. Casebolt Co. v. U.S.*, 421 F.2d 710, 712 (Ct.Cl. 1970); *Torncello v. U.S.*, 681 F.2d 756, 759 (Ct.Cl. 1982).

TERMINATION 149

the contractor because recovery of profit is often less when deducted work is considered a termination for convenience rather than a change order.

While the relevant facts must be considered on a case-by-case basis, there are two objective tests for determining which clause applies: (1) whether the eliminated work is considered minor or major; and (2) the identifiability and ability to segregate the deleted work. For example, a reduction or elimination of a separate portion of the work is generally accomplished under the Termination for Convenience clause, whereas changes to the technical plans or specifications are considered changes under the Changes clause. In addition, where "major" portions of the work are eliminated without substitution of additional work, the termination for convenience clause is generally used.[2]

12-2c. Notice of Termination

Once the government decides to terminate a contract either for default or convenience, the FAR requires formal, written notice to the contractor that the contract is terminated as of a certain date, the grounds, the contractor's appeal rights, special instructions, and so forth (FAR 49.102).

12-3. PRIVATE CLAUSES

Documents issued by the American Institute of Architects (AIA) are recognized standards in private construction contracts. AIA document A201, General Conditions, contains a clause authorizing the owner to terminate "for cause," (¶14.2), which is similar to the federal Termination for Default clause. The 1997 edition of A201 includes both a "Suspension for Convenience" clause (¶14.3) and a "Termination for Convenience" clause (¶14.4). A201 also provides for a contractor's right to terminate (¶14.1). Because of the popularity of the AIA standard form contracts and their similarity to many private contracts based thereon, the AIA termination clauses are discussed below.

Contractors are cautioned strongly, however, to examine carefully the termination language contained in the specific contract in question. Significant variations and deviations from the AIA clauses may substantially affect the contractor's rights and remedies.

12-3a. Termination for Cause

Under ¶14.2 (A201), an owner can terminate a contract if the contractor substantially breaches the contract, if he fails to pay subcontractors, or if he "persistently" disregards applicable laws and regulations or "persistently" fails to supply sufficient workers or materials. In these circumstances, after

---

[2]See, generally, *Ideker, Inc.*, ENG BCA Nos. 4389, 4602, 87-3 BCA ¶20,145 at 101,974.

giving the contractor seven days written notice, the owner may terminate the contract, take possession of the site and the contractor's materials and equipment, and finish the work by any reasonable method the owner deems expedient.

12-3b. Suspension for Convenience

Paragraph 14.3 (A201) authorizes the owner to "suspend, delay or interrupt" the contract without cause or without stating any reason for doing so. The owner must give the contractor written notice of the suspension or delay, and the contractor is entitled to an adjustment for the resulting increased costs of performance. (Under ¶14.1, discussed below, the contractor may terminate the contract if owner suspensions or delays total more than 100% of the total number of days scheduled for completion, or 120 days in any 365-day period, whichever is less.)

12-3c. Termination by Contractor

In general, few circumstances allow a contractor to willfully terminate a contract. Most termination clauses authorize only the owner to terminate and the contractor to recover payment for completed work. However, paragraph 14.1 (A201) includes a provision more favorable to contractors, allowing them to terminate a contract after either a 30-day work stoppage for one of five specified reasons, or a 60-day work stoppage "with respect to matters important to the progress of the Work." In either case, the contractor must give the owner seven days written notice of termination *after* the work has been stopped for the specified number of days.

12-3c.1. After 30-day work stoppage. A contractor may terminate a contract if the work is stopped for 30 days through no fault of the contractor or subcontractors for any of five reasons: (1) issuance of an order by a court or public authority; (2) an act of government making material unavailable; (3) failure of the owner and/or architect to make timely payments; (4) owner suspensions for convenience totaling more than 120 days in any 365-day period or more than 100% of the total number of days scheduled for completion, whichever is less; or (5) failure by the owner to furnish evidence of financial capability to pay, upon the contractor's request for such proof.

After the 30-day work stoppage, the contractor must then give seven days written notice of the termination to the owner and architect.

12-3c.2. After 60-day work stoppage. If the owner fails to fulfill contract obligations "with respect to matters important to the progress of the Work," the contractor can terminate after the work has been stopped for 60 days by then giving seven days written notice.

12-4. CONCLUSION

In addition to these AIA clauses, other private standard form contracts contain variations on the federal termination clauses. For example, Associated General Contractors of America Standard Form 3, "Form of Contract for Engineering Construction Projects," provides that upon written notice of suspension by the owner, the contractor can recover payment for all work done and, in addition, a negotiated percentage to compensate for lost profit and unabsorbed overhead. This provision is far more generous to the contractor than the federal termination for convenience clause, under which the government is never liable for anticipated profits.

The Engineers' Joint Contract Documents Committee Standard Form 1910-8, "Standard General Conditions of the Construction Contract," contains a provision authorizing the owner to terminate upon seven days written notice. In such case, the contractor may recover payment for all work done plus "reasonable termination expenses," defined to include direct, indirect and consequential costs such as professional fees of attorneys, architects, and engineers as well as litigation expenses. While such provision does not include recovery of lost profits, its broad definition of consequential costs is favorable to the contractor.

CHAPTER 13

CONCLUSION

13-1. THE CLAIMS, CHANGES, AND DISPUTE RESOLUTION PROCESS

In summarizing this book as a whole, the claims, changes, and dispute resolution process can be looked at in terms of the flow of the construction contract from start to finish, which includes the following elements:

- Preparing complete contract documents
- Setting up systems to prevent and resolve disputes
- Knowledge and capability to properly prepare change order proposals and claims for equitable adjustment and time extensions
- Negotiation and settlement of claims and changes before they become disputes
- The selection and pursuit of satisfactory and expedient dispute resolution methods.

This flow can be viewed in the context of the various stages of the project, with earlier stages of resolution being preferred over later stages. Figure 13-1 represents the various venues of dispute prevention, administration, and resolution.

13-2. ROLES OF CONSTRUCTION TEAM

Throughout the various stages, each party to the contract has an important role to play in the success of the project. The role of the principal parties in preventing and resolving disputes is summarized here.

Stage 1 Pre-Bid	Stage 2 Pre-Construction	Stage 3 Construction	Stage 4 Post-Construction
<u>Create Contract Documents that are:</u> • Clear • Concise • Complete • Realistic • Conform to Industry Practice <u>Bid Preparation</u> • Provide Ample Time for Contractors to Prepare Bids and Conduct Site Investigations • Provide the best Site Conditions Data possible and allow the contractor to rely on same • Alert Bidders of Intent to Include Partnering and ADR	<u>Disputes Avoidance</u> • Set up Partnering Agreements • Assemble Dispute Resolution Board <u>Contact Administration</u> • Set up documentation and communication systems • Create a detailed and thorough construction schedule	<u>Changes Processing</u> • Maintain Partnering Process • Identify changes • Prepare and Timely Submit Change Order Proposals and Claims • Negotiate Equitable Adjustments and Time Extensions <u>Dispute Resolution Steps</u> • Dispute Resolution Board • Mediator • Third Party Neutral • Binding or Non-binding Arbitration	<u>Non-binding Resolution</u> • Mediation • Mini-trial • Arbitration <u>Binding Resolution</u> • Arbitration • Board of Contract Appeals • Litigation

FIG. 13-1 *Summary Chart—Procedural Stages of Disputes Prevention and Resolution*

13-2a. Contractor's Role

Claims and change order administration involves more than setting up an account number for each item of extra work performed on a contract. It requires a firm knowledge of construction methods and estimating techniques, basic proficiency in construction law, and the application of formal management procedures. Thus, in addition to his own job, the project manager also must be something of an estimator, an engineer, and a lawyer. He is constantly encountering new situations that demand quick decisions and appropriate actions. This handbook should help the contract manager and his staff further their knowledge of the theoretical concept of claims and change orders, as well as the practical knowledge necessary for their administration.

13-2b. Designer's Role

Reading through this book should leave the architect, engineer, and other designers better prepared to meet the challenges of crafting construction documents that will lead to less ambiguous specifications. Errors and omissions can occasionally slip through, but designers must be ready to step up and provide corrections as expeditiously as possible, and advise the owners that extra costs and time may be due the contractor to implement the corrections. By working with the owner and contractor, whether in formal partnering methods or informal efforts, the goal of the designer is to provide ongoing solutions that allow changes to be implemented with as little impact in cost and time as possible yet still provide the owner with a quality product.

13-2c. Owner's and Owner's Representatives' Roles

The owner simply wants a quality product on time and within budget. However, the owner cannot sit back passively and expect perfect conditions and the job to run itself. The owner needs to stay active in the progress of the job and be ready to respond with decisions when needed. The owner's staff or representatives, whether they be construction managers, resident engineers, or third-party consultants, should consider themselves as members of the construction team as well as the owner's advocate. The owner's representatives need their own administration procedures to properly manage the job changes and should allow ample time to respond to the various day-to-day issues that the contractor needs to resolve.

13-3. ROLE OF ALTERNATIVE DISPUTE RESOLUTION

The evolving use of preventative type alternative dispute resolution (ADR) techniques plays an increasingly major role in the ability of contractors and owners alike to effectively deal with construction claims. Partnering

CONCLUSION   155

and dispute resolution boards in particular do much to enhance communications that do not treat claims as contentious issues, but rather as inherent problems of the construction process that need to be mutually solved.

As mentioned in chapter 11, ADR has already proven itself effective in reducing litigation. It is this type of communication and willingness to resolve disputes that will let owners, engineers, and contractors alike mutually focus on the successful completion of a project.

In conclusion, it is fitting to close this chapter by noting a voluntary disputes prevention and resolution commitment made on April 15, 1996, by 40 private and public construction entities. The "declaration of principles" was developed by the Construction Industry Dispute Avoidance and Resolution Task Force, a Washington, D.C.–based nonprofit organization in recognition of the high costs, considerable delays, and damages to the relationship of the parties caused by formal litigation procedures. (See Appendix 19 for the complete declaration and a list of the signees.)

In short, the declaration recommends that participants to the construction contract

1. Engage in partnering or other team-building procedures
2. Agree to resolve disputes that arise during performance through a negotiated resolution using agreed on lines of authority within their respective organizations
3. Agree to consider mediation or other forms of ADR rather than more confrontational or adversarial approaches for resolving disputes that arise after project completion

These principles are intended to encourage the parties to use ADR, but do not replace or invalidate existing contract provisions.

13-4. LEGAL CONSIDERATIONS

Each contract has variations of language that must be read and studied carefully. The contract should be read as a reasonable instrument, or framework, that will guide the manager in understanding his rights and obligations in performing the work. "Reasonable" is a common word often applied in contract law by the boards and courts, and represents a good rule-of-thumb approach in making any decision concerning the future well-being of a project. A significant amount of legal doctrine is available to help the contract manager with the orientation of boards and courts on the administration of construction contracts. These legal decisions serve as a frame of reference when dealing with new problems and can be a starting point for the manager to further research his own ideas. Nevertheless, legal counsel should be sought when questions of significant potential impact to the contract arise.

13-5. USE OF EXPERTS

In making decisions on contract problems or field conditions where the contractor's expertise is limited, "experts" should be consulted. Experts play an important role in helping contractors with technical problems and can also be of great help interpreting contracts.

For instance, a hydrologist may be required for subsurface or surface water problems while a geologist or soils engineer may be needed for problems encountered in rock or soil. In this same vein, metallurgists, chemical engineers, structural engineers, and experts in other related fields can prove very valuable.

Other contractors, and the various construction trade associations, should not be forgotten if it is necessary to establish industry custom or practice, especially in relation to technical wording or a reasonable standard of performance. Textbooks along with data published by the government and private industry can serve as references to support technical positions and pricing methods.

Scheduling consultants can be useful in preparing bids, initial schedules, and periodic updates. Their input in evaluating the effect of changes on the job schedule as well as their assistance in helping the project staff implement the job schedule is usually worth the expense of the consultant's active participation. Construction consultants can aid the busy contractor in performing productivity analysis, providing claims evaluation and preparation services, and can help set up and monitor claims administration programs.

Remember, failure to call in experts at the earliest time may prove to be "penny-wise but pound foolish." Although costly, experts will probably solve a problem in the most economical fashion, and in so doing, also help to reduce or avoid future problems.

13-6. CLAIMS CONSCIOUSNESS

Identification and notification of claims must be a conscious effort—recognizing a problem is the first important step toward resolution. Valid claims may go completely unrecognized. Growing companies hire new personnel inexperienced in claims management, the experienced personnel move up to higher management levels, and the resulting loss of communication between top management and on-site construction personnel can cause even those claims that have been noticed to go unreported.

Even experienced field personnel, anxious to perform a good job, will take responsibility for all problems and deliberately avoid becoming involved with identifying or tracking changes. Similarly, large companies entering new markets may deliberately avoid submission of claims to enhance their image and avoid creating the appearance of being claims oriented.

CONCLUSION

These attitudes are dangerous and frequently backfire when unavoidable delays become apparent, and the contractor is left holding the bag.

The successful contractor employing effective claims management techniques does not permit profits to be consumed by the performance of work at no cost that should be the subject of a change order or other claim. This knowledge and the cost and pricing experience that accompany it allow the well-managed contractor to submit more accurate bids, reduce contingencies, and gain the competitive edge.

The implementation of an active and productive "claims consciousness" program will serve the contractor well. This handbook has introduced the inexperienced engineer and contract manager to the problems that can occur during contract performance. The techniques and guidelines presented will assist in dealing with such problems. As for the experienced manager, he should find it useful in reevaluating and updating his claims administration and resolution program in order to make it more successful, effective, and efficient.

Appendix 1 - Contract Disputes Act of 1978/FAR 33.2

Contract Disputes Act of 1978
(Federal Acquisition Regulation - Subpart 33.2)

This appendix contains the complete **SUBPART 33.2--DISPUTES AND APPEALS** of the **Federal Acquisition Regulation (FAR)**, which is the implementation of the Contract Disputes Act of 1978 along with updates through 1996.

SUBPART 33.2--DISPUTES AND APPEALS

33.201 Definitions.

"Accrual of a claim" occurs on the date when all events, which fix the alleged liability of either the Government or the contractor and permit assertion of the claim, were known or should have been known. For liability to be fixed, some injury must have occurred. However, monetary damages need not have been incurred.

"Alternative dispute resolution (ADR)" means any procedure or combination of procedures voluntarily used to resolve issues in controversy without the need to resort to litigation. These procedures may include, but are not limited to, assisted settlement negotiations, conciliation, facilitation, mediation, fact-finding, minitrials, and arbitration.

"Claim," as used in this part, means a written demand or written assertion by one of the contracting parties seeking, as a matter of right, the payment of money in a sum certain, the adjustment or interpretation of contract terms, or other relief arising under or relating to the contract. A claim arising under a contract, unlike a claim relating to that contract, is a claim that can be resolved under a contract clause that provides for the relief sought by the claimant. However, a written demand or written assertion by the contractor seeking the payment of money exceeding $100,000 is not a claim under the Contract Disputes Act of 1978 until certified as required by the Act and 33.207. A voucher, invoice, or other routine request for payment that is not in dispute when submitted is not a claim. The submission may be converted to a claim, by written notice to the contracting officer as provided in 33.206(a), if it is disputed either as to liability or amount or is not acted upon in a reasonable time.

"Defective certification," as used in this subpart, means a certificate which alters or otherwise deviates from the language in 33.207(c) or which is not executed by a person duly authorized to bind the contractor with respect to the claim. Failure to certify shall not be deemed to be a defective certification.

"Issue in controversy" means a material disagreement between the Government and the contractor which (1) may result in a claim or (2) is all or part of an existing claim.

"Misrepresentation of fact," as used in this part, means a false statement of substantive fact, or any conduct which leads to the belief of a substantive fact material to proper understanding of the matter in hand, made with intent to deceive or mislead.

"Neutral person," as used in this subpart, means an impartial third party, who serves as a mediator, fact finder, or arbitrator, or otherwise functions to assist the parties to resolve the issues in controversy. A neutral person may be a permanent or temporary officer or employee of the Federal Government or any other individual who is acceptable to the parties. A neutral person shall have no official, financial, or personal conflict of interest with respect to the issues in controversy, unless such interest is fully disclosed in writing to all parties and all parties agree that the neutral person may serve (5 U.S.C. 583).

33.202 Contract Disputes Act of 1978.

The Contract Disputes Act of 1978, as amended (41 U.S.C. 601-613) (the Act), establishes procedures and requirements for asserting and resolving claims subject to the Act. In addition, the Act provides for: (a) the payment of interest on contractor claims; (b) certification of contractor claims; and (c) a civil penalty for contractor claims that are fraudulent or based on a misrepresentation of fact.

33.203 Applicability.

(a) Except as specified in paragraph (b) of this section, this part applies to any express or implied contract covered by the Federal Acquisition Regulation.

(b) This subpart does not apply to any contract with (1) a foreign government or agency of that government, or (2) an international organization or a subsidiary body of that organization, if the agency head determines that the application of the Act to the contract would not be in the public interest.

(c) This part applies to all disputes with respect to contracting officer decisions on matters "arising under" or "relating to" a contract. Agency Boards of Contract Appeals (BCA's) authorized under the Act continue to have all of the authority they possessed before the Act with respect to disputes arising under a contract, as well as authority to decide disputes relating to a contract. The clause at 52.233-1, Disputes, recognizes the "all disputes" authority established by the Act and states certain requirements and limitations of the Act for the guidance of contractors and contracting agencies. The clause is not intended to affect the rights and obligations of the parties as provided by the Act or to constrain the authority of the statutory agency BCA's in the handling and deciding of contractor appeals under the Act.

33.204 Policy.

The Government's policy is to try to resolve all contractual issues in controversy by mutual agreement at the contracting officer's level. Reasonable efforts should be made to resolve controversies prior to the submission of a claim. Agencies are encouraged to use ADR procedures to the maximum extent practicable. Certain factors, however, may make the use of ADR inappropriate (see 5 U.S.C. 572(b)). Except for arbitration conducted pursuant to the Administrative Dispute Resolution Act (ADRA), Pub. L. 101-522, agencies have authority which is separate from that provided by the ADRA to use ADR procedures to resolve issues in controversy. Agencies may also elect to proceed under the authority and requirements of the ADRA.

33.205 Relationship of the Act to Public Law 85-804.

(a) Requests for relief under Public Law 85-804 (50 U.S.C. 1431-1435) are not claims within the Contract Disputes Act of 1978 or the Disputes clause at 52.233-1, Disputes, and shall be processed under Part 50, Extraordinary Contractual Actions. However, relief formerly available only under Public Law 85-804; i.e., legal entitlement to rescission or reformation for mutual mistake, is now available within the authority of the contracting officer under the Contract Disputes Act of 1978 and the Disputes clause. In case of a question whether the contracting officer has authority to settle or decide specific types of claims, the contracting officer should seek legal advice.

(b) A contractor's allegation that it is entitled to rescission or reformation of its contract in order to correct or mitigate the effect of a mistake shall be treated as a claim under the Act. A contract may be reformed or rescinded by the contracting officer if the contractor would be entitled to such remedy or relief under the law of Federal contracts. Due to the complex legal issues likely to be associated with allegations of legal entitlement, contracting officers shall make written decisions, prepared with the advice and assistance of legal counsel, either granting or denying relief in whole or in part.

(c) A claim that is either denied or not approved in its entirety under paragraph (b) above may be cognizable as a request for relief under Public Law 85-804 as implemented by Part 50. However, the claim must first be submitted to the contracting officer for consideration under the Contract Disputes Act of 1978 because the claim is not cognizable under Public Law 85-804, as implemented by Part 50, unless other legal authority in the agency concerned is determined to be lacking or inadequate.

33.206 Initiation of a claim.

(a) Contractor claims shall be submitted, in writing, to the contracting officer for a decision within 6 years after accrual of a claim, unless the contracting parties agreed to a shorter time period. This 6-year time period does not apply to contracts awarded prior to October 1, 1995. The contracting officer shall document the contract file with evidence of the date of receipt of any submission from the contractor deemed to be a claim by the contracting officer.

(b) The contracting officer shall issue a written decision on any Government claim initiated against a contractor within 6 years after accrual of the claim, unless the contracting parties agreed to a shorter time period. The 6-year period shall not apply to contracts awarded prior to October 1, 1995, or to a Government claim based on a contractor claim involving fraud.

33.207 Contractor certification.

(a) Contractors shall provide the certification specified in 33.207(c) when submitting any claim--
　(1) Exceeding $100,000; or
　(2) Regardless of the amount claimed when using--
　　(i) Arbitration conducted pursuant to 5 U.S.C. 575-580; or
　　(ii) Any other ADR technique that the agency elects to handle in accordance with the ADRA

(b) The certification requirement does not apply to issues in controversy that have not been submitted as all or part of a claim.

(c) The certification shall state as follows: "I certify that the claim is made in good faith; that the supporting data are accurate and complete to the best of my knowledge and belief; that the amount requested accurately reflects the contract adjustment for which the contractor believes the Government is liable; and that I am duly authorized to certify the claim on behalf of the contractor."

(d) The aggregate amount of both increased and decreased costs shall be used in determining when the

APPENDIX 1—CONTRACT DISPUTES ACT OF 1978 / FAR 33.2   161

dollar thresholds requiring certification are met (see example in 15.804-2(a)(1)(iii) regarding cost or pricing data).

(e) The certification may be executed by any person duly authorized to bind the contractor with respect to the claim.

(f) A defective certification shall not deprive a court or an agency BCA of jurisdiction over that claim. Prior to the entry of a final judgment by a court or a decision by an agency BCA, however, the court or agency BCA shall require a defective certification to be corrected.

33.208 Interest on claims.

(a) The Government shall pay interest on a contractor's claim on the amount found due and unpaid from the date that--

(1) The contracting officer receives the claim (certified if required by 33.207(a)); or

(2) Payment otherwise would be due, if that date is later, until the date of payment.

(b) Simple interest on claims shall be paid at the rate, fixed by the Secretary of the Treasury as provided in the Act, which is applicable to the period during which the contracting officer receives the claim and then at the rate applicable for each 6-month period as fixed by the Treasury Secretary during the pendency of the claim. (See 32.614 for the right of the Government to collect interest on its claims against a contractor.)

(c) With regard to claims having defective certifications, interest shall be paid from either the date that the contracting officer initially receives the claim or October 29, 1992, whichever is later. However, if a contractor has provided a proper certificate prior to October 29, 1992, after submission of a defective certificate, interest shall be paid from the date of receipt by the Government of a proper certificate.

33.209 Suspected fraudulent claims.

If the contractor is unable to support any part of the claim and there is evidence that the inability is attributable to misrepresentation of fact or to fraud on the part of the contractor, the contracting officer shall refer the matter to the agency official responsible for investigating fraud.

33.210 Contracting officer's authority.

Except as provided in this section, contracting officers are authorized, within any specific limitations of their warrants, to decide or resolve all claims arising under or relating to a contract subject to the Act. In accordance with agency policies and 33.214, contracting officers are authorized to use ADR procedures to resolve claims. The authority to decide or resolve claims does not extend to--

(a) A claim or dispute for penalties or forfeitures prescribed by statute or regulation that another Federal agency is specifically authorized to administer, settle, or determine; or

(b) The settlement, compromise, payment, or adjustment of any claim involving fraud.

33.211 Contracting officer's decision.

(a) When a claim by or against a contractor cannot be satisfied or settled by mutual agreement and a decision on the claim is necessary, the contracting officer shall--

(1) Review the facts pertinent to the claim;

(2) Secure assistance from legal and other advisors;

(3) Coordinate with the contract administration office or contracting office, as appropriate; and

(4) Prepare a written decision that shall include a--

(i) Description of the claim or dispute;

(ii) Reference to the pertinent contract terms;

(iii) Statement of the factual areas of agreement and disagreement;

(iv) Statement of the contracting officer's decision, with supporting rationale;

(v) Paragraph substantially as follows: "This is the final decision of the Contracting Officer. You may appeal this decision to the agency board of contract appeals. If you decide to appeal, you must, within 90 days from the date you receive this decision, mail or otherwise furnish written notice to the agency board of contract appeals and provide a copy to the Contracting Officer from whose decision this appeal is taken. The notice shall indicate that an appeal is intended, reference this decision, and identify the contract by number. With regard to appeals to the agency board of contract appeals, you may, solely at your election, proceed under the board's small claim procedure for claims of $50,000 or less or its accelerated procedure for claims of $100,000 or less. Instead of appealing to the agency board of contract appeals, you may bring an action directly in the United States Court of Federal Claims (except as provided in the Contract Disputes Act of 1978, 41 U.S.C. 603, regarding Maritime Contracts) within 12 months of the date you receive this decision"; and

(vi) Demand for payment prepared in accordance with 32.610(b) in all cases where the decision results in a finding that the contractor is indebted to the Government.

(b) The contracting officer shall furnish a copy of the decision to the contractor by certified mail, return receipt requested, or by any other method that provides evidence of receipt. This requirement shall apply to decisions on claims initiated by or against the contractor.

(c) The contracting officer shall issue the decision within the following statutory time limitations:

(1) For claims of $100,000 or less, 60 days after receiving a written request from the contractor that a decision be rendered within that period, or within a reasonable time after receipt of the claim if the contractor does not make such a request.

(2) For claims over $100,000, 60 days after receiving a certified claim; provided, however, that if a decision will not be issued within 60 days, the contracting officer shall notify the contractor, within that period, of the time within which a decision will be issued.

(d) The contracting officer shall issue a decision within a reasonable time, taking into account--

(1) The size and complexity of the claim;

(2) The adequacy of the contractor's supporting data; and

(3) Any other relevant factors.

(e) The contracting officer shall have no obligation to render a final decision on any claim exceeding $100,000 which contains a defective certification, if within 60 days after receipt of the claim, the contracting officer notifies the contractor, in writing, of the reasons why any attempted certification was found to be defective.

(f) In the event of undue delay by the contracting officer in rendering a decision on a claim, the contractor may request the tribunal concerned to direct the contracting officer to issue a decision in a specified time period determined by the tribunal.

(g) Any failure of the contracting officer to issue a decision within the required time periods will be deemed a decision by the contracting officer denying the claim and will authorize the contractor to file an appeal or suit on the claim.

(h) The amount determined payable under the decision, less any portion already paid, should be paid, if otherwise proper, without awaiting contractor action concerning appeal. Such payment shall be without prejudice to the rights of either party.

33.212 Contracting officer's duties upon appeal.

To the extent permitted by any agency procedures controlling contacts with agency BCA personnel, the contracting officer shall provide data, documentation, information, and support as may be required by the agency BCA for use on a pending appeal from the contracting officer's decision.

33.213 Obligation to continue performance.

(a) In general, before passage of the Act, the obligation to continue performance applied only to claims arising under a contract. However, Section 6(b) of the Act authorizes agencies to require a contractor to continue contract performance in accordance with the contracting officer's decision pending final decision on a claim relating to the contract. In recognition of this fact, an alternate paragraph is provided for paragraph (h) of the clause at 52.233-1, Disputes. This paragraph shall be used only as authorized by agency procedures.

(b) In all contracts that include the clause at 52.233-1, Disputes, with its Alternate I, in the event of a dispute not arising under, but relating to, the contract, the contracting officer shall consider providing, through appropriate agency procedures, financing of the continued performance; provided, that the Government's interest is properly secured.

33.214 Alternative dispute resolution (ADR).

(a) The objective of using ADR procedures is to increase the opportunity for relatively inexpensive and expeditious resolution of issues in controversy. Essential elements of ADR include--

(1) Existence of an issue in controversy;

(2) A voluntary election by both parties to participate in the ADR process;

(3) An agreement on alternative procedures and terms to be used in lieu of formal litigation;

(4) Participation in the process by officials of both parties who have the authority to resolve the issue in controversy; and

(5) Certification by the contractor in accordance with 33.207 when using ADR procedures to resolve all or part of a claim under the authority of the ADRA.

(b) If the contracting officer rejects a request for ADR from a small business contractor, the contracting officer shall provide the contractor written explanation citing one or more of the conditions in 5 U.S.C. 572(b) or such other specific reasons that ADR procedures are inappropriate for the resolution of the dispute. In any case where a contractor rejects a request of an agency for ADR proceedings, the contractor shall inform the agency in writing of the contractor's specific reasons for rejecting the request.

(c) ADR procedures may be used at any time that

the contracting officer has authority to resolve the issue in controversy. If a claim has been submitted, ADR procedures may be applied to all or a portion of the claim. When ADR procedures are used subsequent to the issuance of a contracting officer's final decision, their use does not alter any of the time limitations or procedural requirements for filing an appeal of the contracting officer's final decision and does not constitute a reconsideration of the final decision.

(d) When appropriate, a neutral person may be used to facilitate resolution of the issue in controversy using the procedures chosen by the parties.

(e) The confidentiality of ADR proceedings shall be protected consistent with 5 U.S.C. 574.

33.215 Contract clause.

The contracting officer shall insert the clause at 52.233-1, Disputes, in solicitations and contracts, unless the conditions in 33.203(b) apply. If it is determined under agency procedures that continued performance is necessary pending resolution of any claim arising under or relating to the contract, the contracting officer shall use the clause with its Alternate I.

> Appendix 2 - FAR 52.2 Text of Provisions and Clauses

The Federal Acquisition Regulation (FAR) – Select Clauses

This appendix contains select clauses from the **Federal Acquisition Regulation (FAR)**. This set of clauses is from *Subpart 52 - Text of Provisions and Clauses*, which represent the "General Conditions" of the contract. **Table A4-1** contains a summary of the clauses in this section. This is followed by a Table A4-2 containing a more comprehensive listing of most of the standard clauses used on construction contracts, including a cross reference to their counterparts from the old Standard Form 23.

Notes on the F.A.R.

The Federal Acquisition Regulation System is established for the codification and publication of uniform policies and procedures for acquisition by all executive agencies. The Federal Acquisition Regulation System consists of the Federal Acquisition Regulation (FAR), which is the primary document, and agency acquisition regulations that implement or supplement the FAR. The FAR System does not include internal agency guidance of the type described in 1.301(a)(2).

The FAR is prepared, issued, and maintained, and the FAR System is prescribed, jointly by the Secretary of Defense, the Administrator of General Services, and the Administrator, National Aeronautics and Space Administration, under their several statutory authorities.

Copies of the FAR in Federal Register, loose-leaf, and CFR form may be purchased from the Superintendent of Documents, Government Printing Office (GPO), Washington, DC 20402. Additionally, the FAR is maintained on the Internet at /www.arnet.gov/far.

APPENDIX 2—FAR 52.2 TEXT OF PROVISIONS & CLAUSES

Selected Federal Acquisition Regulation (F.A.R.) Clauses

F.A.R. Clause No.	Description	Appendix 2 Page No.
52.211-12	Liquidated Damages–Construction	167
52.211-13	Time Extensions	167
52.211-18	Variation in Estimated Quantity	167
52.222-11	Subcontracts (Labor Standards)	167
52.222-12	Contract Termination - Debarment	167
52.231-3	Site Investigations	167
52.232-27	Prompt Payment	167
52.233-1	Disputes	171
52.236-1	Performance of work by the Contractor	172
52.236-2	Differing Site Conditions	172
52.236-3	Site Investigations and Conditions Affecting the Work	172
52.236-4	Physical Data	172
52.236-5	Materials and Workmanship	172
52.236-6	Superintendence by Contractor	173
52.236-7	Permits and Responsibilities	173
52.236-15	Schedules for Construction Contracts	173
52.236-16	Quality Surveys	173
52.236-21	Specifications and Drawings for Construction	174
52.242-14	Suspension of Work	175
52.242-15	Stop Work Order	175
52.243-4	Changes	175
52.244-1	Subcontractors	176
52.246-12	Inspection of Construction	177
52.246-21	Warranty of Construction	177
52.248-3	Value Engineering Incentive	178
52.249-2 (ALT. I)	Termination for Convenience of the Government	180
52.249-10	Termination for Default - Damages for Delay-Time Extensions	183
52.249-14	Excusable Delays	184

Reference List F.A.R. Clauses and Previous Standard Form 23

Form 23	Description	F.A.R. No.
1.1 & 1.2	Definitions	52.202-1
2.	Specifications and Drawings	52.236-21
3.	Changes	52.243-4
4.	Differing Site Conditions	52.236-2
5.	Termination for Default - Damages for Delay - Time Extensions	52.249-10
6.	Disputes	52.233-1
7.	Payments to contractor	52.232-5
8.	Assignment of Claims	52.232-23
9.	Materials and Workmanship	52.236-5
10.	Inspection and Acceptance	52.246-12
11.	Superintendence by Contractor	52.236-6
12.	Permits and Responsibilities	52.236-7
13.	Conditions Affecting the Work	
14.	Other Contracts	52.236-8
15.	Patent Indemnity	52.227-14
16.	Additional Bond Security	52.228-2
17.	Covenant Against Contingent Fees	52.203-5
18.	Officials Not to Benefit	52.203-6
19.	Buy American Act	52.225-5
20.	Convict Labor	52.222-3
21.	Equal Opportunity	52.222-26
22.	Utilization of Small Business Concerns	52.219-8
23.	Suspension of Work	52.242-14
24.	Davis-Bacon Act	52.222-6
25.	Contract Work Hours and Safety Standards Act - Overtime Compensation	52.223-4
26.	Apprentices and Trainees	52.232-9
27.	Payrolls and Basic Records	52.232-8
28.	Compliance With Copeland Regulations	52.222-10
29.	Withholding of Funds	52.222-7
30.	Subcontracts	52.222-11
31.	Contract Termination - Debarment	52.222-12
32.	Contractor Inspection System	52.246-12
33.	Gratuities	52.203-3
34.	Small Business Subcontracting Program (Maintenance, Repair and Construction)	52.219-9
35.	Federal, State and Local Taxes	52.229-3
36.	Renegotiation	
37.	Termination for Convenience of the Government	52.249-2 (ALT. I)
38.	Notice and Assistance Regarding Patent and Copyright Infringement	52.227-2
39.	Authorization and Consent	52.227-1
40.	Composition of Contractor	
41.	Site Investigation	52.231-3
42.	Protection of Existing Vegetation, Structures, Utilities, and Improvements	52.236-9
43.	Operations and Storage Areas	52.236-10
44.	Modification Proposals - Price Breakdown	
45.	Subcontractors	52.244-1
46.	Use and Possession Prior to Completions	52.236-11
47.	Cleaning Up	52.236-12
48.	Additional Definitions	
49.	Accident Prevention	52.236-13
50.	Government Inspectors	52.246-12
51.	Rights in Shop Drawings	
52.	Affirmative Action for Handicapped Workers	52.222-36
53.	Clean Air and Water	52.223-2
54.	Notice to the Government of Labor Disputes	
55.	Contract Prices - Bidding Schedule	
56.	Examination of Records by Comptroller General	
57.	Priorities, Allocations, and Allotments	
58.	Price Reduction for Defective Cost or Pricing Data - Price Adjustments	52.215-23
59.	Interest	52.237-17
60.	Audit by Department of Defense	
61.	Subcontractor Cost or Pricing Data - Price Adjustments	52.215-25
62.1	Government - Furnished Property (Short Form)	52.245-4
62.2	Government Property (Fixed Price)	52.245-2
63.	Disputes Concerning Labor Standards	
64.	Variations in Estimated Quantities	52.211-18
65.	Progress Charts and Requirements for Overtime Work	
66.	Value Engineering Incentive	52.243-3
67.	Pricing of Adjustments	
68.	Listing of Employment Openings	
69.	Utilization of Minority Business Enterprises	
70.	Minority Business Enterprises Subcontracting Program	
71.	Payment of Interest on Contractors Claims	
72.	Environmental Litigation	

APPENDIX 2—FAR 52.2 TEXT OF PROVISIONS & CLAUSES 167

52.211-12 Liquidated Damages--Construction.

(APR 1984)

(a) If the Contractor fails to complete the work within the time specified in the contract, or any extension, the Contractor shall pay to the Government as liquidated damages, the sum of _____ [*Contracting Officer insert amount*] for each day of delay.

(b) If the Government terminates the Contractor's right to proceed, the resulting damage will consist of liquidated damages until such reasonable time as may be required for final completion of the work together with any increased costs occasioned the Government in completing the work.

(c) If the Government does not terminate the Contractor's right to proceed, the resulting damage will consist of liquidated damages until the work is completed or accepted.

(End of clause)

Alternate I (APR 1984). If different completion dates are specified in the contract for separate parts or stages of the work, revise paragraph (a) of the clause to state the amount of liquidated damages for delay of each separate part or stage of the work.

52.211-13 Time Extensions.

(APR 1984)

Notwithstanding any other provisions of this contract, it is mutually understood that the time extensions for changes in the work will depend upon the extent, if any, by which the changes cause delay in the completion of the various elements of construction. The change order granting the time extension may provide that the contract completion date will be extended only for those specific elements so delayed and that the remaining contract completion dates for all other portions of the work will not be altered and may further provide for an equitable readjustment of liquidated damages under the new completion schedule.

(End of clause)

52.211-18 Variation in Estimated Quantity.

(APR 1984)

If the quantity of a unit-priced item in this contract is an estimated quantity and the actual quantity of the unit-priced item varies more than 15 percent above or below the estimated quantity, an equitable adjustment in the contract price shall be made upon demand of either party. The equitable adjustment shall be based upon any increase or decrease in costs due solely to the variation above 115 percent or below 85 percent of the estimated quantity. If the quantity variation is such as to cause an increase in the time necessary for completion, the Contractor may request, in writing, an extension of time, to be received by the Contracting Officer within 10 days from the beginning of the delay, or within such further period as may be granted by the Contracting Officer before the date of final settlement of the contract. Upon the receipt of a written request for an extension, the Contracting Officer shall ascertain the facts and make an adjustment for extending the completion date as, in the judgement of the Contracting Officer, is justified.

(End of clause)

52.222-11 Subcontracts (Labor Standards).

(FEB 1988)

(a) The Contractor or subcontractor shall insert in any subcontracts the clauses entitled Davis-Bacon Act, Contract Work Hours and Safety Standards Act--Overtime Compensation, Apprentices and Trainees, Payrolls and Basic Records, Compliance with Copeland Act Requirements, Withholding of Funds, Subcontracts (Labor Standards), Contract Termination--Debarment, Disputes Concerning Labor Standards, Compliance with Davis-Bacon and Related Act Regulations, and Certification of Eligibility, and such other clauses as the Contracting Officer may, by appropriate instructions, require, and also a clause requiring subcontractors to include these clauses in any lower tier subcontracts. The Prime Contractor shall be responsible for compliance by any subcontractor or lower tier subcontractor with all the contract clauses cited in this paragraph.

(b)(1) Within 14 days after award of the contract, the Contractor shall deliver to the Contracting Officer a completed Statement and Acknowledgment Form (SF 1413) for each subcontract, including the subcontractor's signed and dated acknowledgment that the clauses set forth in paragraph (a) of this clause have been included in the subcontract.

(2) Within 14 days after the award of any subsequently awarded subcontract the Contractor shall deliver to the Contracting Officer an updated completed SF 1413 for such additional subcontract.

(End of clause)

52.222-12 Contract Termination--Debarment.

(FEB 1988)

A breach of the contract clauses entitled *Davis-Bacon Act, Contract Work Hours and Safety Standards Act--Overtime Compensation, Apprentices and Trainees, Payrolls and Basic Records, Compliance with Copeland Act Requirements, Subcontracts (Labor Standards), Compliance with Davis-Bacon and Related Act Regulations, or Certification of Eligibility* may be grounds for termination of the contract, and for debarment as a Contractor and subcontractor as provided in 29 CFR 5.12.

(End of clause)

52.232-27 Prompt Payment for Construction Contracts.

(MAR 1994)

Notwithstanding any other payment terms in this contract, the Government will make invoice payments and contract financing payments under the terms and conditions specified in this clause. Payment shall be considered as being made on the day a check is dated or an electronic funds transfer is made. Definitions of pertinent terms are set forth in 32.902. All days referred to in this clause are calendar days, unless otherwise specified.

(a) Invoice Payments.

(1) For purposes of this clause, there are several types of invoice payments which may occur under this contract, as follows:

(i) Progress payments, if provided for elsewhere in this contract, based on Contracting Officer approval of the estimated amount and value of work or services performed, including payments for reaching milestones in any project:

(A) The due date for making such payments shall be 14 days after receipt of the payment request by the designated billing office. However, if the designated billing office fails to annotate the payment request with the actual date of receipt, the payment due date shall be deemed to be the 14th day after the date the Contractor's payment request is dated, provided a proper payment request is received and there is no disagreement over quantity, quality, or Contractor compliance with contract requirements.

(B) The due date for payment of any amounts retained by the Contracting Officer in accordance with the clause at 52.232-5, Payments Under Fixed-Price Construction Contracts, shall be as specified in the contract or, if not specified, 30 days after approval for release to the Contractor by the Contracting Officer.

(ii) Final payments based on completion and acceptance of all work and presentation of release of all claims against the Government arising by virtue of the contract, and payments for partial deliveries that have been accepted by the Government (e.g., each separate building, public work, or other division of the contract for which the price is stated separately in the contract):

(A) The due date for making such payments shall be either the 30th day after receipt by the designated billing office of a proper invoice from the Contractor, or the 30th day after Government acceptance of the work or services completed by the Contractor, whichever is later. However, if the designated billing office fails to annotate the invoice with the date of actual receipt, the invoice payment due date shall be deemed to be the 30th day after the date the Contractor's invoice is dated, provided a proper invoice is received and there is no disagreement over quantity, quality, or Contractor compliance with contract requirements.

(B) On a final invoice where the payment amount is subject to contract settlement actions (e.g., release of claims), acceptance shall be deemed to have occurred on the effective date of the contract settlement.

(2) An invoice is the Contractor's bill or written request for payment under the contract for work or serv-ices performed under the contract. An invoice shall be prepared and submitted to the designated billing office. A proper invoice must include the items listed in subdivisions (a)(2)(i) through (a)(2)(ix) of this clause. If the invoice does not comply with these requirements, the Contractor will be notified of the defect within 7 days after receipt of the invoice at the designated billing office. Untimely notification will be taken into account in the computation of any interest penalty owed the Contractor in the manner described in subparagraph (a)(4) of this clause:

(i) Name and address of the Contractor.

(ii) Invoice date.

(iii) Contract number or other authorization for work or services performed (including order number and contract line item number).

(iv) Description of work or services performed.

(v) Delivery and payment terms (e.g., prompt payment discount terms).

(vi) Name and address of Contractor official to whom payment is to be sent (must be the same as that in the contract or in a proper notice of assignment).

(vii) Name (where practicable), title, phone number, and mailing address of person to be notified in event of a defective invoice.

(viii) For payments described in subdivision (a)(1)(i) of this clause, substantiation of the amounts requested and certification in accordance with the requirements of the clause at 52.232-5, Payments Under Fixed-Price Construction Contracts.

(ix) Any other information or documentation required by the contract.

(3) An interest penalty shall be paid automatically by the designated payment office, without request from the Contractor, if payment is not made by the due date and the conditions listed in subdivisions (a)(3)(i) through (a)(3)(iii) of this clause are met, if applicable.

(i) A proper invoice was received by the designated billing office.

(ii) A receiving report or other Government documentation authorizing payment was processed and there was no disagreement over quantity, quality, Contractor compliance with any contract term or condition, or requested progress payment amount.

(iii) In the case of a final invoice for any balance of funds due the Contractor for work or services performed, the amount was not subject to further contract settlement actions between the Government and the Contractor.

(4) The interest penalty shall be at the rate established by the Secretary of the Treasury under section 12 of the Contract Disputes Act of 1978 (41 U.S.C. 611) that is in effect on the day after the due date, except where the interest penalty is prescribed by other governmental authority. This rate is referred to as the "Renegotiation Board Interest Rate," and it is published in the Federal Register semiannually on or about January 1 and July 1. The interest penalty shall accrue daily on the invoice payment amount approved by the Government and be compounded in 30-day increments inclusive from the first day after the due date through the payment date. That is, interest accrued at the end of any 30-day period will be added to the approved invoice payment amount and be subject to interest penalties if not paid in the succeeding 30-day period. If the designated billing office failed to notify the Contractor of a defective invoice within the periods prescribed in sub-paragraph (a)(2) of this clause, then the due date on the corrected invoice will be adjusted by subtracting the number of days taken beyond the prescribed notification of defects period. Any interest penalty owed the Contractor will be based on this adjusted due date. Adjustments will be made by the designated payment office for errors in calculating interest penalties, if requested by the Contractor.

(i) For the sole purpose of computing an interest penalty that might be due the Contractor for payments described in subdivision (a)(1)(ii) of this clause, Government acceptance or approval shall be deemed to have occurred constructively on the

7th day after the Contractor has completed the work or services in accordance with the terms and conditions of the contract. In the event that actual acceptance or approval occurs within the constructive acceptance or approval period, the determination of an interest penalty shall be based on the actual date of acceptance or approval. Constructive acceptance or constructive approval requirements do not apply if there is a disagreement over quantity, quality, or Contractor compliance with a contract provision. These requirements also do not compel Government officials to accept work or services, approve Contractor estimates, perform contract administration functions, or make payment prior to fulfilling their responsibilities.

(ii) The following periods of time will not be included in the determination of an interest penalty:

(A) The period taken to notify the Contractor of defects in invoices submitted to the Government, but this may not exceed 7 days.

(B) The period between the defects notice and resubmission of the corrected invoice by the Contractor.

(iii) Interest penalties will not continue to accrue after the filing of a claim for such penalties under the clause at 52.233-1, Disputes, or for more than 1 year. Interest penalties of less than $1.00 need not be paid.

(iv) Interest penalties are not required on payment delays due to disagreement between the Government and Contractor over the payment amount or other issues involving contract compliance, or on amounts temporarily withheld or retained in accordance with the terms of the contract. Claims involving disputes, and any interest that may be payable, will be resolved in accordance with the clause at 52.233-1, Disputes.

(5) An interest penalty shall also be paid automatically by the designated payment office, without request from the Contractor, if a discount for prompt payment is taken improperly. The interest penalty will be calculated on the amount of discount taken for the period beginning with the first day after the end of the discount period through the date when the Contractor is paid.

(6) If this contract was awarded on or after October 1, 1989, a penalty amount, calculated in accordance with regulations issued by the Office of Management and Budget, shall be paid in addition to the interest penalty amount if the Contractor--

(i) Is owed an interest penalty;

(ii) Is not paid the interest penalty within 10 days after the date the invoice amount is paid; and

(iii) Makes a written demand, not later than 40 days after the date the invoice amount is paid, that the agency pay such a penalty.

(b) Contract Financing Payments.

(1) For purposes of this clause, if applicable, "contract financing payment" means a Government disbursement of monies to a Contractor under a contract clause or other authorization prior to acceptance of supplies or services by the Government, other than progress payments based on estimates of amount and value of work performed. Contract financing payments include advance payments and interim payments under cost-type contracts.

(2) If this contract provides for contract financing, requests for payment shall be submitted to the designated billing office as specified in this contract or as directed by the Contracting Officer. Contract financing payments shall be made on the (insert day as prescribed by Agency head; if not prescribed, insert 30th day) day after receipt of a proper contract financing request by the designated billing office. In the event that an audit or other review of a specific financing request is required to ensure compliance with the terms and conditions of the contract, the designated payment office is not compelled to make payment by the due date specified. For advance payments, loans, or other arrangements that do not involve recurrent submissions of contract financing requests, payment shall be made in accordance with the corresponding contract terms or as directed by the Contracting Officer. Contract financing payments shall not be assessed an interest penalty for payment delays.

(c) The Contractor shall include in each subcontract for property or services (including a material supplier) for the purpose of performing this contract the following:

(1) A payment clause which obligates the Contractor to pay the subcontractor for satisfactory performance under its subcontract not later than 7 days from receipt of payment out of such amounts as are paid to the Contractor under this contract.

(2) An interest penalty clause which obligates the Contractor to pay to the subcontractor an interest penalty for each payment not made in accordance with the payment clause--

(i) For the period beginning on the day after the required payment date and ending on the date on which payment of the amount due is made; and

(ii) Computed at the rate of interest established by the Secretary of the Treasury, and published in the Federal Register, for interest payments under section 12 of the Contract Disputes Act of 1978 (41 U.S.C. 611) in effect at the time the Contractor accrues the obligation to pay an interest penalty.

(3) A clause requiring each subcontractor to include a payment clause and an interest penalty clause conforming to the standards set forth in subparagraphs (c)(1) and (c)(2) of this clause in each of its subcontracts, and to require each of its subcontractors to include such clauses in their subcontracts with each lower-tier subcontractor or supplier.

(d) The clauses required by paragraph (c) of this clause shall not be construed to impair the right of Contractor or a subcontractor at any tier to negotiate, and to include in their subcontract, provisions which--

(1) Permit the Contractor or a subcontractor to retain (without cause) a specified percentage of each progress payment otherwise due to a subcontractor for satisfactory performance under the subcontract without incurring any obligation to pay a late payment interest penalty, in accordance with terms and conditions agreed to by the parties to the subcontract, giving such recognition as the parties deem appropriate to the ability of a subcontractor to furnish a performance bond and a payment bond;

(2) Permit the Contractor or subcontractor to make a determination that part or all of the subcontractor's request for payment may be withheld in accordance with the subcontract agreement; and

(3) Permit such withholding without incurring any obligation to pay a late payment penalty if--

(i) A notice conforming to the standards of paragraph (g) of this clause has been previously furnished to the subcontractor; and

(ii) A copy of any notice issued by a Contractor pursuant to subdivision (d)(3)(i) of this clause has been furnished to the Contracting Officer.

(e) If a Contractor, after making a request for payment to the Government but before making a payment to a subcontractor for the subcontractor's performance covered by the payment request, discovers that all or a portion of the payment otherwise due such subcontractor is subject to withholding from the subcontractor in accordance with the subcontract agreement, then the Contractor shall--

(1) Furnish to the subcontractor a notice conforming to the standards of paragraph (g) of this clause as soon as practicable upon ascertaining the cause giving rise to a withholding, but prior to the due date for subcontractor payment;

(2) Furnish to the Contracting Officer, as soon as practicable, a copy of the notice furnished to the subcontractor pursuant to subparagraph (e)(1) of this clause;

(3) Reduce the subcontractor's progress payment by an amount not to exceed the amount specified in the notice of withholding furnished under subparagraph (e)(1) of this clause;

(4) Pay the subcontractor as soon as practicable after the correction of the identified subcontract performance deficiency, and--

(i) Make such payment within--

(A) Seven days after correction of the identified subcontract performance deficiency (unless the funds therefor must be recovered from the Government because of a reduction under subdivision (e)(5)(i) of this clause; or

(B) Seven days after the Contractor recovers such funds from the Government; or

(ii) Incur an obligation to pay a late payment interest penalty computed at the rate of interest established by the Secretary of the Treasury, and published in the *Federal Register*, for interest payments under section 12 of the Contracts Disputes Act of 1978 (41 U.S.C. 611) in effect at the time the Contractor accrues the obligation to pay an interest penalty;

(5) Notify the Contracting Officer upon--

(i) Reduction of the amount of any subsequent certified application for payment; or

(ii) Payment to the subcontractor of any withheld amounts of a progress payment, specifying--

(A) The amounts withheld under subparagraph (e)(1) of this clause; and

(B) The dates that such withholding began and ended; and

(6) Be obligated to pay to the Government an amount equal to interest on the withheld payments (computed in the manner provided in 31 U.S.C. 3903(c)(1)), from the 8th day after receipt of the withheld amounts from the Government until--

(i) The day the identified subcontractor performance deficiency is corrected; or

(ii) The date that any subsequent payment is reduced under subdivision (e)(5)(i) of this clause.

(f)(1) If a Contractor, after making payment to a first-tier subcontractor, receives from a supplier or subcontractor of the first-tier subcontractor (hereafter referred to as a "second-tier subcontractor") a written notice in accordance with section 2 of the Act of August 24, 1935 (40 U.S.C. 270b, Miller Act), asserting a deficiency in such first-tier subcontractor's performance under the contract for which the Contractor may be ultimately liable, and the Contractor determines that all or a portion of future payments otherwise due such first-tier subcontractor is subject to withholding in accordance with the subcontract agreement, then the Contractor may, without incurring an obligation to pay an interest penalty under subparagraph (e)(6) of this clause--

(i) Furnish to the first-tier subcontractor a notice conforming to the standards of paragraph (g) of this clause as soon as practicable upon making such determination; and

(ii) Withhold from the first-tier subcontractor's next available progress payment or payments an amount not to exceed the amount specified in the notice of withholding furnished under subdivision (f)(1)(i) of this clause.

(2) As soon as practicable, but not later than 7 days after receipt of satisfactory written notification that the identified subcontract performance deficiency has been corrected, the Contractor shall pay the amount withheld under subdivision (f)(1)(ii) of this clause to such first-tier subcontractor, or shall incur an obligation to pay a late payment interest penalty to such first-tier subcontractor computed at the rate of interest established by the Secretary of the Treasury, and published in the *Federal Register*, for interest payments under section 12 of the Contracts Disputes Act of 1978 (41 U.S.C. 611) in effect at the time the Contractor accrues the obligation to pay an interest penalty.

(g) A written notice of any withholding shall be issued to a subcontractor (with a copy to the Contracting Officer of any such notice issued by the Contractor), specifying--

(1) The amount to be withheld;

(2) The specific causes for the withholding under the terms of the subcontract; and

(3) The remedial actions to be taken by the subcontractor in order to receive payment of the amounts withheld.

(h) The Contractor may not request payment from the Government of any amount withheld or retained in accordance with paragraph (d) of this clause until such time as the Contractor has determined and certified to the Contracting Officer that the subcontractor is entitled to the payment of such amount.

(i) A dispute between the Contractor and subcontractor relating to the amount or entitlement of a subcontractor to a payment or a late payment interest penalty under a clause included in the subcontract pursuant to paragraph (c) of this clause does not constitute a dispute to which the United States is a party. The United States may not be interpleaded in any judicial or administrative proceeding involving such a dispute.

APPENDIX 2—FAR 52.2 TEXT OF PROVISIONS & CLAUSES

(j) Except as provided in paragraph (i) of this clause, this clause shall not limit or impair any contractual, administrative, or judicial remedies otherwise available to the Contractor or a subcontractor in the event of a dispute involving late payment or nonpayment by the Contractor or deficient subcontract performance or nonperformance by a subcontractor.

(k) The Contractor's obligation to pay an interest penalty to a subcontractor pursuant to the clauses included in a subcontract under paragraph (c) of this clause shall not be construed to be an obligation of the United States for such interest penalty. A cost reimbursement claim may not include any amount for reimbursement of such interest penalty.

(End of clause)

52.233-1 Disputes.

(OCT 1995)

(a) This contract is subject to the Contract Disputes Act of 1978, as amended (41 U.S.C. 601-613).

(b) Except as provided in the Act, all disputes arising under or relating to this contract shall be resolved under this clause.

(c) "Claim," as used in this clause, means a written demand or written assertion by one of the contracting parties seeking, as a matter of right, the payment of money in a sum certain, the adjustment or interpretation of contract terms, or other relief arising under or relating to this contract. A claim arising under a contract, unlike a claim relating to that contract, is a claim that can be resolved under a contract clause that provides for the relief sought by the claimant. However, a written demand or written assertion by the Contractor seeking the payment of money exceeding $100,000 is not a claim under the Act until certified as required by subparagraph (d)(2) of this clause. A voucher, invoice, or other routine request for payment that is not in dispute when submitted is not a claim under the Act. The submission may be converted to a claim under the Act, by complying with the submission and certification requirements of this clause, if it is disputed either as to liability or amount or is not acted upon in a reasonable time.

(d)(1) A claim by the Contractor shall be made in writing and, unless otherwise stated in this contract, submitted within 6 years after accrual of the claim to the Contracting Officer for a written decision. A claim by the Government against the Contractor shall be subject to a written decision by the Contracting Officer.

(2)(i) Contractors shall provide the certification specified in subparagraph (d)(2)(iii) of this clause when submitting any claim--

(A) Exceeding $100,000; or

(B) Regardless of the amount claimed, when using--

(1) Arbitration conducted pursuant to 5 U.S.C. 575-580; or

(2) Any other alternative means of dispute resolution (ADR) technique that the agency elects to handle in accordance with the Administrative Dispute Resolution Act (ADRA).

(ii) The certification requirement does not apply to issues in controversy that have not been submitted as all or part of a claim.

(iii) The certification shall state as follows: "I certify that the claim is made in good faith; that the supporting data are accurate and complete to the best of my knowledge and belief; that the amount requested accurately reflects the contract adjustment for which the Contractor believes the Government is liable; and that I am duly authorized to certify the claim on behalf of the Contractor."

(3) The certification may be executed by any person duly authorized to bind the Contractor with respect to the claim.

(e) For Contractor claims of $100,000 or less, the Contracting Officer must, if requested in writing by the Contractor, render a decision within 60 days of the request. For Contractor-certified claims over $100,000, the Contracting Officer must, within 60 days, decide the claim or notify the Contractor of the date by which the decision will be made.

(f) The Contracting Officer's decision shall be final unless the Contractor appeals or files a suit as provided in the Act.

(g) If the claim by the Contractor is submitted to the Contracting Officer or a claim by the Government is presented to the Contractor, the parties, by mutual consent, may agree to use ADR. If the Contractor refuses an offer for alternative disputes resolution, the Contractor shall inform the Contracting Officer, in writing, of the Contractor's specific reasons for rejecting the request. When using arbitration conducted pursuant to 5 U.S.C. 575-580, or when using any other ADR technique that the agency elects to handle in accordance with the ADRA any claim, regardless of amount, shall be accompanied by the certification described in subparagraph (d)(2)(iii) of this clause, and executed in accordance with subparagraph (d)(3) of this clause.

(h) The Government shall pay interest on the amount found due and unpaid from (1) the date that the Contracting Officer receives the claim (certified, if required); or (2) the date that payment otherwise would be due, if that date is later, until the date of payment. With regard to claims having defective certifications, as defined in FAR 33.201, interest shall be paid from the date that the Contracting Officer initially receives the claim. Simple interest on claims shall be paid at the rate, fixed by the Secretary of the Treasury as provided in the Act, which is applicable to the period during which the Contracting Officer receives the claim and then at the rate applicable for each 6-month period as fixed by the Treasury Secretary during the pendency of the claim.

(i) The Contractor shall proceed diligently with performance of this contract, pending final resolution of any request for relief, claim, appeal, or action arising under the contract, and comply with any decision of the Contracting Officer.

(End of clause)

Alternate I (DEC 1991). If it is determined under agency procedures, that continued performance is necessary pending resolution of any claim arising under or relating to the contract, substitute the following paragraph (i) for the paragraph (i) of the basic clause:

(i) The Contractor shall proceed diligently with performance of this contract, pending final resolution of any request for relief, claim, appeal, or action arising under or relating to the contract, and comply with any decision of the Contracting Officer.

52.236-1 Performance of Work by the Contractor.

(APR 1984)

The Contractor shall perform on the site, and with its own organization, work equivalent to at least _____ [*insert the appropriate number in words followed by numerals in parentheses*] percent of the total amount of work to be performed under the contract. This percentage may be reduced by a supplemental agreement to this contract if, during performing the work, the Contractor requests a reduction and the Contracting Officer determines that the reduction would be to the advantage of the Government.

(End of clause)

52.236-2 Differing Site Conditions.

(APR 1984)

(a) The Contractor shall promptly, and before the conditions are disturbed, give a written notice to the Contracting Officer of (1) subsurface or latent physical conditions at the site which differ materially from those indicated in this contract, or (2) unknown physical conditions at the site, of an unusual nature, which differ materially from those ordinarily encountered and generally recognized as inhering in work of the character provided for in the contract.

(b) The Contracting Officer shall investigate the site conditions promptly after receiving the notice. If the conditions do materially so differ and cause an increase or decrease in the Contractor's cost of, or the time required for, performing any part of the work under this contract, whether or not changed as a result of the conditions, an equitable adjustment shall be made under this clause and the contract modified in writing accordingly.

(c) No request by the Contractor for an equitable adjustment to the contract under this clause shall be allowed, unless the Contractor has given the written notice required; provided, that the time prescribed in paragraph (a) of this clause for giving written notice may be extended by the Contracting Officer.

(d) No request by the Contractor for an equitable adjustment to the contract for differing site conditions shall be allowed if made after final payment under this contract.

(End of clause)

52.236-3 Site Investigation and Conditions Affecting the Work.

(APR 1984)

(a) The Contractor acknowledges that it has taken steps reasonably necessary to ascertain the nature and location of the work, and that it has investigated and satisfied itself as to the general and local conditions which can affect the work or its cost, including but not limited to (1) conditions bearing upon transportation, disposal, handling, and storage of materials; (2) the availability of labor, water, electric power, and roads; (3) uncertainties of weather, river stages, tides, or similar physical conditions at the site; (4) the conformation and conditions of the ground; and (5) the character of equipment and facilities needed preliminary to and during work performance. The Contractor also acknowledges that it has satisfied itself as to the character, quality, and quantity of surface and subsurface materials or obstacles to be encountered insofar as this information is reasonably ascertainable from an inspection of the site, including all exploratory work done by the Government, as well as from the drawings and specifications made a part of this contract. Any failure of the Contractor to take the actions described and acknowledged in this paragraph will not relieve the Contractor from responsibility for estimating properly the difficulty and cost of successfully performing the work, or for proceeding to successfully perform the work without additional expense to the Government.

(b) The Government assumes no responsibility for any conclusions or interpretations made by the Contractor based on the information made available by the Government. Nor does the Government assume responsibility for any understanding reached or representation made concerning conditions which can affect the work by any of its officers or agents before the execution of this contract, unless that understanding or representation is expressly stated in this contract.

(End of clause)

52.236-4 Physical Data.

(APR 1984)

Data and information furnished or referred to below is for the Contractor's information. The Government shall not be responsible for any interpretation of or conclusion drawn from the data or information by the Contractor.

(a) The indications of physical conditions on the drawings and in the specifications are the result of site investigations by . . . . [*insert a description of investigational methods used, such as surveys, auger borings, core borings, test pits, probings, test tunnels*].

(b) Weather conditions . . . . [*insert a summary of weather records and warnings*].

(c) Transportation facilities . . . . [*insert a summary of transportation facilities providing access from the site, including information about their availability and limitations*].

(d) . . . . [*insert other pertinent information*].

(End of clause)

52.236-5 Material and Workmanship.

(APR 1984)

(a) All equipment, material, and articles incorporated into the work covered by this contract shall be new and of the most suitable grade for the purpose intended, unless otherwise specifically provided in this contract. References in the specifications to equipment, material, articles, or patented processes by trade name, make, or catalog number, shall be regarded as establishing a standard of quality and shall not be construed as limiting competition. The Contractor may, at its option, use any equipment, material, article, or process that, in

APPENDIX 2—FAR 52.2 TEXT OF PROVISIONS & CLAUSES   173

the judgment of the Contracting Officer, is equal to that named in the specifications, unless otherwise specifically provided in this contract.

(b) The Contractor shall obtain the Contracting Officer's approval of the machinery and mechanical and other equipment to be incorporated into the work. When requesting approval, the Contractor shall furnish to the Contracting Officer the name of the manufacturer, the model number, and other information concerning the performance, capacity, nature, and rating of the machinery and mechanical and other equipment. When required by this contract or by the Contracting Officer, the Contractor shall also obtain the Contracting Officer's approval of the material or articles which the Contractor contemplates incorporating into the work. When requesting approval, the Contractor shall provide full information concerning the material or articles. When directed to do so, the Contractor shall submit samples for approval at the Contractor's expense, with all shipping charges prepaid. Machinery, equipment, material, and articles that do not have the required approval shall be installed or used at the risk of subsequent rejection.

(c) All work under this contract shall be performed in a skillful and workmanlike manner. The Contracting Officer may require, in writing, that the Contractor remove from the work any employee the Contracting Officer deems incompetent, careless, or otherwise objectionable.

(End of clause)

52.236-6 Superintendence by the Contractor.

(APR 1984)

At all times during performance of this contract and until the work is completed and accepted, the Contractor shall directly superintend the work or assign and have on the worksite a competent superintendent who is satisfactory to the Contracting Officer and has authority to act for the Contractor.

(End of clause)

52.236-7 Permits and Responsibilities.

(NOV 1991)

The Contractor shall, without additional expense to the Government, be responsible for obtaining any necessary licenses and permits, and for complying with any Federal, State, and municipal laws, codes, and regulations applicable to the performance of the work. The Contractor shall also be responsible for all damages to persons or property that occur as a result of the Contractor's fault or negligence. The Contractor shall also be responsible for all materials delivered and work performed until completion and acceptance of the entire work, except for any completed unit of work which may have been accepted under the contract.

(End of clause)

52.236-15 Schedules for Construction Contracts.

(APR 1984)

(a) The Contractor shall, within five days after the work commences on the contract or another period of time determined by the Contracting Officer, prepare and submit to the Contracting Officer for approval three copies of a practicable schedule showing the order in which the Contractor proposes to perform the work, and the dates on which the Contractor contemplates starting and completing the several salient features of the work (including acquiring materials, plant, and equipment). The schedule shall be in the form of a progress chart of suitable scale to indicate appropriately the percentage of work scheduled for completion by any given date during the period. If the Contractor fails to submit a schedule within the time prescribed, the Contracting Officer may withhold approval of progress payments until the Contractor submits the required schedule.

(b) The Contractor shall enter the actual progress on the chart as directed by the Contracting Officer, and upon doing so shall immediately deliver three copies of the annotated schedule to the Contracting Officer. If, in the opinion of the Contracting Officer, the Contractor falls behind the approved schedule, the Contractor shall take steps necessary to improve its progress, including those that may be required by the Contracting Officer, without additional cost to the Government. In this circumstance, the Contracting Officer may require the Contractor to increase the number of shifts, overtime operations, days of work, and/or the amount of construction plant, and to submit for approval any supplementary schedule or schedules in chart form as the Contracting Officer deems necessary to demonstrate how the approved rate of progress will be regained.

(c) Failure of the Contractor to comply with the requirements of the Contracting Officer under this clause shall be grounds for a determination by the Contracting Officer that the Contractor is not prosecuting the work with sufficient diligence to ensure completion within the time specified in the contract. Upon making this determination, the Contracting Officer may terminate the Contractor's right to proceed with the work, or any separable part of it, in accordance with the default terms of this contract.

(End of clause)

52.236-16 Quantity Surveys.

(APR 1984)

(a) Quantity surveys shall be conducted, and the data derived from these surveys shall be used in computing the quantities of work performed and the actual construction completed and in place.

(b) The Government shall conduct the original and final surveys and make the computations based on them. The Contractor shall conduct the surveys for any periods for which progress payments are requested and shall make the computations based on these surveys. All surveys conducted by the Contractor shall be conducted under the direction of a representative of the Contracting Officer, unless the Contracting Officer waives this requirement in a specific instance.

(c) Promptly upon completing a survey, the Contractor shall furnish the originals of all field notes and all other records relating to the survey or to the layout of the work to the Contracting Officer, who shall use them as necessary to determine the amount of progress payments. The Contractor shall retain copies of all such material furnished to the Contracting Officer.

(End of clause)

Alternate I (APR 1984). If it is determined at a level above that of the Contracting Officer that it is impracticable for Government personnel to perform the original and final surveys, and the Government wishes the Contractor to perform these surveys, substitute the following paragraph (b) for paragraph (b) of the basic clause:

(b) The Contractor shall conduct the original and final surveys and surveys for any periods for which progress payments are requested. All these surveys shall be conducted under the direction of a representative of the Contracting Officer, unless the Contracting Officer waives this requirement in a specific instance. The Government shall make such computations as are necessary to determine the quantities of work performed or finally in place. The Contractor shall make the computations based on the surveys for any periods for which progress payments are requested.

52.236-21 Specifications and Drawings for Construction.

(FEB 1997)

(a) The Contractor shall keep on the work site a copy of the drawings and specifications and shall at all times give the Contracting Officer access thereto. Anything mentioned in the specifications and not shown on the drawings, or shown on the drawings and not mentioned in the specifications, shall be of like effect as if shown or mentioned in both. In case of difference between drawings and specifications, the specifications shall govern. In case of discrepancy in the figures, in the drawings, or in the specifications, the matter shall be promptly submitted to the Contracting Officer, who shall promptly make a determination in writing. Any adjustment by the Contractor without such a determination shall be at its own risk and expense. The Contracting Officer shall furnish from time to time such detailed drawings and other information as considered necessary, unless otherwise provided.

(b) Wherever in the specifications or upon the drawings the words "directed", "required", "ordered", "designated", "prescribed", or words of like import are used, it shall be understood that the "direction", "requirement", "order", "designation", or "prescription", of the Contracting Officer is intended and similarly the words "approved", "acceptable", "satisfactory", or words of like import shall mean "approved by," or "acceptable to", or "satisfactory to" the Contracting Officer, unless otherwise expressly stated.

(c) Where "as shown," as indicated", "as detailed", or words of similar import are used, it shall be understood that the reference is made to the drawings accompanying this contract unless stated otherwise. The word "provided" as used herein shall be understood to mean "provide complete in place," that is "furnished and installed".

(d) Shop drawings means drawings, submitted to the Government by the Contractor, subcontractor, or any lower tier subcontractor pursuant to a construction contract, showing in detail (1) the proposed fabrication and assembly of structural elements, and (2) the installation (i.e., fit, and attachment details) of materials or equipment. It includes drawings, diagrams, layouts, schematics, descriptive literature, illustrations, schedules, performance and test data, and similar materials furnished by the contractor to explain in detail specific portions of the work required by the contract. The Government may duplicate, use, and disclose in any manner and for any purpose shop drawings delivered under this contract.

(e) If this contract requires shop drawings, the Contractor shall coordinate all such drawings, and review them for accuracy, completeness, and compliance with contract requirements and shall indicate its approval thereon as evidence of such coordination and review. Shop drawings submitted to the Contracting Officer without evidence of the Contractor's approval may be returned for resubmission. The Contracting Officer will indicate an approval or disapproval of the shop drawings and if not approved as submitted shall indicate the Government's reasons therefor. Any work done before such approval shall be at the Contractor's risk. Approval by the Contracting Officer shall not relieve the Contractor from responsibility for any errors or omissions in such drawings, nor from responsibility for complying with the requirements of this contract, except with respect to variations described and approved in accordance with (f) below.

(f) If shop drawings show variations from the contract requirements, the Contractor shall describe such variations in writing, separate from the drawings, at the time of submission. If the Contracting Officer approves any such variation, the Contracting Officer shall issue an appropriate contract modification, except that, if the variation is minor or does not involve a change in price or in time of performance, a modification need not be issued.

(g) The Contractor shall submit to the Contracting Officer for approval four copies (unless otherwise indicated) of all shop drawings as called for under the various headings of these specifications. Three sets (unless otherwise indicated) of all shop drawings, will be retained by the Contracting Officer and one set will be returned to the Contractor.

(End of clause)

Alternate I (APR 1984). When record shop drawings are required and reproducible shop drawings are needed, add the following sentences to paragraph (g) of the basic clause:

Upon completing the work under this contract, the Contractor shall furnish a complete set of all shop drawings as finally approved. These drawings shall show all changes and revisions made up to the time the equipment is completed and accepted.

Alternate II (APR 1984). When record shop drawings are required and reproducible shop drawings are not needed, the following sentences shall be added to paragraph (g) of the basic clause:

Upon completing the work under this contract, the Contractor shall furnish _____ [*Contracting Officer complete by inserting desired amount*] sets of prints of all shop drawings as finally approved. These drawings shall show changes and revisions made up to the time the equipment is completed and accepted.

(End of clause)

APPENDIX 2—FAR 52.2 TEXT OF PROVISIONS & CLAUSES

52.242-14 Suspension of Work.

(APR 1984)

(a) The Contracting Officer may order the Contractor, in writing, to suspend, delay, or interrupt all or any part of the work of this contract for the period of time that the Contracting Officer determines appropriate for the convenience of the Government.

(b) If the performance of all or any part of the work is, for an unreasonable period of time, suspended, delayed, or interrupted (1) by an act of the Contracting Officer in the administration of this contract, or (2) by the Contracting Officer's failure to act within the time specified in this contract (or within a reasonable time if not specified), an adjustment shall be made for any increase in the cost of performance of this contract (excluding profit) necessarily caused by the unreasonable suspension, delay, or interruption, and the contract modified in writing accordingly. However, no adjustment shall be made under this clause for any suspension, delay, or interruption to the extent that performance would have been so suspended, delayed, or interrupted by any other cause, including the fault or negligence of the Contractor, or for which an equitable adjustment is provided for or excluded under any other term or condition of this contract.

(c) A claim under this clause shall not be allowed (1) for any costs incurred more than 20 days before the Contractor shall have notified the Contracting Officer in writing of the act or failure to act involved (but this requirement shall not apply as to a claim resulting from a suspension order), and (2) unless the claim, in an amount stated, is asserted in writing as soon as practicable after the termination of the suspension, delay, or interruption, but not later than the date of final payment under the contract.

(End of clause)

52.242-15 Stop-Work Order.

(AUG 1989)

(a) The Contracting Officer may, at any time, by written order to the Contractor, require the Contractor to stop all, or any part, of the work called for by this contract for a period of 90 days after the order is delivered to the Contractor, and for any further period to which the parties may agree. The order shall be specifically identified as a stop-work order issued under this clause. Upon receipt of the order, the Contractor shall immediately comply with its terms and take all reasonable steps to minimize the incurrence of costs allocable to the work covered by the order during the period of work stoppage. Within a period of 90 days after a stop-work is delivered to the Contractor, or within any extension of that period to which the parties shall have agreed, the Contracting Officer shall either--

(1) Cancel the stop-work order; or

(2) Terminate the work covered by the order as provided in the Default, or the Termination for Convenience of the Government, clause of this contract.

(b) If a stop-work order issued under this clause is canceled or the period of the order or any extension thereof expires, the Contractor shall resume work. The Contracting Officer shall make an equitable adjustment in the delivery schedule or contract price, or both, and the contract shall be modified, in writing, accordingly, if--

(1) The stop-work order results in an increase in the time required for, or in the Contractor's cost properly allocable to, the performance of any part of this contract; and

(2) The Contractor asserts its right to the adjustment within 30 days after the end of the period of work stoppage; *provided*, that, if the Contracting Officer decides the facts justify the action, the Contracting Officer may receive and act upon the claim submitted at any time before final payment under this contract.

(c) If a stop-work order is not canceled and the work covered by the order is terminated for the convenience of the Government, the Contracting Officer shall allow reasonable costs resulting from the stop-work order in arriving at the termination settlement.

(d) If a stop-work order is not canceled and the work covered by the order is terminated for default, the Contracting Officer shall allow, by equitable adjustment or otherwise, reasonable costs resulting from the stop-work order.

(End of clause)

52.243-4 Changes.

(AUG 1987)

(a) The Contracting Officer may, at any time, without notice to the sureties, if any, by written order designated or indicated to be a change order, make changes in the work within the general scope of the contract, including changes--

(1) In the specifications (including drawings and designs);

(2) In the method or manner of performance of the work;

(3) In the Government-furnished facilities, equipment, materials, services, or site; or

(4) Directing acceleration in the performance of the work.

(b) Any other written or oral order (which, as used in this paragraph (b), includes direction, instruction, interpretation, or determination) from the Contracting Officer that causes a change shall be treated as a change order under this clause; *Provided*, that the Contractor gives the Contracting Officer written notice stating (1) the date, circumstances, and source of the order and (2) that the Contractor regards the order as a change order.

(c) Except as provided in this clause, no order, statement, or conduct of the Contracting Officer shall be treated as a change under this clause or entitle the Contractor to an equitable adjustment.

(d) If any change under this clause causes an increase or decrease in the Contractor's cost of, or the time required for, the performance of any part of the work under this contract, whether or not changed by any such order, the Contracting Officer shall make an equitable adjustment and modify the contract in writing. However, except for an adjustment based on defective specifications, no adjustment for any change under paragraph (b) of this clause shall be made for any costs incurred more than 20 days before the Contractor gives written notice as required. In the case of defective specifications for which the

Government is responsible, the equitable adjustment shall include any increased cost reasonably incurred by the Contractor in attempting to comply with the defective specifications.

(e) The Contractor must assert its right to an adjustment under this clause within 30 days after (1) receipt of a written change order under paragraph (a) of this clause or (2) the furnishing of a written notice under paragraph (b) of this clause, by submitting to the Contracting Officer a written statement describing the general nature and amount of the proposal, unless this period is extended by the Government. The statement of proposal for adjustment may be included in the notice under paragraph (b) above.

(f) No proposal by the Contractor for an equitable adjustment shall be allowed if asserted after final payment under this contract.

(End of clause)

52.244-1 Subcontracts (Fixed-Price Contracts).

(FEB 1995)

(a) This clause does not apply to firm-fixed-price contracts and fixed-price contracts with economic price adjustment. However, it does apply to subcontracts resulting from unpriced modifications to such contracts.

(b) "Subcontract," as used in this clause, includes but is not limited to purchase orders, and changes and modifications to purchase orders. The Contractor shall notify the Contracting Officer reasonably in advance of entering into any subcontract if the Contractor does not have an approved purchasing system and if the subcontract--

(1) Is proposed to exceed $100,000; or

(2) Is one of a number of subcontracts with a single subcontractor, under this contract, for the same or related supplies or services, that in the aggregate are expected to exceed $100,000.

(c) The advance notification required by paragraph (b) above shall include--

(1) A description of the supplies or services to be subcontracted;

(2) Identification of the type of subcontract to be used;

(3) Identification of the proposed subcontractor and an explanation of why and how the proposed subcontractor was selected, including the competition obtained;

(4) The proposed subcontract price and the Contractor's cost or price analysis;

(5) The subcontractor's current, complete, and accurate cost or pricing data and Certificate of Current Cost or Pricing Data, if required by other contract provisions;

(6) The subcontractor's Disclosure Statement or Certificate relating to Cost Accounting Standards when such data are required by other provisions of this contract; and

(7) A negotiation memorandum reflecting--

(i) The principal elements of the subcontract price negotiations;

(ii) The most significant considerations controlling establishment of initial or revised prices;

(iii) The reason cost or pricing data were or were not required;

(iv) The extent, if any, to which the Contractor did not rely on the subcontractor's cost or pricing data in determining the price objective and in negotiating the final price;

(v) The extent, if any, to which it was recognized in the negotiation that the subcontractor's cost or pricing data were not accurate, complete, or current; the action taken by the Contractor and subcontractor; and the effect of any such defective data on the total price negotiated;

(vi) The reasons for any significant difference between the Contractor's price objective and the price negotiated; and

(vii) A complete explanation of the incentive fee or profit plan when incentives are used. The explanation shall identify each critical performance element, management decisions used to quantify each incentive element, reasons for the incentives, and a summary of all trade-off possibilities considered.

(d) The Contractor shall obtain the Contracting Officer's written consent before placing any subcontract for which advance notification is required under paragraph (b) above. However, the Contracting Officer may ratify in writing any such subcontract. Ratification shall constitute the consent of the Contracting Officer.

(e) Even if the Contractor's purchasing system has been approved, the Contractor shall obtain the Contracting Officer's written consent before placing subcontracts identified below:

_____

(f) Unless the consent or approval specifically provides otherwise, neither consent by the Contracting Officer to any subcontract nor approval of the Contractor's purchasing system shall constitute a determination (1) of the acceptability of any subcontract terms or conditions, (2) of the acceptability of any subcontract price or of any amount paid under any subcontract, or (3) to relieve the Contractor of any responsibility for performing this contract.

(g) No subcontract placed under this contract shall provide for payment on a cost-plus-a-percentage-of-cost basis, and any fee payable under cost-reimbursement subcontracts shall not exceed the fee limitations in subsection 15.903(d) of the Federal Acquisition Regulation (FAR).

(h) The Government reserves the right to review the Contractor's purchasing system as set forth in FAR Subpart 44.3.

(End of clause)

Alternate I (APR 1984). If the Contracting Officer elects to delete the requirement for advance notification of, or consent to, any subcontracts that were evaluated during negotiations (this election is not authorized for acquisition of major systems and subsystems or their components), add the following paragraph (i) to the basic clause:

(i) Paragraphs (b) and (c) of this clause do not apply to the following subcontracts, which were evaluated during negotiations: [*list subcontracts*]

APPENDIX 2—FAR 52.2 TEXT OF PROVISIONS & CLAUSES

52.246-12 Inspection of Construction.

As prescribed in 46.312, insert the following clause:

INSPECTION OF CONSTRUCTION (AUG 1996)

(a) Definition. "Work" includes, but is not limited to, materials, workmanship, and manufacture and fabrication of components.

(b) The Contractor shall maintain an adequate inspection system and perform such inspections as will ensure that the work performed under the contract conforms to contract requirements. The Contractor shall maintain complete inspection records and make them available to the Government. All work shall be conducted under the general direction of the Contracting Officer and is subject to Government inspection and test at all places and at all reasonable times before acceptance to ensure strict compliance with the terms of the contract.

(c) Government inspections and tests are for the sole benefit of the Government and do not--

(1) Relieve the Contractor of responsibility for providing adequate quality control measures;

(2) Relieve the Contractor of responsibility for damage to or loss of the material before acceptance;

(3) Constitute or imply acceptance; or

(4) Affect the continuing rights of the Government after acceptance of the completed work under paragraph (i) of this section.

(d) The presence or absence of a Government inspector does not relieve the Contractor from any contract requirement, nor is the inspector authorized to change any term or condition of the specification without the Contracting Officer's written authorization.

(e) The Contractor shall promptly furnish, at no increase in contract price, all facilities, labor, and material reasonably needed for performing such safe and convenient inspections and tests as may be required by the Contracting Officer. The Government may charge to the Contractor any additional cost of inspection or test when work is not ready at the time specified by the Contractor for inspection or test, or when prior rejection makes reinspection or retest necessary. The Government shall perform all inspections and tests in a manner that will not unnecessarily delay the work. Special, full size, and performance tests shall be performed as described in the contract.

(f) The Contractor shall, without charge, replace or correct work found by the Government not to conform to contract requirements, unless in the public interest the Government consents to accept the work with an appropriate adjustment in contract price. The Contractor shall promptly segregate and remove rejected material from the premises.

(g) If the Contractor does not promptly replace or correct rejected work, the Government may (1) by contract or otherwise, replace or correct the work and charge the cost to the Contractor or (2) terminate for default the Contractor's right to proceed.

(h) If, before acceptance of the entire work, the Government decides to examine already completed work by removing it or tearing it out, the Contractor, on request, shall promptly furnish all necessary facilities, labor, and material. If the work is found to be defective or nonconforming in any material respect due to the fault of the Contractor or its subcontractors, the Contractor shall defray the expenses of the examination and of satisfactory reconstruction. However, if the work is found to meet contract requirements, the Contracting Officer shall make an equitable adjustment for the additional services involved in the examination and reconstruction, including, if completion of the work was thereby delayed, an extension of time.

(i) Unless otherwise specified in the contract, the Government shall accept, as promptly as practicable after completion and inspection, all work required by the contract or that portion of the work the Contracting Officer determines can be accepted separately. Acceptance shall be final and conclusive except for latent defects, fraud, gross mistakes amounting to fraud, or the Government's rights under any warranty or guarantee.

(End of clause)

52.246-21 Warranty of Construction.

(MAR 1994)

(a) In addition to any other warranties in this contract, the Contractor warrants, except as provided in paragraph (i) of this clause, that work performed under this contract conforms to the contract requirements and is free of any defect in equipment, material, or design furnished, or workmanship performed by the Contractor or any subcontractor or supplier at any tier.

(b) This warranty shall continue for a period of 1 year from the date of final acceptance of the work. If the Government takes possession of any part of the work before final acceptance, this warranty shall continue for a period of 1 year from the date the Government takes possession.

(c) The Contractor shall remedy at the Contractor's expense any failure to conform, or any defect. In addition, the Contractor shall remedy at the Contractor's expense any damage to Government-owned or controlled real or personal property, when that damage is the result of--

(1) The Contractor's failure to conform to contract requirements; or

(2) Any defect of equipment, material, workmanship, or design furnished.

(d) The Contractor shall restore any work damaged in fulfilling the terms and conditions of this clause. The Contractor's warranty with respect to work repaired or replaced will run for 1 year from the date of repair or replacement.

(e) The Contracting Officer shall notify the Contractor, in writing, within a reasonable time after the discovery of any failure, defect, or damage.

(f) If the Contractor fails to remedy any failure, defect, or damage within a reasonable time after receipt of notice, the Government shall have the right to replace, repair, or otherwise remedy the failure, defect, or damage at the Contractor's expense.

(g) With respect to all warranties, express or implied, from subcontractors, manufacturers, or suppliers for work performed and materials furnished under this contract, the Contractor shall--

(1) Obtain all warranties that would be given in normal commercial practice;

(2) Require all warranties to be executed, in writing, for the benefit of the Government, if directed by the Contracting Officer; and

(3) Enforce all warranties for the benefit of the Government, if directed by the Contracting Officer.

(h) In the event the Contractor's warranty under paragraph (b) of this clause has expired, the Government may bring suit at its expense to enforce a subcontractor's, manufacturer's, or supplier's warranty.

(i) Unless a defect is caused by the negligence of the Contractor or subcontractor or supplier at any tier, the Contractor shall not be liable for the repair of any defects of material or design furnished by the Government nor for the repair of any damage that results from any defect in Government-furnished material or design.

(j) This warranty shall not limit the Government's rights under the Inspection and Acceptance clause of this contract with respect to latent defects, gross mistakes, or fraud.

(End of clause)

Alternate I (APR 1984). If the Government specifies in the contract the use of any equipment by "brand name and model," the contracting officer may add a paragraph substantially the same as the following paragraph (k) to the basic clause:

(k) Defects in design or manufacture of equipment specified by the Government on a "brand name and model" basis, shall not be included in this warranty. In this event, the Contractor shall require any subcontractors, manufacturers, or suppliers thereof to execute their warranties, in writing, directly to the Government.

52.248-3 Value Engineering--Construction.

(MAR 1989)

(a) *General*. The Contractor is encouraged to develop, prepare, and submit value engineering change proposals (VECP's) voluntarily. The Contractor shall share in any instant contract savings realized from accepted VECP's, in accordance with paragraph (f) below.

(b) *Definitions*. "Collateral costs," as used in this clause, means agency costs of operation, maintenance, logistic support, or Government-furnished property.

"Collateral savings," as used in this clause, means those measurable net reductions resulting from a VECP in the agency's overall projected collateral costs, exclusive of acquisition savings, whether or not the acquisition cost changes.

"Contractor's development and implementation costs," as used in this clause, means those costs the Contractor incurs on a VECP specifically in developing, testing, preparing, and submitting the VECP, as well as those costs the Contractor incurs to make the contractual changes required by Government acceptance of a VECP.

"Government costs," as used in this clause, means those agency costs that result directly from developing and implementing the VECP, such as any net increases in the cost of testing, operations, maintenance, and logistic support. The term does not include the normal administrative costs of processing the VECP.

"Instant contract savings," as used in this clause, means the estimated reduction in Contractor cost of performance resulting from acceptance of the VECP, minus allowable Contractor's development and implementation costs, including subcontractors' development and implementation costs (see paragraph (h) below).

"Value engineering change proposal (VECP)" means a proposal that--

(1) Requires a change to this, the instant contract, to implement; and

(2) Results in reducing the contract price or estimated cost without impairing essential functions or characteristics; *provided*, that it does not involve a change--

(i) In deliverable end item quantities only; or

(ii) To the contract type only.

(c) *VECP preparation*. As a minimum, the Contractor shall include in each VECP the information described in subparagraphs (1) through (7) below. If the

APPENDIX 2—FAR 52.2 TEXT OF PROVISIONS & CLAUSES

proposed change is affected by contractually required configuration management or similar procedures, the instructions in those procedures relating to format, identification, and priority assignment shall govern VECP preparation. The VECP shall include the following including any suggested specification revisions.

(3) A separate, detailed cost estimate for (i) the affected portions of the existing contract requirement and (ii) the VECP. The cost reduction associated with the VECP shall take into account the Contractor's allowable development and implementation costs, including any amount attributable to subcontracts under paragraph (h) below.

(4) A description and estimate of costs the Government may incur in implementing the VECP, such as test and evaluation and operating and support costs.

(5) A prediction of any effects the proposed change would have on collateral costs to the agency.

(6) A statement of the time by which a contract modification accepting the VECP must be issued in order to achieve the maximum cost reduction, noting any effect on the contract completion time or delivery schedule.

(7) Identification of any previous submissions of the VECP, including the dates submitted, the agencies and contract numbers involved, and previous Government actions, if known.

(d) *Submission.* The Contractor shall submit VECP's to the Resident Engineer at the worksite, with a copy to the Contracting Officer.

(e) *Government action.* (1) The Contracting Officer shall notify the Contractor of the status of the VECP within 45 calendar days after the contracting office receives it. If additional time is required, the Contracting Officer shall notify the Contractor within the 45-day period and provide the reason for the delay and the expected date of the decision. The Government will process VECP's expeditiously; however, it shall not be liable for any delay in acting upon a VECP.

(2) If the VECP is not accepted, the Contracting Officer shall notify the Contractor in writing, explaining the reasons for rejection. The Contractor may withdraw any VECP, in whole or in part, at any time before it is accepted by the Government. The Contracting Officer may require that the Contractor provide written notification before undertaking significant expenditures for VECP effort.

(3) Any VECP may be accepted, in whole or in part, by the Contracting Officer's award of a modification to this contract citing this clause. The Contracting Officer may accept the VECP, even though an agreement on price reduction has not been reached, by issuing the Contractor a notice to proceed with the change. Until a notice to proceed is issued or a contract modification applies a VECP to this contract, the Contractor shall perform in accordance with the existing contract. The Contracting Officer's decision to accept or reject all or part of any VECP shall be final and not subject to the Disputes clause or otherwise subject to litigation under the Contract Disputes Act of 1978 (41 U.S.C. 601-613).

(f) *Sharing.* (1) *Rates.* The Government's share of savings is determined by subtracting Government costs from instant contract savings and multiplying the result by (i) 45 percent for fixed-price contracts or (ii) 75 percent for cost-reimbursement contracts.

(2) *Payment.* Payment of any share due the Contractor for use of a VECP on this contract shall be authorized by a modification to this contract to--

(i) Accept the VECP;

(ii) Reduce the contract price or estimated cost by the amount of instant contract savings; and

(iii) Provide the Contractor's share of savings by adding the amount calculated to the contract price or fee.

(g) *Collateral savings.* If a VECP is accepted, the instant contract amount shall be increased by 20 percent of any projected collateral savings determined to be realized in a typical year of use after subtracting any Government costs not previously offset. However, the Contractor's share of collateral savings shall not exceed (1) the contract's firm-fixed-price or estimated cost, at the time the VECP is accepted, or (2) $100,000, whichever is greater. The Contracting Officer shall be the sole determiner of the amount of collateral savings, and that amount shall not be subject to the Disputes clause or otherwise subject to litigation under 41 U.S.C. 601-613.

(h) *Subcontracts.* The Contractor shall include an appropriate value engineering clause in any subcontract of $50,000 or more and may include one in subcontracts of lesser value. In computing any adjustment in this contract's price under paragraph (f) above, the Contractor's allowable development and implementation costs shall include any subcontractor's allowable development and implementation costs clearly resulting from a VECP accepted by the Government under this contract, but shall exclude any value engineering incentive payments to a subcontractor. The Contractor may choose any arrangement for subcontractor value engineering incentive payments; *provided,* that these payments shall not reduce the Government's share of the savings resulting from the VECP.

(i) *Data.* The Contractor may restrict the Government's right to use any part of a VECP or the supporting data by marking the following legend on the affected parts:

"These data, furnished under the Value Engineering--Construction clause of contract _____ , shall not be disclosed outside the Government or duplicated, used, or disclosed, in whole or in part, for any purpose other than to evaluate a value engineering change proposal submitted under the clause. This restriction does not limit the Government's right to use information contained in these data if it has been obtained or is otherwise available from the Contractor or from another source without limitations."

If a VECP is accepted, the Contractor hereby grants the Government unlimited rights in the VECP and supporting data, except that, with respect to data qualifying and submitted as limited rights technical data, the Government shall have the rights specified in the contract modification implementing the VECP and shall appropriately mark the data. (The terms "unlimited rights" and "limited rights" are defined in Part 27 of the Federal Acquisition Regulation.)

(End of clause)

Alternate I (APR 1984). When the head of the contracting activity determines that the cost of calculating and tracking collateral savings will exceed the benefits to be derived in a construction contract, delete paragraph (g) from the basic clause and redesignate the remaining paragraphs accordingly.

52.249-2 Termination for Convenience of the Government (Fixed-Price).

(SEP 1996)

(a) The Government may terminate performance of work under this contract in whole or, from time to time, in part if the Contracting Officer determines that a termination is in the Government's interest. The Contracting Officer shall terminate by delivering to the Contractor a Notice of Termination specifying the extent of termination and the effective date.

(b) After receipt of a Notice of Termination, and except as directed by the Contracting Officer, the Contractor shall immediately proceed with the following obligations, regardless of any delay in determining or adjusting any amounts due under this clause:

(1) Stop work as specified in the notice.

(2) Place no further subcontracts or orders (referred to as subcontracts in this clause) for materials, services, or facilities, except as necessary to complete the continued portion of the contract.

(3) Terminate all subcontracts to the extent they relate to the work terminated.

(4) Assign to the Government, as directed by the Contracting Officer, all right, title, and interest of the Contractor under the subcontracts terminated, in which case the Government shall have the right to settle or to pay any termination settlement proposal arising out of those terminations.

(5) With approval or ratification to the extent required by the Contracting Officer, settle all outstanding liabilities and termination settlement proposals arising from the termination of subcontracts; the approval or ratification will be final for purposes of this clause.

(6) As directed by the Contracting Officer, transfer title and deliver to the Government (i) the fabricated or unfabricated parts, work in process, completed work, supplies, and other material produced or acquired for the work terminated, and (ii) the completed or partially completed plans, drawings, information, and other property that, if the contract had been completed, would be required to be furnished to the Government.

(7) Complete performance of the work not terminated.

(8) Take any action that may be necessary, or that the Contracting Officer may direct, for the protection and preservation of the property related to this contract that is in the possession of the Contractor and in which the Government has or may acquire an interest.

(9) Use its best efforts to sell, as directed or authorized by the Contracting Officer, any property of the types referred to in subparagraph (b)(6) of this clause; *provided*, however, that the Contractor (i) is not required to extend credit to any purchaser and (ii) may acquire the property under the conditions prescribed by, and at prices approved by, the Contracting Officer. The proceeds of any transfer or disposition will be applied to reduce any payments to be made by the Government under this contract, credited to the price or cost of the work, or paid in any other manner directed by the Contracting Officer.

(c) The Contractor shall submit complete termination inventory schedules no later than 120 days from the effective date of termination, unless extended in writing by the Contracting Officer upon written request of the Contractor within this 120-day period.

(d) After expiration of the plant clearance period as defined in Subpart 45.6 of the Federal Acquisition Regulation, the Contractor may submit to the Contracting Officer a list, certified as to quantity and quality, of termination inventory not previously disposed of, excluding items authorized for disposition by the Contracting Officer. The Contractor may request the Government to remove those items or enter into an agreement for their storage. Within 15 days, the

APPENDIX 2—FAR 52.2 TEXT OF PROVISIONS & CLAUSES

Government will accept title to those items and remove them or enter into a storage agreement. The Contracting Officer may verify the list upon removal of the items, or if stored, within 45 days from submission of the list, and shall correct the list, as necessary, before final settlement.

(e) After termination, the Contractor shall submit a final termination settlement proposal to the Contracting Officer in the form and with the certification prescribed by the Contracting Officer. The Contractor shall submit the proposal promptly, but no later than 1 year from the effective date of termination, unless extended in writing by the Contracting Officer upon written request of the Contractor within this 1-year period. However, if the Contracting Officer determines that the facts justify it, a termination settlement proposal may be received and acted on after 1 year or any extension. If the Contractor fails to submit the proposal within the time allowed, the Contracting Officer may determine, on the basis of information available, the amount, if any, due the Contractor because of the termination and shall pay the amount determined.

(f) Subject to paragraph (e) of this clause, the Contractor and the Contracting Officer may agree upon the whole or any part of the amount to be paid or remaining to be paid because of the termination. The amount may include a reasonable allowance for profit on work done. However, the agreed amount, whether under this paragraph (f) or paragraph (g) of this clause, exclusive of costs shown in subparagraph (g)(3) of this clause, may not exceed the total contract price as reduced by (1) the amount of payments previously made and (2) the contract price of work not terminated. The contract shall be modified, and the Contractor paid the agreed amount. Paragraph (g) of this clause shall not limit, restrict, or affect the amount that may be agreed upon to be paid under this paragraph.

(g) If the Contractor and the Contracting Officer fail to agree on the whole amount to be paid because of the termination of work, the Contracting Officer shall pay the Contractor the amounts determined by the Contracting Officer as follows, but without duplication of any amounts agreed on under paragraph (f) of this clause:

(1) The contract price for completed supplies or services accepted by the Government (or sold or acquired under subparagraph (b)(9) of this clause) not previously paid for, adjusted for any saving of freight and other charges.

(2) The total of--

(i) The costs incurred in the performance of the work terminated, including initial costs and preparatory expense allocable thereto, but excluding any costs attributable to supplies or services paid or to be paid under subparagraph (g)(1) of this clause;

(ii) The cost of settling and paying termination settlement proposals under terminated subcontracts that are properly chargeable to the terminated portion of the contract if not included in subdivision (g)(2)(i) of this clause; and

(iii) A sum, as profit on subdivision (g)(2)(i) of this clause, determined by the Contracting Officer under 49.202 of the Federal Acquisition Regulation, in effect on the date of this contract, to be fair and reasonable; however, if it appears that the Contractor would have sustained a loss on the entire contract had it been completed, the Contracting Officer shall allow no profit under this subdivision (iii) and shall reduce the settlement to reflect the indicated rate of loss.

(3) The reasonable costs of settlement of the work terminated, including--

(i) Accounting, legal, clerical, and other expenses reasonably necessary for the preparation of termination settlement proposals and supporting data;

(ii) The termination and settlement of subcontracts (excluding the amounts of such settlements); and

(iii) Storage, transportation, and other costs incurred, reasonably necessary for the preservation, protection, or disposition of the termination inventory.

(h) Except for normal spoilage, and except to the extent that the Government expressly assumed the risk of loss, the Contracting Officer shall exclude from the amounts payable to the Contractor under paragraph (g) of this clause, the fair value, as determined by the Contracting Officer, of property that is destroyed, lost, stolen, or damaged so as to become undeliverable to the Government or to a buyer.

(i) The cost principles and procedures of Part 31 of the Federal Acquisition Regulation, in effect on the date of this contract, shall govern all costs claimed, agreed to, or determined under this clause.

(j) The Contractor shall have the right of appeal, under the Disputes clause, from any determination made by the Contracting Officer under paragraph (e), (g), or (l) of this clause, except that if the Contractor failed to submit the termination settlement proposal or request for equitable adjustment within the time provided in paragraph (e) or (l), respectively, and failed to request a time extension, there is no right of appeal.

(k) In arriving at the amount due the Contractor under this clause, there shall be deducted--

(1) All unliquidated advance or other payments to the Contractor under the terminated portion of this contract;

(2) Any claim which the Government has against the Contractor under this contract; and

(3) The agreed price for, or the proceeds of sale of, materials, supplies, or other things acquired by the Contractor or sold under the provisions of this clause and not recovered by or credited to the Government.

(l) If the termination is partial, the Contractor may file a proposal with the Contracting Officer for an equitable adjustment of the price(s) of the continued portion of the contract. The Contracting Officer shall make any equitable adjustment agreed upon. Any proposal by the Contractor for an equitable adjustment under this clause shall be requested within 90 days from the effective date of termination unless extended in writing by the Contracting Officer.

(m)(1) The Government may, under the terms and conditions it prescribes, make partial payments and payments against costs incurred by the Contractor for the terminated portion of the contract, if the Contracting Officer believes the total of these payments will not exceed the amount to which the Contractor will be entitled.

(2) If the total payments exceed the amount finally determined to be due, the Contractor shall repay the excess to the Government upon demand, together with interest computed at the rate established by the Secretary of the Treasury under 50 U.S.C. App. 1215(b)(2). Interest shall be computed for the period from the date the excess payment is received by the Contractor to the date the excess is repaid. Interest shall not be charged on any excess payment due to a reduction in the Contractor's termination settlement proposal because of retention or other disposition of termination inventory until 10 days after the date of the retention or disposition, or a later date determined by the Contracting Officer because of the circumstances.

(n) Unless otherwise provided in this contract or by statute, the Contractor shall maintain all records and documents relating to the terminated portion of this contract for 3 years after final settlement. This includes all books and other evidence bearing on the Contractor's costs and expenses under this contract. The Contractor shall make these records and documents available to the Government, at the Contractor's office, at all reasonable times, without any direct charge. If approved by the Contracting Officer, photographs, microphotographs, or other authentic reproductions may be maintained instead of original records and documents.

(End of clause)

Alternate I (SEP 1996). If the contract is for construction, substitute the following paragraph (g) for paragraph (g) of the basic clause:

(g) If the Contractor and Contracting Officer fail to agree on the whole amount to be paid the Contractor because of the termination of work, the Contracting Officer shall pay the Contractor the amounts determined as follows, but without duplication of any amounts agreed upon under paragraph (f) of this clause:

(1) For contract work performed before the effective date of termination, the total (without duplication of any items) of--

(i) The cost of this work;

(ii) The cost of settling and paying termination settlement proposals under terminated subcontracts that are properly chargeable to the terminated portion of the contract if not included in subdivision (g)(1)(i) of this clause; and

(iii) A sum, as profit on subdivision (g)(1)(i) of this clause, determined by the Contracting Officer under 49.202 of the Federal Acquisition Regulation, in effect on the date of this contract, to be fair and reasonable; however, if it appears that the Contractor would have sustained a loss on the entire contract had it been completed, the Contracting Officer shall allow no profit under this subdivision (iii) and shall reduce the settlement to reflect the indicated rate of loss.

(2) The reasonable costs of settlement of the work terminated, including--

(i) Accounting, legal, clerical, and other expenses reasonably necessary for the preparation of termination settlement proposals and supporting data;

(ii) The termination and settlement of subcontracts (excluding the amounts of such settlements); and

(iii) Storage, transportation, and other costs incurred, reasonably necessary for the preservation, protection, or disposition of the termination inventory.

Alternate II (SEP 1996). If the contract is with an agency of the U.S. Government or with State, local, or foreign governments or their agencies, and if the Contracting Officer determines that the requirement to pay interest on excess partial payments is inappropriate, delete subparagraph (m)(2) of the basic clause.

Alternate III (SEP 1996). If the contract is for construction and with an agency of the U.S. Government or with State, local, or foreign governments or their agencies, substitute the following paragraph (g) for paragraph (g) of the basic clause. Subparagraph (m)(2) may be deleted from the basic clause if the Contracting Officer determines that the requirement to pay interest on excess partial payments is inappropriate.

(g) If the Contractor and Contracting Officer fail to agree on the whole amount to be paid the Contractor because of the termination of work, the Contracting Officer shall pay the Contractor the amounts determined as follows, but without duplication of any amounts agreed upon under paragraph (f) of this clause:

(1) For contract work performed before the effective date of termination, the total (without duplication of any items) of--

(i) The cost of this work;

(ii) The cost of settling and paying termination settlement proposals under terminated subcontracts that are properly chargeable to the terminated portion of the contract if not included in subdivision (g)(1)(i) of this clause; and

(iii) A sum, as profit on subdivision (g)(1)(i) of this clause, determined by the Contracting Officer under 49.202 of the Federal Acquisition Regulation, in effect on the date of this contract, to be fair and reasonable; however, if it appears that the Contractor would have sustained a loss on the entire contract had it been completed, the Contracting Officer shall allow no profit under this subdivision (iii) and shall reduce the settlement to reflect the indicated rate of loss.

(2) The reasonable costs of settlement of the work terminated, including--

(i) Accounting, legal, clerical, and other expenses reasonably necessary for the preparation of termination settlement proposals and supporting data;

(ii) The termination and settlement of subcontracts (excluding the amounts of such settlements); and

(iii) Storage, transportation, and other costs incurred, reasonably necessary for the preservation, protection, or disposition of the termination inventory.

52.249-10 Default (Fixed-Price Construction).

(APR 1984)

(a) If the Contractor refuses or fails to prosecute the work or any separable part, with the diligence that will insure its completion within the time specified in this contract including any extension, or fails to complete the work within this time, the Government may, by written notice to the Contractor, terminate the right to proceed with the work (or the separable part of the work) that has been delayed. In this event, the Government may take over the work and complete it by contract or otherwise, and may take possession of and use any materials, appliances, and plant on the work site necessary for completing the work. The Contractor and its sureties shall be liable for any damage to the Government resulting from the Contractor's refusal or failure to complete the work within the specified time, whether or not the Contractor's right to proceed with the work is terminated. This liability includes any increased costs incurred by the Government in completing the work.

(b) The Contractor's right to proceed shall not be terminated nor the Contractor charged with damages under this clause, if--

(1) The delay in completing the work arises from unforeseeable causes beyond the control and without the fault or negligence of the Contractor. Examples of such causes include (i) acts of God or of the public enemy, (ii) acts of the Government in either its sovereign or contractual capacity, (iii) acts of another Contractor in the performance of a contract with the Government, (iv) fires, (v) floods, (vi) epidemics, (vii) quarantine restrictions, (viii) strikes, (ix) freight embargoes, (x) unusually severe weather, or (xi) delays of subcontractors or suppliers at any tier arising from unforeseeable causes beyond the control and without the fault or negligence of both the Contractor and the subcontractors or suppliers; and

(2) The Contractor, within 10 days from the beginning of any delay (unless extended by the Contracting Officer), notifies the Contracting Officer in writing of the causes of delay. The Contracting Officer shall ascertain the facts and the extent of delay. If, in the judgment of the Contracting Officer, the findings of fact warrant such action, the time for completing the work shall be extended. The findings of the Contracting Officer shall be final and conclusive on the parties, but subject to appeal under the Disputes clause.

(c) If, after termination of the Contractor's right to proceed, it is determined that the Contractor was not in default, or that the delay was excusable, the rights and obligations of the parties will be the same as if the termination had been issued for the convenience of the Government.

(d) The rights and remedies of the Government in this clause are in addition to any other rights and remedies provided by law or under this contract.

(End of clause)

Alternate I (APR 1984). If the contract is for dismantling, demolition, or removal of improvements, substitute the following paragraph (a) for paragraph (a) of the basic clause:

(a)(1) If the Contractor refuses or fails to prosecute the work, or any separable part, with the diligence that will insure its completion within the time specified in this contract, including any extension, or fails to complete the work within this time, the Government may, by written notice to the Contractor, terminate the right to proceed with the work or the part of the work that has been delayed. In this event, the Government may take over the work and complete it by contract or otherwise, and may take possession of and use any materials, appliances, and plant on the work site necessary for completing the work.

(2) If title to property is vested in the Contractor under this contract, it shall revest in the Government regardless of any other clause of this contract, except for property that the Contractor has disposed of by bona fide sale or removed from the site.

(3) The Contractor and its sureties shall be liable for any damage to the Government resulting from the Contractor's refusal or failure to complete the work within the specified time, whether or not the Contractor's right to proceed with the work is terminated. This liability includes any increased costs incurred by the Government in completing the work.

Alternate II (APR 1984). If the contract is to be awarded during a period of national emergency, subparagraph (b)(1) below may be substituted for subparagraph (b)(1) of the basic clause:

(1) The delay in completing the work arises from causes other than normal weather beyond the control and without the fault or negligence of the Contractor. Examples of such causes include (i) acts of God or of the public enemy, (ii) acts of the Government in either its sovereign or contractual capacity, (iii) acts of another Contractor in the performance of a contract with the Government, (iv) fires, (v) floods, (vi) epidemics, (vii) quarantine restrictions, (viii) strikes, (ix) freight embargoes, (x) unusually severe weather, or (xi) delays of subcontractors or suppliers at any tier arising from causes other than normal weather beyond the control and without the fault or negligence of both the Contractor and the subcontractors or suppliers; and

Alternate III (APR 1984). If the contract is for dismantling, demolition, or removal of improvements and is to be awarded during a period of national emergency, substitute the following paragraph (a) for paragraph (a) of the basic clause. The following subparagraph (b)(1) may be substituted for subparagraph (b)(1) of the basic clause:

(a)(1) If the Contractor refuses or fails to prosecute the work, or any separable part, with the diligence that will insure its completion within the time specified in this contract, including any extension, or fails to complete the work within this time, the Government may,by written notice to the Contractor, terminate the right to proceed with the work or the part of the work that has been delayed. In this event, the Government may take over the work and complete it by contract or otherwise, and may take possession of and use any materials, appliances, and plant on the work site necessary for completing the work.

(2) If title to property is vested in the Contractor under this contract, it shall revest in the Government regardless of any other clause of this contract, except for property that the Contractor has disposed of by bona fide sale or removed from the site.

(3) The Contractor and its sureties shall be liable for any damage to the Government resulting from the Contractor's refusal or failure to complete the work within the specified time, whether or not the Contractor's right to proceed with the work is terminated. This liability includes any increased costs incurred by the Government in completing the work.

(b) The Contractor's right to proceed shall not be terminated nor the Contractor charged with damages under this clause, if--

(1) The delay in completing the work arises from causes other than normal weather beyond the control and without the fault or negligence of the Contractor. Examples of such causes include (i) acts of God or of the public enemy, (ii) acts of the Government in either its sovereign or contractual capacity, (iii) acts of another Contractor in the performance of a contract with the Government, (iv) fires, (v) floods, (vi) epidemics, (vii) quarantine restrictions, (viii) strikes, (ix) freight embargoes, (x) unusually severe weather, or (xi) delays of subcontractors or suppliers at any tier arising from causes other than normal weather beyond the control and without the fault or negligence of both the Contractor and the subcontractors or suppliers; and

52.249-14 Excusable Delays.

As prescribed in 49.505(d), insert the following clause in solicitations and contracts for supplies, services, construction, and research and development on a fee basis whenever a cost-reimbursement contract is contemplated. Also insert the clause in time-and-material contracts, labor-hour contracts, consolidated facilities contracts, and facilities acquisition contracts. When used in construction contracts, substitute the words "completion time" for "delivery schedule" in the last sentence of the clause. When used in facilities contracts, substitute the words "termination of work" for "termination" in the last sentence of the clause.

EXCUSABLE DELAYS (APR 1984)

(a) Except for defaults of subcontractors at any tier, the Contractor shall not be in default because of any failure to perform this contract under its terms if the failure arises from causes beyond the control and without the fault or negligence of the Contractor. Examples of these causes are (1) acts of God or of the public enemy, (2) acts of the Government in either its sovereign or contractual capacity, (3) fires, (4) floods, (5) epidemics, (6) quarantine restrictions, (7) strikes, (8) freight embargoes, and (9) unusually severe weather. In each instance, the failure to perform must be beyond the control and without the fault or negligence of the

Contractor. "Default" includes failure to make progress in the work so as to endanger performance.

(b) If the failure to perform is caused by the failure of a subcontractor at any tier to perform or make progress, and if the cause of the failure was beyond the control of both the Contractor and subcontractor, and without the fault or negligence of either, the Contractor shall not be deemed to be in default, unless--

(1) The subcontracted supplies or services were obtainable from other sources;

(2) The Contracting Officer ordered the Contractor in writing to purchase these supplies or services from the other source; and

(3) The Contractor failed to comply reasonably with this order.

(c) Upon request of the Contractor, the Contracting Officer shall ascertain the facts and extent of the failure. If the Contracting Officer determines that any failure to perform results from one or more of the causes above, the delivery schedule shall be revised, subject to the rights of the Government under the termination clause of this contract.

(End of clause)

Appendix 3 - AIA A201

AIA - A201 General Conditions - Selected Clauses

This Appendix contains selected clauses from the Standard General Conditions of the Construction Contract (1997 Edition) prepared by the American Institute of Architects.[1] The clauses included here are:

Article 4 - Administration of the Contract
4.3 Claims and Disputes
4.4 Resolution of Claims and Disputes
4.5 Mediation
4.6 Arbitration

Article 7 - Changes in the Work
7.1 General
7.2 Change Orders
7.3 Construction Change Directives
7.4 Minor Changes in the Work

Article 8 - Time
8.1 Definitions
8.2 Progress and Completion
8.3 Delays and Extensions of Time

Article 14 Termination or Suspension of the Contract
14.1 Termination by the Contractor
14.2 Termination by the Owner for Cause
14.3 Suspension by the Owner for Convenience
14.4 Termination by the Owner for Convenience

ARTICLE 4   ADMINISTRATION OF THE CONTRACT

4.3   CLAIMS AND DISPUTES

4.3.1   Definition. A Claim is a demand or assertion by one of the parties seeking, as a matter of right, adjustment or interpretation of Contract terms, payment of money, extension of time or other relief with respect to the terms of the Contract. The term "Claim" also includes other disputes and matters in question between the Owner and Contractor arising out of or relating to the Contract. Claims must be made by written notice. The responsibility to substantiate Claims shall rest with the party making the Claim.

4.3.2   Time Limits on Claims. Claims by either party must be made within 21 days after occurrence of the event giving rise to such Claim or within 21 days after the claimant first recognizes the condition giving rise to the Claim, whichever is later. Claims must be initiated by written notice to the Architect and the other party.

4.3.3   Continuing Contract Performance. Pending final resolution of a Claim except as otherwise agreed in writing or as provided in Subparagraph 9.7.1 and Article 14, the Contractor shall proceed diligently with performance of the Contract and the Owner shall continue to make payments in accordance with the Contract Documents.

4.3.4   Claims for Concealed or Unknown Conditions. if conditions are encountered at the site which are (1) subsurface or otherwise concealed physical conditions which differ materially from those indicated in the Contract Documents or (2) unknown physical conditions of an unusual nature, which differ materially from those ordinarily found to exist and generally recognized as inherent in construction activities of the character provided for in the Contract Documents, then notice by the observing party shall be given to the other party promptly before conditions are disturbed and in no event later than 21 days after first observance of the conditions. The Architect will promptly investigate such conditions and, if they differ materially and cause an increase or decrease in the Contractor's cost of, or time required for, performance of any part of the Work, will recommend an equitable adjustment in the Contract Sum or Contract Time, or both. If the Architect determines that the conditions at the site are not materially different from those indicated in the Contract Documents and that no change in the terms of the Contract is justified, the Architect shall so notify the Owner and Contractor in writing, stating the reasons. Claims by either party in opposition to such determination must be made within 21 days after the Architect has given notice of the decision. If the conditions encountered are materially different, the Contract Sum and Contract Time shall be equitably adjusted, but if the Owner and Contractor cannot agree on an adjustment in the Contract Sum or Contract Time, the adjustment shall be referred to the Architect for initial determination, subject to further proceedings pursuant to Paragraph 4.4.

4.3.5   Claims for Additional Cost. If the Contractor wishes to make Claim for an increase in the Contract Sum, written notice as provided herein shall be given before proceeding to execute the Work. Prior notice is not required for Claims relating to an emergency endangering life or property arising under Paragraph 10.6.

---

[1] Reprinted with permission, American Institute of Architects, Washington, DC.

APPENDIX 3—AIA A201

4.3.6 If the Contractor believes additional cost is involved for reasons including but not limited to (1) a written interpretation from the Architect, (2) an order by the Owner to stop the Work where the Contractor was not at fault, (3) a written order for a minor change in the Work issued by the Architect, (4) failure of payment by the Owner, (5) termination of the Contract by the Owner, (6) Owner's suspension or (7) other reasonable grounds, Claim shall be filed in accordance with this Paragraph 4.3.

4.3.7 CLAIMS FOR ADDITIONAL TIME
4.3.7.1 If the Contractor wishes to make Claim for an increase in the Contract Time, written notice as provided herein shaft be given. The Contractor's Claim shall include an estimate of cost and of probable effect of delay on progress of the Work. In the case of a continuing delay only one Claim is necessary.

4.3.7.2 If adverse weather conditions are the basis for a Claim for additional time, such Claim shall be documented by data substantiating that weather conditions were abnormal for the period of time and could not have been reasonably anticipated, and that weather conditions had an adverse effect on the scheduled construction.

4.3.8 Injury or Damage to Person or Property. If either party to the Contract suffers injury or damage to person or property because of an act or omission of the other party, or of others for whose acts such party is legally responsible, written notice of such injury or damage, whether or not insured, shall be given to the other party within a reasonable time not exceeding 21 days after first discovery. The notice shall provide sufficient detail to enable the other party to investigate the matter.

4.3.9 If unit prices are stated in the Contract Documents or subsequently agreed upon, and if a proposed Change Order or Construction Change Directive so that application of such unit prices to quantities of Work proposed will cause substantial inequity to the Owner or Contractor, the applicable unit prices shall be equitably adjusted.

4.3.10 Claims for Consequential Damages. The Contractor and Owner waive Claims against each other for consequential damages arising out of or relating to this Contract. This mutual waiver includes:
  .1 damages incurred by the Owner for rental expenses, for losses of use, income, profit, financing, business and reputation, and for loss of management or employee productivity or of the services of such persons; and
  .2 damages incurred by the Contractor for principal office expenses including the compensation of personnel stationed there, for losses of financing, business and reputation, and for loss of profit except anticipated profit arising directly from the Work.

This mutual waiver is applicable, without limitation, to all consequential damages due to either party's termination in accordance with Article 14. Nothing contained in this Subparagraph 4.3.10 shall be deemed to preclude an award of liquidated direct damages, when applicable, in accordance with the requirements of the Contract Documents.

4.4 RESOLUTION OF CLAIMS AND DISPUTES
4.4.1 Decision of Architect. Claims, including those alleging an error or omission by the Architect but excluding those arising under Paragraphs 10.3 through 10.5, shall be referred initially to the Architect for decision. An initial decision by the Architect shall be required as a condition precedent to mediation, arbitration or litigation of all Claims between the Contractor and Owner arising prior to the date final payment is due, unless 30 days have passed after the Claim has been referred to the Architect with no decision having been rendered by the Architect. The Architect will not decide disputes between the Contractor and persons or entities other than the Owner.

4.4.2 The Architect will review Claims and within 10 days of the receipt of the Claim take one or more of the following actions: (1) request additional supporting data from the claimant or a response with supporting data from the other party, (2) reject the Claim in whole or in part, (3) approve the Claim, (4) suggest a compromise, or (5) advise the parties that the Architect is unable to resolve the Claim if the Architect lacks sufficient information to evaluate the merits of the Claim or if the Architect concludes that, in the Architect's sole discretion, it would be inappropriate for the Architect to resolved the Claim.

4.4.3 In evaluating Claims, the Architect may, but shall not be obligated to, consult with or seek information from either party or from persons with special knowledge or expertise who may assist the Architect in rendering a decision. The Architect may request the Owner authorize retention of such persons at the Owner's expense.

4.4.4 If the Architect requests a party to provide a response to a Claim or to furnish additional supporting data, such party shall respond, within ten days after receipt of such request, and shall either provide a response on the requested supporting data, advise the Architect when the response or supporting data will be furnished or advise the Architect that no supporting data will be furnished. Upon receipt of the response or supporting data, if any, the Architect will either reject or approve the Claim in whole or in part.

4.4.5 The Architect will approve or reject Claims by written decision, which shall state the reasons therefor and which shall notify the parties of any change in the Contract Sum or Contract Time or both. The approval or rejection of a Claim by the Architect shall be final and binding on the parties but subject to mediation and arbitration.

4.4.6 When a written decision of the Architect states that (1) the decision is final but subject to mediation and arbitration and (2) a demand for arbitration of a Claim covered by such decision must be made within 30 days after the date on which the party making the demand receives the final written decision, then failure to demand arbitration within said 30 days' period shall result in the Architect's decision becoming final and binding upon the Owner and Contractor. If the Architect renders a decision after arbitration proceedings have been initiated, such decision may be entered as evidence, but shall not supersede arbitration proceedings unless the decision is acceptable to all parties concerned.

4.4.7 Upon receipt of a Claim against the Contractor or at any time thereafter, the Architect or the Owner may, but is not obligated to, notify the surety, if any, of the nature and amount of the Claim. If the Claim relates to a possibility of a Contractor's default, the Architect or the Owner may, but is not obligated to, notify the surety and request the surety's assistance in resolving the controversy.

4.4.8 If a Claim relates to or is the subject of a mechanic's lien, the party asserting such Claim may proceed in accordance with applicable law to comply with the lien notice or filing deadlines prior to resolution of the Claim by the Architect, by mediation or by arbitration.

4.5 MEDIATION

4.5.5 Any Claim arising out of or related to the Contract, except Claims relating to aesthetic effect and except those waived as provided for in Subparagraphs 4.1.10, 9.10.4 and 9.10.5 shall, after initial decision by the Architect or 30 days after submission of the Claim to the Architect, be subject to mediation as a condition precedent to arbitration or the institution of legal or equitable proceedings by either party.

4.5.6 The parties shall endeavor to resolve their Claims by mediation which, unless the parties mutually agree otherwise, shall be in accordance with the Construction Industry Mediation Rules of the American Arbitration Association currently in effect. Request for mediation shall be filed in writing with the other party to the Contract and with the American Arbitration Association. The request may be made concurrently with the filing of a demand for arbitration or legal or equitable proceedings, which shall be stayed pending mediation for a period of 60 days from the date of filing, unless stayed for a longer period by agreement of the parties or court order.

4.5.7 The parties shall share the mediator's fee and any filing fees equally. The mediation shall be held in the place where the Project is located, unless another location is mutually agreed upon. Agreements reached in mediation shall be enforceable as settlement agreements in any court having jurisdiction thereof.

4.6 ARBITRATION

4.6.5 Any Claim arising out of or related to the Contract, except Claims relating to aesthetic effect and except those waived as provided for in Subparagraphs 4.5.10, 9.10.4 and 9.10.5, shall, after decision by the Architect or 30 days after submission of the Claim to the Architect, be subject to arbitration. Prior to arbitration, the parties shall endeavor to resolve disputes by mediation in accordance with the provisions of Paragraph 4.5.

4.6.6 Claims not resolved by mediation shall be decided by arbitration which, unless the parties mutually agree otherwise, shall be in accordance with the Construction Industry Arbitration Rules of the American Arbitration Association currently in effect. The demand for arbitration shall be filed in writing with the other party to the Contract and with the American Arbitration Association, and a copy shall be filed with the Architect.

4.6.7 A demand for arbitration shall be made within the time limits specified in Subparagraphs 4.4.6 and 4.6.1 as applicable, and in other cases within a reasonable time after the Claim has arisen, and in no event shall it be made after the date when institution of legal or equitable proceedings based on such Claim would be barred by the applicable statute of limitations as determined pursuant to Paragraph 13.7.

4.6.8 Limitation on Consolidation or Joinder. No arbitration arising out of or relating to the Contract shall include, by consolidation or joinder or in any other manner, the Architect, the Architect's employees or consultants, except by written consent containing specific reference to the Agreement and signed by the Architect, Owner, Contractor and any other person or entity sought to be joined. No arbitration shall include, by consolidation or joinder or in any other manner, parties other than the Owner, Contractor, a separate contractor as described in Article 6 and other persons substantially involved in a common question of fact or law whose presence is required if complete relief is to be accorded in arbitration. No person or entity other than the Owner, Contractor or a separate contractor as described in Article 6 shall be included as an original third party or additional third party to an arbitration whose interest or responsibility is insubstantial. Consent to arbitration involving an additional person or entity shall not constitute consent to arbitration of a Claim not described therein or with a person or entity not named or described therein. The foregoing agreement to arbitrate and other agreements to arbitrate with an additional person or entity duly consented to by parties to the Agreement shall be specifically enforceable under applicable law in any court having jurisdiction thereof.

4.6.9 Claims and Timely Assertion of Claims. The party filing a notice of demand for arbitration must assert in the demand all Claims then known to that party on which arbitration is permitted to be demanded.

4.6.10 Judgment on Final Award. The award rendered by the arbitrator or arbitrators shall be final, and judgement may be entered upon it in accordance with applicable law in any court having jurisdiction thereof.

ARTICLE 7 CHANGES IN THE WORK

7.1 GENERAL

7.1.1 Changes in the Work may be accomplished after execution of the Contract, and without invalidating the Contract, by Change Order, Construction Change Directive or order for a minor change in the Work, subject to the limitations stated in this Article 7 and elsewhere in the Contract Documents.

7.1.2 A Change Order shall be based upon agreement among the Owner, Contractor and Architect; a Construction Change Directive requires agreement by the Owner and Architect and may or may not be agreed to by the Contractor; an order for a minor change in the Work may be issued by the Architect alone.

7.1.3 Changes in the Work shall be performed under applicable provisions of the Contract Documents, and the Contractor shall proceed promptly, unless otherwise provided in the Change Order, Construction Change Directive or order for a minor change in the Work.

APPENDIX 3—AIA A201

7.2 CHANGE ORDERS

7.2.1 A Change Order is a written instrument prepared by the Architect and signed by the Owner, Contractor and Architect, stating their agreement upon all of the following:
   .1   a change in the Work;
   .2   the amount of the adjustment in the Contract Sum; and
   .3   the extent of the adjustment in the Contract Time.

7.2.2 Methods used in determining adjustments to the Contract Sum may include those listed in Subparagraph.

7.3   CONSTRUCTION CHANGE DIRECTIVES

7.3.1 A Construction Change Directive is a written order prepared by the Architect and signed by the Owner and Architect, directing a change in the Work prior to agreement on adjustment, if any, in the Contract Sum or Contract Time, or both. The Owner may by Construction Change Directive, without invalidating the Contract, order changes in the Work within the general scope of the Contract consisting of additions, deletions or other revisions, the Contract Sum and Contract Time being adjusted accordingly.

7.3.2 A Construction Change Directive shall be used in the absence of total agreement on the terms of a Change Order.

7.3.3 If the Construction Change Directive provides for an adjustment to the Contract Sum, the adjustment shall be based on one of the following methods:
   .1   mutual acceptance of a lump sum property itemized and supported by sufficient substantiating data to permit evaluation;
   .2   unit prices stated in the Contract Documents or subsequently agreed upon;
   .3   cost to be determined in a manner agreed upon by the parties and a mutually acceptable fixed or percentage fee; or
   .4   as provided in Subparagraph 7.3.6.

7.3.4 Upon receipt of a Construction Change Directive, the Contractor shall promptly proceed with the change in the Work involved and advise the Architect of the Contractor's agreement or disagreement with the method, if any, provided in the Construction Change Directive for determining the proposed adjustment in the Contract Sum or Contract Time.

7.3.5 A Construction Change Directive signed by the Contractor indicates the agreement of the Contractor therewith, including adjustment in Contract Sum and Contract Time or the method for determining them. Such agreement shall be effective immediately and shall be recorded as a Change Order.

7.3.6 If the Contractor does not respond promptly or disagrees with the method for adjustment in the Contract Sum, the method and the adjustment shall be determined by the Architect on the basis of reasonable expenditures and savings of those performing the Work attributable to the change, including, in case of an increase in the Contract Sum, a reasonable allowance for overhead and profit. In such case, and also under Clause 7.3.3.3, the Contractor shall keep and present, in such form as the Architect may prescribe, an itemized accounting together with appropriate supporting data. Unless otherwise provided in the Contract Documents, costs for the purposes of this Subparagraph 7.3.6 shall be limited to the following:
   .1   costs of labor, including social security, old age and unemployment insurance, fringe benefits required by agreement or custom, and workers' compensation insurance;
   .2   costs of materials, supplies and equipment, including cost of transportation, whether incorporated or consumed;
   .3   rental costs of machinery and equipment, exclusive of hand tools, whether rented from the Contractor or others;
   .4   costs of premiums for all bonds and insurance, permit fees, and sales, use or similar taxes related to the Work; and
   .5   additional costs of supervision and field office personnel directly attributable to the change.

7.3.7 The amount of credit to be allowed by the Contractor to the Owner for a deletion or change which results in a net decrease in the Contract Sum shall be actual net cost as confirmed by the Architect. When both additions and credits covering related Work or substitutions are involved in a change, the allowance for overhead and profit shall be figured on the basis of net increase, if any, with respect to that change.

7.3.8 Pending final determination of cost a Construction Change Directive to the Owner, amounts not in dispute may be included in Applications for Payment accompanied by a Change Order indicating the parties' agreement with part or all of such costs. For any portion of such cost that remains in dispute, the Architect will make an interim determination for purposes of monthly certification for payment for those costs. That determination of cost shall adjust the Contract Sum on the same basis as a Change Order, subject to the right of either party to disagree and assert a claim in accordance with Article 4.

7.3.9 When the Owner and Contractor agree with the determination made by the Architect concerning the adjustments in the Contract Sum and Contract Time, or otherwise reach agreement upon the adjustments, such agreement shall be effective immediately and shall be recorded by preparation and execution of an appropriate Change Order.

7.4   MINOR CHANGES IN THE WORK

7.4.1 The Architect will have authority to order minor changes in the Work not involving adjustment in the Contract Sum or extension of the Contract Time and not inconsistent with the intent of the Contract Documents. Such changes shall be effected by written order and shall be binding on the Owner and Contractor. The Contractor shall carry out such written orders promptly.

ARTICLE 8   TIME

8.1   DEFINITIONS

8.1.1 Unless otherwise provided, Contract Time is the period of time, including authorized adjustments, allotted in the Contract Documents for Substantial Completion of the Work.

8.1.2   The date of commencement of the Work is the date established in the Agreement.

8.1.3   The date of Substantial Completion is the date certified by the Architect in accordance with Paragraph 9.8.
8.1.4   The term "day" as used in the Contract Documents shall mean calendar day unless otherwise specifically defined.

8.2 PROGRESS AND COMPLETION

8.2.1   Time limits stated in the Contract Documents are of the essence of the Contract. By executing the Agreement the Contractor confirms that the Contract Time is a reasonable period for performing the Work

8.2.2   The Contractor shall not knowingly, except by agreement or instruction of the Owner in writing, prematurely commence operations on the site or elsewhere prior to the effective date of insurance required by Article 11 to be furnished by the Contractor and Owner. The date of commencement of the Work shall not be changed by the effective date of such insurance. Unless the date of commencement is established by the Contract Documents or a notice to proceed given by the Owner, the Contractor shall notify the Owner in writing not less than five days or other agreed period before commencing the Work to permit the timely filing of mortgages, mechanic's liens and other security interests.

8.2.3   The Contractor shall proceed expeditiously with adequate forces and shall achieve Substantial Completion within the Contract Time.

8.3 DELAYS AND EXTENSIONS OF TIME

8.3.1   If the Contractor is delayed at any time in the commencement or progress of the Work by an act or neglect of the Owner or Architect, or of an employee of either, or of a separate contractor employed by the Owner, or by changes ordered in the Work, or by labor disputes, fire, unusual delay in deliveries, unavoidable casualties or other causes beyond the Contractor's control, or by delay authorized by the Owner pending mediation and arbitration, or by other causes which the Architect determines may justify delay, then the Contract Time shall be extended by Change Order for such reasonable time as the Architect may determine.

8.3.2   Claims relating to time shall be made in accordance with applicable provisions of Paragraph 4.3.

8.3.3   This Paragraph 8.3 does not preclude recovery of damages for delay by either party under other provisions of the Contract Documents.

ARTICLE 14   TERMINATION OR SUSPENSION OF THE CONTRACT

14.1 TERMINATION BY THE CONTRACTOR

14.1.1   The Contractor may terminate the Contract if the Work is stopped for a period of 30 days through no act or fault of the Contractor or a Subcontractor, Sub-subcontractor or their agents or employees or any other persons performing portions of the Work under direct or indirect contract with the Contractor for any of the following reasons:

.1   issuance of an order of a court or other public authority having jurisdiction which requires all Work to be stopped;
.2   an act of government, such as a declaration of national emergency which requires all Work to be stopped;
.3   because the Architect has not issued a Certificate for Payment and has not notified the Contractor of the reason for withholding certification as provided in Subparagraph 9.4.1, or because the Owner has not made payment on a Certificate for Payment within the time stated in the Contract Documents; or
.4   the Owner has failed to finish to the Contractor promptly, upon the Contractor's request, reasonable evidence as required by Subparagraph 2.2.1.

14.1.2   The Contractor may terminate the Contract if, through no act or fault of the Contractor or a Subcontractor, Sub-subcontractor or their agents or employees or any other persons or entities performing portions of the Work under direct or indirect contract with the Contractor, repeated suspensions, delays or interruptions of the entire Work by the Owner as described in Paragraph 14.3 constitute in the aggregate more than 100 percent of the total number of days scheduled for completion, or 120 days in any 365-day period, whichever is less.

14.1.3   If one of the reasons described in Subparagraph 14.1.1 or 14.1.2 exists, the Contractor may, upon seven additional days' written notice to the Owner and Architect, terminate the Contract and recover from the Owner payment for Work executed and for proven loss with respect to materials, equipment, tools, and construction equipment and machinery, including reasonable overhead, profit and damages.

14.1.4   If the Work is stopped for a period of 60 days through no act or fault of the Contractor or a Subcontractor or their agents or employees or any other persons performing portions of the Work under contract with the Contractor because the Owner has persistently failed to fulfill the Owner's obligations under the Contract Documents with respect to matters important to the progress of the Work, the Contractor may, upon seven additional days' written notice to the Owner and the Architect, terminate the Contract and recover from the Owner as provided in Subparagraph 14.1.3.

14.2 TERMINATION BY THE OWNER FOR CAUSE

14.2.1   The Owner may terminate the Contract if the Contractor:

.1   persistently or repeatedly refuses or fails to supply enough property skilled workers or proper materials;
.2   fails to make payment to Subcontractors for materials or labor in accordance with the respective agreements between the Contractor and the Subcontractors;
.3   persistently disregards laws, ordinances, or rules, regulations or orders of a public authority, having jurisdiction; or
.4   otherwise is guilty of substantial breach of a provision of the Contract Documents.

APPENDIX 3—AIA A201

14.2.2 When any of the above reasons exist, the Owner, upon certification by the Architect that sufficient cause exists to justify such action, may without prejudice to any other rights or remedies of the Owner and after giving the Contractor and the contractor's surety, if any, seven days' written notice, terminate employment of the Contractor and may, subject to any rights of the surety:
- .1 take possession of the site and of all materials, equipment, tools, and construction equipment and machinery thereon owned by the Contractor;
- .2 accept assignment of subcontracts pursuant to Paragraph 5.4; and
- .3 finish the Work by whatever reasonable method the owner may deem expedient. Upon request of the Contractor, the Owner shall furnish to the Contractor a detailed accounting of the costs incurred by the Owner in finishing the Work.

14.2.3 When the Owner terminates the Contract for one of the reasons stated in Subparagraph 14.2.1, the Contractor shall not be entitled to receive further payment until the Work is finished.

14.2.4 If the unpaid balance of the Contract Sum exceeds costs of finishing the Work, including compensation for the Architect's services and expenses made necessary thereby, and other damages incurred by the Owner and not expressly waived, such excess shall be paid to the Contractor. If such costs and damages exceed the unpaid balance, the Contractor shall pay the difference to the Owner. The amount to be paid to the Contractor or Owner, as the case may be, shall be certified by the Architect, upon application, and this obligation for payment shall survive termination of the Contract.

14.3 SUSPENSION BY THE OWNER FOR CONVENIENCE

14.3.1 The Owner may, without cause, order the Contractor in writing to suspend, delay or interrupt the Work in whole or in part for such period of time as the Owner may determine.

14.3.2 The Contract Sum and Contract Time shall be adjusted for increases in the cost and time caused by the suspension, delay or interruption as described in Subparagraph 14.3.1. Adjustment of the Contract Sum shall include profit. No adjustment shall be made to the extent:
- .1 that performance is, was or would have been so suspended, delayed or interrupted by another cause for which the Contractor is responsible; or
- .2 that an equitable adjustment is made or denied under another provision of the Contract.

14.4 TERMINATION BY THE OWNER FOR CONVENIENCE

14.4.1 The Owner may, at any time, terminate the Contract for the Owner's convenience and without cause.

14.4.2 Upon receipt of written notice from the Owner of such termination for the Owner's convenience, the Contractor shall:
- .1 cease operations as directed by the Owner in the notice; or
- .2 take actions necessary, or that the Owner may direct, for the protection and preservation of the Work; and
- .3 except for Work directed to be performed prior to the effective date of termination stated in the notice, terminate all existing subcontracts and purchase orders and enter into no further subcontracts and purchase orders.

14.4.3 In case of such termination for the Owner's convenience, the Contractor shall be entitled to receive payment for Work executed, and costs incurred by reason of such termination, along with reasonable overhead and profit on the Work not executed.

Appendix 4 - EJCDC 1910-8

Appendix 4 - EJCDC 1910-8 General Conditions - Selected Clauses

This Appendix contains selected clauses from the **Standard General Conditions of the Construction Contract** (1996 Edition) prepared by Engineers Joint Contract Documents Committee.[2] The clauses included here are:

Article 4 - Availability of Lands; Subsurface and Physical Conditions; Reference Points

Article 10 - Changes in the Work, Claims

Article 11 - Cost Of The Work; Cash Allowances; Unit Price Work

Article 12 - Change Of Contract Price; Change Of Contract Times

Article 15 - Suspension Of Work And Termination

Article 16 - Dispute Resolution

Article 17 - Miscellaneous

ARTICLE 4 - AVAILABILITY OF LANDS; SUBSURFACE AND PHYSICAL CONDITIONS; REFERENCE POINTS

4.01 *Availability of Lands*

A. OWNER shall furnish the Site. OWNER shall notify CONTRACTOR of any encumbrances or restrictions not of general application but specifically related to use of the Site with which CONTRACTOR must comply in performing the Work. OWNER will obtain in a timely manner and pay for easements for permanent structures or permanent changes in existing facilities. If CONTRACTOR and OWNER are unable to agree on entitlement to or on the amount or extent, if any, of any adjustment in the Contract Price or Contract Times, or both, as a result of any delay in OWNER's furnishing the Site, CONTRACTOR may make a Claim therefor as provided in paragraph 10.05.

B. Upon reasonable written request, OWNER shall furnish CONTRACTOR with a current statement of record legal title and legal description of the lands upon which the Work is to be performed and OWNER's interest therein as necessary for giving notice of or filing a mechanic's or construction lien against such lands in accordance with applicable Laws and Regulations.

C. CONTRACTOR shall provide for all additional lands and access thereto that may be required for temporary construction facilities or storage of materials and equipment.

4.02 *Subsurface and Physical Conditions*

A. Reports and Drawings: The Supplementary Conditions identify:

.1 those reports of explorations and tests of subsurface conditions at or contiguous to the Site that ENGINEER has used in preparing the Contract Documents; and

.2 those drawings of physical conditions in or relating to existing surface or subsurface structures at or contiguous to the Site (except Underground Facilities) that ENGINEER has used in preparing the Contract Documents.

B. Limited Reliance by CONTRACTOR on Technical Data Authorized: CONTRACTOR may rely upon the general accuracy of the "technical data" contained in such reports and drawings, but such reports and drawings are not Contract Documents. Such "technical data" is identified in the Supplementary Conditions. Except for such reliance on such "technical data," CONTRACTOR may not rely upon or make any Claim against OWNER, ENGINEER, or any of ENGINEER's Consultants with respect to:

1. The completeness of such reports and drawings for CONTRACTOR's purposes, including, but

---

[2]Issued and Published Jointly by *American Consulting Engineers Council*, *National Society of Professional Engineers* and the *American Society of Civil Engineers*. This document has been approved and endorsed by the *Associated General Contractors of America* and the *Construction Specifications Institute*. Reprinted with Permission. Full copies of this document may be ordered directly from any of the participating organizations.

APPENDIX 4—EJCDC 1910-8

not limited to, any aspects of the means, methods, techniques, sequences, and procedures of construction to be employed by CONTRACTOR, and safety precautions and programs incident thereto; or

2. Other data, interpretations, opinions, and information contained in such reports or shown or indicated in such drawings; or

3. Any CONTRACTOR interpretation of or conclusion drawn from any "technical data" or any such other data, interpretations, opinions, or information.

4.03 *Differing Subsurface or Physical Conditions*

A. Notice.- If CONTRACTOR believes that any subsurface or physical condition at or contiguous to the Site that is uncovered or revealed either:

1. Is of such a nature as to establish that any "technical data" on which CONTRACTOR is entitled to rely as provided in paragraph 4.02 is materially inaccurate; or

2. Is of such a nature as to require a change in the Contract Documents; or

3. Differs materially from that shown or indicated in the Contract Documents; or

4. Is of an unusual nature, and differs materially from conditions ordinarily encountered and generally recognized as inherent in work of the character provided for in the Contract Documents; then CONTRACTOR shall, promptly after becoming aware thereof and before further disturbing the subsurface or physical conditions or performing any Work in connection therewith (except in an emergency as required by paragraph 6.16.A), notify OWNER and ENGINEER in writing about such condition. CONTRACTOR shall not further disturb such condition or perform any Work in connection therewith (except as aforesaid) until receipt of written order to do so.

B. ENGINEER's Review: After receipt of written notice as required by paragraph 4.03.A, ENGINEER will promptly review the pertinent condition, determine the necessity of OWNER's obtaining additional exploration or tests with respect thereto, and advise OWNER in writing (with a copy to CONTRACTOR) of ENGINEER's findings and conclusions.

C. Possible Price and Times Adjustments

1. The Contract Price or the Contract Times, or both, will be equitably adjusted to the extent that the existence of such differing subsurface or physical condition causes an increase or decrease in CONTRACTOR's cost of, or time required for, performance of the Work; subject, however, to the following:

a. such condition must meet any one or more of the categories described in paragraph 4.03.A; and

b. with respect to Work that is paid for on a Unit Price Basis, any adjustment in Contract Price will be subject to the provisions of paragraphs 9.08 and 11.03.

2. CONTRACTOR shall not be entitled to any adjustment in the Contract Price or Contract Times if:

a. CONTRACTOR knew of the existence of such conditions at the time CONTRACTOR made a final commitment to OWNER in respect of Contract Price and Contract Times by the submission of a Bid or becoming bound under a negotiated contract; or

b. the existence of such condition could reasonably have been discovered or revealed as a result of any examination, investigation, exploration, test, or study of the Site and contiguous areas required by the Bidding Requirements or Contract Documents to be conducted by or for CONTRACTOR prior to CONTRACTOR's making such commitment; or

c. CONTRACTOR failed to give the written notice within the time and as required by paragraph 4.03.A.

3. If OWNER and CONTRACTOR are unable to agree on entitlement to or on the amount or extent, if any, of any adjustment in the Contract Price or Contract Times, or both, a Claim may be made therefor as provided in paragraph 10.05. However, OWNER, ENGINEER, and ENGINEER's Consultants shall not be liable to CONTRACTOR for any claims, costs, losses, or damages (including but not limited to all fees and charges of engineers, architects, attorneys, and other professionals and all court or arbitration or other dispute resolution costs) sustained by CONTRACTOR on or in connection with any other project or anticipated project.

4.04 *Underground Facilities*

A. Shown or Indicated: The information and data shown or indicated in the Contract Documents with respect to existing Underground Facilities at or contiguous to the Site is based on information and data furnished to OWNER or ENGINEER by the owners of such Underground Facilities, including OWNER, or by others. Unless it is otherwise expressly provided in the Supplementary Conditions:

1. OWNER and ENGINEER shall not be responsible for the accuracy or completeness of any such information or data; and

2. the cost of all of the following will be included in the Contract Price, and CONTRACTOR shall have full responsibility for:

    a. reviewing and checking all such information and data,

    b. locating all Underground Facilities shown or indicated in the Contract Documents,

    c. coordination of the Work with the owners of such Underground Facilities, including OWNER, during construction, and

    d. the safety and protection of all such Underground Facilities and repairing any damage thereto resulting from the Work.

B. Not Shown or Indicated

    1. If an Underground Facility is uncovered or revealed at or contiguous to the Site which was not shown or indicated, or not shown or indicated with reasonable accuracy in the Contract Documents, CONTRACTOR shall, promptly after becoming aware thereof and before further disturbing conditions affected thereby or performing any Work in connection therewith (except in an emergency as required by paragraph 6.16.A), identify the owner of such Underground Facility and give written notice to that owner and to OWNER and ENGINEER. ENGINEER will promptly review the Underground Facility and determine the extent, if any, to which a change is required in the Contract Documents to reflect and document the consequences of the existence or location of the Underground Facility. During such time, CONTRACTOR shall be responsible for the safety and protection of such Underground Facility.

    2. If ENGINEER concludes that a change in the Contract Documents is required, a Work Change Directive or a Change Order will be issued to reflect and document such consequences. An equitable adjustment shall be made in the Contract Price of Contract Times, or both, to the extent that they are attributable to the existence or location of any Underground Facility that was not shown or indicated or not shown or indicated with reasonable accuracy in the Contract Documents and that CONTRACTOR did not know of and could not reasonably have been expected to be aware of or to have anticipated. If OWNER and CONTRACTOR are unable to agree on entitlement to or on the amount or extent, if any, of any such adjustment in Contract Price or Contract Times, OWNER or CONTRACTOR may make a Claim therefor as provided in paragraph 10.05.

4.05   *Reference Points*

A. OWNER shall provide engineering surveys to establish reference points for construction which in ENGINEER's judgment are necessary to enable CONTRACTOR to proceed with the Work. CONTRACTOR shall be responsible for laying out the Work, shall protect and preserve the established reference points and property monuments, and shall make no changes or relocations without the prior written approval of OWNER. CONTRACTOR shall report to ENGINEER whenever any reference point or property monument is lost or destroyed or requires relocation because of necessary changes in grades or locations, and shall be responsible for the accurate replacement or relocation of such reference points or property monuments by professionally qualified personnel.

4.06   *Hazardous Environmental Condition at Site*

A. Reports and Drawings: Reference is made to the Supplementary Conditions for the identification of those reports and drawings relating to a Hazardous Envirorunental Condition identified at the Site, if any, that have been utilized by the ENGINEER in the preparation of the Contract Documents.

B. Limited Reliance by CONTRACTOR on Technical Data Authorized: CONTRACTOR may rely upon the general accuracy of the "technical data" contained in such reports and drawings, but such reports and drawings are not Contract Documents. Such "technical data" is identified in the Supplementary Conditions. Except for such reliance on such "technical data," CONTRACTOR may not rely upon or make any Claim against OWNER, ENGINEER or any of ENGINEER's Consultants with respect to:

    1. the completeness of such reports and drawings for CONTRACTOR's purposes, including, but not limited to, any aspects of the means, methods, techniques, sequences and procedures of construction to be employed by CONTRACTOR and safety precautions and programs incident thereto; or

    2. other data, interpretations, opinions and information contained in such reports or shown or indicated in such drawings; or

    3. any CONTRACTOR interpretation of or conclusion drawn from any "technical data" or any such other data, interpretations, opinions or information.

C. CONTRACTOR shall not be responsible for any Hazardous Environmental Condition uncovered or revealed at the Site which was not shown or indicated in Drawings or Specifications or identified in the Contract Documents to be within the scope of the Work. CONTRACTOR shall be responsible for a Hazardous Environmental Condition created with any materials brought to the Site by CONTRACTOR, Subcontractors, Suppliers, or anyone else for whom CONTRACTOR is responsible.

D. If CONTRACTOR encounters a Hazardous Environmental Condition or if CONTRACTOR or anyone for whom CONTRACTOR is responsible creates a Hazardous Environmental Condition, CONTRACTOR shall immediately: (i) secure or otherwise isolate such condition; (ii) stop all Work in connection with such condition and in any area affected thereby (except in an emergency as required by paragraph 6.16); and (iii) notify OWNER and ENGINEER (and promptly thereafter confirm such notice in writing). OWNER shall promptly consult with ENGINEER concerning the necessity for OWNER to retain a qualified expert to evaluate such condition or take corrective action, if any.

E. CONTRACTOR shall not be required to resume Work in connection with such condition or in any affected area until after OWNER has obtained any required permits related thereto and delivered to CONTRACTOR written notice: (i) specifying that such condition and any affected area is or has been rendered safe for the resumption of Work; or (ii) specifying any special conditions under which such Work may be resumed safely. If OWNER and CONTRACTOR cannot agree as to entitlement to or on the amount or extent, if any, of any adjustment in Contract Price or Contract Times, or both, as a result of such Work stoppage or such special conditions under which Work is agreed to be resumed by CONTRACTOR, either party may make a Claim therefor as provided in paragraph 10.05.

F. If after receipt of such written notice CONTRACTOR does not agree to resume such Work based on a reasonable belief it is unsafe, or does not agree to resume such Work under such special conditions, then OWNER may order the portion of the Work that is in the area affected by such condition to be deleted from the Work.

If OWNER and CONTRACTOR cannot agree as to entitlement to or on the amount or extent, if any, of an adjustment in Contract Price or Contract Times as a result of deleting such portion of the Work, then either party may make a Claim therefor as provided in paragraph 10.05. OWNER may have such deleted portion of the Work performed by OWNER's own forces or others in accordance with Article 7.

G. To the fullest extent permitted by Laws and Regulations, OWNER shall indemnify and hold harmless CONTRACTOR, Subcontractors, ENGINEER, ENGINEER's Consultants and the officers, directors, partners, employees, agents, other consultants, and subcontractors of each and any of them from and against all claims, costs, losses, and damages (including but not limited to all fees and charges of engineers, architects, attorneys, and other professionals and all court or arbitration or other dispute resolution costs) arising out of or relating to a Hazardous Environmental Condition, provided that such Hazardous Environmental Condition: (i) was not shown or indicated in the Drawings or Specifications or identified in the Contract Documents to be included within the scope of the Work, and (ii) was not created by CONTRACTOR or by anyone for whom CONTRACTOR is responsible. Nothing in this paragraph 4.06.E shall obligate OWNER to indemnify any individual or entity from and against the consequences of that individual's or entity's own negligence.

H. To the fullest extent permitted by Laws and Regulations, CONTRACTOR shall indemnify and hold harmless O@ER, ENGINEER, ENGINEER's Consultants, and the officers, directors, partners, employees, agents, other consultants, and subcontractors of each and any of them from and against all claims, costs, losses, and damages (including but not limited to all fees and charges of engineers, architects, attorneys, and other professionals and all court or arbitration or other dispute resolution costs) arising out of or relating to a Hazardous Environmental Condition created by CONTRACTOR or by anyone for whom CONTRACTOR is responsible. Nothing in this paragraph 4.06.F shall obligate CONTRACTOR to indemnify any individual or entity from and against the consequences of that individual's or entity's own negligence.

I. The provisions of paragraphs 4.02, 4.03, and 4.04 are not intended to apply to a Hazardous Environmental Condition uncovered or revealed at the Site.

ARTICLE 10 - CHANGES IN THE WORK; CLAIMS

10.01   *Authorized Changes in the Work*

A. Without invalidating the Agreement and without notice to any surety, OWNER may, at any time or from time to time, order additions, deletions, or revisions in the Work by a Written Amendment, a Change Order, or a Work Change Directive. Upon receipt of any such document, CONTRACTOR shall promptly proceed with the Work involved which will be performed under the applicable conditions of the Contract Documents (except as otherwise specifically provided).

B. If OWNER and CONTRACTOR are unable to agree on entitlement to, or on the amount or extent, if any, of an adjustment in the Contract Price or Contract Times, or both, that should be allowed as a result of a Work Change Directive, a Claim may be made therefor as provided in paragraph 10.05.

10.02   *Unauthorized Changes in the Work*

A. CONTRACTOR shall not be entitled to an increase in the Contract Price or an extension of the Contract Times with respect to any work performed that is not required by the Contract Documents as amended, modified, or supplemented as provided in paragraph 3.04, except in the case of an emergency as provided in paragraph 6.16 or in the case of uncovering Work as provided in paragraph 13.04.B.

10.03   *Execution of Change Orders*

A. OWNER and CONTRACTOR shall execute appropriate Change Orders recommended by ENGINEER (or Written Amendments) covering:

1. changes in the Work which are: (i) ordered by OWNER pursuant to paragraph 10.01.A, (ii) required

because of acceptance of defective Work under paragraph 13.08.A or OWNER's correction of defective Work under paragraph 13.09, or (iii) agreed to by the parties;

2. changes in the Contract Price or Contract Times which are agreed to by the parties, including any undisputed sum or amount of time for Work actually performed in accordance with a Work Change Directive; and

3. changes in the Contract Price or Contract Times which embody the substance of any written decision rendered by ENGINEER pursuant to paragraph 10.05; provided that, in lieu of executing any such Change Order, an appeal may be taken from any such decision in accordance with the provisions of the Contract Documents and applicable Laws and Regulations, but during any such appeal, CONTRACTOR shall carry on the Work and adhere to the progress schedule as provided in paragraph 6.18.A.

10.04   *Notification to Surety*

A. If notice of any change affecting the general scope of the Work or the provisions of the Contract Documents (including, but not limited to, Contract Price or Contract Times) is required by the provisions of any Bond to be given to a surety, the giving of any such notice will be CONTRACTOR's responsibility. The amount of each applicable Bond will be adjusted to reflect the effect of any such change.

10.05   *Claims and Disputes*

A. Notice: Written notice stating the general nature of each Claim, dispute, or other matter shall be delivered by the claimant to ENGINEER and the other party to the Contract promptly (but in no event later than 30 days) after the start of the event giving rise thereto. Notice of the amount or extent of the Claim, dispute, or other matter with supporting data shall be delivered to the ENGINEER and the other party to the Contract within 60 days after the start of such event (unless ENGINEER allows additional time for claimant to submit additional or more accurate data in support of such Claim, dispute, or other matter). A Claim for an adjustment in Contract Price shall be prepared in accordance with the provisions of paragraph 12.01.B. A Claim for an adjustment in Contract Time shall be prepared in accordance with the provisions of paragraph 12.02.B. Each Claim shall be accompanied by claimant's written statement that the adjustment claimed is the entire adjustment to which the claimant believes it is entitled as a result of said event. The opposing party shall submit any response to ENGINEER and the claimant within 30 days after receipt of the claimant's last submittal (unless ENGINEER allows additional time).

B. ENGINEER's Decision: ENGINEER will render a formal decision in writing within 30 days after receipt of the last submittal of the claimant or the last submittal of the opposing party, if any. ENGINEER's written decision on such Claim, dispute, or other matter will be final and binding upon OWNER and CONTRACTOR unless:

1. an appeal from ENGINEER's decision is taken within the time limits and in accordance with the dispute resolution procedures set forth in Article 16; or

2. if no such dispute resolution procedures have been set forth in Article 16, a written notice of intention to appeal from ENGINEER's written decision is delivered by OWNER or CONTRACTOR to the other and to ENGINEER within 30 days after the date of such decision, and a formal proceeding is instituted by the appealing party in a forum of competent jurisdiction within 60 days after the date of such decision or within 60 days after Substantial Completion, whichever is later (unless otherwise agreed in writing by OWNER and CONTRACTOR), to exercise such rights or remedies as the appealing party may have with respect to such Claim, dispute, or other matter in accordance with applicable Laws and Regulations.

C. If ENGINEER does not render a formal decision in writing within the time stated in paragraph 10.05.B, a decision denying the Claim in its entirety shall be deemed to have been issued 31 days after receipt of the last submittal of the claimant or the last submittal of the opposing party, if any.

D. No Claim for an adjustment in Contract Price or Contract Times (or Milestones) will be valid if not submitted in accordance with this paragraph 10.05.

ARTICLE 11 - COST OF THE WORK; CASH ALLOWANCES; UNIT PRICE WORK

11.01   *Cost of the Work*

A. Costs Included: The term Cost of the Work means the sum of all costs necessarily incurred and paid by CONTRACTOR in the proper performance of the Work. When the value of any Work covered by a Change Order or when a Claim for an adjustment in Contract Price is determined on the basis of Cost of the Work, the costs to be reimbursed to CONTRACTOR will be only those additional or incremental costs required because of the change in the Work or because of the event giving rise to the Claim. Except as otherwise may be agreed to in writing by OWNER, such costs shall be in amounts no higher than those prevailing in the locality of the Project, shall include only the following items, and shall not include any of the costs itemized in paragraph 11.01.B.

APPENDIX 4—EJCDC 1910-8

1. Payroll costs for employees in the direct employ of CONTRACTOR in the performance of the Work under schedules of job classifications agreed upon by OWNER and CONTRACTOR. Such employees shall include without limitation superintendents, foremen, and other personnel employed full time at the Site. Payroll costs for employees not employed full time on the Work shall be apportioned on the basis of their time spent on the Work. Payroll costs shall include, but not be limited to, salaries and wages plus the cost of fringe benefits, which shall include social security contributions, unemployment, excise, and payroll taxes, workers' compensation, health and retirement benefits, bonuses, sick leave, vacation and holiday pay applicable thereto. The expenses of performing Work outside of regular working hours, on Saturday, Sunday, or legal holidays, shall be included in the above to the extent authorized by OWNER.

2. Cost of all materials and equipment furnished and incorporated in the Work, including costs of transportation and storage thereof, and Suppliers' field services required in connection therewith. All cash discounts shall accrue to CONTRACTOR unless OWNER deposits funds with CONTRACTOR with which to make payments, in which case the cash discounts shall accrue to OWNER. All trade discounts, rebates and refunds and returns from sale of surplus materials and equipment shall accrue to OWNER, and CONTRACTOR shall make provisions so that they may be obtained.

3. Payments made by CONTRACTOR to Subcontractors for Work performed by Subcontractors. If required by OWNER, CONTRACTOR shall obtain competitive bids from subcontractors acceptable to OWNER and CONTRACTOR and shall deliver such bids to OWNER, who will then determine, with the advice of ENGINEER, which bids, if any, will be acceptable. If any subcontract provides that the Subcontractor is to be paid on the basis of Cost of the Work plus a fee, the Subcontractor's Cost of the Work and fee shall be determined in the same manner as CONTRACTOR's Cost of the Work and fee as provided in this paragraph 11.01.

4. Costs of special consultants (including but not limited to engineers, architects, testing laboratories, surveyors, attorneys, and accountants) employed for services specifically related to the Work.

5. Supplemental costs including the following:

  a. The proportion of necessary transportation, travel, and subsistence expenses of CONTRACTOR's employees incurred in discharge of duties connected with the Work.

  b. Cost, including transportation and maintenance, of all materials, supplies, equipment, machinery, appliances, office, and temporary facilities at the Site, and hand tools not owned by the workers, which are consumed in the performance of the Work, and cost, less market value, of such items used but not consumed which remain the property of CONTRACTOR.

  c. Rentals of all construction equipment and machinery, and the parts thereof whether rented from CONTRACTOR or others in accordance with rental agreements approved by OWNER with the advice of ENGINEER, and the costs of transportation, loading, unloading, assembly, dismantling, and removal thereof. All such costs shall be in accordance with the terms of said rental agreements. The rental of any such equipment, machinery, or parts shall cease when the use thereof is no longer necessary for the Work.

  d. Sales, consumer, use, and other similar taxes related to the Work, and for which CONTRACTOR is liable, imposed by Laws and Regulations.

  e. Deposits lost for causes other than negligence of CONTRACTOR, any Subcontractor, or anyone directly or indirectly employed by any of them or for whose acts any of them may be liable, and royalty payments and fees for permits and licenses.

  f. Losses and damages (and related expenses) caused by damage to the Work, not compensated by insurance or otherwise, sustained by CONTRACTOR in connection with the performance of the Work (except losses and damages within the deductible amounts of property insurance established in accordance with paragraph 5.06.D), provided such losses and damages have resulted from causes other than the negligence of CONTRACTOR, any Subcontractor, or anyone directly or indirectly employed by any of them or for whose acts any of them may be liable. Such losses shall include settlements made with the written consent and approval of OWNER. No such losses, damages, and expenses shall be included in the Cost of the Work for the purpose of determining CONTRACTOR's fee.

  g. The cost of utilities, fuel, and sanitary facilities at the Site.

  h. Minor expenses such as telegrams, long distance telephone calls, telephone service at the Site, expressage, and similar petty cash items in connection with the Work.

  i. When the Cost of the Work is used to determine the value of a Change Order or of a Claim, the cost of premiums for additional Bonds and insurance required because of the changes in the Work or caused by the event giving rise to the Claim.

j. When all the Work is performed on the basis of cost-plus, the costs of premiums for all Bonds and insurance CONTRACTOR is required by the Contract Documents to purchase and maintain.

B. *Costs Excluded*: The term Cost of the Work shall not include any of the following items:

1. Payroll costs and other compensation of CONTRACTOR's officers, executives, principals (of partnerships and sole proprietorships), general managers, engineers, architects, estimators, attorneys, auditors, accountants, purchasing and contracting agents, expediters, timekeepers, clerks, and other personnel employed by CONTRACTOR, whether at the Site or in CONTRACTOR's principal or branch office for general administration of the Work and not specifically included in the agreed upon schedule of job classifications referred to in paragraph 11.01.A.1 or specifically covered by paragraph 11.01.A.4, all of which are to be considered administrative costs covered by the CONTRACTOR's fee.

2. Expenses of CONTRACTOR's principal and branch offices other than CONTRACTOR's office at the Site.

3. Any part of CONTRACTOR's capital expenses, including interest on CONTRACTOR's capital employed for the Work and charges against CONTRACTOR for delinquent payments.

4. Costs due to the negligence of CONTRACTOR, any Subcontractor, or anyone directly or indirectly employed by any of them or for whose acts any of them may be liable, including but not limited to, the correction of defective Work, disposal of materials or equipment wrongly supplied, and making good any damage to property.

5. Other overhead or general expense costs of any kind and the costs of any item not specifically and expressly included in paragraphs 11.01.A and 11.01.B.

C. CONTRACTOR's Fee: When all the Work is performed on the basis of cost-plus, CONTRACTOR's fee shall be determined as set forth in the Agreement. When the value of any Work covered by a Change Order or when a Claim for an adjustment in Contract Price is determined on the basis of Cost of the Work, CONTRACTOR's fee shall be determined as set forth in paragraph 12.01.C.

D. Documentation: Whenever the Cost of the Work for any purpose is to be determined pursuant to paragraphs 11.01.A and 11.01.B, CONTRACTOR will establish and maintain records thereof in accordance with generally accepted accounting practices and submit in a form acceptable to ENGINEER an itemized cost breakdown together with supporting data.

11.02   *Cash Allowances*

A. It is understood that CONTRACTOR has included in the Contract Price all allowances so named in the Contract Documents and shall cause the Work so covered to be performed for such sums as may be acceptable to OWNER and ENGINEER. CONTRACTOR agrees that:

1. the allowances include the cost to CONTRACTOR (less any applicable trade discounts) of materials and equipment required by the allowances to be delivered at the Site, and all applicable taxes; and

2. CONTRACTOR's costs for unloading and handling on the Site, labor, installation costs, overhead, profit, and other expenses contemplated for the allowances have been included in the Contract Price and not in the allowances, and no demand for additional payment on account of any of the foregoing will be valid.

B. Prior to final payment, an appropriate Change Order will be issued as recommended by ENGINEER to reflect actual amounts due CONTRACTOR on account of Work covered by allowances, and the Contract Price shall be correspondingly adjusted.

11.03   *Unit Price Work*

A. Where the Contract Documents provide that all or part of the Work is to be Unit Price Work, initially the Contract Price will be deemed to include for all Unit Price Work an amount equal to the sum of the unit price for each separately identified item of Unit Price Work times the estimated quantity of each item as indicated in the Agreement. The estimated quantities of items of Unit Price Work are not guaranteed and are solely for the purpose of comparison of Bids and determining an initial Contract Price. Determinations of the actual quantities and classifications of Unit Price Work performed by CONTRACTOR will be made by ENGINEER subject to the provisions of paragraph 9.08.

B. Each unit price will be deemed to include an amount considered by CONTRACTOR to be adequate to cover CONTRACTOR's overhead and profit for each separately identified item.

C. OWNER or CONTRACTOR may make a Claim for an adjustment in the Contract Price in accordance with paragraph 10.05 if:

1. the quantity of any item of Unit Price Work performed by CONTRACTOR differs materially and significantly from the estimated quantity of such item indicated in the Agreement; and

APPENDIX 4—EJCDC 1910-8

2. there is no corresponding adjustment with respect any other item of Work; and

3. if CONTRACTOR believes that CONTRACTOR is entitled to an increase in Contract Price as a result of having incurred additional expense or OWNER believes that OWNER is entitled to a decrease in Contract Price and the parties are unable to agree as to the amount of any such increase or decrease.

ARTICLE 12 - CHANGE OF CONTRACT PRICE; CHANGE OF CONTRACT TIMES

12.01 *Change of Contract Price*

A. The Contract Price may only be changed by a Change Order or by a Written Amendment. Any Claim for an adjustment in the Contract Price shall be based on written notice submitted by the party making the Claim to the ENGINEER and the other party to the Contract in accordance with the provisions of paragraph 10.05.

B. The value of any Work covered by a Change Order or of any Claim for an adjustment in the Contract Price will be determined as follows:

1. where the Work involved is covered by unit prices contained in the Contract Documents, by application of such unit prices to the quantities of the items involved (subject to the provisions of paragraph 11.03); or

2. where the Work involved is not covered by unit prices contained in the Contract Documents, by a mutually agreed lump sum (which may include an allowance for overhead and profit not necessarily in accordance with paragraph 12.01.C.2); or

3. where the Work involved is not covered by unit prices contained in the Contract Documents and agreement to a lump sum is not reached under paragraph 12.01.B.2, on the basis of the Cost of the Work (determined as provided in paragraph 11.01) plus a CONTRACTOR's fee for overhead and profit (determined as provided in paragraph 12.01. C).

C. *CONTRACTOR's Fee:* The CONTRACTOR's fee for overhead and profit shall be determined as follows:

1. a mutually acceptable fixed fee; or

2. if a fixed fee is not agreed upon, then a fee based on the following percentages of the various portions of the Cost of the Work:

a. for costs incurred under paragraphs 11.01.A.1 and 11.01.A.2, the CONTRACTOR's fee shall be 15 percent;

199

b. for costs incurred under paragraph 11.01.A.3, the CONTRACTOR's fee shall be five percent;

c. where one or more tiers of subcontracts are on the basis of Cost of the Work plus a fee and no fixed fee is agreed upon, the intent of paragraph 12.01.C.2.a is that the Subcontractor who actually performs the Work, at whatever tier, will be paid a fee of 15 percent of the costs incurred by such Subcontractor under paragraphs 11.01.A.1 and 11.01.A.2 and that any higher tier Subcontractor and CONTRACTOR will each be paid a fee of five percent of the amount paid to the next lower tier Subcontractor;

d. no fee shall be payable on the basis of costs itemized under paragraphs 11.01.A.4, 11.01.A.5, and 11.01.B;

e. the amount of credit to be allowed by CONTRACTOR to OWNER for any change which results in a net decrease in cost will be the amount of the actual net decrease in cost plus a deduction in CONTRACTOR's fee by an amount equal to five percent of such net decrease; and

f. when both additions and credits are involved in any one change, the adjustment in CONTRACTOR's fee shall be computed on the basis of the net change in accordance with paragraphs 12.01.C.2.a through 12.01.C.2.e, inclusive.

12.02 *Change of Contract Times*

A. The Contract Times (or Milestones) may only be changed by a Change Order or by a Written Amendment. Any Claim for an adjustment in the Contract Times (or Milestones) shall be based on written notice submitted by the party making the claim to the ENGINEER and the other party to the Contract in accordance with the provisions of paragraph 10.05.

B. Any adjustment of the Contract Times (or Milestones) covered by a Change Order or of any Claim for an adjustment in the Contract Times (or Milestones) will be determined in accordance with the provisions of this Article 12.

12.03 *Delays Beyond CONTRACTOR's Control*

A. Where CONTRACTOR is prevented from completing any part of the Work within the Contract Times (or Milestones) due to delay beyond the control of CONTRACTOR, the Contract Times (or Milestones) will be extended in an amount equal to the time lost due to such delay if a Claim is made therefor as provided in paragraph 12.02.A. Delays beyond the control of CONTRACTOR shall include, but not be limited to, acts or neglect by OWNER, acts or neglect of utility owners or other contractors performing other work as contemplated by Article 7, fires, floods, epidemics, abnormal weather conditions, or acts of God.

12.04   *Delays Within CONTRACTOR's Control*

A. The Contract Times (or Milestones) will not be extended due to delays within the control of CONTRACTOR. Delays attributable to and within the control of a Subcontractor or Supplier shall be deemed to be delays within the control of CONTRACTOR.

12.05   *Delays Beyond OWNER's and CONTRACTOR's Control*

A. Where CONTRACTOR is prevented from completing any part of the Work within the Contract Times (or Milestones) due to delay beyond the control of both OWNER and CONTRACTOR, an extension of the Contract Times (or Milestones) in an amount equal to the time lost due to such delay shall be CONTRACTOR's sole and exclusive remedy for such delay.

12.06   *Delay Damages*

A. In no event shall OWNER or ENGINEER be liable to CONTRACTOR, any Subcontractor, any Supplier, or any other person or organization, or to any surety for or employee or agent of any of them, for damages arising out of or resulting from:

1. delays caused by or within the control of CONTRACTOR; or

2. delays beyond the control of both OWNER and CONTRACTOR including but not limited to fires, floods, epidemics, abnormal weather conditions, acts of God, or acts or neglect by utility owners or other contractors performing other work as contemplated by Article 7.

B. Nothing in this paragraph 12.06 bars a change in Contract Price pursuant to this Article 12 to compensate CONTRACTOR due to delay, interference, or disruption directly attributable to actions or inactions of OWNER or anyone for whom OWNER is responsible.

ARTICLE 15 - SUSPENSION OF WORK AND TERMINATION

15.01   *OWNER May Suspend Work*

A. At any time and without cause, OWNER may suspend the Work or any portion thereof for a period of not more than 90 consecutive days by notice in writing to CONTRACTOR and ENGINEER which will fix the date on which Work will be resumed. CONTRACTOR shall resume the Work on the date so fixed. CONTRACTOR shall be allowed an adjustment in the Contract Price or an extension of the Contract Times, or both, directly attributable to any such suspension if CONTRACTOR makes a Claim therefor as provided in paragraph 10.05.

15.02   *OWNER May Terminate for Cause*

A. The occurrence of any one or more of the following events will justify termination for cause:

1. CONTRACTOR's persistent failure to perform the Work in accordance with the Contract Documents (including, but not limited to, failure to supply sufficient skilled workers or suitable materials or equipment or failure to adhere to the progress schedule established under paragraph 2.07 as adjusted from time to time pursuant to paragraph 6.04);

2. CONTRACTOR's disregard of Laws or Regulations of any public body having jurisdiction;

3. CONTRACTOR's disregard of the authority of ENGINEER; or

4. CONTRACTOR's violation in any substantial way of any provisions of the Contract Documents.

B. If one or more of the events identified in paragraph 15.02.A occur, OWNER may, after giving CONTRACTOR (and the surety, if any) seven days written notice, terminate the services of CONTRACTOR, exclude CONTRACTOR from the Site, and take possession of the Work and of all CONTRACTOR's tools, appliances, construction equipment, and machinery at the Site, and use the same to the full extent they could be used by CONTRACTOR (without liability to CONTRACTOR for trespass or conversion), incorporate in the Work all materials and equipment stored at the Site or for which OWNER has paid CONTRACTOR but which are stored elsewhere, and finish the Work as OWNER may deem expedient. In such case, CONTRACTOR shall not be entitled to receive any further payment until the Work is finished. If the unpaid balance of the Contract Price exceeds all claims, costs, losses, and damages (including but not limited to all fees and charges of engineers, architects, attorneys, and other professionals and all court or arbitration or other dispute resolution costs) sustained by OWNER arising out of or relating to completing the Work, such excess will be paid to CONTRACTOR. If such claims, costs, losses, and damages exceed such unpaid balance, CONTRACTOR shall pay the difference to OWNER. Such claims, costs, losses, and damages incurred by OWNER will be reviewed by ENGINEER as to their reasonableness and, when so approved by ENGINEER, incorporated in a Change Order. When exercising any rights or remedies under this paragraph OWNER shall not be required to obtain the lowest price for the Work performed.

C. Where CONTRACTOR's services have been so terminated by OWNER, the termination will not affect any rights or remedies of OWNER against CONTRACTOR then existing or which may thereafter accrue. Any retention or payment of moneys due CONTRACTOR by OWNER will not release CONTRACTOR from liability.

15.03 *OWNER May Terminate For Convenience*

A. Upon seven days written notice to CONTRACTOR and ENGINEER, OWNER may, without cause and without prejudice to any other right or remedy of OWNER, elect to terminate the Contract. In such case, CONTRACTOR shall be paid (without duplication of any items):

1. for completed and acceptable Work executed in accordance with the Contract Documents prior to the effective date of termination, including fair and reasonable sums for overhead and profit on such Work;

2. for expenses sustained prior to the effective date of termination in performing services and furnishing labor, materials, or equipment as required by the Contract Documents in connection with uncompleted Work, plus fair and reasonable sums for overhead and profit on such expenses;

3. for all claims, costs, losses, and damages (including but not limited to all fees and charges of engineers, architects, attorneys, and other professionals and all court or arbitration or other dispute resolution costs) incurred in settlement of terminated contracts with Subcontractors, Suppliers, and others; and

4. for reasonable expenses directly attributable to termination.

B. CONTRACTOR shall not be paid on account of loss of anticipated profits or revenue or other economic loss arising out of or resulting from such termination.

15.04 *CONTRACTOR May Stop Work or Terminate*

A. If, through no act or fault of CONTRACTOR, the Work is suspended for more than 90 consecutive days by OWNER or under an order of court or other public authority, or ENGINEER fails to act on any Application for Payment within 30 days after it is submitted, or OWNER fails for 30 days to pay CONTRACTOR any sum of money determined to be due, then CONTRACTOR may, upon seven days written notice to OWNER and ENGINEER, and provided OWNER or ENGINEER do not remedy such suspension or failure within that time, terminate the Contract and recover from OWNER payment on the same terms as provided in paragraph 15.03. In lieu of terminating the Contract and without prejudice to any other right or remedy, if ENGINEER has failed to act on an Application for Payment within 30 days after it is submitted, or OWNER has failed for 30 days to pay CONTRACTOR any sum finally determined to be due, CONTRACTOR may, seven days after written notice to OWNER and ENGINEER, stop the Work until payment is made of all such amounts due CONTRACTOR, including interest thereon. The provisions of this paragraph 15.04 are not intended to preclude CONTRACTOR from making a Claim under paragraph 10.05 for an adjustment in Contract Price or Contract Times or otherwise for expenses or damage directly attributable to CONTRACTOR's stopping the Work as permitted by this paragraph.

ARTICLE 16 - DISPUTE RESOLUTION

16.01 *Methods and Procedures*

A. Dispute resolution methods and procedures, if any, shall be as set forth in the Supplementary Conditions. If no method and procedure has been set forth, and subject to the provisions of paragraphs 9.09 and 10.05, OWNER and CONTRACTOR may exercise such rights or remedies as either may otherwise have under the Contract Documents or by Laws or Regulations in respect of any dispute.

ARTICLE 17 - MISCELLANEOUS

17.01 *Giving Notice*

A. Whenever any provision of the Contract Documents requires the giving of written notice, it will be deemed to have been validly given if delivered in person to the individual or to a member of the firm or to an officer of the corporation for whom it is intended, or if delivered at or sent by registered or certified mail, postage prepaid, to the last business address known to the giver of the notice.

17.02 *Computation of Times*

A. When any period of time is referred to in the Contract Documents by days, it will be computed to exclude the first and include the last day of such period. If the last day of any such period falls on a Saturday or Sunday or on a day made a legal holiday by the law of the applicable jurisdiction, such day will be omitted from the computation.

17.03 *Cumulative Remedies*

A. The duties and obligations imposed by these General Conditions and the rights and remedies available hereunder to the parties hereto are in addition to, and are not to be construed in any way as a limitation of, any rights and remedies available to any or all of them which are otherwise imposed or available by Laws or Regulations, by special warranty or guarantee, or by other provisions of the Contract Documents, and the provisions of this paragraph will be as effective as if repeated specifically in the Contract Documents in connection with each particular duty, obligation, right, and remedy to which they apply.

17.04   *Survival of Obligations*

   A.   All representations, indemnifications, warranties, and guarantees made in, required by, or given in accordance with the Contract Documents, as well as all continuing obligations indicated in the Contract Documents will survive final payment, completion, and acceptance of the Work or termination or completion of the Agreement.

17.05   *Controlling Law*

   A.   This Contract is to be governed by the law of the state in which the Project is located.

Appendix 5 - Site Investigation Report Form

Site Investigation Report

This outline is for use as a general guide in preparing for and conducting a site visit. It is not all nclusive and should be supplemented for the specific type construction your company performs.

1. Name of Project _____
   Owner _____
   Location of project _____
   Bid Date _____
   Date and times site is available for visit _____
2. Date of visit _____
3. Site Demographics and Access
   Nearest city _____ Distance to this city _____
   Highways (Describe road access, including any bridge or road restrictions, along with seasonal limitations. If haul roads are involved, include a full description on a separate page.):

   Railroad (Describe type and location of loading/unloading locations):

   Airport (Nearest. Include commercial services available): _____

   Water (Describe river or ocean access, harbors, channel depth, etc., including commercial carriers. Use a separate page if more room is required.)

4. Utilities:
   a. Power company (Name, address, telephone and capacities): _____

   b. Telephone company (Name, address, telephone and capacities): _____

   c. Gas company (Name, address, telephone and capacities): _____

   d. Water company (Name, address, telephone and capacities): _____

5. Staging, storage, housing and trailer facilities (Location, availability and cost): _____

6. Working season (Note typical weather patterns, seasons and conditions): _____

7. Local trade association chapters
   a. (List names, addresses and telephone):

b. (Obtain information on unusual working conditions, labor availability, union contacts, pay scales, benefits, etc.)

_____
_____
_____

8. Local subcontractors or suppliers:
   Refer to bid schedule and prepare a separate list of subcontractors and suppliers. Obtain local/regional phone book(s) to begin making contacts.
9. Visit owner's facilities:
   a. List names and titles; telephone numbers of persons contacted

   Name _____
   Title _____ Phone _____
   Name _____
   Title _____ Phone _____

   b. Prepare a list of items to discuss with owner during site visit. If possible, provide list to owner and request written response. Include items such as general job requirements, questions about the drawings and specifications, local geology, ground water situation, availability of special reports, photos, maps, boring logs and other data (obtain copies) both referenced and not referenced in the contract documents, local environmental regulations, safety requirements, easements,
   c. Request conducted tour of proposed work
   d. Examine all cores, test locations and logs of test holes available
10. Describe site: Take photographs. Compare and note both similarities and differences of observations at the site with those specified in the contract drawings and specifications.

_____
_____
_____
_____
_____
_____
_____

11. Initiate site preparation estimate (including location of facilities, foundations, drinking water, etc.):

_____
_____
_____

12. Determine any special conditions that will enhance or prevent usage of special equipment.

_____
_____
_____

Site Investigation Report - Page 2

Appendix 6

RULES OF CONTRACT INTERPRETATION
(Restatement of Contracts)

Primary Rules

a. The ordinary meaning of language throughout the country is given to words unless circumstances show that a different meaning is applicable.

b. Technical terms and words of art are given their technical meaning unless the context or a usage which is applicable indicates a different meaning.

c. A writing is interpreted as a whole and all writings forming part of the same transaction are interpreted together.

d. All circumstances accompanying the transaction may be taken into consideration, except that when the parties adopt a written statement of their agreement, oral statements of their intentions concerning the agreement made prior to, or contemporaneous with, the writing may not generally be considered.

e. If the conduct of the parties subsequent to a manifestation of intention indicates that all the parties placed a particular interpretation upon it, that meaning is adopted if a reasonable person could attach it to the manifestation.

Secondary Rules

a. An interpretation which gives a reasonable, lawful and effective meaning to all manifestations of intention is preferred to an interpretation which leaves a part of such manifestations unreasonable, unlawful or of no effect.

b. The principal apparent purpose of the parties is given great weight in determining the meaning to be given to manifestations of intention or to any part thereof.

c. Where there is an inconsistency between general provisions and specific provisions, the specific provisions ordinarily qualify the meaning of the general provisions.

d. Where words or other manifestations of intention bear more than one reasonable meaning an interpretation is preferred which operates more strongly against the party from whom they proceed, unless their use by him is prescribed by law.

e. Where written provisions are inconsistent with printed provisions, an interpretation is preferred which gives effect to the written provisions.

f. Where a public interest is affected an interpretation is preferred which favors the public.

Copyright 1932 by the American Law Institute. Reprinted with the permission of the American Law Institute.

Appendix 7

Sources of Overtime Statistics

1. "Hours of Work and Output," Bulletin No. 917, United States Department of Labor, Bureau of Labor Statistics, 1947.

2. "How Much Does Overtime Really Cost," Bulletin No. 18A, Management Methods Committee of the Mechanical Contractors Association of America.

3. James Howerton, "Do You Know the Hidden Loss of Overtime?" *Qualified Contractor.*

4. *"Overtime and Productivity in Electrical Construction," A Report on a Continuing Study* by the National Electrical Contractors' Association.

5. "Field Construction, Loss of Productivity Curves," United Engineers and Constructors, Inc.

6. "Scheduled Overtime" *Coming to Grips with Some Major Problems in the Construction Industry*, The Business Roundtable, 1975

Appendix 8 - Sample Daily Prodution Report

Contract 8A0033   WPL Trackwork Constructors, Inc.   **Ballast Track Production Report**

Job #204   Report No. _____   Date __/__/__   Working Day No. _____   Weather _____

Operation	Route	Track	Lane	From	To	Quantity	Comments
Excavation							
Embankment							
Sub-grade preparation							
Sub-ballast							
Top ballast (First lift)							
Distribute Ties & Track Material							
Lay Rail							
Gauge & Spike							
Ballast (Top off)							
Raise & Line							
Adjust & Anchor							
Other Work							

Additional Information:

Contract No. _____   Date: _____   Weather: Temperature Range
                                       AM:
                                       PM:

Contractor's Staff: Supervisory   Craftsman   Job Location   Work Performed

_____
_____
_____
_____
_____
_____
_____

Subcontractors on Job:
Contractor: Supervisory   Craftsman   Job Location   Work Performed

_____
_____
_____
_____
_____

Appendix 9 - Change Order Initiation Form - Instructions

CHANGE ORDER INITIATION (COI) FORM

Instruction Sheet

In order to establish a well organized and complete claims and change order program, it is necessary to have an accurate and detailed history of each change. To insure that such a history is set up and maintained, the attached form shall be put into effect each time a potential claim or change order is identified. This form should be made out by the project engineer or his staff.

Such a record will insure that all necessary background information is documented and that necessary actions are taken. Such a record will greatly aid in the composition of proposals and in support of negotiations. It will also assist the project engineer in ascertaining that supervisors and subcontractors are aware of changes and that proper actions on their part are being taken. Last, such a record will help in making and maintaining more accurate cost-revenue forecasts.

A work order number should be established each time a potential claim or change is identified, or a change order issued, whether or not there will be any costs. This will insure that every contract modification will have a cost account number to facilitate job accounting procedures.

The attached form should be attached to each extra work order folder. A separate notebook containing all extra work orders should be maintained for ready reference. Additionally, a copy should be given to the project manager for his information and concurrence upon initiation of each extra work order number.

APPENDIX 9—CHANGE ORDER INITIATION FORM

WPL Trackwork Constructors

CHANGE ORDER INITIATION (COI) FORM

Owner's Change Order No. _____ Date: ___/___/___
Contractor's Extra Work Order No. _____
Contract Modification No. _____ Date Modification Received: ___/___/___

Title of Change _____

Description: (What, where, which, why, who, how; refer to specification and contract drawing

Directed to do work_____ Date ___/___/___
                        (whom & how)
Notice given to owner_____ Date ___/___/___

Proposal Submitted_____ Date ___/___/___

Proposal Resubmitted_____ Date ___/___/___

Negotiations Begun_____ Date ___/___/___

Negotiations Complete_____ Date ___/___/___

Settlement Amount _____ Time Extension _____ (Calendar Days)

CHANGE ORDER INITIATION (COI) FORM - Page 2

Notification to Staff & Supervisors _____
_____
_____

Distribution of Drawings _____
_____
_____

Potential Effect on Subcontractors _____
_____
_____

Response from Subcontractors _____
_____
_____

Potential Time and Cost Impact on Job (Refer to CPM Schedule)_____
_____
_____

Estimated Cost (Ballpark figure) $ _____ Time _____ (Calendar Days)
Comments: _____
_____
_____
_____
_____
_____
_____
_____
_____
_____
_____
_____

Concurrence: Project Engineer_____ Date ___/___/_____
Project Manager_____ Date ___/___/_____

> Appendix 10 - Change Order Status Cover Letter

WPL TRACKWORK CONSTRUCTORS, INC.
P.O. Box 1617
Washington, D.C. 20002

April 8, 1997
Ref #: 433

Owner's Representative, Inc.
Main Rail Yard Project
400 New York Ave. N.E.
Washington, D.C. 20002

Attention: Mr. B.P. Pong
                Resident Engineer

RE: Contract Number 8C0033
             Change Order Status Report No. 24

Gentlemen:

Submitted herewith is our monthly *Change Order Status Report No. 24* outlining the current status of all unresolved claims and change orders. We call your attention to the following figures and request you take whatever action necessary to process these items into contract modifications.

1. Outstanding Change Orders _____ .

2. Outstanding Work Order Accounts _____ . These _____ represent, in addition to the outstanding change orders in (1) above, a combination of: directives by the Resident Engineer (RE), claims by WPL Trackwork, and changes initiated by us with the RE's concurrence. All but _____ of these have been reduced to writing yet there have been no change orders issued for any of them by the owner.

3. WPL Trackwork has submitted cost proposals for _____ outstanding change orders (totaling $_____) and _____ outstanding work orders (totaling $_____) for a total dollar value of $_____ .

4. The remaining claims and change orders represents a projected total dollar value of $_____ , of which $_____ has been expended by us to date. We expect to have proposals for these items to you shortly.

We look forward to your earliest attention to these open items. Thank you.

Very truly yours,

A. Romeo
Project Manager

Appendix 11 - Sample Schecule Cover Letter

WPL TRACKWORK CONSTRUCTORS, INC.
P.O. Box 1617
Washington, D.C. 20002

February 8, 1997
Ref #: 467

Owner's Representative, Inc.
Main Rail Yard Project
400 New York Ave. N.E.
Washington, D.C. 20002

Attention: Mr. B.P. Pong
                Resident Engineer

RE: Contract Number 8CO033 CPM Schedule

Gentlemen:

Enclosed please find our proposed CPM schedule submitted in accordance with Section 6 of the Special Conditions.

Except for contractual milestone dates required by the contract documents, the duration times shown on the attached schedules are not commitments. These times are estimates based on presently known or represented conditions and any changes therein may result in changes to the overall schedule. Please note those items of work which are dependent on the owner's actions or those of other contractors performing work for the owner. Reliance on those dates has been placed by us in preparing both our bid and the enclosed schedule. Delays to some or all of these relied upon dates may adversely affect the contract completion dates.

We will assume that this schedule is acceptable to you and in conformance with the contract requirements unless notified otherwise within the next 30 days. Thank you.

Very truly yours,

A. Romeo
Project Manager

Appendix 12 - AGC/ASA/ASC

Appendix 12 - AGC/ASA/ASC Standard Form Construction Contract

This Appendix contains selected clauses from the **AGC/ASA/ASC Standard Form Construction Contract** (1994 Edition) developed through the joint efforts of the Associated General Contractors of America, the American Subcontractors Association, Inc. and the Associated Specialty Contractors. The clauses included here are:

Article 6 - Performance of Work

    6.2   Schedule of Work

Article 7 - Subcontract Interpretation

    7.1   Inconsistencies and Omissions

Article 8 - Contractor's Obligations

    8.3   Timely Communications

Article 9 - Subcontractor's Obligations

    9.2   Subcontractor's Obligations for Site Visitation

Article 13 - Changes, Claims and Delays

- 13.1 Changes
- 13.2 Claims
- 13.3 Delay

Article 15 - Dispute Resolution

- 15.1 Initial Dispute Resolution
- 15.2 Agreement to Arbitrate
- 15.3 Stay of Proceedings and Consolidation
- 15.4 Notice of Demand
- 15.5 Award
- 15.6 Work Continuation and Payment
- 15.7 No Limitation of Rights and Remedies
- 15.8 Same Arbitrators

Article 16 - Recourse by Contractor

- 16.1 Failure of Performance
- 16.2 Bankruptcy
- 16.3 Stoppage of Work
- 16.4 Suspension by Owner for Convenience
- 16.5 Termination by Owner
- 16.6 Contingent Assignment of Subcontract
- 16.7 Suspension by Contractor for Convenience

Article 17 - Termination by Subcontra

Reprinted with permission of the Associated General Contractors of America (AGC), the American Subcontractors Association, Inc. (ASA), and the Associated Specialty Contractors (ASC).
Copies of current forms may be obtained from:

AGC Publications Department, 1957 E Street N.W., Washington, DC 20006,
(202) 393-2040; ASA Education Department, 1004 Duke Street, Alexandria, VA
22314-3588, (703) 684-3450; or ASC, 3 Bethesda Metro Center Suite 1100, Bethesda, MD
20814-5372, (301) 657-3110.

ARTICLE 6
PERFORMANCE OF WORK

6.2 SCHEDULE OF WORK In a timely fashion, the Subcontractor shall provide the Contractor with any scheduling information proposed by the Subcontractor for the Subcontract Work. In consultation with the Subcontractor, the Contractor shall prepare the schedule for performance of the Contract (hereinafter called the "Schedule of Work") and shall revise and update such schedule, as necessary, as the work progresses. Both the Contractor and the Subcontractor shall be bound by the Schedule of Work. The Schedule of Work and all subsequent changes and additional details thereto shall be submitted to the Subcontractor promptly and reasonably in advance of the required performance. The Contractor shall have the right to determine and, if necessary, change the time, order and priority in which the various portions of the work shall be performed and all other matters relative to the timely and orderly conduct of the Subcontract Work.

ARTICLE 7
SUBCONTRACT INTERPRETATION

7.1 INCONSISTENCIES AND OMISSIONS Should inconsistencies or omissions appear in the Subcontract Documents, it shall be the duty of the Subcontractor to so notify the Contractor in writing within three (3) working days of the Subcontractor's discovery thereof. Upon receipt of said notice, the Contractor shall instruct the Subcontractor as to the measures to be taken and the Subcontractor shall comply with the Contractor's instructions. If the Subcontractor performs work knowing it to be contrary to any applicable laws, statutes, ordinances, building codes, rules or regulations without notice to the Contractor and advance approval by appropriate authorities, including the Contractor, then the Subcontractor shall assume full responsibility for such work and shall bear all associated costs, charges, fees and expenses necessarily incurred to remedy the violation.

ARTICLE 8
CONTRACTOR'S OBLIGATIONS

8.3 TIMELY COMMUNICATIONS The Contractor, with reasonable promptness, shall transmit to the appropriate parties all submittals, transmittals, and written approvals relating to the Subcontract Work. Unless otherwise specified in the Subcontract Documents, communications by and with the Subcontractor's subcontractors, materialmen and suppliers shall be through the Subcontractor.

ARTICLE 9
SUBCONTRACTOR'S OBLIGATIONS

9.2 SUBCONTRACTOR'S OBLIGATIONS FOR SITE VISITATION The Subcontractor acknowledges that it has visited the Project site and visually inspected the general and local conditions which could affect the Subcontract Work. Any failure of the Subcontractor to reasonably ascertain from a visual inspection of the site, the general and local conditions which could affect the Subcontract Work, will not relieve the Subcontractor from its responsibility to properly complete the Subcontract Work without additional expense to the Contractor.

ARTICLE 13
CHANGES, CLAIMS AND DELAYS

13.1 CHANGES

13.1.1 SUBCONTRACT CHANGE A Subcontract Change is any change in the Subcontract Work within the general scope of the Subcontract including a change in the drawings, specifications or technical requirements of the Subcontract and/or a change in the Schedule of Work affecting the performance of the Subcontract.

13.1.2 CHANGE ORDER When the Contractor orders in writing, the Subcontractor, without nullifying this Subcontract, shall make any and all changes in the Subcontract Work which are within the general scope of this Subcontract. Adjustments in the Subcontract Price or Subcontract Time, if any, resulting from such changes shall be set forth in a Subcontract Change Order or a Subcontract Construction Change Directive pursuant to the Subcontract Documents. No such adjustments shall be made for any changes performed by the Subcontractor that have not been ordered by the Contractor. A Subcontract Change Order is a written instrument prepared by the Contractor and signed by the Subcontractor stating their agreement upon the change in the scope of the Subcontract Work, adjustment in the Subcontract Price and/or Subcontract Time. A Subcontract Construction Change Directive is a written instrument prepared by the Contractor directing a change in the Subcontract Work and stating a proposed adjustment, if any, in the Subcontract Price or Subcontract Time or both. A Subcontract Construction Change Directive shall be used in the absence of agreement on the terms of a Subcontract Change Order.

13.1.3 SUBCONTRACT CONSTRUCTION CHANGE DIRECTIVE The Subcontractor shall comply with all Subcontract Construction Change Directives received from the Contractor and perform the required changes in the Subcontract Work in a prompt and expeditious manner. The Subcontractor shall evaluate the proposed adjustment in the Subcontract Price or Subcontract Time, if any, as set forth in the Subcontract Construction Change Directive and respond, in writing, to the Contractor stating the Subcontractor's acceptance or rejection of the proposed adjustment and the reasons therefor.

APPENDIX 12—AGC/ASA/ASC   215

The Subcontractor may agree to the Subcontract Construction Change Directive and the terms of the proposed adjustment, if any, by signing the Subcontract Construction Change Directive and returning it forthwith to the Contractor. Subcontract Construction Change Directives agreed to by the Subcontractor are effective immediately and become Subcontract Change Orders in accordance with their terms.

13.1.4 ADJUSTMENT IN SUBCONTRACT PRICE If a Subcontract Change Order or Subcontract Construction Change Directive requires an adjustment in the Subcontract Price, the adjustment shall be established by one of the following methods:

(a) Mutual agreement on a lump sum with sufficient information to substantiate the amount;

(b) Unit prices already established in the Subcontract Documents or if not established by the Subcontract Documents then established by mutual agreement for the adjustment;

(c) A mutually determined cost plus a jointly acceptable markup for overhead and profit; or

(d) As may otherwise be required by the Subcontract Documents.

13.1.5 SUBSTANTIATION OF ADJUSTMENT If the Subcontractor does not advise the Contractor promptly of the Subcontractor's agreement or disagreement with a proposed adjustment, or if the Subcontractor disagrees with the proposed method of adjustment, the method and the adjustment shall be determined by the Contractor on the basis of reasonable Subcontractor expenditures and savings attributable to the change, including, in the case of an increase in the Subcontract Price, a reasonable markup for overhead and profit. The Subcontractor may contest the reasonableness of any adjustment determined by the Contractor. Pending final determination of costs to the Contractor and/or Owner, the Subcontractor may include in Subcontractor Applications for Payment to Contractor amounts not in dispute for work performed pursuant to properly authorized Subcontract Construction Change Directives.

13.1.6 INCIDENTAL CHANGES IN THE SUBCONTRACT WORK The Contractor may direct the Subcontractor to perform incidental changes in the Subcontract Work which do not involve adjustments in the Subcontract Price or Subcontract Time. Incidental changes shall be consistent with the scope and intent of the Subcontract Documents. The Contractor shall initiate an incidental change in the Subcontract Work by issuing a written order to the Subcontractor. Such written orders shall be carried out promptly and are binding on the parties.

13.2 CLAIMS

13.2.1 CLAIM A claim is a demand or assertion made in writing by the Contractor or the Subcontractor seeking an adjustment in the Subcontract Price and/or Subcontract Time, an adjustment or interpretation of the Subcontract terms, or other relief arising under or relating to this Subcontract, including the resolution of any matters in dispute between the Contractor and Subcontractor in connection with the Project.

13.2.2 CLAIMS RELATING TO OWNER The Subcontractor agrees to make all claims against the Contractor for which the Owner is or may be liable in the same manner and within the time limits provided in the Contract for like claims by the Contractor against the Owner and in sufficient time for the Contractor to make such claims against the Owner in accordance with the Contract. The Contractor agrees to permit the Subcontractor to prosecute a claim in the name of the Contractor for the use and benefit of the Subcontractor in the manner provided in the Contract for like claims by the Contractor against Owner. The Contractor shall make available to the Subcontractor, prior to the execution of this Subcontract Agreement, copies of all Contract provisions pertaining to claims by the Contractor against the Owner.

13.2.3 CLAIMS RELATING TO CONTRACTOR The Subcontractor shall give the Contractor written notice of all claims not included in Subparagraph 13.2.2 or 16.7.3 within seven (7) calendar days of the date when the Subcontractor knew of the facts giving rise to the event for which claim is made; otherwise, such claims shall not be valid.

13.2.4 UNRESOLVED CLAIMS, DISPUTES AND OTHER MATTERS All unresolved claims, disputes and other matters in question between the Contractor and the Subcontractor, not relating to claims included in Paragraph 12.5, shall be resolved in the manner provided in Article 15 herein.

13.3 DELAY

13.3.1 If the Subcontractor is delayed in the performance of the Subcontract Work for any reason beyond the Subcontractor's control, and without the Subcontractor's fault or negligence, including delays caused in whole or in part by the Contractor, Owner, Architect or any other persons, entities or events, or if the Subcontract Work is delayed by order of the Contractor, Owner or an authorized representative of either, or if the Subcontract Work is delayed for any reason or cause for which the Contractor, Owner or Architect concludes has resulted in excusable delay, then the Subcontractor is entitled to an extension of the Subcontract Time in which to complete its work. Said extension shall be set forth in a Subcontract Change Order for such time as the parties may agree is reasonable.

13.3.2 Claims relating to time shall be made in accordance with applicable provisions of the Subcontract Documents. This Article 13 does not preclude recovery of damages for delay by either party.

13.3.3 LIQUIDATED DAMAGES If the Contract provides for liquidated or other damages for delay beyond the completion date set forth in the Contract, and such damages are assessed by the Owner against the Contractor, then the

Contractor may assess such damages against the Subcontractor in proportion to its share of the responsibility for such delay and damage, but no more. The amount of such assessment against the Subcontractor, if any, shall not exceed the Subcontractor's proportionate share of the responsibility for such delay and damage and shall never exceed the amount assessed against the Contractor by the Owner.

Nothing in Subparagraph 13.3.3 shall limit the Contractor's right to claim all actual damages sustained by the Contractor as a result of Subcontractor delay.

ARTICLE 15
DISPUTE RESOLUTION

15.1 INITIAL DISPUTE RESOLUTION If a dispute arises out of or relates to this Subcontract, or the breach thereof, the parties may endeavor to settle the dispute first through direct discussions. If the dispute cannot be settled through direct discussions, the parties may endeavor to settle the dispute by mediation before recourse to arbitration. Unless the parties agree otherwise, the mediation shall be conducted in accordance with the Construction Mediation Rules of the American Arbitration Association. Mediation will be commenced within the time limits for arbitration stipulated in the Subcontract Documents. The time limits for any subsequent arbitration will be extended for the duration of the mediation process plus fourteen (14) calendar days, or as otherwise provided in the Subcontract Documents. Issues to be mediated are subject to the exceptions in Paragraph 15.3 for arbitration. The location of the mediation shall be the same as the location for arbitration identified in Paragraph 15.4.

15.2 AGREEMENT TO ARBITRATE All claims, disputes and other matters in question arising out of, or relating to, this Subcontract, or the breach thereof, except for claims which have been waived by the making or acceptance of final payment, shall be decided by arbitration in accordance with the Construction Industry Arbitration Rules of the American Arbitration Association then in effect unless the parties mutually agree otherwise. Notwithstanding other provisions in this Subcontract, or choice of law provisions to the contrary, this agreement to arbitrate shall be governed by the Federal Arbitration Act, 9 U.S.C. §1 *et seq.*, which shall not be superseded or supplemented by any other arbitration act, statute or regulation.

15.3 STAY OF PROCEEDINGS AND CONSOLIDATION In the event the Contractor and Subcontractor determine that all or a portion of any claim, dispute or other matter in question between them is the responsibility in whole or in part of a person or entity who is under no obligation to arbitrate said claim, dispute or matter with Contractor and Subcontractor in the same proceeding, then the Contractor and Subcontractor may agree in writing to delay or stay any arbitration between them pending the determination, in a separate proceeding, of the responsibility and liability of said person or entity for the claim, dispute or matter involved. The Subcontractor agrees that any arbitration instituted under this Article 15 may, at the Contractor's election, be consolidated with any other arbitration proceeding involving a common question of fact or law between the Contractor and any other subcontractors performing work in connection with the Contract.

In any dispute concerning the application of this paragraph 15.3, the question of arbitrability shall be decided by the appropriate court and not by arbitration.

15.4 NOTICE OF DEMAND Notice of the demand for arbitration shall be filed in writing with the other party to this Subcontract and with the American Arbitration Association. The demand for arbitration shall be made as required in the Subcontract Documents or within a reasonable time after written notice of the claim, dispute or other matter in question has been given, but in no event shall it be made when institution of legal or equitable proceedings based on such claim, dispute or other matter in question would be barred by the applicable statutes of limitation. The location of the arbitration proceedings shall be at the office of the American Arbitration Association nearest the Project site, unless the parties agree otherwise.

15.5 AWARD The award rendered by the arbitrators shall be final and judgment may be entered upon it in accordance with the Federal Arbitration Act in any court having jurisdiction.

15.6 WORK CONTINUATION AND PAYMENT The Subcontractor shall carry on the Subcontract Work and maintain the Schedule of Work pending final resolution of a claim including arbitration, unless the Subcontract has been terminated or the Subcontract Work suspended as provided for in the Subcontract, or the parties otherwise agree in writing to a partial or total suspension of the Subcontract Work. If the Subcontractor is continuing to perform in accordance with the Subcontract, the Contractor shall continue to make payments as required by the Subcontract.

15.7 NO LIMITATION OF RIGHTS AND REMEDIES Nothing in this Article shall limit any rights or remedies not expressly waived by the Subcontractor which the Subcontractor may have under lien laws or surety bonds.

15.8 SAME ARBITRATORS To the extent not prohibited by their contracts with others, the claims and disputes of the Owner, Contractor, Subcontractor and others involved with the Project, concerning a common question of fact or law, shall be heard by the same arbitrators in a single proceeding.

ARTICLE 16
RECOURSE BY CONTRACTOR

16.1 FAILURE OF PERFORMANCE

16.1.1 NOTICE TO CURE If the Subcontractor refuses or fails to supply enough properly skilled workers, proper materials, or maintain the Schedule of Work, or it fails to make prompt payment to its workers, subcontractors or suppliers,

APPENDIX 12—AGC/ASA/ASC   217

disregards laws, ordinances, rules, regulations or orders of any public authority having jurisdiction, or otherwise is guilty of a material breach of a provision of this Subcontract, the Subcontractor may be deemed in default of this Subcontract. If the Subcontractor fails within three (3) working days after written notification to commence and continue satisfactory correction of such default, with diligence and promptness, then the Contractor without prejudice to any other rights or remedies, shall have the right to any or all of the following remedies:

(a) Supply such number of workers and quantity of materials, equipment and other facilities as the Contractor deems necessary for the satisfactory correction of such default, which the Subcontractor has failed to complete or perform after the aforesaid notice, and charge the cost thereof to the Subcontractor, who shall be liable for the payment of same including reasonable overhead, profit and attorneys' fees;

(b) Contract with one or more additional contractors, to perform such part of the Subcontract Work as the Contractor shall determine will provide the most expeditious correction of the default and charge the cost thereof to the Subcontractor;

(c) Withhold payment of moneys due the Subcontractor in accordance with Subparagraph 14.1.3 of this Subcontract Agreement; and

(d) In the event of an emergency affecting the safety of persons or property, the Contractor may proceed to commence and continue satisfactory correction of such default, without first giving three (3) working days' written notice to the Subcontractor, but shall give prompt written notice of such action to the Subcontractor.

16.1.2 TERMINATION BY CONTRACTOR If the Subcontractor fails to commence and satisfactorily continue correction of a default within three (3) working days after written notification issued under Subparagraph 16.1.1, then the Contractor may, in lieu of or in addition to the remedies set forth in Subparagraph 16.1.1, issue a second written notification to the Subcontractor and the Subcontractor's surety, if any. Such notice shall state that if the Subcontractor fails to commence and continue correction of the default within seven (7) working days of the second written notification, the Subcontract maybe terminated and the Contractor may use any materials, implements, equipment, appliances or tools furnished by or belonging to the Subcontractor to complete the Subcontract Work. A written notice of termination shall be issued by the Contractor to the Subcontractor at the time the Subcontract is terminated.

The Contractor also may furnish those materials, equipment and/or employ such workers or subcontractors as the Contractor deems necessary to maintain the orderly progress of the work.

All costs incurred by the Contractor in performing the Subcontract Work, including reasonable overhead, profit and attorneys' fees, shall be deducted from any moneys due or to become due the Subcontractor under this Subcontract. The Subcontractor shall be liable for the payment of any amount by which such expense may exceed the unpaid balance of the Subcontract Price. If the unpaid balance of the Subcontract Price exceeds the expense of finishing the Subcontract Work, such excess shall be paid to the Subcontractor.

16.1.3 USE OF SUBCONTRACTOR'S EQUIPMENT If the Contractor performs work under this Article, or subcontracts such work to be so performed, the Contractor and/or the persons to whom work has been subcontracted shall have the right to take and use any materials, implements, equipment, appliances or tools furnished by, belonging or delivered to the Subcontractor and located at the Project for the purpose of completing any remaining Subcontract Work. Immediately upon completion of the Subcontract Work, any remaining materials, implements, equipment, appliances or tools not consumed or incorporated in performance of the Subcontract Work, and furnished by, belonging to, or delivered to the Project by or on behalf of the Subcontractor, shall be returned to the Subcontractor in substantially the same condition as when they were taken, normal wear and tear excepted.

16.2 BANKRUPTCY

16.2.1 TERMINATION ABSENT CURE If Subcontractor files a petition under the Bankruptcy Code, this Subcontract shall terminate if the Subcontractor or the Subcontractor's trustee rejects the Subcontract or, if there has been a default, the Subcontractor is unable to give adequate assurance that the Subcontractor will perform as required by this Subcontract or otherwise is unable to comply with the requirements for assuming this Subcontract under the applicable provisions of the Bankruptcy Code.

16.2.2 INTERIM REMEDIES If the Subcontractor is not performing in accordance with the Schedule of Work at the time a petition in bankruptcy is filed, or at any subsequent time, the Contractor, while awaiting the decision of the Subcontractor or its trustee to reject or to assume this Subcontract and provide adequate assurance of its ability to perform hereunder, may avail itself of such remedies under this Article as are reasonably necessary to maintain the Schedule of Work.

The Contractor may offset against any sums due or to become due the Subcontractor under this Subcontract all costs incurred in pursuing any of the remedies provided hereunder, including, but not limited to, reasonable overhead, profit and attorneys' fees.

The Subcontractor shall be liable for the payment of any amount by which such expense may exceed the unpaid balance of the Subcontract Price.

16.3 STOPPAGE OF WORK Should the Owner order the Contractor in writing to stop the performance of the Contract or any portion which affects the Subcontract Work due to any act or omission of the Contractor, or any other person or entity for whose acts or omissions the Contractor may be liable, then the Contractor shall so notify the Subcontractor in writing and upon written notification the Subcontractor shall stop that portion of the Subcontract Work as ordered by the Contractor.

16.4 SUSPENSION BY OWNER FOR CONVENIENCE

16.4.1 Should the Owner order the Contractor in writing to suspend, delay, or interrupt the performance of the Contract or any part which affects the Subcontract Work for such period of time as may be determined to be appropriate for the convenience of the Owner, and not due to any act or omission of the Contractor, or any other person or entity for whose acts or omissions the Contractor maybe liable, then the Contractor shall so notify the Subcontractor in writing and, upon written notification, the Subcontractor shall immediately suspend, delay or interrupt that portion of the Subcontract Work as ordered by Contractor.

16.4.2 In the event of an Owner suspension, delay or interruption for convenience as described in Subparagraph 16.4.1, the Contractor's liability to the Subcontractor for any damages caused by said order, including any claims for adjustments in the Subcontract Price and/or Subcontract Time, shall be extinguished by the Contractor pursuing said damages and claims against the Owner, on the Subcontractor's behalf, and by awarding and paying over to the Subcontractor any additional time and/or money obtained from the Owner on the Subcontractor's behalf, if accepted by the Subcontractor.

16.4.3 If the Subcontractor's damages and claims resulting from an Owner suspension, delay or interruption for convenience as described in Subparagraph 16.4.1, cannot be resolved through negotiation under the Contract, then the Contractor agrees to cooperate with the Subcontractor, at the Subcontractor's expense, in the prosecution of said damages and claims against the Owner through mediation, arbitration and/or litigation, and to permit the Subcontractor to prosecute said damages and claims, in the name of the Contractor and for the use and benefit of the Subcontractor. The Contractor's liability to the Subcontractor for any damages and claims caused by the Owner suspension, delay or interruption for convenience shall be fully extinguished by the Contractor awarding and paying over to the Subcontractor any additional time and/or money obtained from the Owner on the Subcontractor's behalf through the conclusion of the mediation, arbitration, and/or litigation process.

16.5 TERMINATION BY OWNER

16.5.1 Should the Owner terminate its Contract with the Contractor, or any part which includes the Subcontract Work, the Contractor shall so notify the Subcontractor in writing within three (3) calendar days of the termination and, upon written notification, this Subcontract shall be terminated and the Subcontractor shall immediately stop the Subcontract Work, follow the Contractor's instructions regarding shutdown and termination procedures, and mitigate all costs.

16.5.2 In the event that the Owner terminates its Contract with the Contractor for the convenience of the Owner, and not due to any act or omission of the Contractor, then the Contractor's liability to the Subcontractor for any damages incurred or claims resulting from the Owner termination, shall be extinguished by the Contractor pursuing said damages and claims against the Owner on the Subcontractor's behalf, and by paying over to the Subcontractor any additional money obtained by the Contractor from the Owner on the Subcontractor's behalf, if accepted by the Subcontractor.

16.5.3 In the event that the Owner terminates its Contract with the Contractor for the convenience of the Owner, and the Subcontractor's damages and claims cannot be resolved through negotiation in accordance with the Contract or otherwise, then the Contractor agrees to cooperate with the Subcontractor, at the Subcontractor's expense, in the prosecution of said damages and claims against the Owner through mediation, arbitration and/or litigation, and to permit the Subcontractor to prosecute said damages and claims, in the name of the Contractor and for the use and benefit of the Subcontractor. The Contractor's liability to the Subcontractor for any damages and claims caused by the Owner termination for convenience shall be fully extinguished by the Contractor awarding and paying over to the Subcontractor any additional time and/or money obtained from the Owner on the Subcontractor's behalf through the conclusion of the mediation, arbitration and/or litigation process.

16.6 CONTINGENT ASSIGNMENT OF SUBCONTRACT

The Contractor may assign this Subcontract to the Owner if required under the Contract. The assignment shall be effective only when the Owner: (a) has terminated the Contract for cause, and (b) has accepted the assignment by notifying the Subcontractor in writing. The contingent assignment is subject to the prior rights of a surety that may be obligated under the Contractor's bond, if any. Subcontractor hereby consents to such assignment and agrees to be bound to the Owner, as assignee, by the terms of this Subcontract.

16.7 SUSPENSION BY CONTRACTOR FOR CONVENIENCE

16.7.1 The Contractor may order the Subcontractor in writing to suspend, delay or interrupt all or any part of the Subcontract Work for such period of time as may be determined to be appropriate for the convenience of the Contractor. The short/incidental stoppage of the Subcontract Work, shall not be deemed a suspension, delay or interruption of work.

16.7.2 The Subcontractor shall notify the Contractor in writing within fourteen (14) calendar days after receipt of the Contractor's order of the effect of such order upon the Subcontract Work. The Subcontract Price and/or Subcontract Time shall be adjusted by Subcontract Change Order for any increase in the time and/or cost of performance of this Subcontract caused by such suspension, delay or interruption.

16.7.3 No claim under this Paragraph 16.7 shall be allowed for any costs incurred more than fourteen (14) calendar days prior to the Subcontractor's notice to the Contractor.

16.7.4 The Subcontract Price shall not be adjusted under this Paragraph 16.7 for any suspension, delay or interruption to the extent that the performance of the Subcontractor is, was or would have been so suspended, delayed or interrupted by the fault or neglect of the Subcontractor, by a cause for which the Subcontractor is responsible, or by a cause for which the Subcontractor is entitled only to a time extension under this Subcontract.

ARTICLE 17
TERMINATION BY SUBCONTRACTOR

If the Subcontract Work has been stopped for thirty (30) calendar days because the Subcontractor has not received progress payments as required under Article 14, or has been abandoned or suspended for an unreasonable period of time not due to the fault or neglect of the Subcontractor, then the Subcontractor may terminate this Subcontract upon giving the Contractor seven (7) calendar days' written notice. Upon such termination, Subcontractor shall be entitled to recover from the Contractor payment for all Subcontract Work satisfactorily performed but not yet paid for, including reasonable overhead, profit and damages. However, if the Owner has not paid the Contractor for the satisfactory performance of the Subcontract Work through no fault or neglect of the Contractor, and the Subcontractor terminates the Subcontract under this Article because it has not received corresponding progress payments as required under Article 14, then the Subcontractor shall be entitled to recover from the Contractor, within a reasonable period of time following termination, payment for all Subcontract Work satisfactorily performed but not yet paid for, including reasonable overhead and profit thereon. The Contractor's liability for any other damages claimed by the Subcontractor under such circumstances shall be extinguished by the Contractor pursuing said damages and claims against the Owner, on the Subcontractor's behalf, in the manner provided for in Subparagraphs 16.5.2 and 16.5.3 of this Subcontract Agreement.

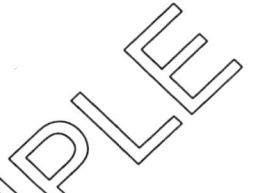

Appendix 13 - Flat Rate Pricing System

FLAT RATE PRICING SYSTEM FOR CHANGES
UNDER $15,000

The Contract is hereby changed as follows

To reduce time and effort for administrative processing of contract modifications, the following "flat rates" are agreed to for computing indirect costs for modification under above contract provisions when the agreed net additional or deductive direct costs do not exceed $15,000.00 and increase or decrease in contract time is within + or - five(5) calendar days if specifically agreed to between the Engineer and the Contractor. When the change in contract time is increased, the change in contract amount will include the indirect impact costs of extended performance and no further consideration of such costs arising from the specific modification and cited change orders will be given.

JOB OFFICE OVERHEAD will be the sum of:

a. 10% of direct labor costs [including fringe benefits, excluding FICA and FUTA, and State Unemployment Insurance (SUI)].

b. 10% of direct material costs.

c. 5% of direct equipment costs. Small tools, defined as equipment less than $1,000 in acquisition cost, are included and computed at 5% of direct base-labor wages.

d. 5% of subcontract costs.

HOME OFFICE GENERAL AND ADMINISTRATIVE COSTS will be 3% of the sum of direct costs and job office overhead costs.

BOND will be allowed at actual cost without mark-up.

In using the above, the following apply:

Payroll Tax (FICA, FUTA, and SUI) amounts are added immediately after all direct and indirect costs are totaled.

Subcontractor indirect costs will be computed in the same manner as above if the subcontractor elects to use the "flat rates." The Contractor agrees to furnish to the Engineer the names of subcontractors who do and do not so elect.

Indirect costs will not be duplicated in direct costs.

The above flat rates are for use *in lieu of the submission of a price breakdown justifying any increases or decreases* to any elements of the Contractor's indirect costs which are caused by a modification to the contract. Under this Agreement the "flat rates" are used for all modifications to this contract where negotiated direct costs do not exceed +$15,000. If a Subcontractor elects not to use the above "flat rates," his proposal for each contract modification shall include a price breakdown justifying the proposed increased indirect costs in accordance with the *General Provisions - Contract Modifications - Requirements for Proposals, Price Breakdown and Negotiation of Profit*.

APPENDIX 13—FLAT RATE PRICING SYSTEM

The Contractor can expect to have the finalized modification form completed within 60 days after the Record of Negotiations is signed by the RE and Project Manager. If he becomes dissatisfied with performance under this criterion, the Contractor may withdraw his election and return to the method (price breakdown) of substantiating increased indirect costs as well as direct costs.

Accepted:

_____ Owner:
      Name of contractor

By: _____   By: _____
    Signature   Date   Signature   Date

_____   _____
    Typed name   Typed name

Appendix 14 - Change Order Proposal Form

PROPOSAL SUMMARY SHEET

Extra Work Order No._____ Change Order No._____ Date_____

Description:

GENERAL CONTRACTOR'S COSTS
Outside Professional Fees   _____
Construction Equipment   _____
Materials   _____
Labor   _____
Fringe Benefits (____%)   _____
Workmen's Comp & Liab Ins (____%) _____
  SUBTOTAL   _____
Home Office Fee (____%)   _____
  SUBTOTAL   _____
Overhead (____%)   _____
  SUBTOTAL   _____
Profit (____%)   _____
FICA & FUTA (____%)   _____
  GENERAL CONTRACTOR'S COSTS   ════════════

SUBCONTRACTOR'S COSTS
Outside Professional Fees   _____
Construction Equipment   _____
Materials   _____
Labor   _____
Fringe Benefits (____%)   _____
Workmen's Comp & Liab Ins (____%) _____
  SUBTOTAL   _____
Overhead (____%)   _____
  SUBTOTAL   _____
Profit (____%)   _____
FICA & FUTA (____%)   _____
  SUBTOTAL - SUBCONTRACTOR'S COSTS   _____
General Contractor's Profit (____%) _____
  TOTAL SUBCONTRACTOR'S COSTS   ════════════

TOTAL COSTS   ════════════

*If overhead costs are in detail, attach supporting computations

Appendix 15

PRICING CHECKLIST

DIRECT COSTS
- Labor
- Equipment
- Plant
- Material: Permanent and Job Supplies; Freight & Storage
- Small Tools
- Subcontractors
- Testing

INDIRECT COSTS
- Management
- Supervision
- Engineering
- Overhead
- Permits
- Depreciation
- Taxes
- Interest
- Insurance
- Bond
- Home Office Fee
- Inspection

IMPACT COSTS
- Time
- Resequencing
- Rescheduling
- Disruption
- Delays
- Acceleration
- Overtime
- Additional Mobilization
- Additional Equipment
- Changed Labor Force
- Increased Workload
- Worker Attitude
- Maintenance and Storage
- Redesign
- Idle Equipment
- Idle Labor
- Escalation

CLAIM PREPARATION COSTS

PROFIT

Appendix 16 - Construction Operations Learning Centers

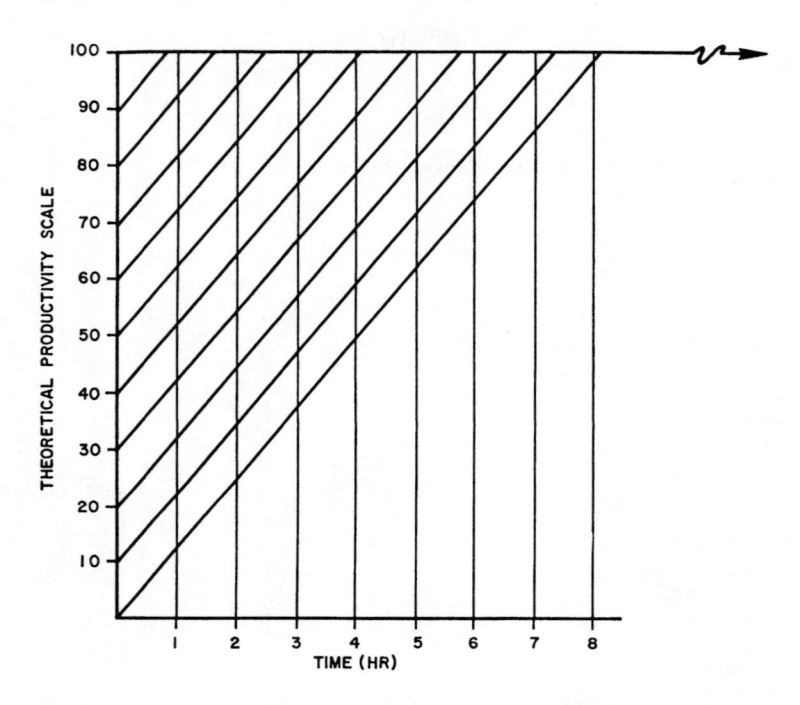

*100 REPRESENTS THE PRODUCTIVITY RATE REQUIRED TO MAINTAIN SCHEDULED PROGRESS

(BASED ON CONSTRUCTION OPERATIONS
ORIENTATION / LEARNING CHART)

PRODUCTIVITY STARTING POINT	DURATION (HR)	AVERAGE LOSS (HR)
100	0	0
90	0.8	04
80	1.6	0.8
70	2.4	1.2
60	3.2	1.6
50	4.0	2.0
40	4.8	2.4
30	5.6	2.8
20	6.4	3.2
10	7.2	3.6
0	8.0	4.0

APPENDIX 16—CONSTRUCTION OPERATIONS LEARNING CHARTS

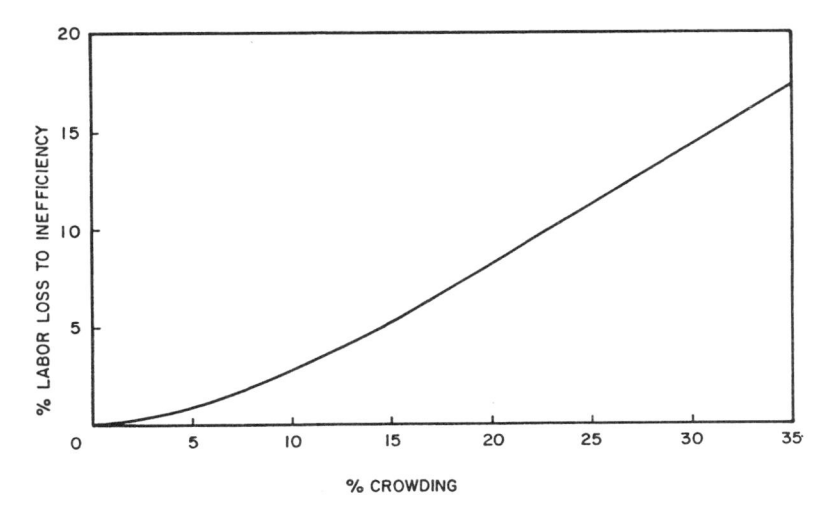

Effect of crowding on labor efficiency.

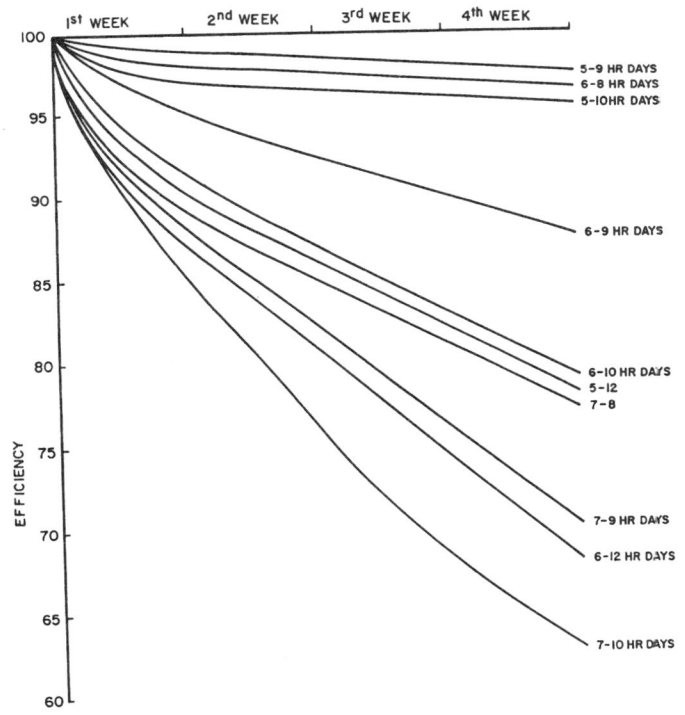

Effect of work schedule on efficiency.

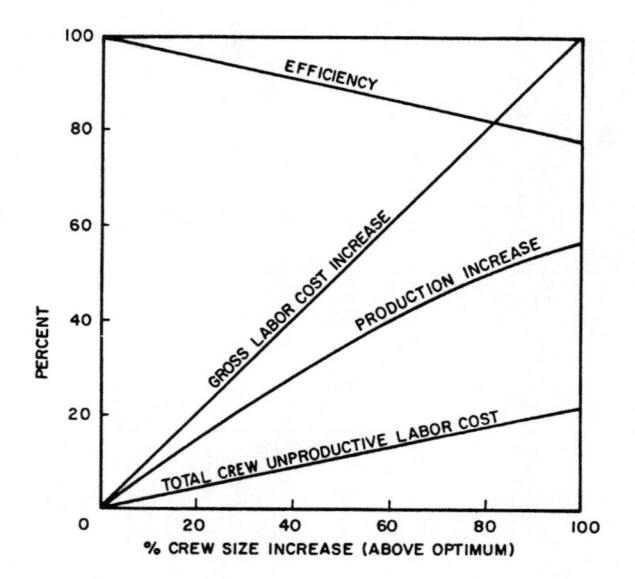

Composite effects of crew overloading

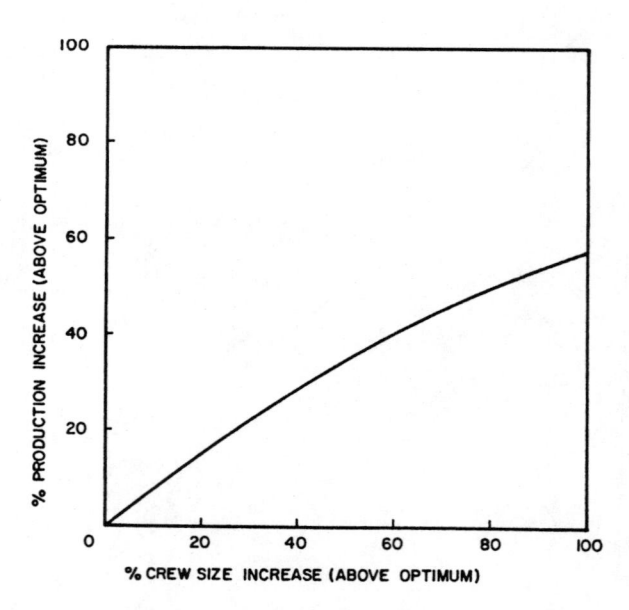

Unproductive labor at crew overloading.

APPENDIX 16—CONSTRUCTION OPERATIONS LEARNING CHARTS

% PRODUCTIVITY

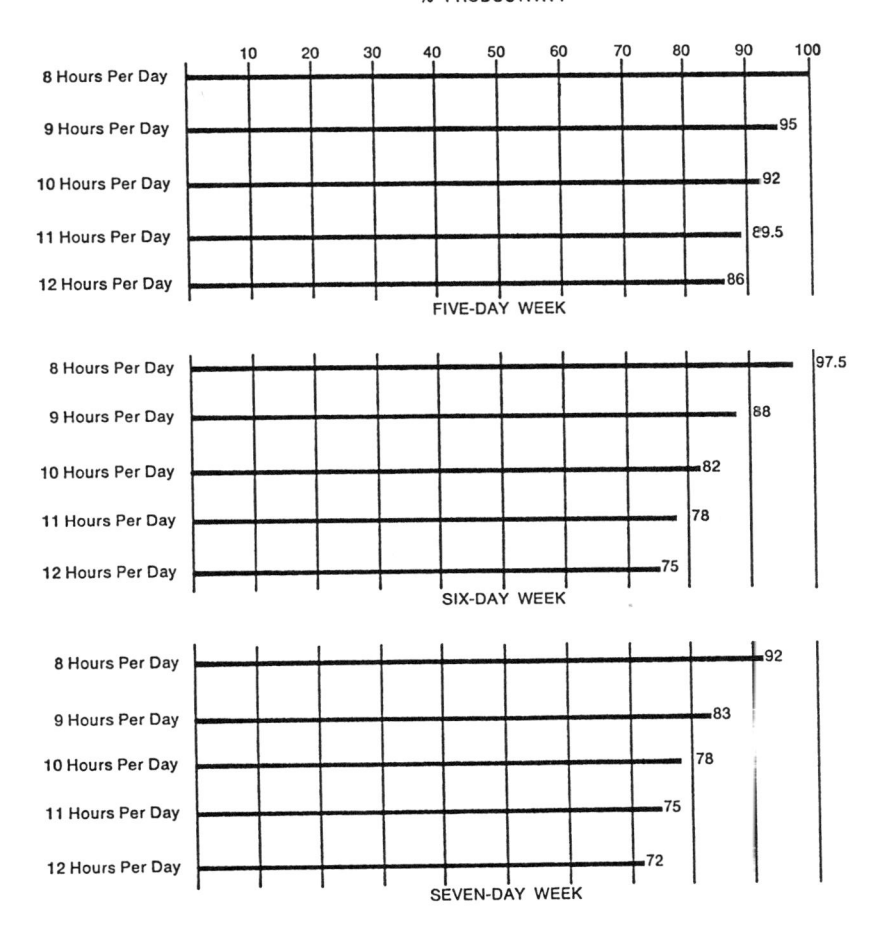

FIVE-DAY WEEK
- 8 Hours Per Day: 100
- 9 Hours Per Day: 95
- 10 Hours Per Day: 92
- 11 Hours Per Day: 89.5
- 12 Hours Per Day: 86

SIX-DAY WEEK
- 8 Hours Per Day: 97.5
- 9 Hours Per Day: 88
- 10 Hours Per Day: 82
- 11 Hours Per Day: 78
- 12 Hours Per Day: 75

SEVEN-DAY WEEK
- 8 Hours Per Day: 92
- 9 Hours Per Day: 83
- 10 Hours Per Day: 78
- 11 Hours Per Day: 75
- 12 Hours Per Day: 72

Figure 1. Productivity as a Function of Work Days Per Week and Work Hours Per Day
(BLS #917 Findings)

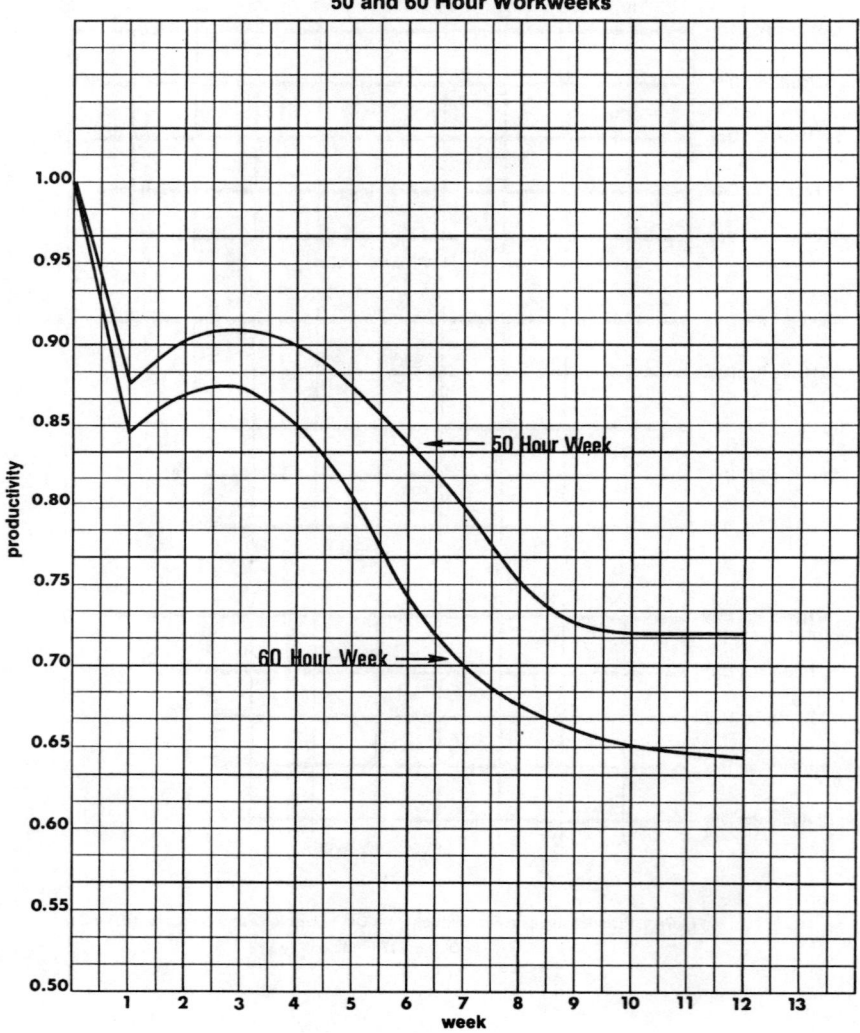

**Figure 2. Cumulative Effect of Overtime on Productivity
50 and 60 Hour Workweeks**

Appendix 17 - Federal Acquisition Regulation

PART 31 – CONTRACT COST PRINCIPLES AND PROCEDURES

This appendix contains sections 31.000 to 31.204 of the Federal Acquisition Regulation Section 31 - *Contract Cost Principles and Procedures*. Intended mainly as guidelines for types of costs allowed on cost reimbursable government contracts, these principles may be used to determine direct and/or indirect costs for contract modifications on fixed price contracts. Section 31.205, due to its length and to its involvement more with cost-reimbursesable "supply" contracts, is not reproduced here. The complete section can be downloaded from the internet at /www.gsa.gov.far/.

FAR Clause No.	Description
31.000	Scope of part.
31.001	Definitions
31.105	Construction and architect-engineer contracts
31.201	General
31.201-1	Composition of total cost
31.201-2	Determining allocability
31.201-3	Determining reasonableness
31.201-4	Determining allocability
31.201-5	Credits
31.201-6	Accounting for unallowable costs
31.201-7	Construction and architect-engineer contracts
31.202	Direct costs
31.203	Indirect costs
31.204	Application of principles and procedures
31.205	Selected costs
31.205-1	Public relations and advertising costs
31.205-2	Automatic data processing equipment leasing costs
31.205-3	Bad debts
31.205-4	Bonding costs
31.205-5	Civil defense costs
31.205-6	Compensation for personal services
31.205-7	Contingencies
31.205-8	Contributions or donations
31.205-9	[Reserved]
31.205-10	Cost of money
31.205-11	Depreciation
31.205-12	Economic planning costs
31.205-13	Employee morale, health, welfare, food service, and dormitory costs and credits
31.205-14	Entertainment costs
31.205-15	Fines, penalties, and mischarging costs
31.205-16	Gains and losses on disposition of depreciable property or capital assets
31.205-17	Idle facilities and idle capacity costs
31.205-18	Independent research and development and bid and proposal costs

FAR Clause No.	Description
31.205-19	Insurance and indemnification
31.205-20	Interest and other financial costs
31.205-21	Labor relations costs
31.205-22	Legislative lobbying costs
31.205-23	Losses on other contracts
31.205-24	Maintenance and repair costs
31.205-25	Manufacturing and production engineering costs
31.205-26	Material costs
31.205-27	Organization costs
31.205-28	Other business expenses
31.205-29	Plant protection costs
31.205-30	Patent costs
31.205-31	Plant reconversion costs
31.205-32	Precontract costs
31.205-33	Professional and consultant service costs
31.205-34	Recruitment costs
31.205-35	Relocation costs
31.205-36	Rental costs
31.205-37	Royalties and other costs for use of patents
31.205-38	Selling costs
31.205-39	Service and warranty costs
31.205-40	Special tooling and special test equipment costs
31.205-41	Taxes
31.205-42	Termination costs
31.205-43	Trade, business, technical, and professional activity costs
31.205-44	Training and education costs
31.205-45	Transportation costs
31.205-46	Travel costs
31.205-47	Costs related to legal and other proceedings
31.205-48	Deferred research and development costs
31.205-49	Goodwill
31.205-50	Executive lobbying costs
31.205-51	Costs of alcoholic beverages
31.205-52	Asset valuations resulting from business combinations

31.000 Scope of part.

This part contains cost principles and procedures for (a) the pricing of contracts, subcontracts, and modifications to contracts and subcontracts whenever cost analysis is performed (see 15.805-3) and (b) the determination, negotiation, or allowance of costs when required by a contract clause.

31.001 Definitions.

"Accrued benefit cost method" means an actuarial cost method under which units of benefit are assigned to each cost accounting period and are valued as they accrue; i.e., based on the services performed by each employee in the period involved. The measure of normal cost under this method for each cost accounting period is the present value of the units of benefit deemed to be credited to employees for service in that period. The measure of the actuarial liability at a plan's inception date is the present value of the units of benefit credited to employees for service prior to that date. (This method is also known as the unit credit cost method.)

"Accumulating costs" means collecting cost data in an organized manner, such as through a system of accounts.

"Actual cash value" means the cost of replacing damaged property with other property of like kind and quality in the physical condition of the property immediately before the damage.

"Actual costs," as used in this part (other than Subpart 31.6), means amounts determined on the basis of costs incurred, as distinguished from forecasted costs. Actual costs include standard costs properly adjusted for applicable variances.

"Actuarial assumption" means a prediction of future conditions affecting pension costs; e.g., mortality rate, employee turnover, compensation levels, pension fund earnings, and changes in values of pension funds assets.

"Actuarial cost method" means a technique which uses actuarial assumptions to measure the present value of future pension benefits and pension fund administrative expenses, and which assigns the cost of such benefits and expenses to cost accounting periods.

"Actuarial gain and loss" means the effect on pension cost resulting from differences between actuarial assumptions and actual experience.

"Actuarial liability" means pension cost attributable, under the actuarial cost method in use, to years before the date of a particular actuarial valuation. As of such date, the actuarial liability represents the excess of the present value of the future benefits and administrative expenses over the present value of future contributions, for the normal cost for all plan participants and beneficiaries. The excess of the actuarial liability over the value of the assets of a pension plan is the unfunded actuarial liability.

"Actuarial valuation" means the determination, as of a specified date, of the normal cost, actuarial liability, value of the assets of a pension fund, and other relevant values for the pension plan.

"Allocate" means to assign an item of cost, or a group of items of cost, to one or more cost objectives. This term includes both direct assignment of cost and the reassignment of a share from an indirect cost pool.

"Business unit" means any segment of an organization, or an entire business organization which is not divided into segments.

"Compensated personal absence" means any absence from work for reasons such as illness, vacation, holidays, jury duty, military training, or personal activities for which an employer pays compensation directly to an employee in accordance with a plan or custom of the employer.

"Cost input" means the cost, except general and administrative (G&A) expenses, which for contract costing purposes is allocable to the production of goods and services during a cost accounting period.

"Cost objective," as used in this part (other than Subpart 31.6), means a function, organizational subdivision, contract, or other work unit for which cost data are desired and for which provision is made to accumulate and measure the cost of processes, products, jobs, capitalized projects, etc.

"Cost of capital committed to facilities" means an imputed cost determined by applying a cost of money rate to facilities capital.

"Deferred compensation" means an award made by an employer to compensate an employee in a future cost accounting period or periods for services rendered in one or more cost accounting periods before the date of the receipt of compensation by the employee. This definition shall not include the amount of year end accruals for salaries, wages, or bonuses that are to be paid within a reasonable period of time after the end of a cost accounting period.

"Defined-benefit pension plan" means a pension plan in which the benefits to be paid, or the basis for determining such benefits, are established in advance and the contributions are intended to provide the stated benefits.

"Defined-contribution pension plan" means a pension plan in which the contributions to be made are established in advance and the benefits are determined thereby.

"Directly associated cost" means any cost which is generated solely as a result of the incurrence of another cost, and which would not have been incurred had the other cost not been incurred.

"Estimating costs" means the process of forecasting a future result in terms of cost, based upon information available at the time.

"Expressly unallowable cost" means a particular item or type of cost which, under the express provisions of an applicable law, regulation, or contract, is specifically named and stated to be unallowable.

APPENDIX 17—CONTRACT COST PRINCIPLES AND PROCEDURES 231

"Facilities capital" means the net book value of tangible capital assets and of those intangible capital assets that are subject to amortization.

"Final cost objective," as used in this part (other than Subparts 31.3 and 31.6), means a cost objective that has allocated to it both direct and indirect costs and, in the contractor's accumulation system, is one of the final accumulation points.

"Fiscal year," as used in this part, means the accounting period for which annual financial statements are regularly prepared, generally a period of 12 months, 52 weeks, or 53 weeks.

"Funded pension cost," as used in this part, means the portion of pension costs for a current or prior cost accounting period that has been paid to a funding agency.

"General and administrative (G&A) expense" means any management, financial, and other expense which is incurred by or allocated to a business unit and which is for the general management and administration of the business unit as a whole. G&A expense does not include those management expenses whose beneficial or causal relationship to cost objectives can be more directly measured by a base other than a cost input base representing the total activity of a business unit during a cost accounting period.

"Home office" means an office responsible for directing or managing two or more, but not necessarily all, segments of an organization. It typically establishes policy for, and provides guidance to, the segments in their operations. It usually performs management, supervisory, or administrative functions, and may also perform service functions in support of the operations of the various segments. An organization which has intermediate levels, such as groups, may have several home offices which report to a common home office. An intermediate organization may be both a segment and a home office.

"Immediate-gain actuarial cost method" means any of the several actuarial cost methods under which actuarial gains and losses are included as part of the unfunded actuarial liability of the pension plan, rather than as part of the normal cost of the plan.

"Independent research and development (IR&D) cost" means the cost of effort which is neither sponsored by a grant, nor required in performing a contract, and which falls within any of the following four areas: (a) basic research, (b) applied research, (c) development, and (d) systems and other concept formulation studies.

"Indirect cost pools," as used in this part (other than Subparts 31.3 and 31.6), means groupings of incurred costs identified with two or more cost objectives but not identified specifically with any final cost objective.

"Insurance administration expenses" means the contractor's costs of administering an insurance program; e.g., the costs of operating an insurance or risk-management department, processing claims, actuarial fees, and service fees paid to insurance companies, trustees, or technical consultants.

"Intangible capital asset" means an asset that has no physical substance, has more than minimal value, and is expected to be held by an enterprise for continued use or possession beyond the current accounting period for the benefits it yields.

"Job," as used in this part, means a homogeneous cluster of work tasks, the completion of which serves an enduring purpose for the organization. Taken as a whole, the collection of tasks, duties, and responsibilities constitutes the assignment for one or more individuals whose work is of the same nature and is performed at the same skill/responsibility level--as opposed to a position, which is a collection of tasks assigned to a specific individual. Within a job, there may be pay categories which are dependent on the degree of supervision required by the employee while performing assigned tasks which are performed by all persons with the same job.

"Job class of employees," as used in this part, means employees performing in positions within the same job.

"Labor cost at standard" means a preestablished measure of the labor element of cost, computed by multiplying labor-rate standard by labor-time standard.

"Labor market," as used in this part, means a place where individuals exchange their labor for compensation. Labor markets are identified and defined by a combination of the following factors: (1) geography, (2) education and/or technical background required, (3) experience required by the job, (4) licensing or certification requirements, (5) occupational membership, and (6) industry.

"Labor-rate standard" means a preestablished measure, expressed in monetary terms, of the price of labor.

"Labor-time standard" means a preestablished measure, expressed in temporal terms, of the quantity of labor.

"Material cost at standard" means a preestablished measure of the material elements of cost, computed by multiplying material-price standard by material-quantity standard.

"Material-price standard" means a preestablished measure, expressed in monetary terms, of the price of material.

"Material-quantity standard" means a preestablished measure, expressed in physical terms, of the quantity of material.

"Moving average cost" means an inventory costing method under which an average unit cost is computed after each acquisition by adding the cost of the newly acquired units to the cost of the units of inventory on hand and dividing this figure by the new total number of units.

"Normal cost" means the annual cost attributable, under the actuarial cost method in use, to years subsequent to a particular valuation date.

"Original complement of low cost equipment" means a group of items acquired for the initial outfitting of a tangible capital asset or an operational unit, or a new addition to either. The items in the group individually cost less than the minimum amount established by the contractor for capitalization for the classes of assets acquired but in the aggregate they represent a material investment. The group, as a complement, is expected to be held for continued service beyond the current period. Initial outfitting of the unit is completed when the unit is ready and available for normal operations.

"Pay-as-you-go cost method" means a method of recognizing pension cost only when benefits are paid to retired employees or their beneficiaries.

"Pension plan" means a deferred compensation plan established and maintained by one or more employers to provide systematically for the payment of benefits to plan participants after their retirements; provided, that the benefits are paid for life or are payable for life at the option of the employees. Additional benefits such as permanent and total disability and death payments, and survivorship payments to beneficiaries of deceased employees may be an integral part of a pension plan.

"Pension plan participant" means any employee or former employee of an employer or any member or former member of an employee organization, who is or may become eligible to receive a benefit from a pension plan which covers employees of such employer or members of such organization who have satisfied the plan's participation requirements, or whose beneficiaries are receiving or may be eligible to receive any such benefit. A participant whose employment status with the employer has not been terminated is an active participant of the employer's pension plan.

"Pricing" means the process of establishing a reasonable amount or amounts to be paid for supplies or services.

"Profit center," as used in this part (other than Subparts 31.3 and 31.6), means the smallest organizationally independent segment of a company charged by management with profit and loss responsibilities.

"Projected average loss" means the estimated long-term average loss per period for periods of comparable exposure to risk of loss.

"Projected benefit cost method" means any of the several actuarial cost methods which distribute the estimated total cost of all the employees' prospective benefits over a period of years, usually their working careers.

"Proposal" means any offer or other submission used as a basis for pricing a contract, contract modification, or termination settlement or for securing payments thereunder.

"Residual value" means the proceeds, less removal and disposal costs, if any, realized upon disposition of a tangible capital asset. It usually is measured by the net proceeds from the sale or other disposition of the asset, or its fair value if the asset is traded in on another asset. The estimated residual value is a current forecast of the residual value.

"Segment" means one of two or more divisions, product departments, plants, or other subdivisions of an organization reporting directly to a home office, usually identified with responsibility for profit and/or producing a product or service. The term includes Government-owned contractor-operated (GOCO) facilities, and joint ventures and subsidiaries (domestic and foreign) in which the organization has a majority ownership. The term also includes those joint ventures and subsidiaries (domestic and foreign) in which the organization has less than a majority of ownership, but over which it exercises control.

"Self-insurance" means the assumption or retention of the risk of loss by the contractor, whether voluntarily or involuntarily. Self-insurance includes the deductible portion of purchased insurance.

"Self-insurance charge" means a cost which represents the projected average loss under a self-insurance plan.

"Service life" means the period of usefulness of a tangible capital asset (or group of assets) to its current owner. The period may be expressed in units of time or output. The estimated service life of a tangible capital asset (or group of assets) is a current forecast of its service life and is the period over which depreciation cost is to be assigned.

"Spread-gain actuarial cost method" means any of the several projected benefit actuarial cost methods under which actuarial gains and losses are included as part of the current and future normal costs of the pension plan.

"Standard cost" means any cost computed with the use of preestablished measures.

"Tangible capital asset" means an asset that has physical substance, more than minimal value, and is expected to be held by an enterprise for continued use or possession beyond the current accounting period for the services it yields.

"Termination gain or loss" means an actuarial gain or loss resulting from the difference between the assumed and actual rates at which pension plan participants separate from employment for reasons other than retirement, disability, or death.

"Unallowable cost" means any cost which, under the provisions of any pertinent law, regulation, or contract, cannot be included in prices, cost-reimbursements, or settlements under a Government contract to which it is allocable.

"Unfunded pension plan," as used in this part, means a defined benefit pension plan for which no funding agency is established for the accumulation of contributions.

"Variance" means the difference between a preestablished measure and an actual measure.

"Weighted average cost" means an inventory costing method under which an average unit cost is computed periodically by dividing the sum of the cost of

APPENDIX 17—CONTRACT COST PRINCIPLES AND PROCEDURES   233

beginning inventory plus the cost of acquisitions by the total number of units included in these two categories.

31.002 Availability of accounting guide.

Contractors needing assistance in developing or improving their accounting systems and procedures may request a copy of the guide entitled "Guidance for New Contractors" (DCAAP 7641.90). The guide is available from: Headquarters, Defense Contract Audit Agency, Operating Administrative Office, 8725 John J. Kingman Road, Suite 2135, Fort Belvoir, Virginia 22060-6219; Telephone No. (703) 767-1066; Telefax No. (703) 767-1061.

SUBPART 31.1–APPLICABILITY

31.100 Scope of subpart.

This subpart describes the applicability of the cost principles and procedures in succeeding subparts of this part to various types of contracts and subcontracts. It also describes the need for advance agreements.

31.101 Objectives.

In recognition of differing organizational characteristics, the cost principles and procedures in the succeeding subparts are grouped basically by organizational type; e.g., commercial concerns and educational institutions. The overall objective is to provide that, to the extent practicable, all organizations of similar types doing similar work will follow the same cost principles and procedures. To achieve this uniformity, individual deviations concerning cost principles require advance approval of the agency head or designee. Class deviations for the civilian agencies require advance approval of the Civilian Agency Acquisition Council. Class deviations for the National Aeronautics and Space Administration require advance approval of the Associate Administrator for Procurement. Class deviations for the Department of Defense require advance approval of the Director of Defense Procurement, Office of the Under Secretary of Defense for Acquisition and Technology.

31.105 Construction and architect-engineer contracts.

(a) This category includes all contracts and contract modifications negotiated on the basis of cost with organizations other than educational institutions (see 31.104), State and local governments (see 31.107), and nonprofit organizations except those exempted under OMB Circular A-122 (see 31.108) for construction management or construction, alteration or repair of buildings, bridges, roads, or other kinds of real property. It also includes architect-engineer contracts related to construction projects. It does not include contracts for vessels, aircraft, or other kinds of personal property.

(b) Except as otherwise provided in (d) below, the cost principles and procedures in Subpart 31.2 shall be used in the pricing of contracts and contract modifications in this category if cost analysis is performed as required by 15.805-3.

(c) In addition, the contracting officer shall incorporate the cost principles and procedures in Subpart 31.2 (as modified by (d) below) by reference in contracts in this category as the basis for--

(1) Determining reimbursable costs under cost-reimbursement contracts, including cost-reimbursement subcontracts thereunder;

(2) Negotiating indirect cost rates;

(3) Proposing, negotiating, or determining costs under terminated contracts;

(4) Price revision of fixed-price incentive contracts; and

(5) Pricing changes and other contract modifications.

(d) Except as otherwise provided in this paragraph (d), the allowability of costs for construction and architect-engineer contracts shall be determined in accordance with Subpart 31.2.

(1) Because of widely varying factors such as the nature, size, duration, and location of the construction project, advance agreements as set forth in 31.109, for such items as home office overhead, partners' compensation, employment of consultants, and equipment usage costs, are particularly important in construction and architect-engineer contracts. When appropriate, they serve to express the parties' understanding and avoid possible subsequent disputes or disallowances.

(2) "Construction equipment," as used in this section, means equipment (including marine equipment) in sound workable condition, either owned or controlled by the contractor or the subcontractor at any tier, or obtained from a commercial rental source, and furnished for use under Government contracts.

(i) Allowable ownership and operating costs shall be determined as follows:

(A) Actual cost data shall be used when such data can be determined for both ownership and operations costs for each piece of equipment, or groups of similar serial or series equipment, from the contractor's accounting records. When such costs cannot be so determined, the contracting agency may specify the use of a particular schedule of predetermined rates or any part thereof to determine ownership and operating costs of construction equipment (see subdivisions (d)(2)(i)(B) and (C) of this section). However, costs otherwise unallowable under this part shall not become allowable through the use of any schedule (see 31.109(c)). For example, schedules need to be adjusted for Government contract costing purposes if they are based on replacement cost, include unallowable interest costs, or use improper cost of money rates or computations. Contracting officers should review the computations and factors included within the specified schedule and ensure that unallowable or unacceptably computed factors are not allowed in cost submissions.

(B) Predetermined schedules of construction equipment use rates (e.g., the Construction Equipment Ownership and Operating Expense Schedule, published by the U.S. Army Corps of Engineers, industry sponsored construction equipment cost guides, or commercially published schedules of construction equipment use cost) provide average ownership and operating rates for construction equipment. The allowance for operating costs may include costs for such items as fuel, filters, oil, and grease; servicing, repairs, and maintenance; and tire wear and repair. Costs of labor, mobilization, demobilization, overhead, and profit are generally not reflected in schedules, and separate consideration may be necessary.

(C) When a schedule of predetermined use rates for construction equipment is used to determine direct costs, all costs of equipment that are included in the cost allowances provided by the schedule shall be identified and eliminated from the contractor's other direct and indirect costs charged to the contract. If the contractor's accounting system provides for site or home office overhead allocations, all costs which are included in the equipment allowances may need to be included in any cost input base before computing the contractor's overhead rate. In periods of suspension of work pursuant to a contract clause, the allowance for equipment ownership shall not exceed an amount for standby cost as determined by the schedule or contract provision.

(ii) Reasonable costs of renting construction equipment are allowable (but see paragraph (C) of this subsection).

(A) Costs, such as maintenance and minor or running repairs incident to operating such rented equipment, that are not included in the rental rate are allowable.

(B) Costs incident to major repair and overhaul of rental equipment are unallowable.

(C) The allowability of charges for construction equipment rented from any division, subsidiary, or organization under common control, will be determined in accordance with 31.205-36(b)(3).

(3) Costs incurred at the job site incident to performing the work, such as the cost of superintendence, timekeeping and clerical work, engineering, utility costs, supplies, material handling, restoration and cleanup, etc., are allowable as direct or indirect costs, provided the accounting practice used is in accordance with the contractor's established and consistently followed cost accounting practices for all work.

(4) Rental and any other costs, less any applicable credits incurred in acquiring the temporary use of land, structures, and facilities are allowable. Costs, less any applicable credits, incurred in constructing or fabricating structures and facilities of a temporary nature are allowable.

SUBPART 31.2—CONTRACTS WITH COMMERCIAL ORGANIZATIONS

31.201 General.

31.201-1 Composition of total cost.

(a) The total cost of a contract is the sum of the direct and indirect costs allocable to the contract, incurred or to be incurred, less any allocable credits, plus any allocable cost of money pursuant to 31.205-10. In ascertaining what constitutes a cost, any generally accepted method of determining or estimating costs that is equitable and is consistently applied may be used, including standard costs properly adjusted for applicable variances. See 31.201-2(b) and (c) for Cost Accounting Standards (CAS) requirements.

(b) While the total cost of a contract includes all costs properly allocable to the contract, the allowable costs to the Government are limited to those allocable costs which are allowable pursuant to Part 31 and applicable agency supplements.

31.201-2 Determining allowability.

(a) The factors to be considered in determining whether a cost is allowable include the following:
 (1) Reasonableness.
 (2) Allocability.
 (3) Standards promulgated by the CAS Board, if applicable; otherwise, generally accepted accounting principles and practices appropriate to the particular circumstances.
 (4) Terms of the contract.
 (5) Any limitations set forth in this subpart.

(b) Certain cost principles in this subpart incorporate the measurement, assignment, and allocability rules of selected CAS and limit the allowability of costs to the amounts determined using the criteria in those selected standards. Only those CAS or portions of standards specifically made applicable by the cost principles in this subpart are mandatory unless the contract is CAS-covered (see Part 30). Business units that are not otherwise subject to these standards under a CAS clause are subject to the selected standards only for the purpose of determining allowability of costs on Government contracts. Including the selected standards in the cost principles does not subject the business unit to any other CAS rules and regulations. The applicability of the CAS rules and regulations is determined by the CAS clause, if any, in the contract and the requirements of the standards themselves.

(c) When contractor accounting practices are inconsistent with this Subpart 31.2, costs resulting from such inconsistent practices shall not be allowed in excess of the amount that would have resulted from using practices consistent with this subpart.

APPENDIX 17—CONTRACT COST PRINCIPLES AND PROCEDURES

(d) A contractor is responsible for accounting for costs appropriately and for maintaining records, including supporting documentation, adequate to demonstrate that costs claimed have been incurred, are allocable to the contract, and comply with applicable cost principles in this subpart and agency supplements. The contracting officer may disallow all or part of a claimed cost which is inadequately supported.

31.201-3 Determining reasonableness.

(a) A cost is reasonable if, in its nature and amount, it does not exceed that which would be incurred by a prudent person in the conduct of competitive business. Reasonableness of specific costs must be examined with particular care in connection with firms or their separate divisions that may not be subject to effective competitive restraints. No presumption of reasonableness shall be attached to the incurrence of costs by a contractor. If an initial review of the facts results in a challenge of a specific cost by the contracting officer or the contracting officer's representative, the burden of proof shall be upon the contractor to establish that such cost is reasonable.

(b) What is reasonable depends upon a variety of considerations and circumstances, including--

(1) Whether it is the type of cost generally recognized as ordinary and necessary for the conduct of the contractor's business or the contract performance;

(2) Generally accepted sound business practices, arm's-length bargaining, and Federal and State laws and regulations;

(3) The contractor's responsibilities to the Government, other customers, the owners of the business, employees, and the public at large; and

(4) Any significant deviations from the contractor's established practices.

31.201-4 Determining allocability.

A cost is allocable if it is assignable or chargeable to one or more cost objectives on the basis of relative benefits received or other equitable relationship. Subject to the foregoing, a cost is allocable to a Government contract if it--

(a) Is incurred specifically for the contract;

(b) Benefits both the contract and other work, and can be distributed to them in reasonable proportion to the benefits received; or

(c) Is necessary to the overall operation of the business, although a direct relationship to any particular cost objective cannot be shown.

31.201-5 Credits.

The applicable portion of any income, rebate, allowance, or other credit relating to any allowable cost and received by or accruing to the contractor shall be credited to the Government either as a cost reduction or by cash refund.

See 31.205-6(j)(4) for rules related to refund or credit to the Government upon termination of an over-funded defined benefit pension plan.

31.201-6 Accounting for unallowable costs.

(a) Costs that are expressly unallowable or mutually agreed to be unallowable, including mutually agreed to be unallowable directly associated costs, shall be identified and excluded from any billing, claim, or proposal applicable to a Government contract. A directly associated cost is any cost which is generated solely as a result of incurring another cost, and which would not have been incurred had the other cost not been incurred. When an unallowable cost is incurred, its directly associated costs are also unallowable.

(b) Costs which specifically become designated as unallowable or as unallowable directly associated costs of unallowable costs as a result of a written decision furnished by a contracting officer shall be identified if included in or used in computing any billing, claim, or proposal applicable to a Government contract. This identification requirement applies also to any costs incurred for the same purpose under like circumstances as the costs specifically identified as unallowable under either this paragraph or paragraph (a) above.

(c) The practices for accounting for and presentation of unallowable costs will be those as described in 48 CFR 9904.405, Accounting for Unallowable Costs.

(d) If a directly associated cost is included in a cost pool which is allocated over a base that includes the unallowable cost with which it is associated, the directly associated cost shall remain in the cost pool. Since the unallowable costs will attract their allocable share of costs from the cost pool, no further action is required to assure disallowance of the directly associated costs. In all other cases, the directly associated costs, if material in amount, must be purged from the cost pool as unallowable costs.

(e)(1) In determining the materiality of a directly associated cost, consideration should be given to the significance of (i) the actual dollar amount, (ii) the cumulative effect of all directly associated costs in a cost pool, or (iii) the ultimate effect on the cost of Government contracts.

(2) Salary expenses of employees who participate in activities that generate unallowable costs shall be treated as directly associated costs to the extent of the time spent on the proscribed activity, provided the costs are material in accordance with subparagraph (e)(1) above (except when such salary expenses are, themselves, unallowable). The time spent in proscribed activities should be compared to total time spent on company activities to determine if the costs are material. Time spent by employees outside the normal working hours should not be considered except when it is evident that an employee engages so frequently in company activities during periods outside normal working hours as to indicate that such activities are a part of the employee's regular duties.

(3) When a selected item of cost under 31.205 provides that directly associated costs be unallowable, it is intended that such directly associated costs be unallowable only if determined to be material in amount in accordance with the criteria provided in subparagraphs (e)(1) and (e)(2) above, except in those situations where allowance of any of the directly associated costs involved would be considered to be contrary to public policy.

31.201-7 Construction and architect-engineer contracts.

Specific principles and procedures for evaluating and determining costs in connection with contracts and subcontracts for construction, and architect-engineer contracts related to construction projects, are in 31.105. The applicability of these principles and procedures is set forth in 31.000 and 31.100.

31.202 Direct costs.

(a) A direct cost is any cost that can be identified specifically with a particular final cost objective. No final cost objective shall have allocated to it as a direct cost any cost, if other costs incurred for the same purpose in like circumstances have been included in any indirect cost pool to be allocated to that or any other final cost objective. Costs identified specifically with the contract are direct costs of the contract and are to be charged directly to the contract. All costs specifically identified with other final cost objectives of the contractor are direct costs of those cost objectives and are not to be charged to the contract directly or indirectly.

(b) For reasons of practicality, any direct cost of minor dollar amount may be treated as an indirect cost if the accounting treatment--

(1) Is consistently applied to all final cost objectives; and

(2) Produces substantially the same results as treating the cost as a direct cost.

31.203 Indirect costs.

(a) An indirect cost is any cost not directly identified with a single, final cost objective, but identified with two or more final cost objectives or an intermediate cost objective. It is not subject to treatment as a direct cost. After direct costs have been determined and charged directly to the contract or other work, indirect costs are those remaining to be allocated to the several cost objectives. An indirect cost shall not be allocated to a final cost objective if other costs incurred for the same purpose in like circumstances have been included as a direct cost of that or any other final cost objective.

(b) Indirect costs shall be accumulated by logical cost groupings with due consideration of the reasons for incurring such costs. Each grouping should be determined so as to permit distribution of the grouping on the basis of the benefits accruing to the several cost objectives. Commonly, manufacturing overhead, selling expenses, and general and administrative (G&A) expenses are separately grouped. Similarly, the particular case may require subdivision of these groupings, e.g., building occupancy costs might be separable from those of personnel administration within the manufacturing overhead group. This necessitates selecting a distribution base common to all cost objectives to which the grouping is to be allocated. The base should be selected so as to permit allocation of the grouping on the basis of the benefits accruing to the several cost objectives. When substantially the same results can be achieved through less precise methods, the number and composition of cost groupings should be governed by practical considerations and should not unduly complicate the allocation.

(c) Once an appropriate base for distributing indirect costs has been accepted, it shall not be fragmented by removing individual elements. All items properly includable in an indirect cost base should bear a pro rata share of indirect costs irrespective of their acceptance as Government contract costs. For example, when a cost input base is used for the distribution of G&A costs, all items that would properly be part of the cost input base, whether allowable or unallowable, shall be included in the base and bear their pro rata share of G&A costs.

(d) The contractor's method of allocating indirect costs shall be in accordance with standards promulgated by the CAS Board, if applicable to the contract; otherwise, the method shall be in accordance with generally accepted accounting principles which are consistently applied. The method may require examination when--

(1) Substantial differences occur between the cost patterns of work under the contract and the contractor's other work;

(2) Significant changes occur in the nature of the business, the extent of subcontracting, fixed-asset improvement programs, inventories, the volume of sales and production, manufacturing processes, the contractor's products, or other relevant circumstances; or

(3) Indirect cost groupings developed for a contractor's primary location are applied to offsite locations. Separate cost groupings for costs allocable to offsite locations may be necessary to permit equitable distribution of costs on the basis of the benefits accruing to the several cost objectives.

(e) A base period for allocating indirect costs is the cost accounting period during which such costs are incurred and accumulated for distribution to work performed in that period. The criteria and guidance in 30.406 for selecting the cost accounting periods to be used in allocating indirect costs are incorporated herein for application to contracts subject to full CAS coverage. For contracts subject to modified CAS coverage and for non-CAS-covered contracts, the base period for allocating indirect costs will normally be the contractor's fiscal year. But a shorter period may be appropriate (1) for contracts in which performance involves only a minor portion of the fiscal year, or (2) when it is general practice in the industry to use a shorter period. When a

APPENDIX 17—CONTRACT COST PRINCIPLES AND PROCEDURES

contract is performed over an extended period, as many base periods shall be used as are required to represent the period of contract performance.

(f) Special care should be exercised in applying the principles of paragraphs (b), (c), and (d) above when Government-owned contractor-operated (GOCO) plants are involved. The distribution of corporate, division, or branch office G&A expenses to such plants operating with little or no dependence on corporate administrative activities may require more precise cost groupings, detailed accounts screening, and carefully developed distribution bases.

31.204 Application of principles and procedures.

(a) Costs shall be allowed to the extent they are reasonable, allocable, and determined to be allowable under 31.201, 31.202, 31.203, and 31.205. These criteria apply to all of the selected items that follow, even if particular guidance is provided for certain items for emphasis or clarity.

(b) Costs incurred as reimbursements or payments to a subcontractor under a cost-reimbursement, fixed-price incentive, or price redeterminable type subcontract of any tier above the first firm-fixed-price subcontract or fixed-price subcontract with economic price adjustment provisions are allowable to the extent that allowance is consistent with the appropriate subpart of this Part 31 applicable to the subcontract involved. Costs incurred as payments under firm-fixed-price subcontracts or fixed-price subcontracts with economic price adjustment provisions or modifications thereto, when cost analysis was performed under 15.805-3, shall be allowable only to the extent that the price was negotiated in accordance with 31.102.

(c) Section 31.205 does not cover every element of cost. Failure to include any item of cost does not imply that it is either allowable or unallowable. The determination of allowability shall be based on the principles and standards in this subpart and the treatment of similar or related selected items. When more than one subsection in 31.205 is relevant to a contractor cost, the cost shall be apportioned among the applicable subsections, and the determination of allowability of each portion shall be based on the guidance contained in the applicable subsection. When a cost, to which more than one subsection in 31.205 is relevant, cannot be apportioned, the determination of allowability shall be based on the guidance contained in the subsection that most specifically deals with, or best captures the essential nature of, the cost at issue.

Appendix 18 - ASBCA ADR Sample Forms

ARMED SERVICES BOARD OF CONTRACT APPEALS
SKYLINE SIX
5109 LEESBURG PIKE
FALLS CHURCH, VA 22041-3208

NOTICE REGARDING ALTERNATIVE METHODS OF DISPUTE RESOLUTION

The Contract Disputes Act of 1978, 41 U.S.C. § 607, states that boards of contract appeals "shall provide to the fullest extent practicable, informal, expeditious, and inexpensive resolution of dispute all. Resolution of a dispute at the earliest stage feasible, by the fastest and least expensive method possible, benefits both parties. To that end, the Board suggests that the parties consider Alternative Disputes Resolution (ADR) procedures.

The ADR methods described in this Notice are intended to suggest techniques which have worked in the past. Any method which brings the parties together in settlement, or partial settlement, of their disputes is a good method. The ADR methods listed are not intended to preclude the parties' use of other ADR techniques which do not require the Board's participation, such as settlement negotiations, fact finding conferences or procedures, mediation, or minitrial not involving use of the Board's personnel. The ADR methods described below are designed to supplement existing "extrajudicial" settlement techniques, not to replace them. Any method, or combination of methods, including one which will result in a binding decision, may be selected by the parties without regard to the dollar amount in dispute.

Requests to the Board to utilize ADR procedures must be made jointly by the parties. If an ADR method involving the Board's participation Is requested by the parties, the presiding administrative judge or member of the Board's legal staff will forward the request to the Board's Chairman for consideration. Unilateral requests or motions seeking ADR will not be considered. The presiding administrative judge or member of the Board's legal staff may also schedule a conference to explore the desirability and selection of an ADR method. if a non-binding ADR method involving the Board's participation is requested and approved by the Chairman, a settlement judge or a neutral advisor will be appointed. Usually the person appointed will be an administrative judge or hearing examiner employed by the Board.

If a non-binding ADR method fails to resolve the dispute, the appeal will be restored to the active docket for processing under the Board's Rules. To facilitate full, frank and open discussion and presentations, any settlement judge or neutral advisor who has participated in a non-binding ADR procedure which has failed to resolve the underlying dispute will ordinarily not participate in the restored appeal. Further, the judge or advisor will not discuss the merits of the appeal or substantive matters involved in the ADR proceedings with other Board personnel. Unless the parties explicitly request to the contrary, and such request is approved by the Chairman, the assigned ADR settlement judge or neutral advisor will be recused from consideration of the restored appeal.

Written material prepared specifically for use in an ADR proceeding, oral presentations made at an ADR proceeding, and all discussions in connection with such proceedings between representatives of the parties and a settlement judge or a neutral advisor are confidential and, unless otherwise specifically agreed by the parties, inadmissible as evidence in any pending or future Board proceeding involving the parties or matter in dispute. However, evidence otherwise admissible before the Board is not rendered inadmissible because of its use in a ADR proceeding.

Guidelines, procedures, and requirements implementing the ADR method selected will be prescribed by agreement of the parties and the settlement judge or neutral advisor. ADR methods can be used successfully at any stage of the litigation. Adoption of an ADR method as early in the appeal process as feasible will eliminate substantial cost and daisy. Generally, ADR proceedings will be concluded within 120 days following approval of their use by the Chairman.

APPENDIX 18—ASBCA ADR SAMPLE FORMS

The following ADR methods are consensual and voluntary. Both parties and the Board must agree to use of any of these methods.

1. <u>Settlement Judge</u>: A settlement judge, is an administrative judge or hearing examiner who will not hear or have any formal or informal decision-making authority in the appeal and who is appointed for the purpose of facilitating settlement. In many circumstances, settlement can be fostered by a frank, in-depth discussion of the strengths and weaknesses of each party's position with the settlement judge. The agenda for meetings with the settlement judge will be flexible to accommodate the requirements of the individual appeal. To further the settlement effort, the settlement judge may meet with the parties either jointly or individually. A settlement judge's recommendations are not binding on the parties.

2. <u>Minitrial</u>: The minitrial is a highly flexible, expedited, but structured, procedure where each party presents an abbreviated version of its position to principals of the parties who have full contractual authority to conclude a settlement and to a Board-appointed neutral advisor. The parties determine the form of presentation without regard to customary judicial proceedings and rules of evidence. Principals and the neutral advisor participate during the presentation of evidence in accordance with their advance agreement on procedure. Upon conclusion of these presentations, settlement negotiations are conducted. The neutral advisor may assist the parties in negotiating a settlement. The procedures for each minitrial will be designed to meet the needs of the individual appeal. The neutral advisor's recommendations are not binding.

3. <u>Summary Trial With Binding Decision</u>: A summary trial with binding decision Is a procedure whereby the scheduling of the appeal is expedited and the parties try their appeal informally before an administrative judge or panel of Judges. A summary, "bench" decision generally will be issued upon conclusion of the trial or a summary written decision will be issued no later than ten days following the Later of conclusion of the trial or receipt of a trial transcript. The parties must agree that all decisions, rulings, and orders by the Board under this method shall be final conclusive, not appealable, and may not be set aside, except for fraud. All such decisions, rulings, and orders will have no precedential value. The length of trial and the extent to which scheduling of the appeal is expedited will be tailored to the needs of each particular appeal. Pretrial, trial, and post-trial procedures and rules applicable to appeals generally will be modified or eliminated to expedite resolution of the appeal.

4. <u>Other Agreed Methods</u>: The parties and the Board may agree upon other Informal methods which are structured and tailored to suit the requirements of the individual appeal.

The above-listed ADR procedures are intended to shorten and simplify the Board's more formalized procedures. Generally, if the parties resolve their dispute by agreement, they benefit in terms of cost and time savings and maintenance or restoration of amicable relations. The Board will not view the parties, participation in ADR proceedings as a sign of weakness. Any method adopted for dispute resolution depends upon both parties having a firm, good faith commitment to resolve their differences. Absent such intention, the best structured dispute resolution procedure is unlikely to be successful.

These documents are provided for reference only and are subject to change. Reprinted with permission of the <u>Armed Services Board of Contract Appeals</u>. 1997

ARMED SERVICES BOARD OF CONTRACT APPEALS
SKYLINE SIX
5109 LEESBURG PIKE
FALLS CHURCH, VA 22041-3208

14 December 1993

[NOTE: The following sample agreement is provided in response to requests the Board receives for examples of ADR agreements that may be suitable for use in ADR proceedings under the Board's "Notice Regarding Alternative Methods of Dispute Resolution." This sample is offered as an aid to the parties in focusing their thoughts on the ground rules that will best serve their interests in resolving a particular dispute. The Board recognizes that one of the strengths of the ADR process would be lost if the same procedural format were insisted on in every case. Thus, the Board by offering this sample does not intend to restrict the parties' discretion in tailoring the agreement to meet their particular needs. Paragraphs 13 and 14, however, are key features of the Summary Trial with Binding Decision Method of ADR. In all cases consultation with the presiding judge is encouraged.]

SAMPLE

AGREEMENT TO UTILIZE THE PROCEDURE OF SUMMARY TRIAL WITH BINDING DECISION UNDER THE ASBCA'S "NOTICE REGARDING ALTERNATIVE METHODS OF DISPUTE RESOLUTION

THIS AGREEMENT is entered into by and between _____ (hereinafter "Appellant") and the Department of _____ (hereinafter the "Government").

WHEREAS, Appellant and the Government entered into Contract No: _____; and

WHEREAS, Appellant filed with the Armed Services Board of Contract Appeals (hereinafter the "ASBCA") an appeal under said contract; and

WHEREAS, said appeal is designated ASBCA No._____ and

WHEREAS, ASBCA No. _____ involves claims by [Appellant for] [Government for] in the amount of $_____; and

WHEREAS, the parties wish to resolve the appeal by alternative dispute resolution, specifically summary trial with binding decision, under the Contract Disputes Act; and

WHEREAS, the ASBCA is authorized to resolve disputes by alternative disputes resolution under its Charter and the Contract Disputes Act; and

NOW THEREFORE, the parties mutually stipulate and agree as follows:

1. Motion practice in this appeal is waived.

2. Discovery will be concluded by _____.

3. The documentary record will be limited to those documents which have been submitted, identified and indexed pursuant to Rule 4 or as exhibits no later than _____

[NOTE: The parties may agree to have the appeal decided on the documentary record in accordance with ASBCA Rule 11. If so, such procedure may be provided in additional paragraphs and should include the concepts in ¶¶ 12-14 below modified as may be necessary. If the parties seek an oral hearing on the appeal, the following ADR paragraphs should be considered:]

4. Each party's hearing presentation will be limited to _____ hours [day], including time for examination of witnesses, presentation of rebuttal evidence and oral argument, if any.

5. The appeal shall be tried informally, and the rules of evidence are waived. The parties agree, nonetheless, that the presiding judge shall retain discretion to limit evidence where necessary for the reasonable conduct of the hearing.

APPENDIX 18—ASBCA ADR SAMPLE FORMS

6. Witnesses shall be examined orally under oath or affirmation. A party shall be allowed to cross-examine the adverse party's witnesses.

7. Pre- and post-hearing briefs are waived. [A very brief (three to five page) preheating submission is often useful to the presiding judge.]

8. A transcript of the proceedings will be prepared. [Preparation of a transcript is waived.]

9. Each party will bear its own fees and expenses, including but not limited to attorney and agent fees and compensation for witnesses, incurred incidental to the ADR proceeding;

10. The hearing on this appeal is scheduled for ____ day(s), namely: _____;

11. The issues in dispute shall be presented in the following order:

    a. _____
    b. _____
    c. _____
    d. _____
       and
    e. [Other issues, if any]

12. The Board shall issue a bench decision at the conclusion of the hearing, or, at the option of the presiding judge, no later than business days after receipt of the transcript [or conclusion of the hearing if no transcript].

13. The decision will contain no findings of fact or conclusions of law.

14. The Board's decision shall be final, conclusive, not subject to reconsideration or appeal, and may not be set aside, except for fraud. The decision shall have no precedential value.

APPELLANT   GOVERNMENT AGENCY

By:_____   By:_____
Dated _____   Dated _____

ARMED SERVICES BOARD OF CONTRACT APPEALS
SKYLINE SIX
5109 LEESBURG PIKE
FALLS CHURCH, VA 22041-3208

14 May 1994

[NOTE: The following sample agreement is provided in response to requests the Board receives for examples of ADR agreements that may be suitable for use in ADR proceedings under the Board's "Notice Regarding Alternative Methods of Dispute Resolution." This sample is offered solely as an aid to the parties in focusing their thoughts on the ground rules that will best serve their interests in resolving a particular dispute. The Board recognizes that one of the strengths of the ADR process would be lost if the same procedural format were insisted on in every case. Thus, the Board by offering this sample does not intend to restrict the parties' discretion in tailoring the agreement to meet their particular needs. Paragraphs 2, 6 and 9, however, are key features of the settlement judge method of ADR. In all cases consultation with the presiding judge is encouraged.]

SAMPLE
AGREEMENT TO UTILIZE THE PROCEDURE OR SETTLEMENT JUDGE UNDER THE ASBCA'S "NOTICE REGARDING ALTERNATIVE METHODS Of DISPUTE RESOLUTION"

THIS AGREEMENT is entered into by and between _____ (hereinafter "Appellant") and the Department of _____ (hereinafter the "Government").

WHEREAS, Appellant and the Government entered into Contract No. _____ ; and

WHEREAS, Appellant filed with the Armed Services Board of Contract Appeals (hereinafter the "ASBCA") an appeal under said contract; and

WHEREAS, said appeal is designated ASBCA No. _____ and

WHEREAS, ASBCA No. _____ involves claims [Appellant for][Government for] in the amount of $ _____ ; and

WHEREAS, the parties wish to resolve the appeal by alternative dispute resolution, specifically with the assistance of a settlement judge, under the Contract Disputes Act; and

WHEREAS, the ASBCA is authorized to resolve disputes by alternative disputes resolution under its Charter and the Contract Disputes Act; and

NOW THEREFORE, the parties mutually stipulate and agree as follows:

1. Schedule. The ADR proceeding on the appeal is scheduled _____ for days(s), namely: _____, at the Board (or other agreed location).
2. Settlement judge. The judge's role will be to facilitate the parties' settlement efforts. The judge may meet with the parties either jointly or individually and to the extent necessary to foster a negotiated settlement of the dispute. The judge's recommendations are not binding on the parties. [Note: The settlement judge will normally not participate further in the appeal if the parties' efforts are unsuccessful, unless the parties seek the continued involvement of the judge.]
3. Record. (The parties should agree on what documents will be included in the record for consideration by the settlement judge in assessing the merits of the parties' positions)
4. Transcript. A transcript of the proceedings will not be prepared.
5. Agenda. The presentations of the parties will be informal and the rules of evidence are waived. The settlement judge may, nonetheless, guide the presentation of evidence. [The parties should spell out how they wish to make their informal presentations and agree on time to be allotted to various phases of the process. It is often helpful for each party to submit a brief position paper (3 to 5 pages) sufficiently in advance of the proceeding for the judge to consider it in connection with the record agreed to by the parties.]
6. Participants. Each party will include among its representatives a principal with authority to settle the appeal.
7. Use of statements and documents. The admissibility of statements made or documents used in connection with the ADR proceeding will be governed by Federal Rule of Evidence 408.
8. Fees and expenses. Each party will bear its own fees and expenses, including but not limited to attorney and agent fees and compensation for witnesses, incurred incidental to the ADR proceeding.
9. Good faith. All participants in the ADR proceeding agree to act in good faith in all aspects of the proceeding with the view of resolving the dispute.

APPELLANT   GOVERNMENT AGENCY

By:_____   By:_____
Dated _____   Dated _____

APPENDIX 18—ASBCA ADR SAMPLE FORMS

ARMED SERVICES BOARD OF CONTRACT APPEALS
SKYLINE SIX
5109 LEESBURG PIKE
FALLS CHURCH, VA 22041-3208

25 October 1996

[NOTE: The following sample agreement is provided in response to requests the Board receives for examples of agreements that may be suitable for use in Alternative Dispute Resolution (ADR) proceedings under the Board's "Notice Regarding Alternative Methods of Dispute Resolution." This sample is offered as an aid to the parties in focusing their thoughts on the ground rules that will best serve their interests in resolving a particular dispute. The Board recognizes that one of the strengths of the ADR process would be lost if the same procedural format were insisted on in every case. Thus, the Board by offering this sample does not intend to restrict the parties' discretion in tailoring the agreement to meet their particular needs. Paragraphs 2, 3 and 4, however, are key features of the minitrial method of ADR. In all cases consultation with the presiding judge is encouraged.]

SAMPLE

AGREEMENT TO UTILIZE THE MINITRIAL PROCEDURE
UNDER THE ASBCA'S "NOTICE REGARDING
ALTERNATIVE METHODS OF DISPUTE RESOLUTION"

THIS AGREEMENT is entered into by and between _____ (hereinafter the Appellant) and (hereinafter the Government).

WHEREAS, the Appellant and the Government entered into contract No. _____ ; and

WHEREAS, the Appellant and the Government are currently engaged in litigation before the Armed Services Board of Contract Appeals (ASBCA or Board), which is docketed as ASBCA No(s) _____ ; and

WHEREAS, the Appellant and the Government wish to resolve their dispute through the use of the minitrial method of alternative dispute resolution (ADR) under the Contract Disputes Act; and

WHEREAS, the ASBCA is authorized to resolve disputes by ADR under its Charter and the Contract Disputes Act;

NOW THEREFORE, the Appellant and the Government mutually stipulate and agree as follows:

1. Scope of the ADR. The Appellant and the Government will voluntarily engage in a non-binding minitrial on the claim(s) of _____ . [Spell out the parties' claims (including the amounts) that are to be resolved during the proceeding to a level of detail that satisfies the parties.]

2. Good Faith Efforts to Resolve the Dispute. The goal of the ADR proceeding is to resolve the matters in dispute between the parties through negotiation by the parties' principal representatives, guided as necessary by a neutral advisor. To this end the minitrial proceeding will be aimed at informing the principal representatives and the neutral advisor of the underlying bases of the parties' positions. Each party will have the opportunity and responsibility to present its "best case" on entitlement and quantum. The presentations will be made primarily through the parties' counsel. Other persons may attend in the discretion of each party. All participants in the ADR proceeding agree to act in good faith in all aspects of the proceeding with the goal of resolving the dispute.

3. The Principal Representatives. The principal representatives for the purpose of this proceeding will be:

For the Appellant:

For the Government:

Each party represents that its principal representative will come to the ADR proceeding with full authority to settle the matter, and that it will obtain any required reviews or approvals in advance of the proceeding. Each party will bear its own expenses associated with the ADR proceeding.

4. The Neutral Advisor. The ASBCA will designate the neutral advisor. The neutral advisor will preside during the ADR proceeding and will participate in the negotiations between the parties. The neutral advisor may comment on any of the issues involved and may express an opinion on the relative strength and weaknesses of positions taken by either or both of the parties. The neutral advisor may meet with the parties or their counsel, jointly or individually, to the extent the neutral advisor deems desirable to foster a negotiated settlement of the dispute. The neutral advisor's recommendations are not binding on the parties. In the event the ADR proceeding does not result in settlement of the issues in dispute, the neutral advisor will not participate further in the appeal. (Recusal is the normal practice if the ADR is unsuccessful; however, the parties may seek the continued involvement of the neutral advisor.] The neutral advisor will serve at no expense to either party.

5. Discovery. [Parties should take into account the discovery necessary for the minitrial. Board practice is to stay discovery during the ADR proceeding if it is reasonable to do so.] Discovery will be stayed from the date of this Agreement. If this matter is not resolved as a result of the ADR

proceeding, the Board will lift the stay. The Appellant and the Government will remain entitled to pursue such additional discovery as they believe necessary and as the Board may allow.

6. <u>The Record for Purpose of the ADR Proceeding</u>. The Appellant and the Government in consultation with the neutral advisor will agree on the composition of the record upon which the ADR proceeding will be based. (Generally, the parties will designate key portions of the R4 file and often prepare special exhibits. The extent of the record and the time of its submission to the parties' representatives and the neutral advisor is left to the parties, keeping in mind that the record must be manageable and the time to assimilate it sufficient.) No later than _____ weeks prior to commencement of the minitrial proceeding, the parties will provide to the neutral advisor and exchange copies of all documentary evidence proposed for utilization at the conference, inclusive of a listing of all witnesses with a brief statement of the subject matter of their testimony.

7. <u>The Position Paper</u>. No later than _____ weeks prior to commencement of the proceeding, the parties will exchange and submit to the principal representatives and the neutral advisor a position paper of no more than 30 double-spaced pages. The position paper will spell out a party's factual and legal position on each claim to be resolved. Each party may submit a reply of no more than 10 pages not later than weeks prior to the commencement of the proceeding.

8. <u>The Schedule</u>. The minitrial will be held on _____, at _____ [a mutually agreed location or the offices of the Board]. The ADR proceeding will take _____ day(s). The parties have agreed to the following schedule [sample one day schedule]:

MINITRIAL CONFERENCE SCHEDULE

Day 1
9:00 a.m. - 10:30 a.m.   Appellant's statement of case & presentation of position
10:45 a.m. - 12:15 p.m.   Government's Rebuttal
12:15 p.m. - 1:00 p.m.   Lunch
1:00 p.m. - 2:00 p.m.   Appellant's Reply
2:15 p.m. - 3:15 p.m.   Open question & answer period
3:15 p.m. - 5:00 p.m.   Negotiations/Discussions between parties and neutral advisor

If the parties are unable to resolve the dispute, the minitrial shall be deemed terminated and the appeal will continue.

9. <u>Manner of Proceeding</u>. At the ADR proceeding counsel for the parties have the discretion to structure the content of their presentations as they desire. The presentations may include, for example, remarks by fact or expert witnesses, audio-visual aids, demonstrative evidence, affidavits, and oral argument. The rules of evidence will not apply and witnesses may provide testimony in narrative form. The principal representatives and the neutral advisor may ask any relevant question of the witnesses that they deem appropriate.

10. <u>Record of the Proceeding</u>. No transcript or recording shall be made of the ADR proceeding.

11. <u>Use of Statements and Documents</u>. The admissibility of statements made and documents used in connection with the ADR proceeding will be governed by Federal Rule of Evidence 408.

12. <u>Termination of the ADR Proceeding</u>. Each party has the right to terminate the minitrial at any time for any reason. The neutral advisor may terminate the proceeding if he/she believes that one or both of the parties are not committed to the process.

Dated: Dated:

By:_____   By:_____
Principal Representative for   Principal Representative for
Government   Appellant

_____   _____
Attorney for the Government   Attorney for the Appellant

Dated _____   Dated _____

Appendix 19 - DART Declaration

DART

DART DECLARATION
Principles for Prevention and Resolution of Disputes in the
Construction Industry

This Declaration has been prepared by the Dispute Avoidance and Resolution Task Force (DART) of the Construction Industry and has been endorsed by organizations listed below. Members of the Industry are encouraged to express their good faith commitment to adopt it wherever they build.

IMPORTANT NOTICE

This Declaration is solely concerned with voluntary participation in techniques and processes designed to prevent and resolve construction disputes without the need to resort to formal, binding dispute resolution processes. Therefore, it is important to understand that this Declaration is not a contract and does not change contract provisions. In addition, all provisions of a construction contract regarding disputes and the manner of dispute resolution remain in full force and effect. In the event that the parties avail themselves of the procedures provided in this Declaration and they are not successful, the rights of the parties are governed entirely by their contract

ABA Forum on Construction Industry	Engineers Joint Contract Document Committee
ABA Public Contracts Section	General Services Administration
Air Conditioning Contractors of America	Independent Electrical Contractors
American Arbitration Association	Mechanical Contractors Association of America
American College of Construction Lawyers	National Association of Minority Contractors
American Consulting Engineering Council	National Association of Surety Bond Producers
American Institute of Architects	National Association of Women to Construction
American Road & Transportation Builders Association	National Concrete Masonry Association
American Society of Civil Engineers	National Contractors Association
American Subcontractors Association	National Electrical Contractors Association
Associated Builders & Contractors	National Roofing Contractors Association
Associated General Contractors of America	National Society of Professional Engineers
Associated Specialty Contractors	National Utility Contractors Association
Association of the Wall & Ceiling Industries International	North American Society of Trenchless Technology
Building Future's Council	Office of Federal Procurement Policy
Business Roundtable, Construction Section	Painting & Decorating Contractors of America
Construction Financial Management Association	Power & Communication Contractors Association
Construction Management Association of America	Specialized Carriers & Rigging Association
Construction Specifications Institute	Victor O. Schinnerer & Company, Inc.
Design Build Institute	US Army Corps of Engineers
DPIC Companies	US Department of Defense

Produced by the Dispute Avoidance and Resolution Task Force, Washington DC, April 15, 1996

DART

THE DART DECLARATION OF PRINCIPLES

The Construction Industry acknowledges that problems and disputes can arise on construction projects. The Industry further acknowledges that these problems and potential disputes do not need to result in litigation or other formal binding dispute resolution processes. It is in the best interests of all industry members to resolve problems and potential disputes in a non adversarial manner and in a way more constructive to the relationships among the participants in the project.

The industry recommends that participants in a project consider the following principles:

PRINCIPLES FOR THE PREVENTION AND RESOLUTION OF DISPUTES

TEAM BUILDING

Participation in "Partnering" or other team-building procedures with participants in a project tends to establish relationships based upon mutual respect for the legitimate concerns and goals of each of the participants in the project. These efforts are likely to directly contribute to a successful completion of a project. Since there will be some expense and substantial dedication of effort required in order for it to be successful, participants desiring to employ Partnering should agree in advance on a fair sharing of the cost involved. The parties also may wish to consider the establishment of a standing Neutral, a Dispute Review Board, or other similar non-binding processes to facilitate dispute avoidance and resolution.

DISPUTES DURING PERFORMANCE

Disputes may arise during the performance of a project. Failure to resolve disputes early may have an adverse impact on the best interests of the project and the parties themselves. Therefore, the Industry recommends that in the event of a dispute during performance of a project the parties dedicate appropriate efforts to achieve a negotiated resolution using lines of authority within their respective organizations as may be agreed. The parties may identify individuals from their organizations who are not directly involved in the project but who have the authority to resolve disputes during performance. It is recommended that the individuals named below be of equivalent authority and at a level within their respective organizations so that they may exercise independence and objectivity. The efforts to achieve a negotiated resolution should take into consideration prior discussions between the parties and any subsequent recommendations of a Standing Neutral, or Dispute Review Board used on the project.

_____ is designated for _____
_____ is designated for _____

In the event that parties, by their designated representatives, are unable to reach resolution of a dispute within thirty days, it is recommended that the parties submit that dispute to Mediation following the on procedures included in the construction documents, if any.

POST PERFORMANCE DISPUTES

If a dispute arises after the project has been completed, it is recommended that the parties consider Mediation before they engage in the formal, binding dispute resolution procedure provided in the Contract documents. In appropriate circumstances, mediation is a demonstrated method to facilitate successful settlement of disputes. Where technical matters, such as statutes of limitation, govern the commencement of a lawsuit or arbitration, the parties should nonetheless consider Mediation or some other form of Alternative Dispute Resolution (ADR) during the pendency of the matter before engaging in expensive and highly adversarial procedures.

AN ACKNOWLEDGMENT

Participants in a construction project may evidence their support of these Principles by signing this Declaration. By doing so, the parties are not entering into a binding agreement. This Declaration is rather an expression by each party to the other of their serious and good faith desire to cooperatively achieve solutions to problems and resolution of claims and disputes in a manner which will avoid engaging in formal dispute resolution procedures.

We, the undersigned, have read this Declaration, accept the importance of its purposes, and pledge our good faith efforts to cooperate with one another in achieving those purposes.

Party _____   Party _____

Produced by the Dispute Avoidance and Resolution Task Force, Washington, DC, April 15, 1996

Appendix 20

INDEX TO LEGAL CITATIONS

A.S. Wikstrom, Inc. v. State, N.Y. Supreme Court, App. Div. (April 8, 1976). p. 47.
Aerodex, Inc. v. U.S., 189 Ct. Cl. 344 (1969). p. 40.
American Dredging Co. v. U.S., 207 Ct. Cl. 1010 (1977). p. 48.
American Dredging Co., ENGBCA Nos. 2920 et al. 72-1 BCA ¶9316. p. 48.
American Structures, Inc. & Mining Equipment Manufacturing Cooperation, ENGBCA 3408 75-1 BCA ¶11,283. p. 25.
Batteast Construction Co., Inc., ASBCA No. 35818 (December 31, 1991). p. 113.
Beacon Construction Co. v. U.S., 161 Ct. Cl. 1 (1963). p. 44.
Bechtold Paving, Inc. v. City of Kenmore, 446 N.W.2d(N.D. 1989). p. 49.
Bill Strong Enterprises, Inc. v. Shannon, 49 F.3d 15431 (Fed Cir. 1995). p. 118.
Blake Construction Co., Inc., GSBCA 1345, 65-1 BCA ¶4624. p. 33.
Blake Construction Co., Inc., ASBCA No. 39937 (July 24, 1990). p. 63.
Blount Bros. Const. Co., 171 Ct.Cl.478, 496, 346 F.2d 962,973 (1965). p. 45, 46.
Blount Brothers Corporation, NASA BCA 865-29, 67-2 BCA ¶6562. p. 33.
Brock & Blevins Co. v. U.S., 170 Ct. Cl. 52 (1965). p. 63.
Bromley Contracting Co., ASBCA 14884, 72-1 BCA ¶9252. p. 39.
Bruce-Anderson Co., Inc., ASBCA No. 29411 (August 1, 1988). p. 44.
Bruno Law & Richard Marlink, Trustees v. U.S., 195 Ct. Cl. 370 (1971). p. 113.
C & C Plumbing and Heating, ASBCA No. 44270 (July 29, 1994). p. 58.
C.H. Leavell & Co., ASBCA 16099, 72-2 BCA ¶9694. p. 17.
C.A. Fielland, Inc., GSBCA 2903, 71-1 ¶BCA 8734. p. 60.
Capital Electric Co. v. United States, 729 F.2d 743 (Fed.Cir. 1984). p. 111.
Centex Construction Co., Inc., ASBCA No. 29323 (September 30, 1985). p. 41.
Century Construction Company v. U.S., 22 Cl. Ct. 63 (1990). p. 21.
Chaney & James Co. v. United States, 190 Ct. Cl. 699 (1970). p. 77.
Chaney & James Construction Company v. U.S., 190 Ct. Cl. 699 (1970). p. 56.
Commonwealth of Pennsylvania DOT v. Mitchell's Structural Steel Painting Co., 336A2-913 Commonwealth Court of Pennsylvania (1975). p. 30.
Continental Consolidated Corp., Ct. Cl. 214-69, 17 CCF ¶81,1137. p. 62.
Co-Operative C. Store Builders, Inc. v. Arcadia Foods, Inc., 291 So. 2d 403 (La. App. 1974). p. 17.
Corbetta Construction Co. v. U.S., 198 Ct. Cl. 712 (1972). p. 33.
D'Annunzio Brothers, Inc. v. New Jersey Transit Corp., 586 A.2d 301 (N.J.Super.A.D. 1991). p. 17.
Delcon Construction v. U.S., 27 Fed. Cl. 634 (1993). p. 29.
Department of Transportation v. Mosites Construction Co., 494 A.2d 41 (Pa.Cmwlth. 1985). p. 37.

Department of Transportation v. Semanderes, 5-31 A.2d 815 (Pa.Cmwlth. 1987). p. 34.
Donald R. Stewart & Associates, AGBCA No. 89-222-1 (January 16, 1992). p. 62.
E. W. Bliss Company, ASBCA 9489, 68-1 BCA ¶6906. p. 59.
Eichleay Company, ASBCA 5183, 60-2 BCA ¶2688. p. 110.
Electronic & Missile Facilities, ASBCA 9031, 1964 BCA ¶4338. p. 63.
Firestone Tire & Rubber Co. v. U.S., 195 Ct. Cl. 21 (1971). p. 34.
Fort Mechanical, Inc., GSBCA No. 6350 (July 18, 1983). p. 35.
Frank Briscoe Company, Inc., GSBCA 3330, 72-2 BCA ¶9714. p. 60.
G.C. Casebolt Co. v. United States, 421 F.2d 710, 712 (Ct.Cl. 1970). p. 148.
Gaston & Associates v. U.S., 27 Fed Cl. 243 (1992). p. 45.
Gaudelli Brothers, Inc., GSBCA No. 7123 (March 5, 1984). p. 48.
George Bennett v. U.S., 178 Ct. Cl. p. 37.
Gevyn Construction Corp. v. United States, 827 F.2d 752 (Fed.Cir. 1987). p. 117.
Gholson, Byars and Holmes Construction Co. v. U.S., 173 Ct. Cl. 374 (1965). p. 36.
Gibbs v. U.S., 175 Ct. Cl. 411 (1966). p. 36.
Gilbane Building Co. v. U.S., 166 Ct. Cl. 347 (1964). p. 56.
Gordon H. Ball, Inc., ENGBCA No. 3563, 78-1 BCA. p. 29.
Granite Construction Co., ENGBCA No. 3561, 76-1 11,748. p. 49.
Green Construction Co. v. Department of Transportation, 643 A.2d 1129 (Pa. Cmwlth. 1994). p. 30.
Green Construction Co. v. Kansas Power & Light Co., 1 F.3d 1005 (10th Cir. 1993). p. 25.
Griffin and Dickvon, AGBCA No. 74-104-4 (December 4, 1985). p. 104.
H.A. Kaufman Co., GSBCA No. 10687 (December 20, 1990). p. 56.
H.N. Bailey & Associates v. U.S., 196 Ct. Cl. 166 (1971). p. 42.
Harrison Western/Franki-Denys, Inc., ENGBCA No. 552-3 (Nov. 22, 1991). p. 39.
Harrod & Williams, Inc., DOT BCA 72-10, 73-2 BCA ¶10,266. p. 60.
Head Construction Company, ENG BCA 3537, 77-1 BCA ¶12,226. p. 57.
Hedin Construction Co. v. U.S., 171 Ct. Cl. 70 (1965). p. 104.
Helene Curtis Industries, Inc. v. U.S., 160 Ct. Cl. 437 (1963). p. 42.
Helene Curtis Industries, Inc. v. U.S., 160 Ct. Cl. 437 (1963). p. 46.
Hibbitts Construction Co., Inc., ASBCA No. 37070 (January 4, 1990). p. 60.
Hicks Corp., ASBCA 10760, 66-1 BCA ¶5469. p. 59.
Hills Materials Co. v. Rice, 982 F.2d 514 (Fed. Cir. 1992). p. 35.
Hol-Gar Manufacturing Corp. v. U.S., 169 Ct. Cl. 384 (1965). p. 35.
Hull-Hazard, Inc., ASBCA No. 34645 (June 29, 1990). p. 35.
Hyde Construction Co., ASBCA 8393, 1963 BCA ¶3911. p. 62.
Hydromar Corp. v. U.S., 25 Cl. Ct. 555 (1992). p. 29.
Hydrospace Electronics & Instrument Corp., ASBCA 17922, 74-2 BCA ¶10682. p. 49.
Ideker, Inc., ENG BCA Nos. 4389, 4602, 87-3 BCA ¶20,145 at 101,974. p. 149.
Interstate General Government Contractors, Inc. v. West, 12 F.3d 1053 (Fed.Cir. 1993). p. 111.
J.A. Tobin Construction Co. v. State Highway, Commission of Missouri, 680 S.W.2d 183 (Mo.App. 1984). p. 57.
J.J. Brown Co. v. J.L. Simmons Co., 2 111. App. 2d. 132,118 N.W. 2d 781 (1954). p. 90.

J.W. Bateson Co., Inc., VABCA No. 1148 (December 4, 1985). p. 117.
Jarbet Co., ASBCA 14554, 72-1 BCA ¶9379. p. 35.
John A. Johnson & Sons v. U.S. (12 CCF 81,196), 180 Ct. Cl. 969 990. p. 58.
John A. Johnson Contracting Co. v. U.S., 132 Ct. Cl. 645, (1955). p. 26.
Joseph Bell v. United States, 404 F.2d 975 (Fed.Cir. 1969). p. 117.
Kammer Construction Co. v. U.S., 203 Ct. Cl. 182 (1973). p. 50.
Keco Industries, Inc., ASBCA 15131, 72-1 9262. p. 69.
Keco Industries, Inc., ASBCA 15181, 15,547, 72-1 9576. p. 69.
Kelley Control Systems, Inc., VABCA No. 2,337 (July 24, 1987). p. 50.
Kirk Brothers Mechanical Contractors, Inc., ASBCA No. 35771. p. 118.
Koppers/Clough, a Joint Venture v. U.S., 201 Ct. Cl. 344 (1973). p. 57.
Laburnum Construction Corp. v. U.S., 163 Ct. Cl. 339 (1963). p. 43.
Lakeview Construction Co. v. U.S., 21 Cl. Ct. 269 (1990). p. 20.
Lewis v. Anchorage Asphalt Paving Co., F. 2d 1188 (Alaska 1975). p. 46.
M.I.T. Alaska, PSBCA No. 1348 (September 3, 1986). p. 56.
Machinery Associates, Inc., ASBCA 14510, 72-2 BCA ¶9476. p. 17.
Massachusetts Port Authority v. U.S., 197 Ct. Cl. 721 (1972). p. 34.
Max Drill, Inc. v. U.S., 192 Ct. Cl. 608 (1970). p. 39.
Maxima Corporation v. United States, 847 F.2d 1549, 1553 (Fed Cir. 1988). p. 148.
Maxwell Dynometer Co. v. U.S., 181 Ct. Cl. 607 (1967). p. 38.
Metropolitan Sewerage Commission v. R.W. Construction, Inc., 241 N.W 2d 371, (1976). p. 28.
Minter Roofing Co., Inc., ASBCA No. 31137 (August 24, 1989). p. 25.
Missouri Research Lab Inc., ASBCA 12355, 69-1 BCA ¶7762. p. 16.
Mobil Chemical Co. v. Blount Brothers Corp., 809 F.2d 1175 (5th Cir. 1987). p. 62.
Monitor Plastics Co., ASBCA 11 187, 67-2 BCA ¶6408. p. 48.
Moorhead Construction Co., Inc. v. City of Grand Forks, 508 F. 2d 1008 (8th Circuit, 1975). p. 25.
Mountain Home Contractors v. U.S., 192 Ct. Cl. 16, 425 F.2d 1264. p. 45.
Natus Corporation v. U.S., 178 Ct. Cl. 1 (1967). p. 41.
Neal & Co. v. U.S., 19 Cl. Ct. 463 (1990). p. 41.
Oneida Construction Co., Inc./David Boland, Inc., Joint Venture, ASBCA No. 44194 (October 6, 1994). p. 43.
P.T. & L. Construction Co. v. State of New Jersey, Department of Transportation, 5-31 A.2d 1330 (N.J. 1987). p. 29.
Peter Kiewit Sons' Co. v. U.S., 109 Ct. Cl. 517 (1947). p. 37.
Peterson Construction Co., Inc., ASBCA No. 44197 (November 12, 1992). p. 26.
Phillips Construction Co. v. U.S., 184 Ct. Gl. 249 (1968). p. 26.
Pool & Canfield, Inc., ASBCA No. 4-3399 (March 4, 1992). p. 33.
Reliance Insurance Company v. U.S., 20 Cl. Ct. 715 (1990). p. 53.
River Construction Corp. v. U.S., 159 Ct. Cl. 254 (1962). p. 104.
Royal Painting Co., Inc., ASBCA 20034, 75-1 BCA ¶11,311. p. 56.
S. O. G. of Arkansas v. U.S., Ct. Cl. 546 F 2d 367 (Dec. 15, 1976). p. 45.
Saddler v. U.S., 287 F.2d 411 (Ct. Cl. 1961). p. 39.
Santa Fe, Inc., VABCA No. 2167. p. 36.
Sante Fe Engineers, Inc. v. U.S., 801 F.2d 379 (Fed. Cir. 1986). p. 53.
Servidone Construction Corp. v. United States, 931 F.2d 860 (Fed.Cir. 1991). p. 104.

Severin v. U.S., 99 Ct. Cl. No. 435 (1943). p. 95.
Sherman Construction Corp., VABCA No. 1942 (December 13, 1984). p. 44.
Sun Electric Corporation, ASBCA 13031, 70-2 8371. p. 69.
Sylvania Electric Products, Inc. v. U.S., 198 Ct. Cl. 106 (1972). p. 36.
Sylvania Electric Products, Inc., ASBCA 11206, 67-2 BCA ¶6428. p. 63.
Teichert & Son, Inc., ASBCA 10265, et al., 68-2 BCA ¶1175. p. 62.
Tele-Sentry Security, Inc., GSBCA No. 7037 (May 7, 1984). p. 118.
The Little Susitna Co., PSBCA No. 2216 (May 24, 1990). p. 17.
Titan Mountain States Construction Corp., ASBCA No. 2-3095 p. 77.
Titan Pacific Construction Corp. v. United States, 17 Cl. Ct. 630 p. 77.
Torncello v. United States, 681 F.2d 756, 759 (Ct. Cl. 1982). p. 148.
U.S. for the Use & Benefit of Leonardo Mariana v. piracci Construction Co., Inc., 405 F. Supp. 904 (District of Columbia, 1975). p. 96.
U.S. for the Use and Benefit of Superior Insulation Co., Inc. v. Robert E. McKee, Inc., 702 F.Supp. 1298 (N.D.Tex. 1988). p. 96.
U.S. v. Spearin, 248 U.S. 132 (1918). p. 39.
Uhley v. Tapio Construction Co., Inc., 573 So.2d 391 (Fla.App. 1991). p. 42.
Unicon Management Corp. v. U.S., 179 Ct. Cl. 534 (1967). p. 34.
Unis v. JTS Constructors/Managers, Inc., 541 So.2d 278 (La.App. 1989). p. 90.
United States v. Turner Construction Co., 827 F.2d (Fed.Cir.1987). p. 21.
Vanlar Construction, Inc. v. County of Los Angeles, 217 Cal.Rptr. 53 (Cal.App. 1985). p. 60.
W.G. Cornell Co. v. U.S., 179 Ct. Cl. 651 (1967). p. 36.
Weaver-Bailey Contractors, Inc. v. U.S., 19 Cl. Ct. 474 (1990). p. 60, 82–83.
Weeks Dredging and Contracting, Inc. v. United States, 13 Cl. CT. 193 (1987). p. 28.
Wickham Contracting Co., Inc. v. Fischer, 12 F.3d 1574 (Fed. Cir. 1994). p. 111.
WPC Enterprises, Inc. v. U.S., 163 Ct. Cl. 1 (1963). p. 44.
WRB Corp. v. U.S., 183 Ct. Cl. 409 (1968). p. 104.

BIBLIOGRAPHY

Clough, Richard H. Construction Project Management. New York: John Wiley & Sons, Inc. 1972.

Cuneo, Gilbert A. and Ackerly, Robert L. "Acceleration." Government Contracts Monograph No. 9. Washington, D.C.: Government Contracts Program, the George Washington, University. 1975.

Currie, Overton A. and House, Jr., Luther P. "Preparing Construction Claims for Settlement." Briefing Papers #68 5, 1 Briefing Papers Collection. Washington, D.C.

Dees, C. Stanley and Ginsburg, Gilbert J. "Contract Interpretation and Detective Specifications." Government Contracts Monograph No. 4. Washington, D.C.: Government Contracts Program, the George Washington University. 1975.

Driscoll, Thomas J. "Claims." In Contractors Management Handbook, Chapter 16. Edited by James J. O'Brien and R. G. Zilly. New York: McGraw-Hill. 1971.

Essex, Randall J. Geotechnical Baseline Reports for Underground Construction. American Society of Civil Engineers, New York, 1997.

Hynes, Leslie A. "Construction Law." In Contractors Management Handbook. Chapter 22. Edited by James J. O'Brien and R. G. Zilly. New York: McGraw-Hill. 1971.

Jervis, Bruce. Construction Claims Monthly, Business Publishers, Inc. Silver Spring, MD.

Matyas, Mathews, Smith, Sperry. Construction Dispute Review Board Manual. McGraw-Hill Construction Series. 1995.

McNulty, Paul E. "Changed Conditions and Misrepresentations Under Government Construction Contracts." Government Contracts Monograph No. 3. Washington, D.C.: Government Contracts Program, the George Washington University. 1975.

Nash, Jr., Ralph C. Government Contract Changes. Washington, D.C.: Federal Publications, Inc. 1975.

Partnering—A Concept for Success, Associated General Contractors' of America (Sept. 1991).

Pierce, Jr., Jotham D. Construction Contracts, 1976. New York, Practising Law Institute. 1976.

Simon, Michael S. "The Importance of Proper Daily Reports," Constructor, 1976. Associated General Contractors of America.

United States Defense Contract Audit Agency, Audit Guidance Delay and Disruption Claims. 1988.

United States Department of the Army, Office of the Chief of Engineers, Construction Contract Negotiating Guide. Washington, D.C.: Government Printing Office. 1974.

United Sates Department of the Army, Office of the Chief of Engineers, Modification Impact Evaluation Guide. Washington, D.C.: Government Printing Office. 1974.

Waldron, James A. The Legal Implications of a Project Schedule, Haddonfield, N.J. © Waldron Enterprises. 1974.
Warne, Thomas R. Partnering for Success, American Society of Civil Engineers. 1994.
Wickwire, Jon M. and Smith, Richard F. "The Use of Critical Path Method Techniques in Contract Claims." Public Contract Law Journal. Chicago: American Bar Association.

INDEX

Acceleration costs
  constructive, 61, 64, 84
  costs, 64
  directed, 61
  failure to provide time extension, 62
  identification, 62
  three types, 61
  voluntary, 61, 84
Administrative Dispute Resolution Act (ADRA), 141
American Arbitration Association, 138–139
American Institute of Architect (AIA 201A) Clauses
  4.3.1 Definition of claim, 2
  4.3.3 Time Limits, 15
  4.3.6 Concealed or Unknown Conditions, 15, 23
  4.3.8.1 Claims for Additional Time, 15
  8.3 Delays & Time Extensions, 52, 54
  14 Termination, 149–150
American Subcontractor Association
  recommended publications, 97
  standard form contract, 97–98, 213–219
Arbitration, 138–139
Armed Service Board of Contract Appeals ADR survey, 141–142, 238–244
Basic Procedures for Claims Administration, 5
Cardinal Changes, 41
Changes Clause, 11–13
Claims
  Certification, 18, 20, 21
  Consciousness, 8
  Definition, 2
  Policy, 5
  Program, 6

Common law damages, 147
Contract Disputes Act of 1978, 18–21, 143, 159–163
  claims certification, 20, 21
Critical Path Method Scheduling (CPM). See Scheduling
Cure notice, 146
Curtis rule, 42
Default. See Termination
Defective specifications, 39–43
Delays
  compensable time extensions, 52, 53
  concurrent, 58, 84
  defective plans and specifications, 56
  excuseable, 51
  foreseeable, 53
  implied obligation, 54
  liquidated damages, 51, 53. 58
  noncompensable, 52
  nonexcusable, 51, 53
  proving delay & delay costs, 59–60
  site access, 56
  Subcontractor delay damages (Severin Doctrine), 95
  suspension of work. See Suspension of Work
  third party, 58
  unreasonable, 56
Delay costs
  acceleration. See Acceleration.
  direct costs, 60
  differing site conditions, 60
  disruption, 59
  loss of efficiency, 59
  loss of learning curve, 59
  no damage for delay, 61
  out-of-sequence work, 59
  overhead costs, 60
  ripple effect, 59–60
  subcontractor delay damages (Severin Doctrine), 95

Differing Site Conditions
  FAR (52.236-2), 14, 22
  Man-made, 25–26
  Site Investigation, 26–31
  Type one, 22, 23–24
  Type two, 22, 22–25
Dispute Avoidance and Resolution Task Force, 155, 245–246
Dispute review board (DRB), 132–137
Drawing approvals, 94
Duty to clarify, Duty to seek clarification, 30, 43–46
Duty to inform, 46–47
Duty to inspect, 48–50
Duty to proceed, 47–48
  FAR 52.233-1, 48, 164–185
Engineers' Joint Contract Documents Committee General Conditions (EJCDC) 1910-8 Clauses
  4.03 Differing Subsurface or Physical Conditions, 23
  10.05 Claims and Disputes, 16
  12 Delays, 52, 54
Equal Access to Justice Act (EAJA), 118
Escrow bid documents, 137
false claims, 143
FAR. *See* Federal Acquisition Regulation
Federal Acquisition Regulation (FAR)—Clauses
  31.000 Federal Cost Principles, 119
  31.205-47 Legal cost, 118
  33.208 Interest costs, 117
  49.402-3(f) Default procedures, 146
  52.233-1(c) Definition of claim, 2
  52.233-1(i) Duty to proceed, 48
  52.236-2 Differing Site Conditions, 14, 22
  52.236-3 Site Investigation, 27–28
  52.236.15 Schedules, 64
  52.242-14 Suspension of Work, 15, 54
  52.243-4 Changes, 3, 11, 14
  52.249-2 Convenience termination, 145
  52.249-10 Default, 15, 145
  See also page, 000

Federal Streamlining Act of 1994, 18, 143
geotechnical baseline report (GBR), 137
Implied obligation, 54
Implied warranty, 93
Impossibility, 41
Mechanics Liens, 144
Medarb, 141
Mediation, 139–140
Miller Act, 95
Mini-trials, 140
Notice
  failure to Notify, 17
  late notice, 16
  time requirements, 14
Partnering, 129–132
Patent ambiguity—two step test, 45–46
Pricing
  actual cost, 105
  Eichleay formula, 110
  Financing costs, 69
  forward pricing, 100, 101, 122
  home office overhead, 110
  impact costs, 113–117
  inefficiency, 114
  interest, 117
  learning curve, 108, 115
  measured mile, 105
  overhead, 108–111
  overhead—fixed, 109
  overhead—variable, 109
  post pricing, 100, 102
  pricing elements, 106
  production rates, 107
  profit, 108, 111
  reasonable cost, 103, 105
  should cost, 103
  total cost, 102–104, 109
  two types, 100
Principles of Construction Law, 4
Prior knowledge, 57
Proprietary specifications, 93
Purchase orders, 92
Rules of Contract Interpretation
  Against the drafter, 36–37
  Conduct, 37–39

Custom or usage, 35–36
Language, 34–35
Parole evidence rule, 36
Read the contract as a whole, 34
Reasonableness, 33–34
Scheduling
  as-built, 77
  as-planned, 77, 79, 85
  collapsed as-built, 85, 87
  critical path method (CPM), 74
  early completion, 81
  expert analysis, 88
  float, 81
  fragnet, 85
  progress payments, 119
  techniques, 85–88
  time impact analysis, 85, 86
  use in claims analysis, 76
Seek clarification, 29–30
Severin Doctrine, 95
Site Investigation, 26–31
Site investigation form, 30, 203–204
Subcontractor-owner claims, 91

Summary trials, 141
Suspension of work
  compensable time extensions, 53–54
  constructive acceleration, 58
  defective plans and specifications, 56
  prior knowledge, 57
  third-party delay, 58
  unreasonable delays, 56
Termination
  constructive, 148
  convenience, 147
  default, 146–147
  excusable default, 146
  for suspension, 150
  private clauses, 149–150
Time extensions
  changes clause, 53, 54
  compensable, 53, 54
  differing site conditions clause, 53, 54
  suspension of work clause, 53
Two-step test. See Patent Ambiguity
Zone of reasonableness, 44–45